Introduction to Teaching

Becoming a Professional

Don Kauchak
University of Utah

Paul Eggen
University of North Florida

Candice Carter
University of North Florida

Upper Saddle River, New Jersey
Columbus, Ohio

Library of Congress Cataloging-in-Publication Data

Kauchak, Donald P.
Introduction to teaching : becoming a professional / Donald Kauchak, Paul Eggen, Candice Carter.
p. cm.
Includes bibliographical references and index.
ISBN: 0-13-010858-8
1. Teachers. 2. Teaching—Vocational guidance. I. Eggen, Paul D. II. Carter, Candice C. III. Title.

LB1775.K37 2002
371.1'0023'73—dc21 2001036372

Vice President and Publisher: Jeffery W. Johnston
Acquisitions Editor: Debra A. Stollenwerk
Development Editor: Heather Doyle Fraser
Production Editor: Kimberly J. Lundy
Production Coordination: Elm Street Publishing Services, Inc.
Design Coordinator: Diane C. Lorenzo
Photo Coordinator: Nancy Harre Ritz
Cover Designer: Andrew Lundberg
Cover Image: SuperStock
Production Manager: Pamela D. Bennett
Director of Marketing: Kevin Flanagan
Marketing Manager: Krista Groshong
Marketing Services Manager: Barbara Koontz

This book was set in Goudy by Carlisle Communications, Ltd. and was printed and bound by Courier Kendallville, Inc. The cover was printed by The Lehigh Press, Inc.

Photo Credits: PhotoDisc, Inc., pp. 1, 111, 123, 125, 182a, 229, 257, 438; Michael Newman/PhotoEdit, pp. 2, 44, 231, 252, 262, 277, 369, 413, 432; Tom Watson/Merrill, pp. 8, 48, 236, 321, 340; Todd Yarrington/Merrill, pp. 9, 85, 417; Laima Druskis/PH College, pp. 13, 128, 351; Blair Seitz/Photo Researchers, Inc., pp. 16, 386; Scott Cunningham/Merrill, pp. 20, 55, 92, 94, 137, 167, 188, 220, 223, 268, 306, 313, 329, 362; Elena Rooraid/Photo Edit, p. 24; Anthony Magnacca/Merrill, pp. 27, 34, 53, 196, 199, 260, 283, 285, 315, 324, 345, 367, 374, 426; Paul Howell/Liaison Agency, Inc., p. 28; Bonnie Kamin/PhotoEdit, p. 39; Will Hart/PhotoEdit, pp. 51, 70, 214, 295, 355, 419; Cindy Charles/Photo Edit, p. 59; Robin Sachs/PhotoEdit, pp. 61, 106, 408; Zigy Kaluzny/Stone, p. 64; Laura Dwight Photography, p. 69; Mary Kate Denny/PhotoEdit, pp. 74, 131, 272, 348; Bob Daemmrich/The Image Works, pp. 77, 393; Bob Daemmrich/Stock Boston, p. 81; Mark Richards/PhotoEdit, pp. 88, 242; Frank Siteman/PhotoEdit, p. 99; Tony Freeman/PhotoEdit, pp. 115, 169, 359; Amy Etra/PhotoEdit, p. 118; Corbis, p. 138; Library of Congress, pp. 142, 150, 162; Myrleen Ferguson/PhotoEdit, p. 147; Dana White/PhotoEdit, p. 156; Silver Burdett Ginn, pp. 172, 191; Bill Bachman/PhotoEdit, p. 178; Corbis/Stock Market, p. 182b; Robert Brenner/PhotoEdit, p. 186; Susan Oristaglio/PH College, p. 203; David Young-Wolff/PhotoEdit, pp. 210, 296, 425; Richard Hutchings/PhotoEdit, p. 216; Bob Daemmrich Photography, Inc., pp. 235, 247; Corporate Digital Archive, p. 254; PH College, pp. 287, 305; Courtesy SYATP, p. 291; Michelle Bridwell/PhotoEdit, p. 317; Schnepf/Liaison Agency, Inc., p. 331; Cleo Photography/PhotoEdit, p. 333; InFocus, Inc., p. 379; Billy E. Barnes/PhotoEdit, p. 381; Modern Curriculum Press, p. 391; A. Ramey/PhotoEdit, p. 395; Charles Gupton/Corbis/Stock Market, p. 399; Jeff Greenberg/PhotoEdit, p. 402; Larry Hamill/Merrill, p. 407; Bruce Ayres/Stone, p. 414; Spencer Grant/PhotoEdit, p. 434.

Pearson Education Ltd., *London*
Pearson Education Australia Pty. Limited, *Sydney*
Pearson Education Singapore Pte. Ltd.
Pearson Education North Asia Ltd., *Hong Kong*
Pearson Education Canada, Ltd., *Toronto*
Pearson Educación de Mexico, S.A. de C.V.
Pearson Education–Japan, *Tokyo*
Pearson Education Malaysia Pte. Ltd.
Pearson Education, *Upper Saddle River, New Jersey*

10 9 8 7 6 5 4 3
ISBN 0-13-010858-8

PREFACE

INTRODUCTION: A CASE-BASED APPROACH

This highly applied text introduces beginning education students to teaching and attempts to present an honest look at the real world of students, teachers, classrooms, and schools. The topics included in this book and the ways in which they are presented are all designed to answer the question, "What does this have to do with me and my future life as a teacher?"

To answer this question, the authors have developed cases and features that highlight the issues and challenges important in teachers' everyday lives. Each chapter begins with a case study that helps the reader understand how chapter topics relate to the real world of teaching. Then, these cases and vignettes are integrated throughout every chapter to provide concrete frames of reference for educational concepts. Each concept and discussion is framed within a case, so throughout the book students are applying concepts to real situations that teachers face every day.

TEXT THEMES

The book is organized around three themes—Professionalism, Reform, and The Changing Role of Teachers—that provide the threads that bind the topics of the chapters together.

Professionalism

Professionalism ties together topics such as career selection, teacher working conditions, career-long development, teacher evaluation, and relationships with supervisors, peers, students, parents, and the community. The movement towards professionalism provides a tangible goal that can guide beginning teachers as they develop, and it has both short- and long-term potential for improving teaching. Professionalism also provides a framework for examining a number of important issues that developing teachers face, such as more rigorous standards, accountability and testing, and merit pay. At the end of each chapter, *Online Portfolio Activities*, which are connected to INTASC Standards, encourage students to evaluate their own professional growth. *Reflect on This* sections that appear within each chapter contain realistic cases that provide additional opportunities for professional growth through decision making.

Reform

Reform has always been a factor in our educational system, but at no time in the past have so many people called for changes in education. Standards, accountability, and testing—for teachers and students—are being proposed as solutions to both educational and societal problems. Reform efforts have already changed schools and will continue to shape the profession for new teachers. The *Teaching in an Era of Reform* section in each chapter frames a reform issue as it relates to chapter content and asks students to make a personal evaluation of its potential.

The Changing Role of Teachers

Changes in society and in our schools mean changes for teachers. Selected chapters include the feature *Exploring Diversity: Considering Multiple Perspectives*, which helps beginning teachers understand different aspects of diversity and how they can address these differences in their teaching. In addition, *The Changing Role of Teachers* sections translate chapter topics into implications for teachers and teaching as education moves into the 21st century.

FEATURES OF THE TEXT

The book is interactive, encouraging prospective teachers to make conscious decisions about the kind of teacher they want to become. To create this interactive environment, the text uses Theme features, Field Experience features, Video features, and Pedagogical features to enhance the content and aid prospective teachers in their journey.

Theme features highlight the three themes around which the book is organized—Professionalism, Reform, and The Changing Role of Teachers—and present the content in an interactive way.

Exploring Diversity This feature examines an issue related to the chapter's content and for which the increasing diversity in today's students has important implications.

MINORITY TEACHERS AND WHAT THEY BRING TO THE PROFESSION

As the number of minority students in U.S. schools continues to grow, attempts to recruit minority teachers have also increased. Nearly one-third of school-age children in the United States are cultural minorities, compared to only 12 percent of the teaching force (Archer, 2000). Efforts to recruit greater numbers of minority teachers include early recruitment programs aimed at high schoolers, specially targeted scholarship programs, and programs designed to attract older, career-changing minorities.

Why all this interest and effort? What do minority teachers bring to classrooms that is so important? Researchers attempting to answer this question have focused on three areas:

- The need for minority role models.
- The need for effective instructors.
- The need for alternative perspectives.

Let's look at these areas.

Minorities as Role Models

Research clearly indicates that effective role models increase motivation and learning for all children (Bruning et al., 1999; Schunk, 2000). This is particularly important for cultural minorities. Minority teachers demonstrate to minority students that success and professional status are attainable for all people—including cultural minorities. Equally important, they demonstrate that being successful doesn't detract in any way from their cultural identity. For example, a study of Yup'ik Eskimo students in rural Alaska found that the tribe was losing its native language because young children either were not interested in the language or were ashamed of speaking it (Lipka, 1998). The presence of a native Yup'ik teacher reversed the pattern.

We lived right next to the school, and my sister lived with us for the year. We spoke only Yup'ik all of the time, so by the end of the year many of the students were no longer ashamed either to speak, or learn to speak, Yupik. My husband and I felt we had really done something good for those students because they began to identify themselves as Yup'ik and acquired their own language (Lipka, 1998, p. 50).

The importance of modeling is also demonstrated by the fact that many minority teachers say that minority teachers in *their* past were powerful influences on their decision to choose teaching as a career (Gordon, 1993; Toppin & Levine, 1992). Minority students begin believing that they too can succeed academically and become teachers when they see successful minority adult role models.

Minorities as Effective Instructors

Researchers also suggest that minority teachers may bring increased understanding of minority students' backgrounds and needs to learning activities (Villegas, 1991). For example, in a study of instructional styles, effective African American teachers used standard English to give directions and regulate behavior, but used "performances," stylized ways of speaking that resembled African American preaching styles, to motivate students during lessons (Foster, 1992).

As another example, in the study of Yupik instruction mentioned earlier, a Yupik teacher used an interdisciplinary unit on smelting, or drying fish for the winter, as a means to teach geography, science, mathematics, sanitation, family traditions, and cultural values (Lipka, 1998). Students took part in smelting in the classroom through observation, practice, and teaching other students. There was a high degree of interest and participation because the unit was relevant to the students' lives and culture.

Minority Teachers Bring Unique Perspectives to the Profession

Minority teachers also bring valuable alternative perspectives to teaching. Many minority teachers view teaching as a "calling" in which they have opportunities to work with and help minority students (Gordon, 1993). For example, one Chicana student teacher reported, "I began my student teaching experience thinking that minority students had to be saved from a harsh and cruel world which was existent in the schools. Consequently, when I saw the faces of many minority students, I set out to make a difference in their lives" (Kauchak & Burbank, 2000, p. 6). This commitment permeated the teacher's work with students, making her an important advocate for her students.

Minority teachers also help other teachers understand minority students and assist them in looking at the world in different ways. Because they come from minority homes and communities, they can become effective spokespersons for these students (Gordon, 1993; Kauchak & Burbank, 2000; Toppin & Levine, 1992).

Unquestionably, minority students need role models with whom they can identify. Further, diversity and the perspectives people from different backgrounds provide have always been one of our country's strengths. However, all teachers can be role models and effective instructors for African American, Hispanic, Native American, Asian students or other minority students. Further, any intelligent and sensitive teacher can design meaningful interdisciplinary units for their students, such as the one on drying fish that was described earlier.

Just as student diversity can enrich learning for every student, diversity among teachers can add perspectives that make every teacher more effective. The key is professionalism, which is also one of the themes of this book. Professionals—minority and nonminority—have a shared vision; they communicate with and learn from each other; and they're committed to providing the best for all students, not just those whose ethnic and cultural backgrounds are similar to their own.

New Teachers

In 1998, 200,545 new teachers graduated from college, a whopping 49 percent increase from 1983. How do new teachers differ from the existing teacher pool? The answer is more complex than at first glance because the pool of "new" teachers includes newly graduated teachers (approximately 34 percent of the total), recently graduated candidates who delayed entry into teaching (19 percent), persons re-entering the teaching force (30 percent), and transfers from other teaching positions (17 percent)(Darling-Hammond & Sclan, 1996). So, when you go to the orientation meeting at your first school, only 53 percent of the people at the meeting will have never taught; the other 47 percent will be transfers and reentries into the profession.

Market forces both within and outside of education influence the mix of people entering the teaching profession. For example, during the 1980s teaching positions were harder to find, leading many new teachers to accept positions in business and other occupations. During the 1990s, as the demand for more teachers increased, the profession saw more delayed entrants and re-entrant teachers.

How do newly graduated or "newly minted" teachers compare to the existing teaching force? They are more likely to be female (79 percent versus 74 percent for the total teaching force), white (91 percent versus 87 percent), and younger (28 years old versus 43 years old) (Darling-Hammond & Sclan, 1996). An increasing number of students are entering teacher-education programs after they've graduated from college (Bradley, 1999). These post-baccalaureate students tend to be older—around 30—and are more likely to be male than are students in undergraduate programs. In response to this demand, 65 percent of teacher-education programs have special programs for these post-baccalaureate students; approximately 9 percent admit only students who have already graduated from college.

These characteristics are important because they will help to shape the teaching force for the twenty-first century. This teaching force will be your colleagues, the people whom you'll spend significant portions of your school day working with. When you interview for your first teaching position, make a special effort to meet your potential colleagues. They can provide valuable insights into the school you'll be working in as well as help you decide whether your work with them will be productive and enjoyable.

Increasing Understanding 2.21

Think about the class you're in now. Does this national profile match your class? What factors might account for differences?

Teaching in an Era of Reform These special features provide an in-depth analysis of a reform topic related to the content of each chapter. At the end of this section, *You Take a Position* invites the reader to further investigate the reform by going to the *Education Week* Website, reading articles that discuss the reform, and taking a personal position (on the Companion Website) with respect to the issue presented in the chapter.

Teaching *in an* Era *of* Reform

ACCOUNTABILITY AND HIGH-STAKES TESTING

In response to concerns about students graduating from high school without the skills needed to succeed either in college or the workplace, reformers have called for greater accountability for both students and teachers. **Accountability** means that *students are required to demonstrate that they have met specified standards or that they demonstrate understanding of the topics they study as measured by standardized tests, and teachers are being held responsible for students' performance*. Calls for accountability resulted from evidence indicating that students were being promoted from grade to grade without having mastered essential content; some students were graduating from high school barely able to read, write, and do mathematics effectively, and even more had limited scientific literacy and a general lack of understanding of our world.

High-stakes tests are *tests used to determine whether or not students will be promoted from one grade to another, graduate from high school, or have access to specific fields of study*. When students aren't allowed to graduate from high school because they fail a test, for example, the "stakes" are very high, thus the term "high-stakes tests."

High-stakes testing is widespread. For example:

- Every state but Iowa has adopted standards in at least some academic subjects.
- Forty-eight states have testing programs designed, in large part, to measure how well students perform on those standards.
- Twenty-one states plan to issue overall ratings of their schools based largely on their students' performance.
- At least eighteen states have the authority to close, take over, or overhaul schools that are identified as failing (Olson, 2000b).

Putting Reform into Perspective

As you might expect, high-stakes testing is very controversial, with critics arguing that it limits what teachers do. Critics assert that teachers spend too much of their time in school helping students practice for the tests and that teacher creativity is eliminated, because they must narrowly focus their teaching on the content of the tests. Pressure to do well on the tests is so great that some teachers and administrators have been driven to cheat; they help students with the tests or even give them answers (Viadero, 2000b). In Massachusetts, high-stakes testing became so controversial that the state's largest teachers' union, in a highly unusual move, launched a $600,000 television campaign that sharply criticized the *Massachusetts Comprehensive Assessment System* exam, an exam students in the state must pass to graduate (Gehring, 2000).

Increasing Understanding 1.8

Virtually everyone reading this text has taken either the SAT (Scholastic Aptitude Test) or the ACT (American College Testing) program to determine whether you can get into a particular college or university. Are these "high-stakes" tests? Explain.

Advocates of testing, while conceding that teacher preparation, materials, and the tests themselves need to be improved, argue that the tests are the fairest and most effective means of achieving the aims of democratic schooling. Further, they assert, evidence indicates that educational systems that require content standards and use tests that thoroughly measure the extent to which the standards are met greatly improve the achievement for all students, including those from disadvantaged backgrounds (Bishop, 1995, 1998). Hirsch (2000) summarizes the testing advocates' position: "They [standards and tests that measure achievement of the standards] are the most promising educational development in half a century" (p. 64).

You Take a Position

Now it's your turn to take a position on the issue discussed in this section. Go to the *Education Week* Website at **http://www.edweek.com**, find "search" on the first page, and type in one of the following two search terms: *high-stakes tests* or *accountability*. Locate a minimum of three articles on one of these topics and then do the following:

1. Identify the title, author, and date of each article and write a one-paragraph summary of each.
2. Identify a pattern in the articles. (An example of a pattern would be if each article—or even two of the three—suggests that parents approve of high-stakes tests.)
3. After identifying the pattern, take one of the two following positions:
   - The pattern suggested in the articles, if implemented, *is* likely to improve education.
   - The pattern suggested in the articles *is not* likely to improve education.

   State your position in writing and document your position with information taken from the articles. Give your response to your instructor.

To answer these questions online, go to the Take a Position Module in Chapter 1 of the Companion Website.

Reflect on This This feature is an exercise that promotes personal connections by presenting realistic dilemmas in the form of cases that ask students to make professional decisions. Students can then compare their solutions to these educational dilemmas with feedback found on the book's Companion Website.

Reflect *on* This

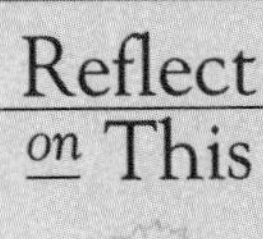

AN ETHICAL DILEMMA

As you're sitting in the teachers' lounge one day, Dana, one of your colleagues, says, "Well, you know that Sheri [another teacher in the school] was brought up on charges of plagiarism when she was working on her master's degree. I guess she got away with it, because her advisor had a lot of political clout, or something, and the whole incident was swept under the rug."

Dana shrugs, gets a cup of coffee, and leaves the room.

Several days later, you hear Dana repeat her story to another teacher in the lounge.

1. Is Dana behaving ethically in making her remarks to you, and later, to the other teacher?
2. As a professional, should you intervene? In other words, should you say something to Dana? Should you say something to Sheri? Should you say anything to the school principal or other administrator?
3. Suppose that Dana's accusations are true, that is, Sheri actually was accused of plagiarism. Is Dana then behaving ethically in making her statements?
4. What would you do in this situation?

To answer these questions online and receive immediate feedback, go to the Reflect on This Module in Chapter 1 of the Companion Website.

The Changing Role of Teachers This chapter-closing section integrates chapter topics into implications for contemporary teachers. Prospective teachers are encouraged to consider the implications these changing roles have for their development as a professional.

The Changing Role of Teachers

Increased accountability and testing for students are reforms that are facts of life for teachers. How will these reforms change your role as a teacher? At least four implications are likely.

First, you'll need to know more. Compared to teachers in the past, you'll be expected to know more English, math, science, history, and geography. The general education requirements for teachers almost certainly will increase, and prospective teachers will be expected to demonstrate their understanding of these subjects on tests before they will be allowed to teach.

Second, you will be held responsible for student learning, and allowances for the increasingly diverse backgrounds of your students probably will not be made. In other words, you will be held responsible for your students' performance regardless of their home environments, background experiences, or motivation. To meet these expectations—in addition to your knowledge of English, history, and other forms of content—your pedagogical content knowledge, general pedagogical knowledge, and knowledge of learners and learning will have to be thorough. In addition, you probably will be tested on the material you learn in your teacher preparation classes. Your performance on these tests may determine if you get a license and whether you will be allowed to teach.

Third, in spite of controversies, testing will be an important part of your teaching life. As we said earlier, you will be tested before you're allowed to enter the profession, and the students you teach will be tested regularly. Proposals are being made to provide merit pay for teachers whose students do well on these tests and to review teachers whose students do not (Bradley, 2000; Hoff, 2000).

Fourth, as you begin your career, you will probably have less autonomy than teachers had 10 or even 5 years ago. You'll be expected to help your students meet the standards mandated by your state or district, so the number of decisions you'll be allowed to make on your own will be reduced. This is a dilemma. As we saw earlier in the chapter, educational leaders are advocating an increase in the professionalization of teaching, and professionals have autonomy. At the same time, other leaders are mandating standards that reduce teacher autonomy, which detracts from professionalism.

Finally, you will need to be highly adaptable. Some specific reforms will be abandoned, only to be replaced by new reforms. Your ability to understand and quickly adapt to these changes will strongly influence your success in and satisfaction with a teaching career.

Online Portfolio Activities Students are encouraged to begin constructing professional portfolio entries tied to each chapter's content. These activities are linked to INTASC Standards and involve students in a range of activities including visiting the websites of professional organizations, beginning work on their philosophy of education, and connecting with local districts and state offices of education.

ONLINE PORTFOLIO ACTIVITIES

To complete these activities online, go to the *Portfolio Activities* Module in Chapter 2 of the Companion Website, and submit your response.

Portfolio Activity 2.1 **Time and Learning**

INTASC Principle 7: *Planning*

Go to the *Portfolio Activities* Module for Chapter 2 of the Companion Website and click on "Time and Organization." Read the information and then write a one- or two-paragraph summary of the section. Then offer at least two specific, concrete ways in which teachers can maximize their *instructional time* and at least two specific, concrete ways in which teachers can maximize *engaged time*.

Field Experience features engage students in real or virtual classroom experiences to enhance their understanding of chapter content.

Going into Schools At the end of each chapter students are invited to apply the information in the chapter to themselves and to school settings. Through focused observations and interviews, students connect to the schools and classrooms in which they'll teach.

GOING INTO SCHOOLS

1. Interview two teachers; if possible, one teacher should be in his or her first year, and the other teacher should have taught for at least five years. Ask them the following questions:
   a. Why did you choose to teach? Please give me all the reasons that apply to your decision.
   b. What are some of the most rewarding aspects of teaching? Please provide some specific examples.
   c. What are some of the most difficult parts of teaching? Please provide some specific examples.
   d. Are you more or less confident in your ability to help kids learn than you were before you started?
   e. How effective was your pre-service teacher-preparation program in helping you learn to teach? What would have made it more effective?
   f. Do you plan to stay in teaching, or do you plan to move to a different job or profession? If you plan to leave teaching, what are your reasons?
   g. In one sentence, please describe the process of teaching.
   h. Do you believe that teaching is a profession? Explain your reasons.
   i. Please rate the importance of each of the following for teachers, using the scale that follows:
   1 = Not at all important
   2 = Not very important
   3 = Somewhat important

Virtual Field Experience This extension of the *Going into Schools* feature allows students who do not have a formal field-experience component as part of their course to explore issues and topics through the Internet. This feature can be found in the *Field Experience* Module of each chapter on the Companion Website.

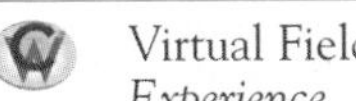

If you would like to participate in a Virtual Field Experience, go to the *Field Experience* Module in Chapter 1 of the Companion Website.

Video features use videos of real-world situations and issues to connect with concepts presented in the text.

Looking Through Classroom Windows Students are provided with realistic glimpses of teachers working in real classrooms. This boxed feature contains a summary of the real-world, unscripted, and unrehearsed video episodes that accompany the text. Students view the video episodes and then respond to questions asking them to apply what they've seen to the content of the chapter. A written transcript of each video episode and feedback for the students are available on the Companion Website. *Looking Through Classroom Windows* features are found in Chapters 1, 6, 10, 11, and 12.

Looking Through Classroom Windows

CLASSROOMS IN ACTION: THE REAL WORLD OF TEACHING

Having looked at the reasons people choose to teach, the rewards and difficulties in teaching, and teacher professionalism, you now have the opportunity to look at three teachers in action. To complete this activity, do the following:

- View the video episodes titled "Classrooms in Action: The Real World of Teaching."
- Read the written transcripts of the three episodes and answer the following questions online by going to the *Classroom Windows* Module in Chapter 1 of the Companion Website at: **http://www.prenhall.com/kauchak.** Go to the Website and follow the directions on your screen.
- Answer the questions that follow:

1. For which of the three teachers are the emotional rewards likely to be the greatest? Explain.
2. For which of the three teachers are the intellectual rewards likely to be the greatest? Explain.
3. Based on what you saw in the episodes, which teacher do you believe has the most difficult job? Explain.
4. For which teacher is knowledge of content most important? Pedagogical content knowledge? General pedagogical knowledge? Knowledge of learners and learning? Explain.
5. How much autonomy do you believe each teacher had in designing and conducting his or her lessons? Explain.
6. To what extent do you believe each teacher demonstrated the characteristics of a professional? Explain.

To answer these questions online and receive immediate feedback, go to the Looking Through Classroom Windows Module in Chapter 1 of the Companion Website.

Video Perspectives Students investigate chapter topics through ABC News video segments focusing on controversial educational issues. Each *Video Perspective* section offers a short summary of the episode and asks students to think about and respond to questions relating to the video and chapter content. *Video Perspectives* are found in Chapters 2, 3, 4, 5, 7, 8, 9, and 13.

Video *Perspectives*

TEACHER SHORTAGE

This ABC News video segment explores the recent teacher shortage from the perspectives of Bob Chase, President of the National Education Association (NEA), and Vicki Rafel of the National Parent Teacher Association (NPTA). Low salaries along with a lack of mentoring and support for beginning teachers are identified as critical reasons for the shortage. Other factors involved, but not discussed, include an aging teacher workforce, a growing student population, and reforms dictating lower student–teacher ratios.

Think about This

1. How might the challenges of the multiple roles of teaching contribute to the teacher shortage?
2. How might the current teacher shortage influence the age, gender, and race–ethnicity of the teaching force?
3. How might the current teacher shortage influence the current profile of "new teachers"?
4. What actions could policy makers take to alleviate the current teacher shortage?

To answer these questions online and receive immediate feedback, go to the Video Perspectives Module in Chapter 2 of the Companion Website.

Video Discussion Questions Students view video clips of educational leaders (such as Theodore Sizer and John Goodlad), answer discussion questions online, and receive immediate feedback through the text's Companion Website (Chapters 1, 2, 4, 7, 8, and 10).

VIDEO DISCUSSION QUESTIONS

The following discussion questions refer to video segments found on the Companion Website. To answer these questions online, view the accompanying video, and receive immediate feedback to your answers, go to the Video Discussion Module in Chapter 1 of the Companion Website at **http://www.prenhall.com/kauchak.**

1. Dr. Urie Triesman is a professor of mathematics at the University of Texas at Austin and director of the Charles A. Dana Center for Math and Science Education. His work focuses on school reform and ways that schools can be helped to improve. He is concerned that individual school and teacher autonomy often conflict with centralized testing programs. What does Dr. Triesman believe is the proper balance between these two forces? Do you think centralized testing jeopardizes school and teacher autonomy? Explain why you believe it does or does not.

Pedagogical features provide additional instructional support for students in their understanding of chapter content.

Chapter Introductions and Focus Questions introduce chapter content and identify major issues and questions.

Integrated Case Studies Each chapter begins with an introductory case study. Additional cases throughout the text provide concrete examples of the topics discussed in the chapter. Within the chapter text, references to case studies are highlighted by a case icon.

Before I became a teacher, I majored in Business Administration in college and worked for 10 and a half years in the banking industry. I held jobs as a receptionist, an accounting clerk, a customer support representative, and a staff auditor. My last job in business—staff auditor—was fun because I got to travel, meet new people, and periodically train other workers. Still, even this wasn't rewarding; I was just a number in a crowd trying to get noticed.

I've always wanted to make a difference, and I've always enjoyed working with young people. Then a couple of years ago I read a book in which the author described the difference between a person's "job" and a person's "work." Your job is how you make money; your work is how you contribute to the world. It really crystalized everything for me. Business, for me, was a job, but I didn't really have any "work," and I longed for it.

In some ways, I think I've always wanted to be a teacher. I remember all the way back to my fourth grade teacher, Mrs. May. She was like my second mother because she was always so willing to help, and she seemed to care about me, just like my mother did at home. And I also remember my tenth-grade history teacher, Mr. Fleming, who explained how important school was for us to develop and grow. We would complain that his tests were so hard, and he would laugh and tell us how good they were for us; he thought history was *so* important. You had to like it, because he loved it so much. All the kids talked about Mr. Fleming and his antics, like when he came into class in his coonskin cap and buckskin outfit. And he asked questions that would make us think, like, "Why does a city way out in Iowa have a French name like Des Moines?" I never fell asleep in his class. I still remember it, and it was years ago.

Increasing Understanding Questions Located in the margins of each chapter, these questions encourage students to think more deeply about chapter content and apply their understanding of the chapter topics to real-world situations. Students can answer these questions and receive immediate feedback on the Companion Website.

Increasing Understanding 2.1

In what kind of districts or schools are you most likely to encounter year-round schools? Why? What implications might these have for you personally?

To answer the "Increasing Understanding" questions online and receive immediate feedback, go to the *Increasing Understanding* Module in Chapter 2 of the Companion Website at **http://www.prenhall.com/kauchak,** type in your response, and then study the feedback.

scheduling in your first job; nearly 1.5 million students in more than 20 states attend public schools on a year-round schedule (National Association for Year-Round Education, 1998). Primary reasons for this schedule change are to alleviate crowding by more efficiently using physical facilities and to minimize the inevitable forgetting (sometimes called "summer loss") that occurs over the summer.

Interestingly, there have been obstacles to year-round schooling; these obstacles come from several different sources. One obstacle is parents; summer has become a time for family vacations and summer camps, and parents resist intrusions on this family time. A second obstacle is the large amounts of money sometimes needed to install and run air conditioning in schools built for cool-weather use. A third obstacle is teachers themselves; many use summers as a time to supplement their teaching salaries or to work on recertification, new areas of certification, or a master's degree.

The School Week

In the United States, the 40-hour workweek is the norm. How does teaching compare to this norm? Study after study shows that the average teacher spends between 45 and 50 hours per week in school-related work, with the average being around 46 hours (Cypher

Chapter Summaries Each chapter concludes with this concise recap of the major ideas discussed within the chapter.

Important Concepts Also located at the end of each chapter, this section lists key concepts that are set in boldface type within the chapter.

Discussion Questions Thought-provoking chapter-end questions provide opportunities for students to integrate and personalize the content in the chapters as they interact with their peers in discussion formats.

ORGANIZATION OF THE TEXT

Part 1, The Profession, includes Chapters 1 and 2. Chapter 1 invites readers to consider their beliefs and reasons for wanting to become a teacher. In addition to describing the themes for the book, the chapter analyzes reasons for entering teaching and factors that influence those reasons. Chapter 2 examines the characteristics of the present teaching force and analyzes teaching using professionalism as a framework. The chapter also considers the complexities of teaching, the multiple roles of teachers, and the characteristics of the present teaching force.

Part 2, Students, includes Chapters 3 and 4. In Chapter 3 learner diversity is described as both a challenge and an opportunity facing tomorrow's teachers. Differences in ability and background knowledge require curricular and instructional adaptations. Cultural diversity, including language differences, requires educational adaptations. In addition, efforts to help both boys and girls as well as students with exceptionalities reach their full potential pose additional challenges. In Chapter 4 the changing American family, shifts in demographic and socioeconomic patterns, and other changes in society are analyzed, and their implications for teaching are discussed. Challenges facing modern youth, including alcohol and drug use, violence, suicide, child abuse, and increased sexuality are discussed. Educational efforts to assist American youth in facing these changes and challenges are described in terms of community, school, and instructional efforts.

Part 3, Foundations, includes Chapters 5 through 9. Chapter 5 discusses the history of education in the United States and focuses on changing conceptions of teachers and teaching. Using the changes in aims of education as a frame of reference, the chapter analyzes the evolving role of education in the United States. Chapter 6 describes the influence of different philosophical movements on schools and schooling. Traditional philosophies, such as idealism, realism, pragmatism, and existentialism, together with their educational counterparts, perennialism, essentialism, progressivism, and postmodernism, are discussed, and their implications for teaching are examined. The final section of the chapter helps developing teachers formulate their own evolving philosophy of teaching.

In Chapter 7 school aims, which were introduced in Chapter 6, are used to analyze different school organizational patterns. Developmental needs of learners and school responses are considered for the preschool, primary, middle, and high school levels. Research on effective schools is discussed and its implications for teaching are presented. Chapter 8 describes the uniquely American configuration of school governance and finance. Constitutional law is used as a framework to analyze the interconnected forces influencing both the governance and finance of American education. Recent innovations such as charter schools, vouchers, and school choice are used to analyze governance and finance issues. Chapter 9 begins by examining how ethics and law influence professional decision making. The U.S. legal system is described as an overlapping and interconnected web of federal, state, and local influences. The concepts of rights and responsibilities are used to frame legal issues for both teachers and students.

Part 4, Teaching, includes Chapters 10 through 12. In Chapter 10 the formal and informal curricula are described, and reform movements in education are placed within a historical context and used to analyze current curricular trends. Curriculum controversies are described using ideological struggles over the control of American education as a framework. Specific examples such as textbooks, banned books, and under-represented minorities are used to illustrate these ideological conflicts. Chapter 11 begins by examining the effective teaching literature and continues with a historical look at two views of learning: behaviorism and cognitive psychology. Implications of the cognitive revolution in teaching are described in terms of learner-centered instruction, learner self-regulation, social influences on learning, and changing views of assessment. Chapter 12 begins with a brief history and overview of technology and teaching. Different ways that technology can influence learning are described and linked to different teaching functions. The chapter concludes with an examination of issues for the future and a look at how technology will change teaching.

Part 5, Careers, is the final part of the text and includes Chapter 13, which examines lifelong teacher development from multiple perspectives. The chapter begins by discussing the types of knowledge teachers must acquire in learning to teach. It continues by examining the characteristics of beginning teachers, including their beliefs, concerns, and experiences. The chapter closes with specific information about finding and obtaining a teaching position.

ANCILLARY MATERIALS FOR THE INSTRUCTOR

The text has the following ancillary materials to assist instructors in their attempts to maximize learning for all students.

Instructor's Manual/Media Guide Concrete suggestions to involve students actively in learning and to promote interactive teaching. This manual contains many aids for instructors as they teach chapter topics and integrate the accompanying media to the fullest extent.

PowerPoint and Acetate Transparencies Instructors can use transparencies to present and elaborate on topics covered in the text. These transparencies are available both on the Companion Website and as acetates.

Test Bank Instructors are given access to multiple choice, critical thinking, and extended response questions for each chapter. These questions are available on CD-ROM in Mac and PC formats.

Looking Through Classroom Windows Case videos, connected to Chapters 1, 6, 10, 11, and 12, provide realistic looks at teachers in classrooms.

ABC News Video Library: Critical Issues in Education, Vol. 1 News segments from ABC television programs such as *Nightline*, *20/20*, and *Good Morning America* are tied to chapter topics and can serve as the focal point for classroom discussions. These appear as Video Perspectives features in Chapters 2, 3, 4, 5, 7, 8, 9, and 13.

Discussion Videos These 15- to 20-minute interviews with John Goodlad, Theodore Sizer, and Uri Treisman can be used to supplement shorter video clips found on the Companion Website or as stand-alone discussion starters.

WEB-BASED ANCILLARIES FOR STUDENTS AND INSTRUCTORS

Companion Website

The Companion Website to accompany this text can be found at **http://www.prenhall.com/kauchak.** Technology is a growing and changing aspect of education that is creating a need for resources. To address this emerging need, Prentice Hall has developed an online learning environment for both students and instructors to support this textbook. In creating the Companion Website, our goal is to embellish what the textbook already offers. For this reason, the content is organized by chapter and provides the instructor and student with a variety of meaningful resources.

For the Instructor Syllabus Manager™ is an online syllabus creation and management instrument with the following capabilities:

- Syllabus Manager™ provides you, the instructor, with a step-by-step process to create and revise syllabi without having to learn HTML. Direct links are provided to the Companion Website and other online content.
- Your completed syllabus is hosted on our servers, allowing convenient updates from any computer on the Internet. Changes you make to your syllabus are immediately available to your students the next time they log on.
- Students may log on to your syllabus at any time. All they need to know is the Web address for the Companion Website and the password you've assigned to your syllabus.
- Clicking on a date, the student is shown the list of activities for that day's assignment. The activities for each assignment are linked directly to text content, which will save students time.

- To add assignments, you simply click on the desired due date and then fill in the details of the assignment.
- Links to other activities can be created easily. If the activity is online, a URL can be entered in the space provided, and it will be linked automatically in the final syllabus.

For the Student The Companion Website provides students with resources and immediate feedback on exercises and other activities linked to the text. In addition, these activities, projects, and resources enhance and extend chapter content to real-world issues and concepts. Each chapter on the Companion Website contains the following modules (or sections) unless specified otherwise:

- **Chapter Overview**—outlines key concepts and issues in the chapter.
- **Self-Assessment**—multiple-choice quizzes with automatic grading provides immediate feedback for students.
- **Web Links**—links to Internet sites that relate to and enhance chapter content.
- **Increasing Understanding**—students can answer these margin questions online and receive immediate feedback.
- **Take a Position**—students can visit the *Education Week* Website, search for information on a chapter-related issue, and then form their own opinions.
- **Reflect on This**—reflection questions that extend chapter feature content.
- **Exploring Diversity**—links to multicultural/diverse content and Websites.
- **Portfolio**—activities and projects that give students the opportunity to begin building their professional portfolios.
- **Field Experience**—projects and activities that create a virtual field experience for students who do not have a formal field experience component as part of the course.
- **Video Perspectives**—thought-provoking questions that correspond to the issue-based ABC News video segments offered with the text (Chapters 2, 3, 4, 5, 7, 8, 9, and 13 only).
- **Classroom Windows**—video transcripts of the *Looking Through Classroom Windows* videos with critical-thinking questions that connect the video and the chapter (Chapters 1, 6, 10, 11, and 12 only).
- **Video Discussion**—streaming video with discussion questions (selected chapters).
- **Message Board**—serves as a virtual bulletin board to post—or respond to—questions or comments to/from a national audience.
- **Chat**—allows anyone who is using the text anywhere in the country to communicate in a real-time environment—ideal for discussion and study groups, class projects, and so on.
- **Other Resources**—users have access to PowerPoint transparencies, the INTASC Standards as they are connected to chapter content and activities, and links to professional organizations.

Online Courses

Online courses for this course are available in two different formats: Blackboard (locally hosted by your school), and CourseCompass (nationally hosted by Prentice Hall).

ACKNOWLEDGMENTS

Every book reflects the work of a team that includes the authors, the staff of editors, and the reviewers. We appreciate the input we've received from the following professors who helped make the book current and true to the realities of teaching Charles Carroll, Lake City Community College; Fred Curtis, Baylor University; Hal E. Jenkins, III, Mississippi University for Women; Jeri A. Carroll, Wichita State University; Consuelo Nieto, California State University, Long Beach; Linda Beath, Central Washington University; Christina Ramirez-Smith, Christopher Newport University; Mary Lou Brotherson, Nova Southeastern University; Leigh Chiarelott, Bowling Green State University; James B. Kracht, Texas A & M University; Carolyn Babione, Indiana Southeast University; Wilford A. Weber, University of Houston; Paul Shore, Saint Louis University; Helen Newcastle, California State University, Long Beach; Philip S. Morse, Suny College at Fredonia; Mary Ann Clark, Brown University; Judith Glies Swearing, Jersey City State College; Alan J. Reiman, North Carolina State University; Ivan W. Banks, Jackson State University; Emma Pitts, Southern University; Harriett D. Hohnson, Emporia State University; William B. Stanley, University of Delaware; Berle Baker, Dekalb College; Scott Willison, Boise State University; Sharon Hobbs, Montana State University—Billings; and Helen S. Faison, Chatham College.

In addition to the reviewers who guided our revisions, our team of editors gave us support in many ways. Heather Doyle Fraser, our development editor, worked miracles putting all the components of the book together. Debbie Stollenwerk, our acquisitions editor, helped guide the book from the beginning. Kim Lundy, our production editor, helped make the book happen in a tight production schedule. Nancy Ritz did a great job with the photographs. Finally, special thanks to our colleague, Mary Burbank, who helped refine the book into the final product you now see.

Our appreciation goes to all these fine people who have taken our words and given them shape. We hope that all our efforts will result in increased learning for students and more rewarding teaching for instructors.

Finally, we would sincerely appreciate any comments or questions about anything that appears in the book or any of its supplements. Please feel free to contact either of us at any time. Our e-mail addresses are kauchak@ed.utah.edu and peggen@nfu.edu.

Good luck.

Don Kauchak
Paul Eggen

BRIEF CONTENTS

CONTENTS

Video Perspectives

PART 1

The Profession

CHAPTER 1

Why Become a Teacher?

Welcome. You're beginning a study of teaching, one of the most interesting, challenging, and noble professions that exists. No one has more potential for touching the personal, social, and intellectual lives of students than do caring and dedicated teachers.

You're probably reading this book for one of two reasons; either you've decided that you want to be a teacher, or you're in the process of deciding. Our purpose in writing this chapter is to provide some information that will shed additional light on that decision, as we try to answer the following questions:

- Why do people decide to teach?
- What are some of the rewards in teaching?
- What are some of the difficulties in teaching?
- Is teaching a profession?
- How will educational reforms affect your life as a teacher?

Case STUDY

Before I became a teacher, I majored in Business Administration in college and worked for 10 and a half years in the banking industry. I held jobs as a receptionist, an accounting clerk, a customer support representative, and a staff auditor. My last job in business—staff auditor—was fun because I got to travel, meet new people, and periodically train other workers. Still, even this wasn't rewarding; I was just a number in a crowd trying to get noticed.

I've always wanted to make a difference, and I've always enjoyed working with young people. Then a couple of years ago I read a book in which the author described the difference between a person's "job" and a person's "work." Your job is how you make money; your work is how you contribute to the world. It really crystalized everything for me. Business, for me, was a job, but I didn't really have any "work," and I longed for it.

In some ways, I think I've always wanted to be a teacher. I remember all the way back to my fourth grade teacher, Mrs. May. She was like my second mother because she was always so willing to help, and she seemed to care about me, just like my mother did at home. And I also remember my tenth-grade history teacher, Mr. Fleming, who explained how important school was for us to develop and grow. We would complain that his tests were so hard, and he would laugh and tell us how good they were for us; he thought history was *so* important. You had to like it, because he loved it so much. All the kids talked about Mr. Fleming and his antics, like when he came into class in his coonskin cap and buckskin outfit. And he asked questions that would make us think, like, "Why does a city way out in Iowa have a French name like Des Moines?" I never fell asleep in his class. I still remember it, and it was years ago.

So, to make a long story short, I went back to school, and this time I did what I've always wanted to do. Of course it's tough some days. The kids are sometimes "off the wall," and I periodically feel like I'm drowning in paperwork, but when you see the light bulb go on for someone, it's all worth it. Now, my job and my work are the same thing. (Suzanne, 35, mother of two and a recent entry into teaching.)

■ ■ ■

Many of you reading this book have characteristics similar to Suzanne's. You're intelligent and introspective, and you've had a number of life experiences. Perhaps you're married, have children, and your spouse is employed successfully in some other profession. You've thought a great deal about becoming a teacher, and you're clear about your reasons for wanting to teach.

Others of you are less certain. You're also intelligent, but you're young, single, and still in the process of deciding what you want to do with your life. You've enjoyed your school experiences, and most of your ideas about teaching are based on them. The idea of working with and helping young people is attractive, but your thinking hasn't gone much past that point.

That's okay. This text is designed to provide you with a close-up and in-depth look at teaching. Either way—if you've already made the decision to teach, or if you're still in the process of deciding—this book will help you understand what teaching is all about: the rewards and difficulties involved in it, the kinds of students you're likely to encounter, what your professional and legal responsibilities to them are, how our schools have evolved to their present state, and a number of other issues that will influence your decision and perhaps ultimately your career.

This chapter is intended to help you begin developing that understanding. Let's get started.

WHY PEOPLE DECIDE TO TEACH

To begin this section, please respond to the Interest in Teaching Inventory that follows.

Interest in Teaching Inventory

Circle the number for each item that best represents your thinking. Use the following scale as a guide.

1 = Strongly disagree
2 = Disagree
3 = Somewhat disagree
4 = Agree and disagree
5 = Somewhat agree
6 = Agree
7 = Strongly agree

1.	A major reason I'm considering becoming a teacher is job security.	1	2	3	4	5	6	7
2.	My family has strongly influenced my decision to become a teacher.	1	2	3	4	5	6	7
3.	Long summer vacations are very important to me as I consider teaching as a career.	1	2	3	4	5	6	7
4.	I've never really considered any other occupation besides teaching.	1	2	3	4	5	6	7
5.	A major reason I'm considering becoming a teacher is my desire to work with young people.	1	2	3	4	5	6	7
6.	I'm thinking of becoming a teacher because I'd like to be of some value or significance to society.	1	2	3	4	5	6	7
7.	A major reason I'm considering becoming a teacher is my own interest in a content or subject matter field.	1	2	3	4	5	6	7
8.	A major reason I'm considering entering teaching is because of the influence of a former elementary or secondary teacher.	1	2	3	4	5	6	7
9.	The opportunity for a lifetime of self-growth is a major reason I'm considering becoming a teacher.	1	2	3	4	5	6	7

Major: Elementary/Secondary (Circle one)

If secondary, what content area? ______________

Gender: Male/Female (Circle one)

Age: _____

We gave this survey to several classes of students taking a course similar to the one you're now in, averaged their responses, and ranked them from most (1) to least (9) important reasons for becoming a teacher. Let's see how your responses compare to our students' answers.

We see from Table 1.1 that the desire to work with young people (Item 5) and to contribute to society (Item 6) were our students' two most important reasons for considering teaching. These reasons are consistent with Suzanne's thinking as she described it in the introduction to the chapter, and they're also consistent with polls conducted by the National Education Association over nearly a 25-year period (National Education Association, 1997).

Table 1.1 **Responses to Interest in Teaching Inventory**

Item	Item Focus	Average Response of Students	Survey Rank
1	Job security	4.3	6
2	Family influence	3.9	8
3	Summer vacations	4.0	7
4	Other careers not considered	2.6	9
5	Work with youth	6.4	1
6	Value to society	6.3	2
7	Content interest	5.4	4
8	Influence of teachers	5.0	5
9	Self-growth	5.5	3

Increasing Understanding 1.1

In Table 1.1 we see that the lowest average response on the Interest in Teaching Inventory is for Item 4, and the highest average responses are for Items 5 and 6. Are these consistent results? Explain.

Let's look more closely at these and other reasons that people go into teaching.

To answer the "Increasing Understanding" questions online and receive immediate feedback, go to the *Increasing Understanding* Module in Chapter 1 of the Companion Website at: **http://www.prenhall.com/kauchak,** type in your response, and then study the feedback.

REWARDS AND DIFFICULTIES IN TEACHING

As with any occupation, people choose to teach because they think it will be rewarding. Some of these rewards are intrinsic—they come from within us—while other rewards are more tangible, like money or free time. Let's look at these rewards in more detail.

Intrinsic Rewards

Intrinsic rewards *are personally satisfying for emotional or intellectual reasons*. A number of people, such as Suzanne and the people in our survey, enter teaching searching for intrinsic rewards; they seek the emotional or intellectual satisfaction that goes with believing they are making a contribution to the world.

Emotional Rewards Let's look at some different ways that teachers receive emotional rewards from their teaching. The following are notes shared with us by teachers. The contents of the notes are taken verbatim.

▪ ▪ ▪

Kasia, 23, calls her boyfriend, Jeff. The middle school in which she teaches has "Teacher Appreciation Week" and she has just received a dozen roses from a group of eight of her third-period, seventh-grade science students.

"I was always on them about whispering, too," she excitedly tells Jeff. "I maybe would have expected this from my fifth period class, but never from this bunch."

"Let me read the note I got from them," she continues. " 'Thank you for all that you've done for us and for all the wonderful things that you've teached [*sic*] us. You are truly an amazing teacher. Thank you again.

Happy Teacher Appreciation Week,

Sincerely,

Alicia, Rosa, Shannon, Tina, Stephanie, Melissa, Jessica, and Becca.' "

"That's wonderful," Jeff laughs. "Good thing you're not their English teacher."

"I know. I showed Isabel [the students' English teacher] the note, and she broke up. 'So much for grammar,' she said."

▪ ▪ ▪

Judy, 32, a teacher in the same school, brought home the following note from two parents.

Dear Mrs. Holmquist,

Thank you very much for working so diligently with Michael this year. I think he now has a better understanding of the world. I hope he told you that he lived in Egypt for nearly two years. We have a large amount of Egyptian souvenirs should your class like to view them. Again, thanks for all of your work day after day.

Sincerely,
Shirley and Bob Wood

▪ ▪ ▪

Miguel Rodriguez, 29, another middle school teacher, received the following note from one of his students.

Mr. Rodriguez,

I wanted to think of some creative way to thank you for being the best teacher I ever had. (But I couldn't ☺ .)

Even though all the geography skills I'll ever use in my life I learned in second grade, I just wanted to say thanks for teaching me how to really prepare for life in the years to come.

Everyday I looked forward to coming to your class (and not just because of Mike [a boy in the class]). I always enjoyed your class, because there was a hidden message about life in there somewhere.

Your [*sic*] my very favorite teacher and you've taught me some of the best lessons in life I could ever learn. Thank you so much.

A grateful student,
Erica Jacobs

(P.S. No, I didn't write this to raise my grade ☺ .)

▪ ▪ ▪

The notes you've just read and the flowers Kasia received symbolize some of the emotional rewards in teaching. Each teacher had an understandably satisfying emotional reaction to the tokens of appreciation. "They're what keep you going," Judy commented matter-of-factly in a discussion of her enjoyment of her work.

Sharon, a first-grade teacher and another veteran, also looks to emotional rewards in her teaching. "The beginning of the day gets me going," she said, smiling, during an interview in which we asked her about her continued commitment to her career. "I stand at the door, and the children give me a hug, a high-five, or a handshake when they come in the room. Even if the previous day was a bad one, all those little faces are enough to get me started all over again."

Sometimes students show their affection in strange ways.

▪ ▪ ▪

Kerry, a first-year teacher, entered her classroom first thing in the morning on her birthday. After entering her room with a custodian's help, Kerry's students had moved *all* the desks to the center of the room and wrapped them together with tape and toilet paper. How would you react?

Kerry was delighted. "I called [the perpetrators] out of class and had them come down and [another teacher] took a picture of them standing out in the middle of it all. I left it here all day. I made them sit on the floor. It was really fun. It was really a fun day" (Bullough, 1989, p. 86).

▪ ▪ ▪

It helps to have a sense of humor when you teach.

All teachers reap emotional rewards from their experiences. Sharon's wide-eyed first graders, a middle school student like Erica Jacobs, or juniors and seniors in high school, who are struggling to become adults, are all sources of emotional satisfaction for teachers.

Increasing Understanding 1.2

For which group of teachers—teachers of elementary school students (grades K–5), middle school students (grades 6–8), or secondary school students (grades 9–12)—are emotional rewards likely to be the greatest? Explain.

Teachers' interactions with their students provide a major source of intrinsic rewards.

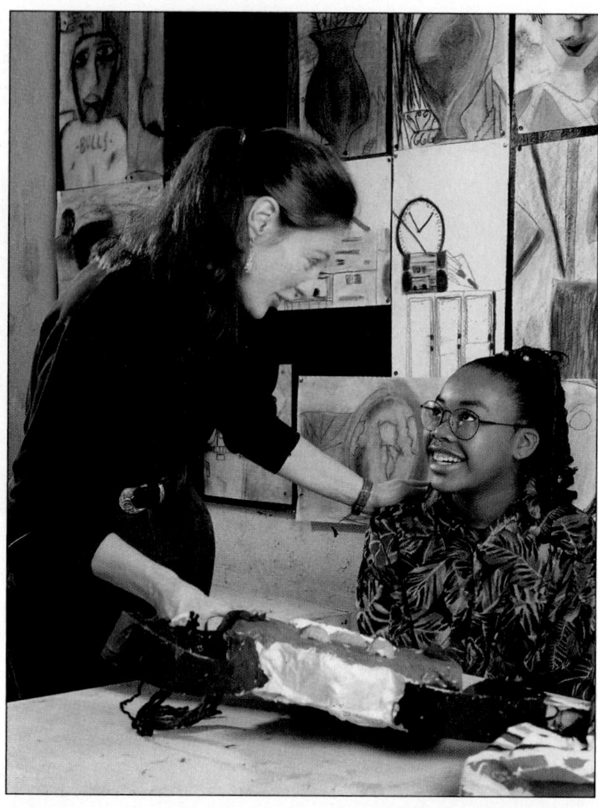

Case STUDY

David Ling, an eighth-grade physical science teacher, enthusiastically says to his students, "Let's think about these questions and try and figure out what they have in common." He then writes the following on the board:

Why do we have seatbelts in our cars?

Why does an automatic washer have holes in the drum?

How does a dog shake the water off itself when it comes out of a pond?

The bemused students look at the list, and after several seconds David continues, "Now, what have we been studying?"

"Inertia," Taneka responds after hesitating briefly.

"Exactly," David smiles. "So, let's review for a minute. What is inertia? . . . Go ahead, Dana."

". . . The tendency . . . of something moving to keep on moving . . . straight."

"Or something not moving to remain still," Jermel adds.

"Excellent, both of you," David nods. "Now, a challenge. Let's answer the questions on the board using the idea of inertia."

With David's guidance, the students conclude that if their cars are suddenly stopped, their bodies have a tendency to keep moving because of their inertia, and the seatbelt stops them, so they don't get hurt. They also conclude that water is separated from clothes in the washer, because the water goes straight out through the holes in the drum, but the clothes are kept in it. Finally, they determine that as the dog shakes one way, and then stops, the water keeps moving, and the same thing happens when it shakes the other way. So, the dog uses the principle of inertia to shake the water from itself.

"Neat," Rebecka says. "Where'd you get that stuff, Mr. Ling?"

"I gradually thought them up," David smiles. "The more I study, the more examples I find. . . . That's what we're here for. We study science, so we can learn how the world around us works."

■ ■ ■

Increasing Understanding 1.3

For which group of teachers—teachers of elementary school students, middle school students, or secondary students—are intellectual rewards likely to be the greatest? Explain.

Intellectual Rewards While some emotional rewards are almost certainly present as well, many teachers teach because they're interested in the content they're teaching and want to share their interest with others. Our survey found that "interest in a content or subject matter field" and "the opportunity for a lifetime of self-growth" were important reasons for considering teaching, ranking 3 and 4 out of 9. Intellectual stimulation, for both you and your students, is an important reason to become a teacher.

A strong sense of personal satisfaction results when someone understands a new idea as a result of a teacher's help. As Suzanne commented, "When you see the light bulb go on for someone, it's all worth it." Sharing with students our love of a content area and seeing students get excited about the same things we do are important intellectual rewards of teaching. Not surprisingly, they are also important reasons veteran teachers remain in the field.

Extrinsic Rewards

In addition to emotional and intellectual rewards, teaching also attracts people for external reasons. **Extrinsic rewards** are *career-linked positive factors such as job security (ranked 6 in our survey) and summer vacations (ranked 7)*. The job security found in teaching is greater than that in most other occupations. For example, after acquiring

Interactions with other teachers provide opportunities for intellectual stimulation and growth.

some experience—usually about three years—teachers are typically awarded tenure. Originally designed to attract good people and protect them from political pressures, tenure provides teachers with job security and is a concrete extrinsic reward. (You will study teacher tenure in detail in Chapter 9.)

In addition to job security, teaching has other extrinsic rewards. According to an old joke, a student was asked to identify three reasons for going into teaching. After pondering the question and being unable to think of any better reasons, the student finally wrote, "June, July, and August."

For some, working in a profession with long vacations is rewarding. In addition to the summer, teachers have vacations at precisely the time when vacations are most attractive—the Friday after Thanksgiving, the winter holiday season, and spring break, for example.

In addition to job security and vacations, additional extrinsic rewards include:

- Work schedules. Because teachers' schedules are similar to students' schedules, many teachers are able to be home after school with their own children.
- Autonomy. **Autonomy,** or *being in control of one's own existence*, has been identified as a basic need by researchers who study human motivation (Ryan & Deci, 1998). Teachers have a great deal of autonomy in their work. In spite of growing concerns about increased regulation and external control, teachers largely decide what and how to teach and, at times, make crucial decisions about students' lives. The autonomy and sense of control over their classrooms allow teachers to express themselves personally and creatively.
- Status. Despite perceptions to the contrary, the teaching profession enjoys considerable occupational status; the public views teaching as not only demanding, but also prestigious (National Education Association, 1993; Rowan, 1994). If you have doubts about teachers' status, think about the trepidation with which parents often approach a parent–teacher conference. They want nothing more than to hear that everything is okay in school and that their child is growing socially and intellectually. Into no other profession's hands is so much care of young people placed.

Increasing Understanding 1.4

Consider medicine, law, and engineering, three other prominent professions. Are the extrinsic rewards in teaching likely to be higher or lower than they are in these professions? Explain.

These intrinsic and extrinsic rewards are not mutually exclusive, of course. The decision to teach or to stay in teaching is influenced by a number of factors; most people choose teaching for both intrinsic and extrinsic reasons, such as the intellectual challenge combined with autonomy.

Case STUDY

Kevin is having a difficult time in James Washington's class. He has missed several days during the grading period, he's disruptive, and he seldom turns in his homework.

James has tried to contact Kevin's mother, a single parent; he left three messages on her answering machine during the last week alone. She hasn't called back.

James works in a school with a large number of underachieving students. Janet Levy, the school principal, is under heavy pressure from the district leadership to raise student test scores, and she is putting similar pressure on the teachers.

"What does Mrs. Levy expect?" James complains to Manuela Martinez, a colleague, after school one day. "Kevin is gone more than he's here; he never turns in his homework; his mom won't call me back. And I'm supposed to get him to learn like those kids in Orange Park [an affluent suburb]. I'm not making enough money to be this stressed. No wonder everyone is trying to transfer out of here."

■ ■ ■

Difficulties in Teaching

James's lament is more common than we would like it to be. In many parts of the country, and particularly in some rural areas and inner cities, teachers face daunting problems. Two of the most common issues involve working conditions and salaries. Let's look at them.

Working Conditions Working conditions are a concern for teachers. School leaders, like Janet Levy, appear unsympathetic; parents or other caregivers, like Kevin's mother, are unresponsive and don't support teachers' efforts; and students are sometimes disruptive or unmotivated. Situations like this are important sources of teacher stress.

Teacher stress has been linked to reduced job satisfaction, poorer relationships with students, decreased teacher effectiveness, and teacher burnout. It is an important reason teachers choose to leave the profession (Abel & Sewell, 1999).

Other difficulties exist. For example, teachers complain about spending so much time on nonteaching requirements and duties, such as filling out student progress reports and other paperwork, monitoring hallways before and after school, checking restrooms for misbehavior, and taking students to and from lunch, that they don't have the time, or energy, to teach effectively. A common lament is, "If they would only give me the time and resources I need, I could teach these students something!"

Salaries Teacher salaries are another concern. Low salaries frequently are cited as a major reason people either avoid teaching as a career or leave teaching after a few years (Metropolitan Life Insurance Company, 1995). Salaries are improving, however. For instance, the average teacher salary in the United States for the 1997–1998 school year was more than $39,000 per year, ranging from a high of more than $50,000 in New Jersey to a low of just below $28,000 in South Dakota. In the same year, the average beginning salary was slightly less than $26,000 (National Center for Educational Statistics, 1999). Beginning teacher salaries for each state in 1997–1998 are shown in Table 1.2.

Your salary will depend on a number of factors, such as the local cost of living and the location of the school district. As you'll see in Chapter 9, property taxes are the major funding source for schools, so teachers' salaries depend, in part, on property values. Also, urban districts typically have higher salaries than their rural counterparts because of the higher cost of living in urban areas.

Other economic factors also exist. Annual salary increases are virtually guaranteed, and, as we said earlier in the chapter, vacation periods are ideal. Medical, dental, and retirement benefits are provided, and job security is high. In addition, teachers are often paid supplements for extra duties, such as club sponsorships, coaching, chairing departments (such as chairing the English department in a middle school), and mentoring beginning teachers (Darling-Hammond, 1998). In schools with year-round schedules, teachers work eleven months of the year—versus nine or ten months—and are paid accordingly.

You might also consider teaching in a private school; approximately 13 percent of all teaching jobs are in private schools (National Center for Educational Statistics, 1997). Their average starting salaries are about 30 percent lower than in public schools, however (Ingersoll, 1997), and the difference increases to more than 40 percent for maximum salaries. Private schools often waive the licensing requirements that public school teachers are required by law to meet, and they usually don't provide the same insurance benefits that public schools provide. One survey, for example, indicated that nearly half of all public schools provide paid medical, dental, and retirement benefits, whereas only about one-fifth of private schools did (Ingersoll, 1997).

Table 1.2 Beginning Teacher Salaries for Each State

State	Salary	State	Salary
Alabama	$27,388	Missouri	$24,125
Alaska	33,162	Montana	21,045
Arizona	24,917	Nebraska	21,949
Arkansas	21,000	Nevada	28,641
California	27,852	New Hampshire	23,927
Colorado	24,867	New Jersey	28,319
Connecticut	29,506	New Mexico	23,297
Delaware	25,493	New York	30,204
District of Columbia	27,234	North Carolina	22,150
Florida	25,266	North Dakota	19,146
Georgia	26,706	Ohio	22,535
Hawaii	26,744	Oklahoma	23,676
Idaho	20,248	Oregon	26,098
Illinois	28,183	Pennsylvania	29,581
Indiana	24,716	Rhode Island	26,300
Iowa	22,475	South Carolina	23,427
Kansas	22,445	South Dakota	20,340
Kentucky	23,536	Tennessee	22,140
Louisiana	22,843	Texas	24,736
Maine	21,554	Utah	22,241
Maryland	27,010	Vermont	25,183
Massachusetts	27,238	Virginia	25,272
Michigan	27,064	Washington	23,860
Minnesota	26,266	West Virginia	22,529
Mississippi	20,630	Wisconsin	24,077
		Wyoming	22,230

Source: From National Center for Educational Statistics. (1999). *Digest of educational statistics.* Washington, D.C.: U.S. Department of Education.

Given these disparities, you might ask, "Why would a teacher choose to teach at a private school?" Some answers include:

- Lack of a licensing requirement
- Commitment to an ideal
- Smaller school bureaucracy
- Smaller classes
- Greater parental involvement

Teachers often choose to work in private schools because they aren't required to take the professional education courses needed for licensing, the school is dedicated to religious or intellectual principles consistent with the teacher's beliefs, communication between administrators and teachers is simpler, and parents whose children attend private schools tend to be more involved in school activities than are parents in public schools.

Whether you plan to teach in a public or private school, choosing any career is ultimately an individual decision, and it depends on a person's values and needs. Whether or not the salaries and benefits in teaching are adequate is a matter of personal judgment.

Putting Rewards and Difficulties into Perspective

Your satisfaction with your teaching career will also be influenced by the specific situation in which you work. **Physical conditions of teaching** are *the school facility and the equipment*

Time spent in administration or noninstructional activities can drain teachers' time and energy.

it contains. The **psychological conditions of teaching** are *the behavioral and emotional characteristics of the students, administrators, and other teachers*. Both can strongly influence student learning as well as teacher satisfaction (Lawrence-Lightfoot, 1983; Metz, 1978).

The student–teacher ratio is one of the most important physical conditions. A survey conducted by the National Center for Education Statistics (1998) showed that from state to state the students-per-teacher ratio ranges from 13.7 to 24.1. These figures can be misleading, however. Because school administrators, counselors, and special educators are counted as "teachers" in the statistics, the actual ratios can be considerably higher; 25 to 35 students in K–12 classes are common.

The social and emotional conditions of teaching are also important. Teaching is heavily interpersonal, and the human-to-human interactions you have with your students, school administrators, and colleagues will have a powerful influence on your satisfaction with your career. Most students and parents are cooperative to work with, and most administrators are cooperative and supportive. Others are similar to Kevin, his mother, and Janet Levy. If the emotional and intellectual rewards of teaching—like those Kasia, Judy, Miguel, and David received—outweigh the frustrations James described, and if the salary and benefits are adequate, it may be a good career choice for you. If not, another career may be preferable.

Increasing Understanding 1.5

As you anticipate a teaching career, do you believe that teaching is more or less difficult than it was ten years ago? Explain.

THE TEACHING PROFESSION

What does it mean to be a professional? Are teachers professionals? Is professionalism more important now than it has been in the past? We try to answer these questions in this section as we look at teaching as a profession.

Characteristics of Professionalism

Researchers examining the concept of *professionalism*, and professions such as medicine and law, identify the following characteristics of a profession (Ingersoll, 1997; Labaree; 1992):

- A specialized body of knowledge
- Extended training for licensure

- Autonomy
- Ethical standards for conduct

A Specialized Body of Knowledge Professionals understand and can utilize a specialized body of knowledge. A physician, for example, can recognize symptoms of diseases and other ailments and is able to prescribe medications, surgical procedures, or other forms of therapy to eliminate the symptoms and their causes. This requires specialized knowledge, and it's a major reason people seek the advice and help of physicians.

Is this true for teaching? Research indicates that effective teachers possess at least four kinds of knowledge (Borko & Putnam, 1996):

- Knowledge of the content they're teaching, such as a thorough understanding of math, science, geography, or literature.
- Pedagogical content knowledge, such as the ability to illustrate concepts like *equivalent fractions* in math or *nationalism* in history, in ways that are understandable to students.
- General pedagogical knowledge, such as the ability to maintain an orderly classroom or guide student learning with questions.
- Knowledge of learners and learning, such as the understanding that learners, even in high school, tend to be egocentric, seeing the world from their own perspectives and often ignoring the views of others.

Increasing Understanding 1.6

Some people believe that teaching isn't a profession because people other than teachers also "teach." For example, young people learn a great deal from their parents, the clergy, and friends. Make an argument both for and against this theory of why teaching isn't a profession. (Use medicine as a point of reference, that is, to what extent do people other than physicians practice medicine?)

A knowledge base allows teachers to make decisions in complex or ill-defined situations, and this decision-making process is one of the differences between a professional and a **technician,** *a person who uses specific skills to complete well-defined tasks*, such as an electrician wiring an outlet. Technical skills are important, of course, but the decision-making process is less complex in technical areas.

Decision making in teaching is incredibly complex. Jackson (1968), in his classic study of elementary classrooms, suggested that teachers make more than 800 decisions a day; Murray (1986) estimated the number at 1,500. Even using the conservative figure, this translates into more than 130 decisions per hour in a 6-hour teaching day!

What kinds of decisions do teachers have to make? Let's look at three examples:

Case STUDY

A kindergarten teacher has just distributed materials for an art project and is surveying the room to see if everyone has started. She notices that Jimmy is staring out the window with his thumb in his mouth and tears in his eyes. It is the beginning of the school year, and Jimmy still isn't used to being away from home. Should the teacher wait a minute and see if the art materials will do the trick, or should she intervene?

■ ■ ■

A middle school teacher is getting frustrated. Mary is obviously more interested in her friends than in English, and the teacher can't keep her from talking. He calls on her; she doesn't hear the question. Should he reprimand her, repeat the question, or go on to another student?

■ ■ ■

A high school teacher has just distributed an assignment. She goes over the work in depth, explaining its importance and how it should be done. She concludes by reminding the class that the grade for the assignment counts as one-fourth of the semester grade. An audible "Who cares?" follows. Should the teacher ignore it and go on, or should she respond? (Kauchak & Eggen, 1998, p. 181).

■ ■ ■

Increasing Understanding 1.7

If you were the middle school teacher, would you reprimand Mary, repeat the question, or go on to another student? Explain your reasoning. (The feedback for this question will give you a research-based answer.)

A teacher's ability to make decisions quickly in circumstances such as these is crucial, and the wisdom of these decisions depends on a teacher's knowledge.

An additional aspect of professional knowledge is the ability and inclination to learn. Just as physicians must continually upgrade their knowledge of therapies, medications, and surgical procedures, teachers must stay abreast of progress in their field. For instance, it makes sense intuitively to encourage students who aren't successful to work harder, but research indicates that this suggestion may be counterproductive. Young children generally believe they're already working hard, so they're bewildered by the suggestion, and older students believe the need to work hard is an indicator of low ability (Tollefson, 2000). Effective teachers stay informed of research in their fields, and they adapt their teaching to reflect this research.

Training for Licensure As with physicians, lawyers, and engineers, teachers must earn a license that allows them to practice their profession. The license is intended to certify that the teacher is knowledgeable and competent and, as with other professions, teachers must renew their licenses to confirm that they are staying current in their fields. Teachers need at least a bachelor's degree prior to licensure, and in many states they must complete the degree in a content area, such as math or English, before they begin teacher preparation experiences. Licensure also requires clinical experiences, such as internships, which are designed to ensure that teachers can apply the professional knowledge they've acquired to the real world of schools.

Autonomy Professionals have the authority to make decisions based on their professional knowledge. When a person sees a physician because of stomach pains, for example, no set of standards mandates treatment or medication; physicians are given the authority to treat patients as they see fit. Those suggesting that teaching isn't a profession argue that states and districts, instead of teachers, are prescribing **curriculum**—*what teachers teach*—and **assessment**—*how student understanding is measured*. This lack of autonomy, they assert, makes teachers technicians instead of professionals.

We disagree. States and districts are indeed prescribing **standards**—*what students should know and what skills they should have upon completing an area of study* (such as fourth grade language arts, or Algebra I)—that must be met before students are allowed to move from one grade to another or to graduate from high school. However, in spite of these mandates, teachers have a great deal of control over what is taught, how they will teach it, and how students will be assessed. Also, the enormous number of decisions teachers make each day depends primarily on their own judgment. Teachers have a great deal of autonomy in their professional lives.

Case STUDY

To begin this section, consider the following examples.

You are an ardent advocate of gun control; you believe that access to guns should be strongly regulated and have said so in class. Eric, one of your students, brings a newspaper editorial to school in which a compelling argument *against* gun control is made. You don't allow the student to share the editorial with the class.

■ ■ ■

Greg is a very difficult student in one of your classes. He is continually disruptive and periodically shouts insults at other students and sometimes even at you. You've tried everything you know to control his behavior, but you've been unsuccessful. Finally, in exasperation one day, another student tells him, "Shut up! I can't think!" after one of his outbursts. To your surprise, Greg is embarrassed and sits quietly for the remainder of the period. Now, finding that public embarrassment seems to be the only way to keep Greg from being disruptive, you use it as a technique to manage his behavior.

Brittany, a student with a specific learning disability in reading, is on the borderline between failing and passing. When final grades are due, you see that she has a failing average. You pass her, reasoning that since she has a disability, she deserves a break. Perhaps she didn't understand the wording on some assignments or quizzes.

■ ■ ■

Professional Ethics Have you behaved "ethically" in these examples? How do you know? **Ethics** *describes moral standards for good behavior;* all professions have a code of ethics intended to guide professionals as they attempt to answer difficult questions like the ones we just asked. Ethical standards are so important to professionals that they are often written into employment contracts.

The National Education Association, the largest professional organization in education, has prepared a code of ethics that is intended as a guide for the professional behavior of teachers in working with their students. It is outlined in Figure 1.1.

Let's look at your actions based on the information in the NEA Code of Ethics. Item 2 in the Commitment to the Student principle (Principle I) in the Code states that a teacher "shall not unreasonably deny the student access to varying points of view." In our first example, you didn't let Eric share the editorial with the other students, so you have denied them access to varying points of view. Whether or not your denial is "unreasonable" is open to interpretation as is the case with ethical standards in any profession.

In the second example, you were desperately searching for a technique to manage Greg's behavior, and you found that embarrassment was the only thing that seemed to work. However, Item 5 in Principle I states that the teacher "shall not intentionally expose the student to embarrassment or disparagement." This case is clear; in your desperation and frustration, you intentionally are using embarrassment as a technique with Greg, so you are in violation of the ethical code.

In the third example, you have given Brittany a break *because* she has a disability. Item 6 in Principle I says the teacher "shall not on the basis of race, color, creed, sex,

Professional knowledge allows teachers to make the split-second decisions essential for effective teaching.

Figure 1.1 **National Education Association Code of Ethics**

Preamble

The educator, believing in the worth and dignity of each human being, recognizes the supreme importance of the pursuit of truth, devotion to excellence, and the nurture of democratic principle. Essential to these goals is the protection of freedom to learn and to teach and the guarantee of equal educational opportunity for all. The educator accepts the responsibility to adhere to the highest ethical standards.

The educator recognizes the magnitude of the responsibility inherent in the teaching process. The desire for the respect and confidence of one's colleagues, of students, of parents, and the members of the community provides the incentive to attain and maintain the highest possible degree of ethical conduct. The Code of Ethics of the Education Profession indicates the aspiration of all educators and provides standards by which to judge conduct.

The remedies specified by the NEA and/or its affiliates for the violation of any provision of this Code shall be exclusive and no such provision shall be enforceable in any form other than one specifically designated by the NEA or its affiliates.

Principle I—Commitment to the Student

The educator strives to help each student realize his or her potential as a worthy and effective member of society. The educator therefore works to stimulate the spirit of inquiry, the acquisition of knowledge and understanding, and the thoughtful formulation of worthy goals.

In fulfillment of the obligation to the student, the educator—

1. Shall not unreasonably restrain the student from independent action in the pursuit of learning.
2. Shall not unreasonably deny the student access to varying points of view.
3. Shall not deliberately suppress or distort subject matter relevant to the student's progress.
4. Shall make reasonable effort to protect the student from conditions harmful to learning or to health and safety.
5. Shall not intentionally expose the student to embarrassment or disparagement.
6. Shall not on the basis of race, color, creed, sex, national origin, marital status, political or religious beliefs, family, social or cultural background, or sexual orientation unfairly:
   a. Exclude any student from participation in any program;
   b. Deny benefits to any student;
   c. Grant any advantage to any student.
7. Shall not use professional relationships with students for private advantage.
8. Shall not disclose information about students obtained in the course of professional service, unless disclosure serves a compelling professional purpose or is required by law.

Principle II—Commitment to the Profession

The education profession is vested by the public with a trust and responsibility requiring the highest ideals of professional service.

In the belief that the quality of the services of the education profession directly influences the nation and its citizens, the educator shall exert every effort to raise professional standards, to promote a climate that encourages the exercise of professional judgment, to achieve conditions which attract persons worthy of the trust to careers in education, and to assist in preventing the practice of the profession by unqualified persons.

In fulfillment of the obligation to the profession, the educator—

1. Shall not in an application for a professional position deliberately make a false statement or fail to disclose a material fact related to competency and qualifications.
2. Shall not misrepresent his/her professional qualifications.
3. Shall not assist entry into the profession of a person known to be unqualified in respect to character, education, or other relevant attribute.
4. Shall not knowingly make a false statement concerning the qualifications of a candidate for a profession position.
5. Shall not assist a noneducator in the unauthorized practice of teaching.
6. Shall not disclose information about colleagues obtained in the course of professional service unless disclosure serves a compelling professional purpose or is required by law.
7. Shall not knowingly make a false or malicious statement about a colleague.
8. Shall not accept any gratuity, gift, or favor that might impair or appear to influence professional decisions or actions.

Source: From National Education Association. (1995). Code of Ethics of the Education Profession, NEA Representative Assembly. Reprinted by permission.

Reflect on This

AN ETHICAL DILEMMA

As you're sitting in the teachers' lounge one day, Dana, one of your colleagues, says, "Well, you know that Sheri [another teacher in the school] was brought up on charges of plagiarism when she was working on her master's degree. I guess she got away with it, because her advisor had a lot of political clout, or something, and the whole incident was swept under the rug."

Dana shrugs, gets a cup of coffee, and leaves the room.

Several days later, you hear Dana repeat her story to another teacher in the lounge.

1. Is Dana behaving ethically in making her remarks to you, and later, to the other teacher?
2. As a professional, should you intervene? In other words, should you say something to Dana? Should you say something to Sheri? Should you say anything to the school principal or other administrator?
3. Suppose that Dana's accusations are true, that is, Sheri actually was accused of plagiarism. Is Dana then behaving ethically in making her statements?
4. What would you do in this situation?

To answer these questions online and receive immediate feedback, go to the Reflect on This Module in Chapter 1 of the Companion Website.

national origin, marital status, political or religious beliefs, family, social or cultural background, or sexual orientation unfairly grant any advantage to any student." As with our first example, a violation of the code of ethics is a matter of interpretation; it isn't clear whether or not you have "unfairly" granted an advantage to Brittany because she has a disability.

The point in these examples is that standards for ethical behavior exist in teaching—even when situations aren't clear-cut—as they do for any other profession.

Are Teachers Professionals?

The information in the preceding section suggests that teaching is a profession and teachers are professionals. Not all people agree, however. Some arguments against teaching being a profession include:

- Lack of rigorous training
- Lack of a unique function
- Lack of autonomy
- Lack of accountability

Lack of Rigorous Training The academic rigor of teachers' professional training has historically been criticized (Gross, 1999; Kramer, 1991). Entrance into teaching isn't highly competitive, particularly on intellectual grounds, and many proposed reforms suggest that pedagogical content knowledge, general pedagogical knowledge, and knowledge of learners and learning be de-emphasized in favor of knowledge of content (Gross, 1999). The argument is often made, though not supported by research, that the only thing that teachers need is knowledge of the subjects they are teaching.

Lack of a Unique Function Whereas only physicians are allowed to practice medicine and only lawyers can legally practice the law, critics suggest that a great many people—other than licensed teachers—practice education. (We addressed this issue initially in Increasing Understanding 1.6). For instance, some young people are involved in formal religious training provided by their churches, where their instructors are certainly acting as teachers, and some children are "home schooled" by their parents, a practice allowed by law.

Lack of Autonomy In an earlier section we argued that teachers have a great deal of autonomy. While we maintain this position, it is important to note that teachers have less autonomy than other professionals. For example, unlike physicians and lawyers, teachers are supervised and evaluated by their immediate school administrators, and a substantial portion of the curriculum is mandated by states or districts. Teachers have little to say about the standards for licensure, and many teachers even have to sign in at the beginning of the day and sign out at the end.

Lack of Accountability Critics also argue that teachers are not accountable for student learning. If a student is unable to read at the end of the third-grade, for example, little consequence exists for the third-grade teacher. Further, when teachers achieve tenure, they are secure in their jobs. Barring a sexual offense or clear incompetence, removing a tenured teacher is extremely difficult.

Putting Teacher Professionalism into Perspective

The issue of whether or not teaching is a profession is controversial, and it won't be resolved in the near future. Without question, the training required for professions like medicine and law is more rigorous than the training required for teaching, though rigor in teacher education is on the rise (Olson, 2000a). Prospective teachers are expected to know and do more, and, increasingly, their understanding and skills are being assessed with tests.

Also, while children are taught by a number of different sources, such as family and the church, the primary institution responsible for helping children learn to read, write, and do math, for example, is the school. Teachers are seen as the people primarily responsible for student learning and intellectual development.

With respect to autonomy, a battle currently is being fought on both sides of the issue. Some would curtail teachers' autonomy by mandating what and how to teach, as well as specifying how to assess student learning. Others argue that this technical view of teaching is unfeasible and unproductive; teaching requires too many decisions to be reduced to mandates, and attempts to do so discourage creative people from considering teaching as a career.

Also, the accountability issue isn't unique to education. Admittedly, teachers don't lose their jobs if their students perform poorly on standardized tests, but similar examples exist in other professions. For instance, physicians don't lose their right to practice medicine if they prescribe an antibiotic for an ear infection, and the infection doesn't go away, and attorneys don't lose their right to practice law if they lose a case.

The issue of professionalism has important implications for teaching and for you as a prospective teacher. One of the most important is this: *If you expect to be treated as a professional, then you must act like a professional.* Commit yourself to academic excellence. Voice your criticisms of courses and experiences that are light on content and low in standards. Make every effort to thoroughly understand the body of knowledge in your profession.

Professional ethics guide teachers in their interactions with students, parents and caregivers, and colleagues.

Looking Through
Classroom Windows

CLASSROOMS IN ACTION: THE REAL WORLD OF TEACHING

Having looked at the reasons people choose to teach, the rewards and difficulties in teaching, and teacher professionalism, you now have the opportunity to look at three teachers in action. To complete this activity, do the following:

- View the video episodes titled "Classrooms in Action: The Real World of Teaching."
- Read the written transcripts of the three episodes and answer the following questions online by going to the *Classroom Windows* Module in Chapter 1 of the Companion Website at: **http://www.prenhall.com/kauchak.** Go to the Website and follow the directions on your screen.
- Answer the questions that follow:

1. For which of the three teachers are the emotional rewards likely to be the greatest? Explain.
2. For which of the three teachers are the intellectual rewards likely to be the greatest? Explain.
3. Based on what you saw in the episodes, which teacher do you believe has the most difficult job? Explain.
4. For which teacher is knowledge of content most important? Pedagogical content knowledge? General pedagogical knowledge? Knowledge of learners and learning? Explain.
5. How much autonomy do you believe each teacher had in designing and conducting his or her lessons? Explain.
6. To what extent do you believe each teacher demonstrated the characteristics of a professional? Explain.

To answer these questions online and receive immediate feedback, go to the Looking Through Classroom Windows Module in Chapter 1 of the Companion Website.

One way of promoting professionalism is to encourage and endorse high standards for licensure. Professional organizations in education historically have been criticized for fighting high standards, but this is now changing (Blair, 2000). Endorse these changes and encourage others to support them as well.

Take your code of ethics seriously. Anything less detracts from the profession and detracts from you as a person and your status as a professional.

BECOMING A TEACHER IN AN ERA OF REFORM

You're beginning your teacher-preparation experience in one of the most tumultuous periods in the history of American education. Critics, both inside and outside the profession, are calling for **reforms,** which are *suggested changes in teaching and teacher preparation intended to increase the amount students learn*. To implement these reforms, teachers must be well-prepared, and leaders in education are saying that we need to professionalize teaching (Blair, 2000). We examine the implications of these reform efforts in this section.

Reform: What Does it Mean?

Educational reform attempts to improve schools through changes in the way they are organized and run. To place recent reform efforts in perspective, we should point out that the process of change and reform has been a part of education throughout its history. From colonial times to the present, schools and teachers have been fair game for outside critics. The openness and accessibility of teaching makes it a unique profession; everyone has been in school. All people have views about teaching, and most of them have opinions about how to improve education. When you study the history of education in Chapter 5, you will see how different reforms have shaped education.

The modern reform movement is often traced to 1983, when the National Commission on Excellence in Education published *A Nation at Risk: The Imperative for Education Reform*. This widely read document suggested that America was "at risk" of being unable to compete in the world economic marketplace because our system of education was inadequate. The terms "at-risk students" and, more recently, "students placed at risk" can also be traced back to this document; these students were at-risk of not acquiring the knowledge and skills needed for success in our modern society. Since 1983 a great many suggestions have been made for improving our nation's schools and the teachers who work in them.

Because discussions of reform are so prominent in education today, we have made it a theme for this book. To introduce you to this theme and the idea of reform, we briefly examine three of the more prominent reforms here:

- Changes in teacher preparation
- Standards-based education
- Accountability and high-stakes testing

Changes in Teacher Preparation Earlier in the chapter we noted increased calls for teacher professionalism, and we examined characteristics of professionalism as they relate to teaching. Reforms in teacher education have implications for the move toward greater teacher professionalism. These reforms include:

- Raising standards for acceptance into teacher-training programs.
- Requiring teachers to take more rigorous courses than they have in the past.
- Requiring higher standards for licensure, including teacher tests.

- Expanding teacher-preparation programs from four years to five.
- Requiring experienced teachers to take more rigorous professional development courses (Blair, 2000).

Some of these suggestions are almost certainly going to affect you. We'll describe two as examples. First, you probably will be required to pass a test before you're awarded your teaching license. At the present time:

- Thirty-nine states require prospective teachers to pass a basic skills test.
- Twenty-nine states require high school teachers to pass tests in the subjects they plan to teach.
- Twenty-seven states require principals to evaluate new teachers (Olson, 2000a).

The American Federation of Teachers, the second largest professional organization for teachers in the United States, recently proposed that prospective teachers pass tests aimed at basic content, such as math and English, as well as tests designed to measure teachers' knowledge of teaching principles (Blair, 2000). This proposal signals a change in policy from the past and suggests that teacher testing is not only here to stay, but is likely to increase.

Second, you will likely be required to take more courses in English, math, science, history, and geography than have been required of teachers in the past. In addition, there is a movement to require all teachers, elementary and secondary, to major in a content area for their undergraduate degree. The rationale behind this push is that teachers can't teach what they don't know themselves.

Whether or not these reforms will result in the hoped-for improvements in education remains to be seen and will continue to be debated. One thing is virtually certain, however. Efforts to reform schools, teachers, and the way teachers are prepared will continue, and you will begin your career as a teacher in the middle of these efforts. Joan Baratz-Snowden, spokesperson for the American Federation of Teachers, summarizes this trend, "It is a new day. Standards-based education is significantly different, and we have to prepare teachers to be successful in it." (Blair, 2000).

Standards-Based Education A great deal has been written about Americans' and American students' lack of knowledge about their world. Research suggests, for example, that 60 percent of adult Americans don't know the name of the president that ordered the dropping of the atomic bomb, 42 percent of college seniors can't place the Civil War in the correct half century, most Americans can't find the Persian Gulf on a map, and 43 percent are unable to find England (Bertman, 2000). While these examples focus on history and geography, even greater concerns have been raised about math, science, and writing. The result has been a move toward **standards-based education,** which is *the process of focusing curriculum and instruction on predetermined standards*. The following are examples of standards for middle school math students created by the National Council of Teachers of Mathematics.

■ ■ ■

Number and Operations Standard for Grades 6–8

Instructional programs from prekindergarten through grade 12 should enable all students to compute fluently and make reasonable estimates:

In grades 6–8 all students should:

- Select appropriate methods and tools for computing with fractions and decimals from among mental computation, estimation, calculators or computers, and paper and pencil, depending on the situation, and apply the selected methods;
- Develop and analyze algorithms for computing with fractions, decimals, and integers and develop fluency in their use;
- Develop and use strategies to estimate the results of rational-number computations and judge the reasonableness of the results;
- Develop, analyze, and explain methods for solving problems involving proportions, such as scaling and finding equivalent ratios. (National Council of Teachers of Mathematics, 2000, p. 214)

■ ■ ■

States also publish standards to guide learning in different content areas:

■ ■ ■

Science: "In Science, students in Missouri public schools will acquire a solid foundation, which includes knowledge of . . . properties and principles of force and motion" (Missouri Department of Elementary and Secondary Education, 1995).

Reading: (Grades 6–8) "Demonstrate inferential comprehension of a variety of printed materials." Grade 8 benchmark: "Identify relationships, images, patterns or symbols and draw conclusions about their meaning" (Oregon Department of Education, 1996).

Social Studies: (Grade 5) "The student will describe colonial America, with emphasis on . . . the principal economic and political connections between the colonies and England" (Virginia Board of Education, 1995).

■ ■ ■

As you can see, these standards are often general and vague. Not until they are translated into specific learning activities or test items do teachers or students have a clear idea of what should be learned or how it will be measured.

The standards movement is widespread; virtually all states have specified standards for at least some of the content areas, and students as well as teachers are being held accountable for meeting these standards.

Teaching in an Era of Reform

We said earlier in this section that we have made *reform* a theme for this book, and you've seen "changes in teacher preparation" and "standards-based education" as two examples. To involve you in examining prominent reforms, we are including a feature in each chapter called "Teaching in an Era of Reform." We will introduce the feature in this chapter and illustrate how you will be asked to respond. The feature includes the following elements:

- A reform issue, such as retaining students who don't pass tests in the same grade (discussed in Chapter 7), or *learner-centered* versus *teacher-centered instruction* (discussed in Chapter 11), is presented and discussed.
- The issue is "put into perspective" by the inclusion of arguments for and against the reform.
- You are then asked to take a position with respect to the issue by going to the Website for *Education Week* (a widely read newspaper devoted to education), studying several articles that discuss the issue, and responding to the articles in writing.

We will illustrate the process in the next section, using "accountability and high-stakes testing" as the reform issue.

Teaching 

in an Era *of* Reform

ACCOUNTABILITY AND HIGH-STAKES TESTING

In response to concerns about students graduating from high school without the skills needed to succeed either in college or the workplace, reformers have called for greater accountability for both students and teachers. **Accountability** means that *students are required to demonstrate that they have met specified standards or that they demonstrate understanding of the topics they study as measured by standardized tests, and teachers are being held responsible for students' performance*. Calls for accountability resulted from evidence indicating that students were being promoted from grade to grade without having mastered essential content; some students were graduating from high school barely able to read, write, and do mathematics effectively, and even more had limited scientific literacy and a general lack of understanding of our world.

High-stakes tests are *tests used to determine whether or not students will be promoted from one grade to another, graduate from high school, or have access to specific fields of study*. When students aren't allowed to graduate from high school because they fail a test, for example, the "stakes" are very high, thus the term "high-stakes tests."

High-stakes testing is widespread. For example:

- Every state but Iowa has adopted standards in at least some academic subjects.
- Forty-eight states have testing programs designed, in large part, to measure how well students perform on those standards.
- Twenty-one states plan to issue overall ratings of their schools based largely on their students' performance.
- At least eighteen states have the authority to close, take over, or overhaul schools that are identified as failing (Olson, 2000b).

Putting Reform into Perspective

As you might expect, high-stakes testing is very controversial, with critics arguing that it limits what teachers do. Critics assert that teachers spend too much of their time in school helping students practice for the tests and that teacher creativity is eliminated, because they must narrowly focus their teaching on the content of the tests.

Standards and the movement toward accountability may require teachers to work individually with students to ensure that all learn essential knowledge and skills.

Pressure to do well on the tests is so great that some teachers and administrators have been driven to cheat; they help students with the tests or even give them answers (Viadero, 2000b). In Massachusetts, high-stakes testing became so controversial that the state's largest teachers' union, in a highly unusual move, launched a $600,000 television campaign that sharply criticized the *Massachusetts Comprehensive Assessment System* exam, an exam students in the state must pass to graduate (Gehring, 2000).

Increasing Understanding 1.8

Virtually everyone reading this text has taken either the SAT (Scholastic Aptitude Test) or the ACT (American College Testing) program to determine whether you can get into a particular college or university. Are these "high-stakes" tests? Explain.

Advocates of testing, while conceding that teacher preparation, materials, and the tests themselves need to be improved, argue that the tests are the fairest and most effective means of achieving the aims of democratic schooling. Further, they assert, evidence indicates that educational systems that require content standards and use tests that thoroughly measure the extent to which the standards are met greatly improve the achievement for all students, including those from disadvantaged backgrounds (Bishop, 1995, 1998). Hirsch (2000) summarizes the testing advocates' position: "They [standards and tests that measure achievement of the standards] are the most promising educational development in half a century" (p. 64).

You Take a Position

Now it's your turn to take a position on the issue discussed in this section. Go to the *Education Week* Website at **http://www.edweek.com**, find "search" on the first page, and type in one of the following two search terms: *high-stakes tests* or *accountability*. Locate a minimum of three articles on one of these topics and then do the following:

1. Identify the title, author, and date of each article and write a one-paragraph summary of each.
2. Identify a pattern in the articles. (An example of a pattern would be if each article—or even two of the three—suggests that parents approve of high-stakes tests.)
3. After identifying the pattern, take one of the two following positions:
   - The pattern suggested in the articles, if implemented, *is* likely to improve education.
   - The pattern suggested in the articles *is not* likely to improve education.

State your position in writing and document your position with information taken from the articles. Give your response to your instructor.

To answer these questions online, go to the Take a Position Module in Chapter 1 of the Companion Website.

Now, let's look at a possible response to this feature. The response consists of three parts:

- A summary of three articles found on the *Education Week* Website (**http://www.edweek.com**). (Remember to double click on "search" on the right side of the page and enter *high-stakes testing* in the box under "Enter your search terms.")
- A description of the pattern found in the articles.
- A position on whether the pattern, if generally implemented, would or would not improve education.

The following is a sample response:

The Three Selected Articles

1. *LA Set To Retain 4th, 8th Graders Based on State Exams* by Erik Robelen, in the May 24, 2000, issue
2. *Arizona Poised to Revisit Graduation Exam* by Darcia Bowman, in the November 29, 2000, issue
3. *Standardized Testing and Its Victims* by Alfie Kohn, in the September 27, 2000, issue

Summary of the Articles

In the first article, Erik Robelen reported that nearly one-third of Louisiana's fourth and eighth graders failed the state's high-stakes test in the spring of 2000. Students who failed will have the opportunity to attend summer school and retake the tests in July, and those who fail a second time face the prospect of repeating a grade next fall. An appeals process exists that allows students who failed the tests, but meet certain other criteria, to request permission to continue to the next grade.

In the second article, Darcia Bowman reported that Arizona education officials are considering delaying a requirement that the state's high school students pass the *Arizona Instrument to Measure Standards* test to graduate, because too many students are failing the test, and large differences exist in the performance of minority and White students. State officials emphasize that this move doesn't imply that Arizona is calling an end to the state's efforts to implement standards and accountability.

In the third article, Alfie Kohn sharply criticizes the increased emphasis on testing and points out that our students are being tested to a greater extent than at any time in history. He is most critical of basing important decisions, such as graduation or promotion, on the results of a single test, and points out that most professional organizations, such as the American Educational Research Association, and the National Council for Teachers of Mathematics hold a similar position. Yet, he notes, just such high-stakes testing is currently taking place, or is scheduled to be introduced soon, in more than half the states.

The Pattern Found in the Articles

A clear pattern exists. States are now implementing high-stakes tests, and several states are also requiring—or are at least considering requiring—that students pass high-stakes tests in order to be promoted to the next grade level or to graduate from high school.

A Possible Position Taken with Respect to the Articles

This pattern—requiring students to pass high-stakes tests to be promoted or graduate—will not help education. As Darcia Bowman points out, not all Arizona students are being taught the content in the standards. Retaining students in a particular grade because they are unable to demonstrate understanding of content they haven't been taught obviously is unfair. Erik Robelen quotes Lorrie A. Shepard, an education professor at the University of Colorado at Boulder: "Every leading body has said you shouldn't make those decisions on the basis of a test alone."

What you've just read is an example that you can use for reference when you're asked to respond to the "Teaching in an Era of Reform" feature in Chapters 2–13. It doesn't mean that your responses must mirror this one. Good luck.

Exploring Diversity: Cultural Minorities and High-Stakes Tests As we saw in the previous section, high-stakes tests are very controversial. An important part of the controversy focuses on critics' claims that these tests are destructive for cultural minorities, particularly Hispanic and African American students who consistently score lower on standardized tests than do their White and Asian counterparts (Bowman, 2000; Viadero & Johnston, 2000). An example of the controversy surrounding the issue occurred in 1999 when the *Mexican-American Legal Defense and Educational Fund* (MALDEF) filed a federal lawsuit seeking to end the practice of requiring students to pass a test to graduate from high school in Texas. MALDEF argued that the Texas Assessment of Academic Skills (TAAS) is unfair to thousands of Hispanic and African-American students (Wildavsky, 1999).

The MALDEF lawsuit was just one case in a long line of controversies over race and testing. All raise the same question: As standardized tests are used increasingly to measure and improve student performance—with important consequences for not measuring up—will historically lower-scoring African-American and Hispanic students be treated fairly? MALDEF's answer to the question is, of course, no, but not all educators—includ-

A major element of many current reform efforts is increased emphasis on testing in schools.

ing some in Texas—agree. For example, one school district in Houston made increased scores on the TAAS a high priority, which resulted in dramatic improvement in the performance of the students, who were 86 percent Hispanic and 88 percent economically disadvantaged (Johnston, 2000).

Other educators have suggested comprehensive strategies for decreasing the achievement gap between minority and nonminority students, and testing is an integral part of those strategies. Increasing minority achievement is the goal, and supporters of testing dismiss criticisms by saying that the critics tacitly assume that eliminating tests will somehow increase achievement; test supporters assert that this simply is not true (Viadero & Johnston, 2000).

However, several issues related to high-stakes testing with minority students remain unanswered. One is whether the tests are sufficiently accurate to justify using the test scores to make important decisions about students' academic lives (Kohn, 2000). A second issue relates to technical problems involved in testing minorities in general (Land, 1997) as well as ESL students, who speak English as a second language (Abedi, 1999). High-stakes test designers need to ensure that test scores reflect differences in achievement rather than cultural or language differences. Finally, deciding student grade promotion or graduation solely on the basis of one test score is being increasingly criticized by a number of prestigious educational professional organizations including the American Educational Research Association and the National Council of Teachers of Mathematics.

Unquestionably, testing is necessary to measure the learning progress of all students, both minorities and nonminorities. Whether or not progress from one grade to another or graduation from high school should be linked to performance on the tests remains an open and troubling question.

The Changing Role of Teachers

Increased accountability and testing for students are reforms that are facts of life for teachers. How will these reforms change your role as a teacher? At least four implications are likely.

First, you'll need to know more. Compared to teachers in the past, you'll be expected to know more English, math, science, history, and geography. The general education requirements for teachers almost certainly will increase, and prospective teachers will be expected to demonstrate their understanding of these subjects on tests before they will be allowed to teach.

Second, you will be held responsible for student learning, and allowances for the increasingly diverse backgrounds of your students probably will not be made. In other words, you will be held responsible for your students' performance regardless of their home environments, background experiences, or motivation. To meet these expectations—in addition to your knowledge of English, history, and other forms of content—your pedagogical content knowledge, general pedagogical knowledge, and knowledge of learners and learning will have to be thorough. In addition, you probably will be tested on the material you learn in your teacher preparation classes. Your performance on these tests may determine if you get a license and whether you will be allowed to teach.

Third, in spite of controversies, testing will be an important part of your teaching life. As we said earlier, you will be tested before you're allowed to enter the profession, and the students you teach will be tested regularly. Proposals are being made to provide merit pay for teachers whose students do well on these tests and to review teachers whose students do not (Bradley, 2000; Hoff, 2000).

Fourth, as you begin your career, you will probably have less autonomy than teachers had 10 or even 5 years ago. You'll be expected to help your students meet the standards mandated by your state or district, so the number of decisions you'll be allowed to make on your own will be reduced. This is a dilemma. As we saw earlier in the chapter, educational leaders are advocating an increase in the professionalization of teaching, and professionals have autonomy. At the same time, other leaders are mandating standards that reduce teacher autonomy, which detracts from professionalism.

Finally, you will need to be highly adaptable. Some specific reforms will be abandoned, only to be replaced by new reforms. Your ability to understand and quickly adapt to these changes will strongly influence your success in and satisfaction with a teaching career.

Despite the negative effects of some reform efforts, teachers still have considerable autonomy in their classrooms.

SUMMARY

Why People Decide to Teach
Research indicates that the most frequently given reason that people choose to teach is their desire to work with young people and make contributions to society. Other reasons to enter teaching include intellectual growth and interest in a content area.

Rewards and Difficulties in Teaching
Teaching is both rewarding and difficult. Intrinsic rewards include helping young people grow emotionally, socially, and intellectually, and extrinsic rewards include desirable vacation times, autonomy, and status. Difficulties include working with students who aren't motivated and are difficult to manage, as well as unresponsive parents, administrators who aren't supportive, and a great many nonteaching duties that are associated with the job.

The Teaching Profession
Professionals in any field understand a specialized body of knowledge, train for licensure, have a great deal of autonomy, and use ethical standards to guide their professional conduct.

Some people argue that teachers are not professionals, suggesting their training isn't rigorous, they don't provide a unique service, they lack autonomy, and accountability is lacking. Others contend that teaching is a developing profession, evolving over time.

Becoming a Teacher in an Era of Reform
The reform movement in education includes emphasis on higher standards for learners and teachers as well as accountability. Prospective teachers will also encounter a number of reforms calling for higher standards, more rigorous training, and increased testing.

The Changing Role of the Teacher
Emphasis on reform is likely to mean that teachers will need to be more knowledgeable, they will be held more responsible for student learning, and testing will be an increasingly important part of their work. Teachers will probably have less autonomy than they have had in the past, and they will need to be increasingly adaptable.

IMPORTANT CONCEPTS

accountability
assessment
autonomy
curriculum
extrinsic rewards
ethics
high-stakes tests
intrinsic rewards
physical conditions of teaching
psychological conditions of teaching
reforms
standards
standards-based education
technician

DISCUSSION QUESTIONS

1. Do the reasons cited in the chapter for becoming a teacher change with the grade level or content area targeted by teachers? Why?
2. Do you believe teaching is more or less rewarding than it was in the past? More or less difficult? Why do you think so?
3. Which of the intrinsic and extrinsic rewards in teaching are likely to become more important in the future? Which are likely to become less important?
4. Is teaching a profession? If not, what would be necessary to make it one?

5. Will the move toward teacher professionalism be beneficial for teachers? Why or why not?
6. Are the different dimensions of reform, such as standards, accountability, and high-stakes testing, good or bad for education? Why do you think so?

VIDEO DISCUSSION QUESTIONS

The following discussion questions refer to video segments found on the Companion Website. To answer these questions online, view the accompanying video, and receive immediate feedback to your answers, go to the Video Discussion Module in Chapter 1 of the Companion Website at **http://www.prenhall.com/kauchak.**

1. Dr. Urie Triesman is a professor of mathematics at the University of Texas at Austin and director of the Charles A. Dana Center for Math and Science Education. His work focuses on school reform and ways that schools can be helped to improve. He is concerned that individual school and teacher autonomy often conflict with centralized testing programs. What does Dr. Triesman believe is the proper balance between these two forces? Do you think centralized testing jeopardizes school and teacher autonomy? Explain why you believe it does or does not.
2. Theodore Sizer is the director of the Coalition for Effective Schools, which attempts to reform high schools. As we've seen in this chapter, testing is being proposed as a major reform tool. In Dr. Sizer's opinion, what questions should people ask when they consider using standardized tests to assess student learning? Do you think Dr. Sizer's cautions are justified? Explain.

GOING INTO SCHOOLS

1. Interview two teachers; if possible, one teacher should be in his or her first year, and the other teacher should have taught for at least five years. Ask them the following questions:
   a. Why did you choose to teach? Please give me all the reasons that apply to your decision.
   b. What are some of the most rewarding aspects of teaching? Please provide some specific examples.
   c. What are some of the most difficult parts of teaching? Please provide some specific examples.
   d. Are you more or less confident in your ability to help kids learn than you were before you started?
   e. How effective was your pre-service teacher-preparation program in helping you learn to teach? What would have made it more effective?
   f. Do you plan to stay in teaching, or do you plan to move to a different job or profession? If you plan to leave teaching, what are your reasons?
   g. In one sentence, please describe the process of teaching.
   h. Do you believe that teaching is a profession? Explain your reasons.
   i. Please rate the importance of each of the following for teachers, using the scale that follows:
      1 = Not at all important
      2 = Not very important
      3 = Somewhat important

4 = Quite important
5 = Extremely important

1. Knowledge of content, such as math, science or language arts.
2. Knowledge of teaching techniques, such as questioning and classroom organization.
3. Knowledge of students, such as how they learn and what motivates them.

Of the three types of knowledge that we see here, which is the most important? Least important? Or are they all equally important?

Compare the two teachers' responses and analyze them in terms of the content in this chapter.

2. Interview a teacher and ask him or her the following questions:

a. To what extent do standards and testing influence what is taught and how it is taught in your school?

b. What are some concrete examples of the standards and how the standards are tested?

c. Has the standards and high-stakes testing movement been good or bad for education? Why do you feel this way?

d. Will the standards, testing, and accountability movement increase or decrease in importance in the next 5 to 10 years? Why do you think so?

e. How have the standards and accountability movements affected your satisfaction as a teacher?

Summarize these responses and explain your personal views on standards and testing.

Virtual Field *Experience*

If you would like to participate in a Virtual Field Experience, go to the *Field Experience* Module in Chapter 1 of the Companion Website.

ONLINE PORTFOLIO ACTIVITIES

Portfolios are collections of a professional's work and evidence of accomplishments, such as a series of pictures that a photographer has taken, together with awards that the photographer has received. Just as photographers, artists, and other professionals develop portfolios to document their personal growth, so can teachers. Teaching portfolios can include evidence of changes in your thinking, such as reflections about your reasons for becoming a teacher (which we suggest in the first activity of this chapter), letters of commendation and recommendation, teaching units you've prepared, and videotapes of lessons you've taught. What you choose to include depends on your personal and professional judgment. (A detailed discussion of teaching portfolios is found in Bullock & Hawl, 2001, Campbell et al., 2001, as well as in Chapter 13 of this text.)

The following are suggested activities that will help you begin. As you continue in your program, you will add a great many items to your portfolio, and you may choose to delete some that you had selected initially.

Each of the activities is linked to an INTASC (Interstate New Teacher Assessment and Support Consortium) principle. The INTASC principles describe what you, as a beginning teacher, should know and be able to do when you first walk into a classroom. You will hear

class and, because he knows his students better, class discussions are more lively, personal, and productive.

From 8:00 A.M. until noon, it's a steady stream of students. Dave has four of his six classes in the morning and teaches 50-minute periods with 5-minute intervals in between. Even between-class intervals are crazy, with both incoming and exiting students wanting to talk about assignments, grades, and sometime even ideas.

Dave eats lunch in his room during his prep period, grading papers as he wolfs down a sandwich. He gave up his formal planning period to take on an additional class for extra pay. The extra money helps, but the extra class means not only one more class to teach but also many more papers to grade. "Why did I ever go into English?" he mutters with a smile, and starts on his next pile of student essays. He recalls the exchange he had the other day with Ricardo, another third-year teacher. They were discussing the relative merits of different kinds of assessments; Ricardo was extolling the benefits of short answer and multiple-choice tests that could be graded quickly. "Maybe Ricardo is right," Dave thinks, "but how are they ever going to learn to write if they don't write a lot?"

At 3:15 P.M., the final class bell rings, and Dave has 15 minutes to prepare materials for Debate Club, which he sponsors. He enjoys working with the students and getting to know them better as people, but jokingly reports to his wife that the $800 they pay him for doing this averages out to less than minimum wage. Her reply, "So, you must not be doing it for the money," causes both of them to laugh.

■ ■ ■

TEACHING: A TIME PERSPECTIVE

Let's think about Maria and Dave. What were their days like? How did they spend most of their time? How do their days compare to a typical day for you?

In this section we use time as a lens through which we'll view teaching. Time is useful for at least three reasons. First, the way we spend our time defines our lives; we spend more of our waking hours involved in our careers than in any other part of life. Once you become a teacher, how you spend your time will greatly influence your satisfaction with your career. Second, the way we spend our time says a great deal about what is important to us; and third, time is a useful way to analyze different teaching situations.

The School Year

Let's begin by looking at the school year. For students, a typical school year lasts 180 days, beginning a few days before or after Labor Day in September and ending in early June. (Some districts are now starting school in early August, so that the first semester is completed before the winter holiday.) For teachers, the school year is several days longer, with time before the students begin allocated to planning, meetings, and getting classrooms ready (for example, putting up bulletin boards, counting books, and requisitioning everyday supplies like paper and scissors). In addition, teachers spend several days after students are finished finalizing grades, packing up their room, and getting organized for next year.

However, this simple picture of 9-months-on, 3-months-off is becoming increasingly clouded by changes in the school calendar. One is **year-round schooling** in which *students spend 3 months on and 1 month off, rather than the traditional 9–3 pattern*. The 9–3 pattern has its historical roots in our agrarian past, when children were needed during the summer months to plant and harvest crops. One of your authors remembers feeling cheated when he visited his farm-living cousins in May and discovered that they were out of school already so they could help with spring planting. You may encounter year-round

Time provides a useful lens through which to analyze the lives of teachers.

Increasing Understanding 2.1

In what kind of districts or schools are you most likely to encounter year-round schools? Why? What implications might these have for you personally?

To answer the "Increasing Understanding" questions online and receive immediate feedback, go to the *Increasing Understanding* Module in Chapter 2 of the Companion Website at **http://www.prenhall.com/kauchak,** type in your response, and then study the feedback.

scheduling in your first job; nearly 1.5 million students in more than 20 states attend public schools on a year-round schedule (National Association for Year-Round Education, 1998). Primary reasons for this schedule change are to alleviate crowding by more efficiently using physical facilities and to minimize the inevitable forgetting (sometimes called "summer loss") that occurs over the summer.

Interestingly, there have been obstacles to year-round schooling; these obstacles come from several different sources. One obstacle is parents; summer has become a time for family vacations and summer camps, and parents resist intrusions on this family time. A second obstacle is the large amounts of money sometimes needed to install and run air conditioning in schools built for cool-weather use. A third obstacle is teachers themselves; many use summers as a time to supplement their teaching salaries or to work on recertification, new areas of certification, or a master's degree.

The School Week

In the United States, the 40-hour workweek is the norm. How does teaching compare to this norm? Study after study shows that the average teacher spends between 45 and 50 hours per week in school-related work, with the average being around 46 hours (Cypher & Willower, 1984; *Metropolitan Life Survey*, 1995; National Center for Education Statistics [NCES], 1997). Thirty-three hours of this is time that teachers are required to be at school, with the remainder spent either with students outside the classroom or at home grading papers or planning.

Bear in mind that these are just averages. In one study, 35 percent of teachers reported working more than 55 hours per week (NCES, 1997). Beginning teachers and experienced teachers changing level or assignment (for example, fourth to first grade or middle school math to science) probably spend considerably more time per week than the average.

Table 2.1 How Teachers Spend Their Time

Activity	Percentage of Day
Working with students	
Instruction	27.5
Testing and monitoring	10.1
Supervision	7.8
Total working with students	45.4
Peer interactions	25.6
Desk and routine work	20.0
Travel	5.3
Private time	3.5

Source: From "The Work Behavior of Secondary School Teachers" by T. Cypher and D. Willower, 1984, *Journal of Research & Development, 18,* pp. 19–20. Reprinted by permission.

Increasing Understanding 2.2

As a group, secondary teachers typically earn slightly more than elementary teachers. Why might this be the case? What implications might this have for a person considering what level to teach at?

These work patterns vary slightly for elementary and secondary teachers (NCES, 1997). As a group, secondary teachers work more hours per week than elementary teachers (46.5 hours versus 44 hours); this difference is largely because secondary teachers supervise more extracurricular activities like sports and clubs. We saw this with Dave Loft, who worked with the Debate Club after his formal teaching day.

The average length of a school teacher's workweek compares favorably with other occupations requiring a bachelor's degree. Managerial positions require the most hours per week at 46 hours, followed by salespeople and service workers (for example, social workers) at 44 hours, and administrative support positions (for example, administrative assistant) at 42 hours.

How do these figures compare with the number of hours worked by teachers in other countries? Primary teachers in 20 industrialized countries worked an average of 829 hours per year; primary teachers in the United States averaged 958 hours per year (NCES, 1997). As we'll see shortly, working conditions and the specifics of teaching also vary considerably from country to country as well as from school to school, within a district, between school districts, and between states. These differences can affect your personal satisfaction with a teaching career, so you need to explore these differences when you seek your first teaching position.

Teaching is a career involving hard work and long hours. Unlike many other occupations, teachers don't punch a time clock and leave their jobs behind when they leave school. Teachers will often talk about their students to spouses and friends (if they'll listen), and many teachers even report dreaming about their classes. If you are looking for a neat 9 to 5 job with few emotional entanglements, teaching may not be for you.

A Typical Workday

What is a typical workday for teachers? How do Maria's and Dave's experiences compare with those of other teachers? Let's look at some national statistics. As we can see from Table 2.1, teachers spend the largest part of their day working with students. Though instruction occupies the majority of that time (27.5 percent), other student-related activities, such as monitoring and supervision, also occupy major chunks of teachers' time. We saw this in Maria's day when she was expected to monitor students on the playground, take her class to lunch, and supervise her students during the assembly.

Peer interactions occupy the next largest chunk (25.6 percent) of teachers' time. Maria and Dave both had meetings before their school day, and Maria had one after. More and more, teachers are being asked to provide input into curricular and instructional issues affecting their teaching, a trend connected to the move toward greater teacher professionalism (Rowan, 1994). In addition, teachers spend a large amount of their day (20 percent) planning, preparing for instruction, and grading student papers and work. In all likelihood, both Maria and Dave took batches of papers with them when they finally left the school building. Teachers' days don't end when students leave or even when they go home. Teachers report they often get lesson ideas while they're driving in their cars or shopping (McCutcheon, 1982). You'll find many teachers grading papers as the rest of the family goes about their regular evening activities. Teaching is a full-time job.

Grade-Level Differences

Increasing Understanding 2.3

The time figures in Table 2.1 are averages for all teachers. How might these figures change for teachers working in learning, enrichment, or pull-out programs? How might they change for teachers in self-contained classrooms? What implications might this have for a person considering different types of teaching positions?

The way teachers spend their day differs dramatically by grade level, and these differences have important implications for you as a teacher. The majority of elementary teachers (62 percent) work in self-contained classrooms, versus only 6 percent of secondary teachers (NCES, 1997). (In all likelihood, this 6 percent is composed of resource or special education teachers.) The remaining elementary teachers not in a self-contained classroom teach in team (9 percent), enrichment (11.2 percent), or pull-out programs (10.5 percent). At the secondary level, over 84 percent of teachers work in departmentalized settings where students rotate to different classes every hour.

The differences in teachers' workdays have implications for you, especially if you are wondering which level is best for you as a teacher. The elementary level, with its emphasis on self-contained classrooms, provides you with greater opportunities to work in-depth with a group of students, getting to know them better than in the departmentalized structure of the secondary level. This is a definite plus; as we saw in Chapter 1, the relationships we form with our students are a major source of satisfaction in teaching.

The secondary level also has advantages. Departmentalization allows you to focus on a specific content area (or areas) and share your interest with your students. Recall from Chapter 1 that interest in a content area and opportunities for self-growth are major intrinsic reasons that people choose teaching as a career. Departmentalization also places you in contact with other people in your school who share your interest in a subject matter area. The 26 percent of the day that secondary teachers spend meeting with others will be more focused on issues related to content in your major or minor. Dave experienced intellectual stimulation during the discussion with his colleagues about the new English curriculum. Recall from Chapter 1 that these intellectual rewards are major factors influencing people to enter and remain in the teaching profession.

Which is better for you? That's a major reason you're taking this course—to decide.

Comparisons with Other Countries

Time comparisons with teachers in other countries are interesting, especially when they come from countries like Japan and China, where students outperform their U.S. counterparts in crucial areas like math and science (Calsyn, Gonzales, & Frase, 1999; Stigler, Gonzales, Kawanaka, Knoll, & Serrano, 1999). The typical Japanese teacher arrives at school around 7:30 A.M., like their U.S. counterparts, but stays there until 6:00 P.M. (Sato & McLaughlin, 1992). Most U.S. teachers are free to leave a half hour after students depart; many teachers leave at that time, preferring to grade papers and plan at home. (This is why you seldom see a teacher leaving school empty-handed—bags, briefcases, and

Teaching 

in an Era *of* Reform

CHANGING THE CLOCK

Among the many reforms suggested for improving schools, one in particular may affect your life as a teacher. It focuses on time and the way it's allocated (National Education Commission on Time and Learning, 1994). Two major reforms with respect to time have been suggested:

1. Lengthen the amount of time students spend in school.
2. Change the way time is scheduled.

Lengthen the Amount of Time Students Spend in School

It makes sense to conclude that the more time students spend in learning activities, the more they will learn; this conclusion is confirmed by research (Karweit, 1989; Nystrand & Gamoran, 1989). In addition, reformers point to other industrialized countries, like Japan and Germany, where the school year is longer (Japan, 240 days, and Germany, 216 days) and test scores on international comparisons are higher (Stigler et al., 1999). As a result, reformers advocate increasing the amount of time students spend in school. This can be accomplished by lengthening the school day, the school year, or both, or by having students attend summer school.

Interestingly, most proposals focus on the school year, leaving the school day relatively unchanged. Most people believe that development places limits on how long students can productively learn and stay in school in one day. Little kids (and big ones, too) tire over the school day, and the last hour of the school day presents special challenges for teachers wanting to motivate their students. However, in many Asian countries, like Japan and Korea, students routinely attend classes all day and then after school go to either enrichment classes in areas like art or music or additional tutoring classes, arriving home hours after school lets out.

A major time reform is the move to additional summer coursework, especially for students who are experiencing problems in school. The prevalence of summer school is expanding rapidly; this expansion is due largely to accountability measures that require students to pass tests before they're promoted to the next grade. "Powerful national movements to end the automatic promotion of students who aren't ready for the next grade and to hold all students to stricter academic standards have converged to swell the ranks of summer school" (Gewertz, 2000, p. 1). Currently 27 percent of school districts have some type of mandatory summer program for failing students, and this number is likely to become larger with the increased emphasis on testing and accountability (Gewertz, 2000). In the summer of 2000, 650,000 students in New York—nearly one-fourth of the district's enrollment—were enrolled in summer school, a sevenfold increase over 1999. Detroit expected a four-fold increase from 1999 to 2000 (Gewertz, 2000). What is not known is what effect programs like this will have on student learning.

Class Scheduling

Schools are also experimenting with different class schedules, particularly in middle schools and high schools. One experiment is **block schedules,** which *increase the length of classes*, often doubling typical periods. The basic purpose behind block scheduling is to minimize disruptions caused by bells and transitions and to provide teachers with not only extended periods of time for teaching but also greater flexibility. Block schedules work especially well in areas like science, home economics, and art, where labs and projects often take longer to complete than the traditional 50-minute period.

Different forms of block schedules exist. For instance, the school year for most high schools is organized into two semesters, and students typically take six classes a day, each of which is about 50–55 minutes in length. A popular variation is called a **four-by-four block schedule,** in which *students take four classes a day, each of which is approximately 90–100 minutes in length.* Courses that took a year in the traditional system are completed in one semester in the four-by-four plan. In an **alternating-day block schedule,** *classes are approximately 90–100 minutes long, students take eight classes a semester, and classes meet* *every other day*. A student's Algebra II class, for example, could meet on Monday, Wednesday, and Friday of one week, Tuesday and Thursday of the next week, Monday, Wednesday, and Friday of the third week, and so on. Like other experiments with school time, the educational benefits of block scheduling are not clear.

Increasing Understanding 2.4

Is block scheduling likely to be more effective for high-SES (socioeconomic status) or for low-SES students? Explain.

Putting Reform into Perspective

Reformers who advocate longer school days, longer school years, or both, commonly point to two sources of information. One is the cross-country comparisons mentioned earlier. Critics argue that one reason students in countries like Japan score higher is because they go to school longer. The second argument for increasing the school day or year is research that shows a link between time studying a subject and the amount learned (Karweit, 1989). When researchers compared elementary teachers who allocated more time to math instruction, for example, they found that their students scored higher on math achievement tests—an intuitively sensible finding. Though the link is not a strong one, there is no denying that more time does provide more opportunities for learning.

However, research indicates that teachers often fail to effectively utilize the time they now have, sometimes spending more than one-third of their class periods on noninstructional activities (Kauchak & Eggen, 1998; Karweit, 1989). If teachers better utilized the time they now have, increasing the length of days and years wouldn't be necessary, experts assert. Further, research on long-term student achievement resulting from programs such as summer school shows mixed results, causing some school leaders to question whether or not the investment in additional time and resources is worth it (Gewertz, 2000).

Block-scheduling advocates argue that time is better utilized with these schedules because students spend less time in transitions, that is, moving from one class to another and getting settled after the move. Also, teachers spend less time in noninstructional activities, such as taking roll and beginning the class. In addition, both students and teachers seem to like block schedules. Students have fewer classes for which they must prepare, and teachers have fewer students per semester, so they get to know the students better, and they have more time for preparation.

These reforms have the potential to change your life as a teacher. For example, summer school and extended school years may result in greater pay; they'll also mean less time for vacations and alternative summer employment. Scheduling changes within the school day will also influence your planning and teaching. The teachers we've talked to about block scheduling either love it or hate it. It does provide more time for teaching, but the longer class periods can be challenging from a motivational perspective.

If teachers tend to primarily lecture, longer class periods can become mind-numbing. In addition, if teachers aren't helped in changing their instruction to better utilize the time, the end of extended periods often gets taken up by students doing homework for the next day. The key, as always, is the orientation and expertise of the teachers. Time and schedules per se do not directly affect learning; teachers who use time effectively can.

You Take a Position

Now it's your turn to take a position on the issues discussed in this section. Go to the *Education Week* Website at **http://www.edweek.com,** find "search" on the first page, and type in one of the following search terms: *school calendar* or *block schedule*. Locate a minimum of three articles on one of these topics and do the following:

1. Identify the title, author, and date of each article and then write a one-paragraph summary of each.
2. Determine if a pattern exists in the articles. (Each article—or even two of the three—suggesting that altering the school calendar is a good idea would be a pattern, for example.)
3. Take one of the two following positions:
   - The pattern suggested in the articles, if implemented, *is* likely to improve education.
   - The pattern suggested in the articles *is not* likely to improve education.

Document your position with information taken from the articles and your study of the text (including this chapter and any other chapter of the text).

To answer these questions online, go to the Take a Position Module in Chapter 2 of the Companion Website.

Increased teacher input into school decisions may positively influence teacher autonomy and professionalism, but may pull teachers away from classrooms and students.

boxes contain the evening's chores.) As opposed to their U.S. counterparts, Japanese teachers work a 240-day school year, but their annual salaries are only about 95 percent of what U.S. teachers make.

There are also major differences in terms of how teachers from these countries spend their time while in school (Ma, 1999; Sato & McLaughlin, 1992). For example, teachers in Japan spend about half as much time as U.S. teachers in direct classroom instruction. The rest of the time is spent in professional planning, conferring with colleagues, and helping to govern their schools. While some reformers advocate moving toward this Asian model, with its emphasis on teacher autonomy, governance, and professionalism, this takes teachers away from their first love—working with students (Lortie, 1975).

This is a real professional dilemma—not only for the profession, but for you as a teacher. At the personal level, do you want to spend more time working with students, working with other teachers on curriculum projects, or helping run the school you work in? At the professional level, greater teacher involvement in school governance is seen as one way for teachers to have greater power and autonomy, resulting in a positive move toward increased teacher professionalism (Rowan, 1994). However, more time spent in governance and working with other teachers means less time spent with students.

The other side of the coin is that teachers *do* want input into decisions that influence their professional life and resent being told to do things without being consulted. Research shows that teachers' satisfaction and their commitment to their school is dependent on their involvement in school decision making (Sergiovanni, Burlingame, Coombs, & Thurstone, 1999). When you interview for your first teaching position, you may want to ask the principal how teachers in the school are involved in decision making and then weigh the principal's response against your personal professional goals.

One of the most important aspects of taking this class is the opportunity to learn more about yourself and how you would enjoy a teaching career. With an understanding of the benefits and liabilities of the profession, you can confirm or reconsider your decision to prepare for and begin a teaching career. We encourage you to seek all the information you can at this point in your education about the nature of current and future teaching opportunities, especially ones which match your interests in working with students and teaching in content areas you're excited about. We write this chapter with this end in mind—to provide a realistic description of the teaching profession and resources you can use in your search for information as you explore a teaching career.

TEACHING: DEALING WITH COMPLEXITIES

What does it feel like to actually teach? What challenges do classrooms and students present? How do teachers deal with these challenges? Let's look at three teachers at different stages of their professional development who also teach at different grade levels.

Ken, an elementary teacher in a third/fourth-grade split classroom shared this incident in his teaching journal:

My class is sitting in a circle. I look up and notice that one of the girls, Sylvia, is crying. Joey, she claims, has called her a fat jerk. The rest of the students all look at me to watch my response. I consider the alternatives: send Joey into the hallway and talk to him in a few minutes; have Joey sit next to me; ask Joey to apologize; direct Sylvia to get a thick skin; ask Sylvia, "How can you solve this problem?"; send Joey to the principal; have Joey write an apology letter; ask Joey, "Why did you do this?"; ignore the situation completely; keep Sylvia and Joey in from recess for a conference; put Joey's name on the board; yell at Joey; send Sylvia and Joey into the hallway to work out the problem; tell them to return to their seats and write in their journals about the problem.

It took me about 10 seconds to run through these alternatives, and after each one I thought of reasons why it wasn't a good idea. By the time I looked up at Sylvia after this brief period of thought, she had stopped crying and was chattering away with a friend about something else. On the surface, the problem had gone away (Adapted from Winograd, 1998, p. 296).

■ ■ ■

Kerry, a first-year middle school English teacher, experienced the following management struggles on the first day back to school after a 4-day holiday (Veteran teachers will attest that students typically are wired the day before as well as the day after a long school holiday.) Kerry knew her students would be excited and she was correct—the students were excited, difficult to settle down, wild. Students chatted excitedly about their weekends and showed one another items they had brought from home, as Kerry vainly shushed and urged them to quiet down. She sensed it was going to be a long day. Finally, she got them settled down and began the day's lesson, but it was a continual struggle to keep their attention.

Throughout the day, the struggle continued. She was constantly surrounded by students who needed help or who did not listen carefully to her directions. As the day progressed, her frustration grew. By afternoon she was nearly frazzled; the students were winning. Seventh period finally arrived, and the end of the day was in sight. P.A. announcements from the office were supposed to begin the period, but they often came late, so teachers never quite knew when to begin class. Kerry waited, while the students talked noisily. Finally the announcements began. Once these were over, she gave the students a quiz on a movie they had seen. This quieted them down. However, as they finished the quiz, the noise level began to creep up. The team leader, whose class was also noisy, walked by and commented, "It's so noisy in here today, I'm going crazy myself!" When the buzzer finally sounded, indicating the day's end, Kerry had "had it"; rather than hold them after class as she had threatened earlier, she let them go, just to get rid of them.

It was, in Kerry's words, a day that nearly drove her "crazy." She was angry and frustrated. "Today they were just screwing off! All these little toys they have. Wanting to look at each other's stuff. Combs. Brushes. I should take them and hit them on the head with the stupid things! It drives you nuts." This was not one of her better days teaching (adapted from Bullough, 1989, p. 73).

■ ■ ■

Two high school student teachers are talking about their frustrations in taking attendance on the day of a special school dance held during regular class hours.

Cheryl: One boy comes in, he's dressed up. He says "I have to go to the dance." Comes in early and tells me, good kid. I'm like, "OK, that's fine Aaron." Then Kent comes in 5 minutes late. This is tall Kent, has his own band, and never lets me mark him tardy even though he's always tardy. He says, "I'm, going to the dance!" After I've already started class! "Ahem. Thank you, Kent. Please sit down." So he's wanting to leave but I can't let him go because he just interrupted my class and . . . I was so mad at him. So I say, "Do you have a ticket?" And he's like, "Well, yeah," and pulls out a ticket from the movie he went to on Friday night and I say, "No, that's not the right ticket." He wasn't . . .

Dani: What color was it?

Cheryl: Pink.

Dani: What was the color for the. . . ?

Cheryl: The other guy who was legit had a gray one. But then, then, I don't know. And I mean WHO KNOWS! I said, "You're not on my excused list" but neither was the other guy and I'm like . . .

Dani: I didn't even get an excused list! I didn't even know this dance was happening . . . I kind of heard something over the intercom (Dulude-Lay, 2000, p. 4).

■ ■ ■

What do these cases have in common? They all illustrate the bewildering and sometimes frustrating world of teaching. Why can teaching be so bewildering and frustrating? Researchers who have analyzed the management demands of teaching identified several dimensions of classroom life that make it complex and demanding (Doyle, 1986). They found that classrooms are:

- **Multidimensional**—*large numbers of events and tasks take place.*
- **Simultaneous**—*many things happen at once.*
- **Immediate**—*classroom events occur rapidly.*
- **Unpredictable**—*classroom events often take unexpected turns.*
- **Public**—*classrooms are public places where teachers are in "fishbowls."*

Let's examine these dimensions more closely.

Multidimensional

Think about all the different roles you'll perform today. You're a student, but you might also be a parent, friend, and co-worker. Your life is multidimensional. In a similar way, at any one time there are likely to be a number of events occurring in your classroom, requiring you to perform multiple roles. While a teacher works with one group of students, other students are working on various assignments. Pull-out programs, which take students needing special help out of the classroom, cause additional logistical problems. Even when teachers try to simplify their instruction with whole-group instruction, each student has a different agenda and may be on a different page, literally and figuratively. Ken found this out when he tried to begin his lesson.

External events, like announcements, assemblies, and school functions, are the bane of teachers because they add to the complexity and also rob teachers of valuable instructional time. Kerry, Cheryl, and Dani had to rearrange their teaching around P.A. announcements and school dances. Teachers often say, "If I only had time to teach." This complaint will become more important as teachers are held increasingly accountable for their students' learning through standards and increased testing.

Simultaneous

Increasing Understanding 2.5

How are the concepts of "multidimensional" and "simultaneous" similar? Different? Which of the two is more alterable by the teacher?

Not only are classrooms multidimensional, busy places, but events in classrooms often occur at the same time. While Cheryl and Dani are trying to take roll and begin class, students come in needing immediate attention, asking questions, showing hall passes, and presenting admission slips if they were absent yesterday. While Kerry and Ken are trying to teach, management problems arise. Knowing which problem to attend to first can be challenging, if not bewildering.

Immediate

Increasing Understanding 2.6

Re-examine Table 2.1, which describes how teachers spend their time. Which of the time categories are subject to the dimension of immediacy? Explain.

We learned in Chapter 1 that teachers make somewhere between 800 and 1,500 decisions everyday. Beyond the sheer numbers, the fact that the decisions need to be made *right now* adds to the demands on the teacher. Sylvia is crying; Ken needs to do something immediately. Kent comes in with a bogus hall pass; Cheryl needs to decide immediately whether to honor it or not. Unfortunately for new teachers, the immediacy of classroom life requires split-second decision making.

Unpredictable

Every teacher plans—not only for instruction but also for management. The better ones plan extensively in an attempt to anticipate unpredictable events.

▪ ▪ ▪

One first-grade teacher, attempting to involve students in a lesson about a story they read about shoes, brought a shoe into class. Pulling it out of a bag, she began, "What can you tell me about this shoe?" "It's red," Mike responded. The shoe was black—there was no sign of red on it anywhere!

▪ ▪ ▪

The teacher had planned extensively, even bringing in concrete objects to illustrate ideas and themes in a story. But she hadn't planned for this response. In a similar way, neither Ken nor Cheryl and Dani could predict events that would require split-second decision making. In teaching, there is little time for thoughtful analysis and consideration of the pros and cons of alternatives as they occur. It is often easy to see after the fact what we should

Classrooms are complex places requiring split-second decision making by teachers.

have done differently, but in the heat of the moment we have to respond immediately to unanticipated events. Classrooms are exciting, unpredictable places—a major reason that people find teaching both interesting and challenging.

Public

When we teach, we teach in front of people. In a sense, we are on stage. Teachers' triumphs and mistakes occur in the public arena for all to see. And mistakes are inevitable. One of the authors, in his first year of teaching, recalls this incident.

■ ■ ■

I was having a rough time quieting my class as they worked on an assignment. After several futile attempts, I said loudly, "All right, this is it! I don't want to hear one more peep out of this class!" The class was momentarily quiet. From behind the cover of held up textbooks came a squeaky "Peep." The class watched and waited while I quickly (and publicly) sorted out my options. Finally, I smiled and said, "Very funny. Now, let's get down to work." This seemed to break the ice, and the students finally settled down. I had learned an important public lesson on ultimatums.

■ ■ ■

As we work with students, we are bound to make mistakes, and our actions can have far-reaching consequences. A teacher ignores one incident of misbehavior—an alternative that Ken considered. What does this communicate to other students—that the teacher condones calling Sylvia a fat jerk and that it's all right to verbally abuse other students? The student teacher allows one high school student to slip out of her class with a bogus pass. What will other students think (and try next time)? A fishbowl is an apt metaphor for classroom teaching; as we swim through our classroom day, not only students but other professionals watch us, as Kerry discovered when a colleague said the noise was bothering her, too.

Does your first year of teaching have to consist of a series of endless, unpredictable decisions? Yes and no. Learning to teach is an exhausting task filled with unanticipated and unpredictable events. One book about the experiences of first year teachers is aptly named *The Roller Coaster Year* (Ryan, 1992). Learning to teach, with all of its emotional ups and downs, can be like a roller coaster. Because of this, your first year will be both exhausting and overwhelming. Take solace in the fact that millions of other beginning teachers have not only survived but flourished.

The teacher-education program that you're in right now or considering entering can help in two major ways. The first is through a series of courses that will provide you with concepts—concepts like withitness and overlapping—to help you understand how experienced teachers appear to teach so effortlessly. **Withitness** is *a teacher's awareness of the multiple activities students are doing simultaneously in a classroom and the ability to communicate that awareness to them*. **Overlapping** is *being able to attend to more than one of their activities at a time*. Neither withitness nor overlapping are effortless; experienced teachers make it appear so because they are knowledgeable and good at what they're doing (Berliner, 1994).

The second way your teacher-education program can assist you in becoming a teacher is through structured clinical experiences in schools (McIntyre, Byrd, & Foxx, 1996). By observing teachers in action, by talking with them about what they're doing and why, and by interacting with students to gauge their reactions to teachers' actions, teacher-education students not only become more knowledgeable but also more skilled. By accessing the wisdom of experienced teachers and trying ideas out for yourself, you'll be able to create and define yourself as a teacher. Again, we wrote this book to assist you in this process.

THE MULTIPLE ROLES OF TEACHING

As we saw in previous sections, teachers perform multiple roles, which take up significant portions of a teacher's day. In this section, we analyze these multiple roles and examine implications these roles have for you, a prospective teacher.

Caring Professionals

Teachers are people who care about their students. Educational researchers have documented the importance of caring for students as a critical, central dimension of teaching (Brint, 1998; Noddings, 1992). **Caring** refers to *teachers' abilities to empathize with and invest in the protection and development of young people* (Chaskin & Rauner, 1995). Caring is more than warm, fuzzy feelings that make people kind. In addition to understanding how students *feel*, caring teachers are committed to their students' growth and development. They attempt to do their very best for the people under their care (Noddings, 1992).The importance of caring is captured in one fourth-grader's comment, "If a teacher doesn't care about you, it affects your mind. You feel like you're a nobody, and it makes you want to drop out of school" (Noblit, Rogers, & McCadden, 1995, p. 683).

To students, a teacher's ability to care is linked closely to how good a teacher he or she is. In one study, students were asked to identify characteristics of a good teacher. "Understanding student problems" and "Being kind and friendly" were rated most important (Boyer, 1995). Knowledge of content and classroom management, dimensions of teaching often cited as essential for learning, were rated as being much less important by students.

Increasing Understanding 2.7

How does the caring dimension of teaching relate to how teachers spend their time during the day? (See Table 2.1.) In terms of this table, what are some different ways that teachers show they care? Explain.

Caring is evidenced in the "people orientation" of teachers and is a major reason they go into teaching. For most teachers, a central source of satisfaction is derived from helping students grow socially and emotionally. Teachers enjoy being with students for the majority of their workday and looking after the needs of their students in a variety of ways.

Let's see what Tangia Anderson, an inner-city high school teacher, has to say about the care-giving dimension of teaching:

■ ■ ■

People ask, "Who are teachers? What does it take to be a teacher?" One reply might be, "Teachers are anyone who can put-up with children." But I would disagree!

Another person might say, "Teachers are people who couldn't survive in the business world." But again, I would disagree! I say that teachers are people who genuinely care about the students they work with (T. Anderson, personal communication, 3/7/99).

■ ■ ■

Can students tell when teachers care? Let's listen to one high school student:

■ ■ ■

Nichole: People here don't have many people to talk to. I don't. The teachers . . . some of them don't care about their students. They say, "They [administrators] want me to teach and I'm going to do it no matter what." I don't like that. I like them to say, "I'm here to teach and help you because I care." That's what I like. But a lot of them are just saying, "I'm here to teach, so I'm gonna teach." I don't think that's right.

Interviewer: Do they actually say that?

Nichole: It's more an attitude, and they do say it. Like Ms. G. She's like . . . she never says it, but you know, she's just there and she just wants to teach, but she doesn't want to explain the whole deal.

Interviewer: How do you know that?

Nichole: I could feel it. The way she acts and the way she does things. She's been here seven years and all the kids I've talked to that have had her before say, "Oooh! You have Ms. G.!" Just like that.

Interviewer: But a teacher who really cares, how do they act?

Nichole: Like Mr. P. He really cares about his students. He's helping me a lot and he tells me, "I'm not angry with you, I just care about you." He's real caring and he does teach me when he cares (Kramer & Colvin, 1991, p. 13).

■ ■ ■

Caring is important for all students; for students on the margins, it often makes the difference between success and failure, between staying in school or dropping out.

What does caring feel like in a fourth-grade classroom? Let's listen to one teacher's perspective.

■ ■ ■

I may not be on the same social studies textbook chapter as the other fourth-grade teachers, and I'll probably be late returning standardized tests to the assistant principal, but I think my kids know they're important to me. I see it in tiny, fleeting moments. I see it when a student says, "Mrs. Carkci, I wish you could come to my house for the weekend. That would be fun." I see it when a boy writes to me to ask if I will take him to the movies, or when a girl gives me a goofy smile after I've led the class down the hall taking giant, silly steps. I'm proud that a girl believes it is okay to ask, "Why in America do people speak lots of languages, while in Vietnam, they only speak one language?" Or that a boy knows I will encourage him to pursue his question, "Who invented the planets?" (Carkci, 1998, p. C3.).

■ ■ ■

Caring not only facilitates learning, it is an integral part of learning.

Caring often involves attending to the physical and emotional needs of our students. Teachers are caretakers who must continually make decisions about the needs and safety of their students. Every age group has risk factors, which the teacher needs to be aware of and closely monitor. A teacher has to be a diagnostician who can recognize the needs of students and find or develop ways to fulfill these needs. To accomplish that, teachers continually have to observe and monitor the physical, emotional, and intellectual well-being of their students. For example, one of the authors took her kindergarten students on frequent walking field trips. She felt these field trips were essential to helping her students see how schoolwork was related to the real world, but she was worried about their physical safety. To keep them together for safety, she used a rope with handle knots that the

Structured clinical experiences during your teacher-education program will provide you with opportunities to experiment with different teaching strategies and ideas.

students had to hold while walking across heavily trafficed streets on their monthly visits to the seashore. Students were told that if anyone let go of the rope, the class had to return to the school (which never happened).

Teachers often have to first take care of the immediate needs of their students in the classroom, and sometimes outside of it, before they can proceed with instruction. Students can't learn when they have pressing problems, such as hunger or safety threats, occupying their minds. Many elementary teachers keep a box of crackers or granola bars in their desks for students who, for whatever reason, didn't have breakfast that morning. Many parents, especially newcomers to the country, are unaware of free breakfast and lunch programs available to low-income families. Caring teachers go the extra mile to make sure their students' families know about and take advantage of these services.

Occasionally, teachers have to be defenders of their students' rights as well as guardians of their safety. Teachers are responsible for the physical and mental safety of their students. Maria Lopez checked on the testing status of one of her students before class and spent time after school working with the parent of another student who needed special services. If teachers don't detect these special student needs, often no one will.

Teachers must also learn the signs of abusive situations that their students might be experiencing at home or school. There are clear guidelines that require teachers to report student abuse in any context and, as we'll see in Chapter 9, teachers are legally required to report this abuse.

Child neglect is an increasing form of abuse that teachers also need to guard against. Several years ago, one of the sixth-grade students in our colleague's class came to school with his pajamas in his backpack. He showed them to his teacher at the end of the school day and asked her not to send him home on the bus, explaining that he wasn't safe at home. Our colleague acted quickly to protect the student by following established procedures. Many abused or neglected students who face emotional or physical abuse at home do not inform their teachers of their personal circumstances, which makes recognition of abuse a difficult, but critical function of a teacher's caretaking role.

Increasing Understanding 2.8

In Chapter 1 we found that knowledge was an essential element of professionalism. How does teacher knowledge affect teachers' ability or capacity to provide care?

The protection of students' rights at school is another dimension of caring that teachers may face when other staff or volunteers make inappropriate decisions. For example, while working in K–12 schools, we have seen staff deny services to students based on their existing placement in one special program. If we had not brought it to the administration's attention that students are entitled to and need *all* the services for which they are qualified, placement in additional, needed programs would not have occurred.

Students with diverse backgrounds, such as English-as-a-Second-Language learners and those with exceptional abilities, are sometimes overlooked or ignored in schools. Teachers are in a unique situation to defend these students' rights to receive the best education a school can provide for them. Teacher caring takes many forms.

Creator of Productive Learning Environments

The design of learning environments that promote student growth and development is the second most important function teachers perform. With the knowledge that students learn best when they enjoy and are involved in learning activities, teachers need to create productive and interesting learning situations.

Motivating students to learn within and outside of their class can be a challenging task. Tangia Anderson, a teacher in a large urban high school, comments,

▪ ▪ ▪

Increasing Understanding 2.9

Identify at least two functions of a teacher that Tangia demonstrated while fostering motivation in her students.

This means we have to dig deep down inside and reach for new strategies and teaching methods that relate to what our students have to face day to day when they are not in a school environment. We often have a student or groups of students who make teaching a challenge. The best thing to remember is to continue to provide a meaningful lesson for the entire class. The student or students who are challenging the teacher may want to use a different strategy. My immediate goal is to get the students participating without making a big issue. For example, in teaching students how to type without looking at their fingers, I always had students that were not motivated to learn the keyboard. So I made the typing assignment like a racing game and told the students to see if they could type without looking at their fingers while racing their classmates. The first three times I participated in the race and then I noticed that my previously idle students started typing to see if they could win. Before I knew it, they were racing with the class and I didn't say a word. Next time we did it, they wanted to start the next race (T. Anderson, personal communication, 3/23/99).

▪ ▪ ▪

In working with students, actions speak louder than words. Tangia comments on the importance of teacher modeling.

▪ ▪ ▪

Increasing Understanding 2.10

Explain how withitness and overlapping relate to the following dimensions of teaching discussed earlier in the chapter: multidimensional, simultaneous, and immediate.

Effective teachers model the expected behaviors or outcomes they want their students to know or learn. Times have long changed from "Do as I say and not as I do," because students will often do the opposite. They will do exactly what they see. When a teacher models for his or her students, students see that the teacher believes in what he or she is doing and the teacher really wants the student to understand the concept or idea. From day one in the classroom, I try to demonstrate the expected behaviors and attitudes I want my students to have. For example, respect for others is an important value I try to teach in my classes. When I teach, I use, as well as visually provide, positive words on the board for my students to use when talking with others and I consciously avoid negative words. Respect for other people's feelings is important and I want my students to know that we can communicate in a positive way to get what we need accomplished without being negative (T. Anderson, personal communication, 5/28/99).

▪ ▪ ▪

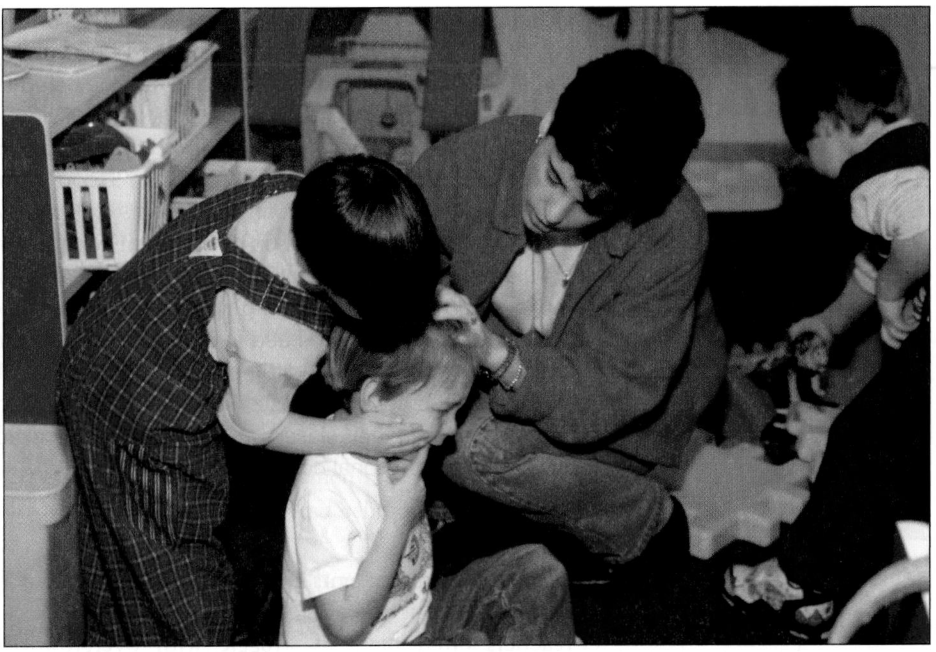

Caring teachers attend to the physical and emotional needs of their students.

Handling students' different needs in a class can be complex and challenging, similar to juggling. To keep lesson momentum and make the constant transitions required both within and between lessons, teachers need both withitness and overlapping (Kounin, 1970). While we observed Tangia teaching, we saw her use both withitness and overlapping in one of her classes.

Case STUDY

Tangia stood in the hallway just outside her classroom door, monitoring students during the passing period as they moved to their next class. In a warm tone, she greeted each student who entered her class with "Good morning." While greeting students, Tangia also monitored the activities of students who had already entered her classroom. Her students settled into their seats before the next bell rang. Students often asked her questions as they entered the classroom. As Tangia monitored both places and listened to her students, she noticed one student approach her desk, which was at the back of the classroom, away from the lesson area. The student eyed a candy jar that was on Tangia's desk along with other personal items, including a gift that had been placed there the previous period. When the student turned back to see if Tangia was watching, he found her looking right at him as she answered questions in the doorway. The student waited a few seconds until she was done speaking, then pointed at her candy jar and said, "Mrs. Anderson, can I have one of these?" Tangia saw the opportunity to address the student's sloppy attire, which was evident in his slouching pants and untucked shirt. She responded, "Yes, if you tuck in your shirt," which the student did with a smile as he took a piece of candy and went to his seat. When the passing-period bell rang, Tangia proceeded to the front of her class and began her lesson (T. Anderson, personal communication, 1/17/99).

To begin, Tangia pointed to a chart of "Acceptable Business Phrases" at the front of her class and discussed various contexts in which the different expressions should be

Economic barriers. Communication and involvement take time, and economic commitments often come first out of necessity. First among these is employment; holding two and even three jobs often prevents parents from helping their children with homework (Ellis, Dowdy, Graham, & Jones, 1992). Often parents lack economic resources, such as child care, transportation, and telephones, that would allow them to participate in school activities. Parents want to be involved in their children's schooling, but schools need to be flexible and provide help and encouragement.

Cultural barriers. Discontinuities between students' home cultures and the culture of the school can also be barriers to home–school cooperation (Delgado-Gaiton, 1992; Harry, 1992). Students may come from homes where the parents experienced schools that were very different from the ones their children have to cope with. Also, some parents may have only gone through the elementary grades or may have had negative school experiences. One researcher described the problem this way:

> Underneath most parents is a student—someone who went to school, sometimes happily, sometimes unhappily. What often happens when the parent-as-adult returns to school, or has dealings with teachers, is that the parent as child/student returns. Many parents still enter school buildings flooded with old memories, angers, and disappointments. Their stomachs churn and flutter with butterflies, not because of what is happening today with their own children, but because of outdated memories and past behaviors (Rich, 1987, p. 24).

Parents like these may require encouragement and support if they are to become involved.

Increasing Understanding 2.14

In what types of educational settings—urban, rural, suburban—are teachers most likely to encounter barriers to greater parent involvement? What implications might this have for you as a first-year teacher?

Language barriers. Language can be another potential barrier to effective home–school cooperation. Parents of bilingual students often do not speak English; this makes home–school communication more difficult. In these situations, the child often has the responsibility of interpreting the message. Homework poses a special problem because parents are unable to interpret assignments or provide help (Delgado-Gaiton, 1992).

Schools often compound the problem by using educational jargon when they send home letters. The problem is especially acute in special education, where legal and procedural safeguards can be bewildering. For example, parents often don't understand Individualized Education Plans or even remember that they've signed one (Harry, 1992). Many parents feel ill-prepared to assist their children with school-related tasks, but suggestions from school describing specific strategies in the home can be effective in bridging the home–school gap (Gorman & Balter, 1997; Hoover-Dempsey, Bassler, & Burow, 1995).

Strategies for Involving Parents The National Parent Teacher Association (PTA) has issued standards for parent/family involvement programs (see Table 2.2). These standards emphasize the central role that parents and caregivers play in their children's education. In addition they suggest broad, comprehensive ways that parents can be involved in their children's schools.

Virtually all schools have formal communication channels; these may include interim progress reports, which tell parents about their children's achievement at the midpoint of each grading period, open houses, during which teachers introduce themselves and describe general guidelines and procedures, parent–teacher conferences, and, of course, report cards. Although these schoolwide processes are valuable, as an individual teacher, you can do more to enhance the communication process in several ways.

- Send home a letter at the beginning of the school year describing your expectations and how parents can assist in their children's learning. Enlist the aid of students, other teachers, or parents to translate the letter into students' home language.

Table 2.2 **National Parent Teacher Association Standards for Parent/Family Involvement Programs**

Standard I	Communication between home and school is regular, two-way, and meaningful.
Standard II	Parenting skills are promoted and supported.
Standard III	Parents play an integral role in assisting student learning.
Standard IV	Parents are welcome in the school, and their support and assistance are sought.
Standard V	Parents are full partners in the decisions that affect children and families.
Standard VI	Community resources are used to strengthen schools, families, and student learning.

Source: From National Parent Teacher Association, (2000). *Standards for Parent/Family Involvement Programs.* [Online]. Available: *http://www.pta.org/programs/INVSTAND.* Reprinted by permission.

- Maintain communication by sending students' work home frequently. Short notes describing upcoming topics and projects along with ways that parents can assist their children communicate caring as well as create a learning partnership with the parents or caregivers.
- Invite parents and caregivers to visit your classroom and contact you if they have questions or concerns.
- Involve parents in school activities by inviting them in to talk about their occupations and asking them to participate in activities like band, chorus, sports and booster clubs.

One first year teacher had this experience in calling parents:

▪ ▪ ▪

I started [calling] because I had some kids right off who really had trouble. So, I felt like I needed to call just so they wouldn't get totally lost so soon. I had to deal with them, somehow. I really like parent/teacher conferences a lot, [but] I've discovered that a phone call is just as good. I've been getting [very] positive feedback from . . . parents. Like, "Oh, I'm so glad you called. Not one teacher called me ever last year. He had so much trouble." I just . . . decided I'm going to call a couple of parents every night. It's really [having] a positive [effect on] what's happening in the classroom. I'm also going to call some parents for positive reasons. There are some kids who really deserve to have a teacher call and say [something good] (Bullough, 1989, p. 112).

▪ ▪ ▪

Increasing Understanding 2.15

Refer to Table 2.1. Identify an additional barrier to increased home–school cooperation. What are some things teachers can do to overcome this barrier?

Research shows that parents want to be involved in their children's education (Elam, Rose, & Gallup, 1995). Teachers can capitalize on this by providing opportunities for parents to learn about and participate in their children's education.

Technology provides another channel for improving communication. A voice-mail system, for example, allows teachers and parents to communicate despite their busy schedules (Cameron & Lee, 1997). One voice-mail system, called the Bridge Project, enables teachers to post daily assignments and reminders about things like field trips on a bulletin board that parents can access 24 hours a day, 7 days a week.

Collaborative Colleague

As we saw earlier, a significant portion of a teacher's time (almost 26 percent) is spent working with peers. Teachers need to be team players as well as colleagues with the other teachers in their schools. They work together cooperatively in committees to accomplish many tasks for their students, school, and district in order to make their instruction more effective and their school a better place in which to learn. Collaboration skills are important for educators in all levels of education. Part of the administrative evaluation of teachers, starting at their job interview, focuses on these collaboration skills. In fact, some

Portfolio Activity 2.1

Time and Learning

INTASC Principle 7: ***Planning***

Go to the *Portfolio Activities* Module for Chapter 2 of the Companion Website and click on "Time and Organization." Read the information and then write a one- or two-paragraph summary of the section. Then offer at least two specific, concrete ways in which teachers can maximize their *instructional time* and at least two specific, concrete ways in which teachers can maximize *engaged time*.

Portfolio Activity 2.2

Caring

INTASC Principle 2: ***Learning***

INTASC Principle 5: ***Motivation and Management***

Explain why a caring teacher will have students who learn more than students taught by a teacher who isn't caring. List at least four specific, concrete things teachers can do to demonstrate that they care about their students.

Portfolio Activity 2.3

Parental Involvement

INTASC Principle 10: ***Partnership***

Write a one-page paper that explains your philosophy with respect to involving parents and caregivers in their children's education. Include in your paper:

- Why you believe parental involvement is important.
- Specific ways in which you will communicate your students' learning progress with parents or other caregivers.
- Specific ways in which you will involve parents or other caregivers.

PART 2

Students

CHAPTER 3

Learner Diversity: Differences in Today's Students

CHAPTER 4

Changes in American Society: Influences on Today's Schools

Teaching in an Era of Reform

BILINGUAL EDUCATION

Bilingual education has been the focus of a number of controversial reform efforts. As you saw earlier, national reform efforts with respect to this issue first began when Congress passed the Bilingual Education Act in 1968, and the 1974 court case *Lau v. Nichols* (the San Francisco case described in the last section) demonstrated the government's commitment to providing services for non-native English speakers.

The magnitude of the challenges involved in this reform is difficult to overstate. For example, in Arizona an estimated 37 percent of the state's ESL students were enrolled in bilingual programs in 1999, and in California, roughly one third of the state's 1.4 million ESL students were enrolled in bilingual education (Schnaiberg, 1999a, 1999b). The Los Angeles Unified School District alone had over 100,000 of its 310,000 ESL students enrolled in bilingual education programs.

As with all reforms, bilingual education has been attacked and criticized, with critics contending that it is:

- Divisive, encouraging non-native English speaking groups to remain separate from mainstream American culture.
- Ineffective, slowing the process of acquiring English for ESL students.
- Inefficient, requiring expenditures for the training of bilingual teachers and materials that could better be spent on quality monolingual programs.

Proponents counter that bilingual programs make sense because they provide a smooth and humane transition to English by building on a student's first language. In addition, they argue that being able to speak two languages has both practical and learning benefits (Garcia, 1993). From a practical standpoint, a truly bilingual person is able to live and communicate in two worlds, which may open economic and career doors. From a learning perspective, there is growing evidence that being able to speak two languages provides intellectual benefits. For example, because of their knowledge of two languages, bilingual students better understand the role of language in communication and how language works (Diaz, 1990).

Critics views prevailed in California; in a 1998 counter-reform, voters passed Proposition 227, a ballot initiative that sharply reduced bilingual education, replacing it with English-only immersion programs for ESL students. A similar measure passed in Arizona in 2000, and other states, such as Utah and Colorado, are considering similar initiatives (Schnaiberg, 1999a; Zehr, 2000a, 2000b).

Putting Reform into Perspective

What does this reform and counter-reform mean? First, the effectiveness of bilingual education is a complicated issue with few absolute answers. Some research indicates that students in bilingual programs score higher in math and reading and have more positive attitudes toward school and themselves (Arias & Casanova, 1993). In addition, contrary to an argument that newcomers to the United States are learning English more slowly than in previous generations, the opposite appears to be true (Waggoner, 1995). Further research indicates that knowledge and skills acquired in a native language—literacy in particular—are "transferable" to the second language (Krashen, 1996), and while conversational English, such as that spoken on the playground, is learned quite quickly, the cognitively demanding language needed for academic success is learned much less rapidly (Peregoy & Boyle, 1997).

However, other research indicates that immersion programs are working. For instance, one California school district reported that standardized test scores for students in the early grades—those most affected by the move from bilingual to immersion programs—improved from the 35th to the 45th percentile in just one year; additional research found similar positive results across California (Barone, 2000). For a report on "The Initial Impact of Proposition 227 on the Instruction of English Learners," go to the *Web Links* Module in Chapter 3 of the Companion Website at **http://www.prenhall.com/kauchak.**

So, what does all this mean for you as a teacher? First, the issue of bilingual education is likely to be a subject of hot debate for years. Second, while bilingual programs have been reduced, they haven't been eliminated, and job opportunities in bilingual education are widespread. For example, there are currently 50,000 bilingual education vacancies in the United States, with 21,000 vacancies in California alone (Sack, 2000b). This is one of the areas of greatest need in education; prospective candidates who speak two languages, especially Spanish, are in high demand across the country. Third, you will almost certainly have non-native English speakers in your classroom, and your ability to make informed professional decisions will be crucial for their learning success.

In working with diverse students, your professionalism will be tested perhaps more than in any other area of your work.

Research offers the following suggestions:

- Create a warm and inviting classroom environment by taking a personal interest in all students and involving everyone in learning activities.
- Mix teacher-centered instruction with cooperative learning groups where students can interact informally, learning English and practicing their language skills as they study content.
- Provide peer tutoring and assistance in which students more proficient in English help their less proficient counterparts. Peer tutoring is also beneficial to the tutor, illustrating the instructional benefits of helping someone else learn (Miller et al., 1994).
- Use many examples and illustrations to provide concrete referents for new ideas and vocabulary (Peregoy & Boyle, 1997; Echevarria & Graves, 1998).

These strategies represent good instruction for all students; for ESL students, they are essential.

You Take a Position

Now it's your turn to take a position on the issues discussed in this section. Go to the *Education Week* Website at **http://www.edweek.com,** find "search" on the first page, and type in one of the following two search terms: *bilingual education* or *Proposition 227*. Locate a minimum of three articles on one of these topics and do the following:

1. Identify the title, author, and date of each article, and then write a one-paragraph summary of each.
2. Determine if a pattern exists in the articles. (Each article—or even two of the three—suggesting that bilingual education be abolished would be a pattern, for example.)
3. Take one of the two following positions:
   - The pattern suggested in the articles, if implemented, *is* likely to improve education.
   - The pattern suggested in the articles *is not* likely to improve education.

Document your position with information taken from the articles and your study of the text (including this chapter and any other chapter of the text).

To answer these questions online, go to the Take a Position Module in Chapter 3 of the Companion Website.

Bilingual education maintains students' first language, using it as the foundation for learning English.

Sexual harassment often occurs in school hallways, and teachers can play a powerful role in preventing it there and in the classrooms.

Several aspects of the study depicted in Figure 3.2 are disturbing. One is the high incidence of sexual harassment that occurs in schools; schools and classrooms should be safe places for learning. Another is a finding that only 7 percent of the harassment cases were reported. In addition, more than half the students surveyed didn't even know if their school had a policy on sexual harassment.

Harassment is a particularly acute problem for homosexual students. One national survey found that 91 percent of gay students had heard anti-gay comments, 69 percent had been verbally abused, and 34 percent reported being verbally abused on a daily basis (Galley, 1999). As the following example shows, sometimes the abuse isn't only verbal.

■ ■ ■

When I was changing classes, I had all the books in my hands. . . . I'd hear someone mutter "faggot" and have my books knocked down. People are walking over me as I'm trying to gather my books. I don't have time to turn around to see who said it (Sears, 1993, p. 129).

■ ■ ■

Students report that harassment such as this makes them feel "sad and worthless," and "powerless" (Shakeshaft et al., 1997). This harassment contributes to higher rates of depression, substance abuse, and suicide for gay students (Berk, 2000).

Schools and teachers need to do a better job of making classrooms and hallways safe. All students—boys and girls, heterosexual and homosexual—have a right to harassment-free schools. Teachers have an important role in ensuring that this happens. Talk with your students about the problem and emphasize that no form of sexual harassment will be tolerated.

ABILITY DIFFERENCES

When you look out at your first class, you'll see obvious similarities and differences. Your students will be about the same age, and their dress and hairstyles will often be similar. They'll come from different cultural backgrounds, and you'll have both boys and girls. Less obvious, however, is their ability to learn. In virtually any class, you'll work with students who master the content effortlessly while others struggle just to keep up. In this section we examine these differences and how schools accommodate them.

What Is Intelligence?

We all have intuitive notions about intelligence; it's how "sharp" people are, how much they know, how quickly and easily they learn, and how perceptive and sensitive they are. But how should intelligence really be defined?

Consider the following questions and decide if they would be included on an intelligence test.

1. On what continent is Brazil?
2. A coat priced $45 is marked one-third off. When it still doesn't sell, the sale price is reduced by half. What is the price after the second discount?
3. Who was Albert Einstein?
4. How far is it from Seattle to Atlanta?
5. How are a river and a plateau alike?

The answer may surprise you. *All* of the items are similar to items found on the Wechsler Intelligence Scale for Children (Wechsler, 1991), one of the most widely used intelligence tests.

Increasing Understanding 3.10

If experience is crucial to performance on tests of learning ability, how might performance be affected by growing up in a minority culture?

Experts define **intelligence** as *the capacity to acquire knowledge, the ability to think and reason in the abstract, and the ability to solve problems* (Snyderman & Rothman, 1987; Sternberg, 1986). What do the test questions that we listed have to do with these three dimensions? First, they suggest that background knowledge and experience are crucial in performance (Perkins, 1995), and second, research consistently indicates that these factors are crucial in people's ability to solve problems and think in the abstract (Bruning, et al., 1999).

Changes in Views of Intelligence

Historically, researchers believed that intelligence was a single trait and that we all exist somewhere along a continuum of general intelligence. This thinking has changed; many researchers now believe that intelligence is composed of several distinct dimensions.

Harvard psychologist Howard Gardner (1983, 1995) illustrates this position. He proposed a theory of **multiple intelligences (MI),** the suggestion that *overall intelligence is composed of eight relatively independent dimensions* (see Table 3.2).

Gardner's theory makes intuitive sense. For example, we all know people who don't seem particularly "sharp" analytically but who excel in getting along with others. This ability serves them well, and in some instances they're more successful than their "brighter" counterparts. Other people seem very self-aware and are able to capitalize on their personal strengths and minimize their weaknesses. Gardner explains these examples by saying the people described are high in interpersonal and intrapersonal intelligence, respectively.

Increasing Understanding 3.11

If educators were to apply Gardner's theory, what would an elementary-level report card look like? A high school report card?

Most classrooms focus heavily on the linguistic and logical-mathematical dimensions and virtually ignore the others. If these other dimensions are to develop, students need experiences with them. For example, cooperative learning activities can help students develop interpersonal intelligence; participation in sports or dance can improve bodily kinesthetic abilities; and playing in the band or singing in choral groups can improve musical intelligence.

Table 3.2 **Gardner's Eight Intelligences**

Dimension	Description	Individuals Who Might Be High in This Dimension
Linguistic intelligence	Sensitivity to the meaning and order of words and the varied uses of language.	Poet, journalist
Logical-mathematical intelligence	The ability to handle long chains of reasoning and to recognize patterns and order in the world.	Scientist, mathematician
Musical intelligence	Sensitivity to pitch, melody, and tone.	Composer, violinist
Spacial intelligence	The ability to perceive the visual world accurately, and to recreate, transform, or modify aspects of the world on the basis of one's perceptions.	Sculptor, navigator
Bodily kinesthetic intelligence	A fine-tuned ability to use the body and to handle objects.	Dancer, athlete
Interpersonal intelligence	An understanding of interpersonal relations and the ability to make distinctions among others.	Therapist, salesperson
Intrapersonal intelligence	Access to one's own "feeling life."	Self-aware individual
Naturalist intelligence	The ability to recognize similarities and differences in the physical world.	Biologist, anthropologist

Source: Adapted from H. Gardner and Hatch, 1989, Multiple intelligences go to school, *Educational Researcher,* 18(8), 4–10; and Chekles, 1997, The first seven . . . and the eighth, *Educational Leadership,* 55, 8–13.

Ability: Nature versus Nurture

No aspect of intelligence has been more hotly debated than the issue of heredity versus environment. The extreme **nature view of intelligence or ability** *asserts that ability is solely determined by genetics;* the **nurture view of intelligence or ability** *emphasizes the influence of the environment.* Differences between these positions are very controversial when race or ethnicity are considered. For example, research indicates that some cultural minority groups collectively score lower on intelligence tests than White American children (Brody, 1992; McLoyd, 1998). People who emphasize the nurture view explain this finding by arguing that minority children have fewer stimulating experiences while they are developing.

People adhering to the nature view argue that heredity is the more important factor. In their highly controversial book *The Bell Curve,* Hernstein and Murray (1994) concluded that the contribution of heredity outweighed environmental factors in influencing the intelligence-test scores of minority populations, especially African Americans. Methodological problems, such as inferring causation from correlational data, caused other experts to reject this position (Jacoby & Glauberman, 1995; Marks, 1995).

In considering the nature–nurture debate, most experts take a position somewhere in the middle, believing that ability is influenced both by heredity and the environment (Yee, 1995). In this view, a person's genes provide the potential for intelligence, and stimulating environments make the most of the raw material.

The opposite is also true; many learning environments don't provide enough stimulation to help children reach their full potential (Ceci, 1990; Loehlin, 1989). For example, researchers tracked children born of low-income parents but adopted as infants into high-income families. The enriched environments resulted in children who scored an average of 14 points higher on intelligence tests than did their comparable siblings (Schiff, Duyme, Dumaret, & Tomkiewicz, 1982).

Formal experiences can also increase intelligence-test scores (Ceci & Williams, 1997). Attempts to directly teach the skills measured by intelligence tests have been successful with preschool and elementary students (Consortium for Longitudinal Studies, 1983; Sprigle &

Schoefer, 1985), adults (Whimbey, 1980), and students with learning disabilities (Brown & Campione, 1986). A longitudinal study of disadvantaged, inner-city children also indicated that early stimulation can have lasting effects on intelligence (Garber, 1988).

Ability Grouping and Tracking

The most common way schools respond to differences in learner ability is by **ability grouping,** which *places students of similar aptitude and achievement histories together and attempts to match instruction to the needs of different groups*.

Ability grouping is popular in elementary schools, and typically exists in two major forms. **Between-class ability grouping** *divides all students in a given grade into high, medium, and low groups;* **within-class ability grouping** *divides all students in a given classroom into high, medium, and low groups*. Most elementary teachers endorse ability grouping, particularly in reading and math.

In middle, junior high, and high schools, ability grouping goes further, with high-ability students studying advanced and college preparatory courses and their low-ability counterparts receiving vocational or work-related instruction. In some cases, students are grouped only in certain areas, such as English or math; in other cases, it exists across all content areas, a practice called **tracking,** which *places students in different classes or curricula on the basis of ability*. Some form of tracking exists in most middle, junior high, and high schools (Braddock, 1990), and tracking has its most negative effect on minorities in the lower tracks (Davenport et al., 1998; Mickelson & Heath, 1999).

Increasing Understanding 3.12

Based on his theory of multiple intelligences, would Howard Gardner favor ability grouping? Explain why or why not. How might he modify ability grouping?

Why is ability grouping so common? Advocates argue that it increases learning by allowing teachers to adjust the pace of instruction, methods, and materials to better meet students' needs. Because pace and assessments are similar for a particular group, instruction is easier for the teacher.

However, research has uncovered the following problems:

- Within-class grouping creates logistical problems for teachers, because different lessons and assignments are required and monitoring students in different tasks is difficult (Good & Brophy, 1997; Oakes, 1992).
- Improper placements occur, and placement tends to become permanent. Cultural minorities are under-represented in high-ability classes and over-represented in lower classes and tracks (Good & Marshall, 1984; Grant & Rothenberg, 1986; Oakes, 1992).
- Low groups are stigmatized; self-esteem and motivation of low groups suffer (Good & Marshall, 1984; Hallinan, 1984).
- Homogeneously grouped low-ability students achieve less than heterogeneously grouped students of similar ability (Good & Brophy, 1997).

Negative effects of grouping are related, in part, to the quality of instruction. Presentations to low groups are more fragmented and vague than those to high groups; they focus more on memorizing than on understanding, problem solving, and "active learning." Students in low-ability classes are often taught by teachers who lack enthusiasm and who stress conformity versus autonomy and the development of self-regulation (Good & Brophy, 1997; Ross, Smith, Loks, & McNelie, 1994).

Grouping also affects the students themselves. In addition to lowered self-esteem and motivation to learn, absentee rates tend to increase. One study found that absenteeism increased from 8 percent to 26 percent after students' transition to a tracked junior high (Slavin & Karweit, 1982), with most of the truants being students in the low-level classes. Tracking can also result in racial or cultural segregation of students, impeding social development and the ability to form friendships across cultural groups (Oakes, 1992).

Teachers minimize the negative effects of ability grouping by using it only in areas where it is absolutely necessary and by adapting instruction to meet the needs of all students.

Increasing Understanding 3.13

What are some possible explanations for the negative effects of ability grouping on students' self-esteem and motivation?

Efforts to reverse the negative effects of grouping and tracking have been positive, but require instructional adaptations. Some of these adaptations for heterogeneously grouped students include the following (Nyberg et al., 1997; Tomlinson, Callahan, & Moon, 1998):

- Giving students who need it more time to complete assignments.
- Providing peer tutors for students requiring extra help.
- Using small group work.
- Providing options on some assignments, such as giving students the choice of presenting a report orally or in writing.
- Breaking large assignments into smaller ones and providing additional scaffolding and support for those who need it.

Effective teachers adapt instruction to meet the needs of all students, with the need being especially acute for low-ability students (Tomlinson et al., 1998).

LEARNING STYLES

Case STUDY

One thing teacher Chris Burnette remembered from his methods classes was the need for variety. He had been primarily using large-group discussions in his junior high social studies class, and most of the students seemed to respond okay. But others seemed disinterested, and their attention often drifted.

Today, Chris decided to try a small-group activity involving problem solving. They had been studying the growth of big cities in America, and he wanted the class to think about some solutions to big cities' problems.

As he watched the small groups interact, he was amazed at what he saw. Some of the quietest, most withdrawn students were leaders in the groups.

"Great!" he thought. But at the same time, he noted that some of his more active students were sitting back and not getting involved.

■ ■ ■

How do you like to study? Do you learn most effectively in groups or alone? Do you prefer teacher presentations or reading a textbook? Your answers to these questions reflect your unique **learning style,** or *your preferred way of learning and processing information.*

We often see differences in learning styles when we present a problem to students; some jump in and try to solve it through trial and error, whereas others sit back and carefully analyze the problem. **Impulsive students** *work quickly but make errors*, and **reflective students** *analyze and deliberate before answering.* Impulsive students concentrate on speed and take chances; reflective students think more and consider alternatives before they answer. Impulsive students perform better on activities requiring factual information; reflective students have an advantage in problem solving.

Increasing Understanding 3.14

Would a field-independent person more likely be impulsive or reflective? Why?

Another difference among students is described as **field dependence/independence,** *an individual's ability to identify relevant information in a complex and potentially confusing background* (Kogan, 1994). Field-dependent people see patterns as wholes; field-independent people are able to analyze complex patterns into their constituent parts. In a math word problem, for example, a field-independent student would be better at breaking a complex problem into subcomponents using relevant information in solving the problem.

Cultural Learning Styles

Learning styles are also influenced by culture and gender. In typical U.S. classrooms, individual initiative and responsibility are emphasized and reinforced by grades and competition. Competition demands successes and failures, and the success of one student can be linked to the failure of another (Cushner, McClelland, & Safford, 1992).

Contrast this orientation with the learning styles of the Hmong, a mountain tribe from Laos that immigrated to the United States after the Vietnam War. The Hmong culture emphasizes cooperation, and Hmong students constantly monitor the learning progress of their peers, offering help and assistance. Individual achievement is de-emphasized in favor of group success.

Case STUDY

When Mee Hang has difficulty with an alphabetization lesson, Pang Lor explains, in Hmong, how to proceed. Chia Ying listens in to Pang's explanation and nods her head. Pang goes back to work on her own paper, keeping an eye on Mee Hang. When she sees Mee looking confused, Pang leaves her seat and leans over Mee's shoulder. She writes the first letter of each word on the line, indicating to Mee that these letters are in alphabetical order and that Mee should fill in the rest of each word. This gives Mee the help she needs and she is able to finish on her own. Mee, in turn, writes the first letter of each word on the line for Chia Ying, passing on Pang Lor's explanation.

Classroom achievement is never personal but always considered to be the result of cooperative effort. Not only is there no competition in the classroom, there is constant denial of individual ability. When individuals are praised by the teacher, they generally shake their heads and appear hesitant to be singled out as being more able than their peers (Hvitfeldt, 1986, p. 70).

■ ■ ■

that significantly contribute to learning. Parents are not just passive onlookers in the process of learning; they contribute substantially in many subtle, and not so subtle, ways to their children's success in school. When you enter your first classroom as a teacher, you will be expected to build upon your students' cultural and linguistic backgrounds and actively involve parents in their children's learning.

Building on Students' Strengths

To build upon students' strengths, you must discover what these strengths are. Effective teachers do this in a number of ways, including talking with previous years' teachers, examining students' cumulative folders, and conducting comprehensive pre-assessments at the beginning of the school year. But effective teachers need to go beyond these traditional strategies and establish human communication links with their students. Ways of doing this include the following:

- Have students write about themselves and their families at the beginning of the school year. Ask them to share their hopes (and anxieties) about the new school year as well as information about themselves as people, like their favorite foods and pastimes and information about their families.
- Spend time with them at lunch and on the playground. This provides you with valuable opportunities to learn about how they act and feel outside the classroom.
- Make yourself available before and after school for school help. When teachers do this, they find that students often want to talk about much more than school-related homework problems.

The goal with all of these strategies is to get to know your students as human beings. Not only will this make you a more effective teacher, but it will also help you enjoy teaching more.

Working with Parents

Learning is a cooperative venture, and teachers, students, and parents are in it together. In a comprehensive review of factors affecting student learning, researchers reached the following conclusions:

■ ■ ■

Because of the importance of the home environment to school learning, teachers must also develop strategies to increase parent involvement in their children's academic life. This means teachers should go beyond traditional once-a-year parent/teacher conferences and work with parents to see that learning is valued in the home. Teachers should encourage parents to be involved with their children's academic pursuits on a day-to-day basis, helping them with homework, monitoring television viewing, reading to their young children, and simply expressing the expectation that their children will achieve academic success (Wang et al., 1993, pp. 278–279).

■ ■ ■

Communication with parents or other primary caregivers is not an appendage to the teaching process; it is an integral part of a teacher's job.

SUMMARY

Cultural Diversity

Due to demographic trends, our schools are becoming increasingly diverse. In the past, schools responded to diversity with the goal of assimilation, hoping to "Americanize" students as quickly as possible. Multicultural education, by contrast, attempts to recognize the contributions of different cultures and build on students' cultural strengths in the classroom.

This increase in diversity is also seen in the languages that students bring to our classrooms. Different approaches to dealing with this language diversity place different amounts of emphasis on maintaining the first language versus learning English as quickly as possible.

Gender

Evidence suggests that both boys and girls encounter problems in today's schools. For girls these problems focus more on achievement, especially in areas like math, science, and computer science, while for boys the problems are more behavioral and connected to learning problems. Causes for these problems range from societal and parental expectations to differential treatment in classrooms. Teachers can play a major role in ensuring that gender differences don't become gender inequalities. Sexual harassment is a problem for both males and females and occurs most often in environments where teachers and administrators allow it to occur.

Ability Differences

A third dimension of diversity found in today's classrooms focuses on students' different abilities to learn. Earlier perspectives viewed ability as unidimensional; the current perspective views ability as multifaceted.

Ability grouping is one of the most common responses to this dimension of diversity. Despite its popularity, research suggests a number of problems with ability grouping, ranging from inappropriate and rigid placements to substandard instruction in some low-ability classrooms.

Learning Styles

Cognitive learning styles emphasize differences in the ways students process information. Cultural learning styles reflect the variety of ways that different groups learn and interact. The concept of learning styles reminds us that all students learn differently; effective teachers are sensitive to these differences and adapt their teaching accordingly.

Students with Exceptionalities

Students with exceptionalities require extra help to reach their full potential. The majority of students with exceptionalities fall into four major categories: gifted and talented, mental retardation, learning disabilities, and behavior disorders. Inclusion is changing the way schools assist students with exceptionalities, providing them with a supporting network of services.

IMPORTANT CONCEPTS

ability grouping
acceleration
assimilation
behavior disorder
between-class ability grouping
culturally responsive teaching
culture

English as a Second Language (ESL)
enrichment
ethnicity
exceptionality
field dependence/independence
gender-role identity
gifted and talented students
immersion programs
impulsive students
inclusion
intelligence
learning disability
learning style
least restrictive environment
mainstreaming
maintenance language programs
mentally retarded students
multicultural education
multiple intelligences
nature view of intelligence or ability
nurture view of intelligence or ability
reflective students
sexual harassment
single-gender classes and schools
special education
students who are gifted and talented
students who are mentally retarded
tracking
transition programs
within-class ability grouping

DISCUSSION QUESTIONS

1. Is multicultural education more important at some grade levels than at others? Why? Is multicultural education more important in some content areas than in others? Why?
2. Experts debate whether teachers should adjust instruction to match student learning styles or teach students to broaden their learning repertoires. Which approach is more desirable? Why?
3. Which approach to teaching English to LEP students makes the most sense in the particular teaching setting you will find yourself in your first job? Why?
4. Are single-gender classrooms a good idea? Why?
5. What are the advantages and disadvantages of full inclusion? Should it be used with all students?
6. What implications does Gardner's theory of multiple intelligences have for you as a teacher? (Be sure to relate your answer to the grade level and content area(s) you'll be teaching.)

GOING INTO SCHOOLS

1. Interview a teacher about the diversity in his or her classroom. Explain how the students differ in terms of the following:
   a. culture
   b. home language
   c. learning styles
   d. multiple intelligences
   e. learning ability

   What does the teacher do to accommodate these differences? Summarize these responses and analyze them using information from this chapter.
2. Observe a classroom and focus on several cultural minority students.
   a. Where do they sit?
   b. Who do they talk to and make friends with?
   c. Do they attend to the class and are they involved?
   d. Do they participate in classroom interaction?

Ask the teacher how these students perform in class and what he or she does to build upon differences in these students. Analyze this response in terms of the information given in this chapter.

3. Ask the teacher to identify several cultural minority students. Interview these students and ask the following questions:
   a. How long have they been at this school?
   b. What do they like the most about school?
   c. What do they like the least about school?
   d. What can teachers do to help them learn better?

   Summarize their responses and suggest several concrete things that teachers can do to make their classrooms better learning environments for cultural minorities.

4. Observe a class during an interactive questioning session.
   a. Note the number of boys and girls in the class.
   b. Where were the boys and girls seated?
   c. Did boys and girls raise their hands to respond equally?
   d. Record the number of times boys and girls were called on. Were they equal?
   e. Did the number of management interventions vary by gender?

   How gender neutral was the class? What can teachers do to make their classes more gender neutral and a better place for both boys and girls to learn?

5. Observe a class working on an in-class assignment. As you do this, circulate around the room so you can observe the work progress of different students. Note the following:
   a. Beginning times—Do all students get immediately to work or do some take their time starting?
   b. On-task behaviors—What percentage of the class stays on task throughout the assignment?
   c. Completions—Do all students complete the assignment? What do they do if they don't complete the work?
   d. Assistance—What forms of help are there for students who need it?
   e. Options—What options are there for students who complete their assignments early?

   From your observations, how diverse is this class in terms of learning ability? What concrete things can teachers do to address this diversity?

6. Interview a teacher to investigate his or her use of the following strategies to deal with differences in learning ability: flexible time requirements, grouping, strategy instruction, and peer tutoring and cooperative learning. Ask these questions:
   a. Are differences in learning ability a problem for the teacher? Explain.
   b. Does the teacher use any of the strategies mentioned in this book? Which ones work and why? Have any been tried that didn't work?
   c. Does the teacher employ any other strategy for dealing with differences in learning ability?

   What implications do the teacher's responses suggest for you and how you would teach in your future classroom?

7. Interview a teacher about working with students with exceptionalities in the classroom. Ask the following questions:
   a. Which students are classified as exceptional? What behaviors led to this classification? What role did the teacher play in identification?

b. In working with students with exceptionalities, what assistance does the classroom teacher receive from the following people?
- Special-education teacher
- School psychologist or school counselor
- Principal

c. What does an Individualized Education Program (IEP) look like ? How helpful is it in working with exceptional students in the classroom?

d. What is the biggest challenge the teacher faces in working with students with exceptionalities?

Summarize your findings. Describe what your approach will be in working with these students.

Virtual Field *Experience*

If you would like to participate in a Virtual Field Experience, go to the *Field Experience* Module in Chapter 1 of the Companion Website.

ONLINE PORTFOLIO ACTIVITIES

To complete these activities online, go to the Portfolio Activities Module in Chapter 3 of the Companion Website, and submit your response.

Portfolio Activity 3.1 **Exploring Cultural Diversity**

INTASC Principle 3: *Adapting Instruction*
The purpose of this activity is to introduce you to the cultural diversity in an area where you might teach. Contact the State Office of Education in a state where you're thinking of teaching. Addresses and Websites can be found in the Companion Website to Chapter 13; school district telephone numbers can be found at the back of the White Pages of the telephone directory in the business section under "Schools." Ask for demographic information on cultural minorities and ESL students. Summarize the information briefly, identifying major cultural groups and possible implications for your teaching.

Portfolio Activity 3.2 **Learning Styles**

INTASC Principle 3: *Adapting Instruction*
The purpose of this activity is to make you more knowledgeable about learning styles. Using the references in this chapter as a starting point, locate and read several articles on learning styles. Write a short paper on the implications of learning styles for your teaching. In your paper include information about the following topics: What are learning styles? Which are most important to teaching and learning? How can teachers adapt their instruction to address students' different learning styles?

Portfolio Activity 3.3 **Exploring Careers in Special Education**

INTASC Principle 9: *Commitment to the Profession*
This activity is designed to acquaint you with teaching career options in special education. Visit the Website for the Council for Exceptional Children, the national profes-

sional organization for special educators (the Website can be found in the *Web Links* Module in Chapter 3 of the Companion Website at **http://www.prenhall.com/kauchak.**) Click on "Student CEC" for information on Tools You Need, Career Info., Goals, Chapter Directory, and Regional Contacts. The *Career Info* Module contains additional information on résumé writing, interviewing, and building a professional portfolio. Write a brief description of career opportunities in special education and how your talents and personality might match these.

Increasing Understanding 4.1

Identify at least two things teachers can do to help parents work with their children more effectively on homework and other academic activities.

To respond to the Increasing Understanding questions in this chapter and receive immediate feedback, go to the *Increasing Understanding* Module in Chapter 4 of the Companion Website at **http://www.prenhall.com/kauchak.**

- Seven out of 10 women with children are in the workforce.
- The divorce rate has quadrupled in the past 20 years; the number of single-parent families is estimated at 25 percent and is expected to increase.
- Sixty-eight percent of all births to teenagers occur out of wedlock.
- The incidence of poverty among single-parent families is between 7 and 8 times higher than in families headed by married couples.
- Sixty percent of teenage families live in poverty, as compared to 14 percent of the total population.

Poverty, divorce, single parents, families where both parents work, and teenage pregnancies pose challenges to parents, their children, and teachers. Work demands for single parents and parents who both work outside the home result in less time being spent with their children in general, as well as less time being spent helping and supervising homework. Research indicates that many parents in today's fast-paced world are spending up to 40 percent less time with their children than parents a generation ago (Kamerman & Kamerman, 1995; Hewlett, 1991). Even when they have time, many parents are uncertain about how to help their children with schoolwork (Gorman, & Balter, 1997).

What does this information imply for teachers? Let's look at an example. One of your authors went to a first volleyball team meeting with his daughter. The team was lined up on the floor and was asked to introduce themselves and their parents/caregivers. The first girl introduced both parents; the second, whose father wasn't there, felt obligated to explain. From that point every girl followed precedent by "explaining" the absence of a parent, and some were embarrassed because their parents were divorced. Teachers can make situations like these easier for students by using words such as, "Would you please introduce your parent, or parents, or caregivers," when asking for introductions. On the surface it may seem like a minor issue, but it is important to students.

Being flexible with meeting times for parent–teacher conferences is another way teachers can accommodate working or single parents. It communicates that you care about your students, you're committed to their education, and you're aware of the pressure of work schedules. In essence, as teachers we should try to be sensitive to these changes in family structure and communicate to our students that we accept and support all types of family patterns.

Child Care When both parents work outside the home or when a single parent leaves the home to make a living, child care becomes an issue. The trend is away from home care; today one-fourth of the children of working parents are cared for in the home compared to 57 percent in 1958 (Leach, 1995).

These trends raise questions about the effects of child care on the emotional and intellectual development of children. Critics contend that young children need the presence of a mother in the home, and child care is not an adequate substitute. Supporters counter that children can adapt to different care patterns and are not jeopardized by alternate child-care arrangements.

Researchers attempting to respond to this issue have focused on the quality of the child care instead of the larger issue of working parents. When children are placed in well-run and supervised child-care facilities, there seem to be few if any adverse effects on the children (Berk, 2000). However, the problem is complicated by the fact that many child-care facilities don't provide high-quality care.

Latchkey Children **Latchkey children,** *children who go home to empty houses after school and who are left alone until parents arrive home from work*, are another work-related prob-

Latchkey children often face long hours of unsupervised care.

lem. There may be as many as 6 million latchkey kids in our country, and almost 50 percent of working parents acknowledge leaving their children unattended for periods of time after school (Leach, 1995). The problem is complex, ranging from concerns about children's safety to questions of supervision, excessive time spent watching television, and lack of help with homework.

Some schools respond with after-hour programs, but a more common solution is for schools to cooperate with community agencies, such as YMCAs or youth clubs, to offer late afternoon programs. In addition to providing safe, supervised environments, these programs teach children how to respond to home emergencies, use the phone to seek help, make healthy snacks, and spend time wisely.

Changing Socioeconomic Patterns

Researchers have found that parents and caregivers from different backgrounds think about and prepare their children for school in different ways. One of the strongest indicators of these differences is **socioeconomic status (SES),** which is *an indicator that combines parents' incomes, occupations, and levels of education.* Teachers, for example, have relatively high socioeconomic status; they have college degrees, they have professional occupations, and they make middle-class incomes. Plumbers, in comparison, tend to have lower socioeconomic status because they don't work in professional occupations, and they usually don't have college degrees (even though they sometimes make more money than teachers do).

Socioeconomic status is commonly described in terms of three levels—upper, middle, and lower class—with finer distinctions within each. The **upper class** is *the smallest segment of the population (less than 15 percent) and is composed of highly educated (usually a college degree), highly paid (typically above $100,000) professionals.* The upper class comprises

Increasing Understanding 4.2

Where do you think most new teaching positions will occur, in schools populated by students from upper, middle, or lower SES backgrounds? Why do you think so?

only a small part of the total population but controls a disproportionate amount of the wealth; the gap between the upper and other classes is growing. For example, in 1979 corporate chief executives earned 29 times as much as their employees; by 1988 the figure had grown to 93 times (Phillips, 1990).

The **middle class** *includes managers, administrators, and white-collar workers who perform nonmanual work.* Teachers are included in this category. Middle-class incomes typically range from $30,000 to $70,000, and about 40 percent of the population falls into this category. (Upper-middle-class groups fall between the $70,000 and $100,000 ranges.)

Families in the lower SES class typically make less than $20,000 per year, have a high-school education or less, and work in blue-collar jobs. About 40 percent of the U.S. population is in this category, and the percentage is increasing. The lowest earning segment of this category often depends upon public assistance to supplement their incomes, and members are often the third or fourth generation to live in poverty. The term **underclass** is used to describe *people with low incomes who have difficulty coping with economic problems;* research indicates that escaping this situation is very difficult (Lind, 1995; Reich, 1995).

Poverty

Case STUDY

When Sally gets a spare moment (and there are precious few of them), she loves to draw, mostly fantasy creatures. "What is your favorite thing to draw?" "A mermaid thing, cuz it's not real—there's no such thing as a mermaid—but I like to draw things that aren't real. Fairy tales. Fairies, monsters." She lights up talking about her creations. But Sally's life is not a fairy tale. With her brother she hurries home from school, immediately does her homework, and "I mean *right* after my homework I have to clean up my room and do the dishes for dinner and cook dinner." "You cook dinner? Every day?" Staring straight across the table separating us, and without blinking her blue eyes, Sally responded slightly defensively, "I'm a good cook." For all the talk about food, Sally's greatest fear, she said, was that she will not get enough to eat and will get sick. Who would take care of the family, then? "I worry . . . I [will] end up getting too skinny and die cuz I'm really skinny. I try to keep my health up, but I don't eat that much." I hesitated, not knowing what to say. "Why?" "I try to eat a lot, but I always have to be served last after dinner, but if there's no food left, I can't eat." "What do you do?" "I go to the store and get me a snack, like an orange or an apple." She began [taking care of her brother and cooking] when she was seven years old. Exhausted, she is in bed by 8:30. Sometimes, before falling asleep, her mother reports, she reads, but there are few books in the house, which disappoints Sally who loves books.

Sally's mother works the early morning shift as a waitress in a large and busy café. She has severe diabetes. Watching her at a distance at work, she moves slowly, deliberately, as though her legs are heavy and getting heavier with each step. Her movements are those of a tired, older woman, not of a young woman, tall, thin, and at one time athletic. She seems to will herself from table to table. Once her ten-hour shift is finished, she laboriously walks the four blocks to her apartment, collapses on the old sofa in the front room nearest the door, smokes a cigarette or two, and sleeps. When she gets home from school, this is how Sally finds her mother (Bullough, 1999, pp. 13–14).

■ ■ ■

The lowest end of the SES continuum is characterized by pervasive **poverty,** which the federal government defines as *earning less than $16,000 for a family of four* (U.S. Census Bureau, 1998).

Figure 4.2 **Poverty Levels by Ethnicity**

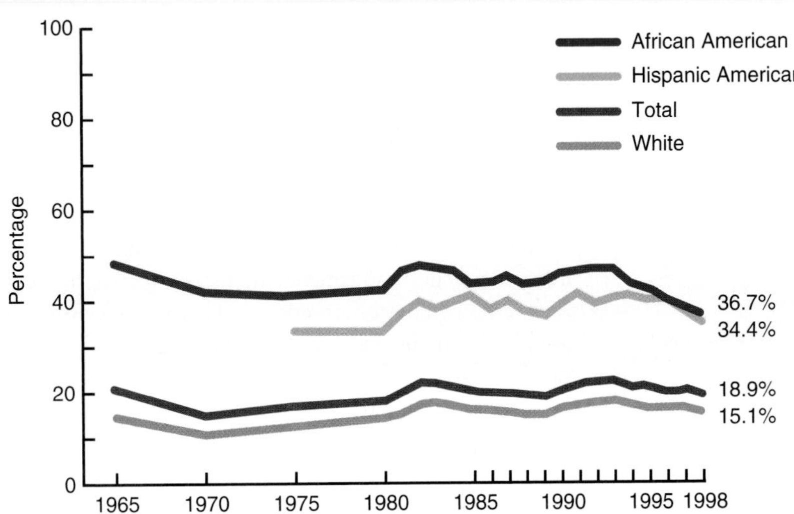

Source: Data from U.S. Census Bureau, 2000, *Historical Poverty Tables, Table 3. Poverty Status of People by Age, Race, and Hispanic Origin: 1959 to 1999.* [Online] Available at http://www.census.gov/hhes/poverty/histpov/hstpov3.html.

Increasing Understanding 4.3

What are some possible ways that poverty can influence learning?

Research on poverty reveals the following patterns:

- Less than 9 percent of America's poor live in inner cities.
- Poverty is most common in small towns and suburban areas (46 percent of all impoverished families live in small towns; 28 percent live in suburban areas).
- Although they comprise only 27 percent of the total population, children constitute 40 percent of the poor.
- Poverty is most common in families headed by single mothers.
- Poverty is more prevalent among minorities than nonminorities (see Figure 4.2).

Some of these results are surprising. For example, many people think that poverty is most prevalent in cities, and most don't realize that 40 percent of our potential leaders for the future are now living in poverty.

The powerful effect that poverty can have on learning is reflected in a recent proposal by Wake County District in North Carolina. This proposal suggests a busing program to ensure that no more than 40 percent of a school's enrollment is composed of students who are eligible for the federal free or reduced-price lunch program (Johnston, 2000b). San Francisco is considering a similar strategy to battle both economic and racial segregation (Kahlenberg, 1999). The programs are based on the belief that high concentrations of students from impoverished backgrounds detract from the students' ability to benefit as much as possible from their school experiences.

Homelessness One of the direct results of poverty is the increase in homelessness. Experts estimate that between one-half and 1 million children are homeless; accurate figures are hard to obtain because of the transient nature of the population (Rafferty, 1995; Gracenin, 1993). Homeless children often come from unstable families, suffer from inadequate diets, and lack medical care (Gracenin, 1993). Because of unstable families, the majority (estimates run as high as 63 percent) of homeless children fail to attend school on a regular basis (Sandham, 2000).

Effective schools attempt to respond to the problem in several ways. Recognizing that the home situation is difficult, they remove barriers by making their admission, attendance, and course requirements flexible (Vissing, Schroepfer, & Bloise, 1994). They also provide outreach services such as counselors, after-school programs, and financial aid for transportation. In addition, school officials coordinate their efforts with other community agencies to ensure that basic needs, such as food and shelter, are met.

One elementary school in Phoenix, Arizona, targets homeless children as its primary clients (Sandham, 2000). It sends school buses around the city to pick up these children and maintains a clothing room that students can visit to pick up fresh underwear and changes of clothes. Volunteer pediatricians staff an on-site clinic that provides free medical care and immunizations. The school even hands out alarm clocks (old-fashioned windups because many of the children don't have access to electricity) to help the children get to school on time in the morning. Teacher dedication and effort make the school work. One teacher commented, "There's something about watching the buses roll out of here, with all the kids' faces pressed against the windows. I get this feeling it's what I should be doing" (Sandham, 2000, p. 29).

Increasing Understanding 4.4

What is the most effective thing teachers can do to demonstrate that they care about a student?

As a teacher, what can you do about homeless children? While seemingly simple and insignificant, the most important responses are to be caring and flexible. Demonstrating that you genuinely care about students and their learning is important for all children. For those that are homeless, it's essential.

Socioeconomic Status and School Success Socorro is a fifth grader who is struggling in school. When a researcher went to her house to learn why, here is what he found.

Case STUDY

During the interview with Socorro's mother, Nick passed through the apartment, apparently returning to work after taking a brief break. The phone rang. Socorro's five-year-old stepbrother curled up in his mother's lap and began talking into her ear. Television was on; there is a television in every room—one is Socorro's. Cable. "I let her do whatever she wants," Socorro's mother exclaims proudly. "She does whatever she wants." Working two jobs, one in housekeeping at a nearby hospital, and another, an evening job as a parking lot attendant to obtain money for a promised trip to Disneyland, leaves her little option: She is not home, often. While at work, her brother, who lives with the family and spends much of his day watching television, tends the children when they are home. Irritated, Socorro says that her uncle expects to be waited on, and she doesn't like it. "I want to support my kids," the mother says, and this requires that she is "never home for them."

Socorro's problem in school, her mother asserts, is that "her mind wanders." Having not read with her daughter nor spoken with her teachers, she is unaware that Socorro cannot read and is struggling; she seems unconcerned that Socorro misses so much school; as her teacher said: "She is out of school more than she is in it." Attending school irregularly, Socorro is slipping further and further behind her classmates. Concerned, teachers made arrangements to place Socorro for part of the day with the special education teacher. They didn't know what else to do, having failed to gain the mother's help getting Socorro to school regularly (Bullough, In press, pp. 48–49).

■ ■ ■

Socioeconomic status is related to school success in several ways. For example, compared to students from low-SES backgrounds, high-SES students score higher on intelligence and achievement tests, get better grades, miss less school, and have fewer suspensions (Macionis, 1997). School dropout rates for students from poor families are twice as high as those for the general population; for students from the poorest families, they exceed 50 percent. The powerful influence of SES on learning can be summarized in one

Poverty can exert a powerful negative influence on school success.

researcher's conclusion, ". . . the relationship between test scores and SES is one of the most widely replicated findings in the social sciences" (Konstantopoulas, 1997, p. 5).

What might cause these differences? At least five factors are likely:

- Basic needs
- Family stability
- School-related experience
- Interaction patterns in the home
- Parental attitudes and values

With respect to basic needs, many low-SES families lack adequate medical care, and an increasing number of children are coming to school without proper nourishment and adequate rest.

SES can also influence the quality of home life. In some low-SES families, unstable work conditions increase economic problems that lead to parental frustration, anger, and depression. These pressures can lead to marital conflicts that result in unstable home environments (Conger et al., 1992). Children then come to school without a sense of safety and security, so they are not as well-equipped to tackle school-related tasks.

Increasing Understanding 4.5

What might kindergarten or first-grade teachers do if they discover that important background learning experiences are lacking?

SES also influences children's background experiences. For example, high-SES parents are more likely than low-SES parents to provide their children with educational activities outside school (for example, visits to art, science, and history museums; attendance at concerts; books bought or borrowed from the library). They are also more likely to have learning materials at home (including computers, pocket calculators, newspapers, encyclopedias, and dictionaries) and to provide educational experiences outside school (such as, art, music, religious, dance, or computer classes). These activities support school learning by providing an experiential base for school activities (Peng & Lee, 1992).

The way parents interact with their children also influences learning (Chance, 1997). Experts estimate that by the age of 3, welfare children have heard 10 million words, compared with 20 million for children from working-class families and 30 million for children from professional homes. In addition, low-SES parents are more likely to "tell" rather than explain and to emphasize conformity and obedience instead of individual responsibility or initiative. Their language is less elaborate, their directions are less clear, and they are less likely to encourage problem solving. High-SES parents talk more with their children, explain ideas and the causes of events, encourage independent thinking, and emphasize individual responsibility (Berk, 2000; Macionis, 1997). These discussions promote language development and prepare children for the kind of verbal interaction found in schools (Heath, 1983). Sometimes called "the curriculum of the home," these rich interaction patterns, together with the enrichment experiences described in the previous paragraph, provide a foundation for reading and vocabulary development (Walberg, 1991).

Finally, the impact of SES is also transmitted through parental attitudes and values. For instance, high-SES parents and caregivers are more likely to read and have books, papers, and magazines around the home. Their children imitate these behaviors, and students who read at home show larger gains in reading achievement than those who don't (Hiebert & Raphael, 1996).

Parents' attitudes are also communicated through their expectations for their children and involvement in their curricular and extracurricular activities. High-SES parents and caregivers expect their children to graduate from high school and attend college and express these expectations in conversations. They communicate the value of a well-rounded education by attending extracurricular activities. One mother commented, "When she sees me at her games, when she sees me going to open house, when I attend her Interscholastic League contests, she knows I am interested in her activities. Plus, we have more to talk about" (Young & Scribner, 1997, p. 12). Unfortunately, research indicates that minority and low-SES students are less likely to participate in extracurricular activities (McNeal, 1997). This is often caused by work demands, transportation problems, or a simple lack of awareness that opportunities to participate exist.

Increasing Understanding 4.6

What do "structure" and "motivational support" mean? Give an example of each to illustrate your explanation.

To succeed in schools, low-SES students often need more structure and motivational support than their high-SES peers. In addition, they may need help in seeing connections between learning tasks and the outside world, as well as in understanding that effort leads to accomplishment.

Changing Student Populations

In the previous sections, we saw how the American family and socioeconomic patterns have changed, and how these changes impact students' chances for success. We now want to look at students themselves, as we examine their sexuality, use of alcohol and other drugs, violence, suicide, and child abuse. These factors are outlined in Figure 4.3 and discussed in the sections that follow.

Changing Sexuality In the past, we tacitly thought of our teenagers as either asexual or restrained. We knew they were going through puberty but assumed that they weren't sexually active (or chose to not think about it).

The facts suggest otherwise. Fifty-three percent of students in grades 9 to 12 have had sexual intercourse (Kann et al., 1993). Everyday in the United States, the following events occur (Children's Defense Fund, 1995):

- 7,742 teenagers become sexually active.
- 2,740 teenagers become pregnant.

Figure 4.3 **Changes in the Student Population**

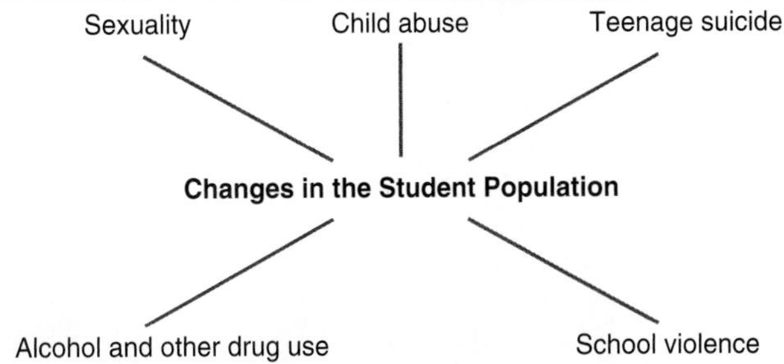

- 1,105 teenagers have abortions.
- 369 teenagers have miscarriages.
- 3 children and youths under age 25 die from AIDS.

Today's students are sexually active, and this activity poses a number of risks, including teenage pregnancy and sexually transmitted diseases.

Teenage pregnancy. Adolescence, a time when most teenagers are focusing on their own development, has become a time when many become pregnant and are forced to turn their attention to the welfare of their babies. Each year, U.S. teenagers give birth to more than 500,000 children, giving the United States the highest teenage birthrate among developed countries. In addition, the percentage of teenagers giving birth out of wedlock has increased from 15 percent in 1960 to 84 percent in 1998 (Children's Defense Fund, 1998; U.S. Department of Health and Human Services, 1996). Greater societal acceptance of teenage sexuality, earlier and more frequent sexual activity among teenagers, and a decrease in early marriages are likely reasons for this increase.

Research indicates that the teenage birthrate has recently declined from 62.1 per 1,000 births in 1991 to 52.3 in 1997, a drop of 16 percent (Coles, 1999a). Experts credit the drop to improved contraception use as well as a slight decline in teenage sexual activity.

For a full report on the latest statistics on teenage sexual behavior, consult the *Web Links* Module in Chapter 4 of the Companion Website at **http://www.prenhall.com/kauchak.**

Teenage pregnancies force students to mature too quickly, diverting energy from their own development to caring for another person. Economics is also a problem; over half of the households headed by teenage mothers live in poverty. Many drop out of school, develop poor work skills, and have limited employment opportunities. They are forced to juggle children with work and, because of inadequate prenatal care, many babies of teenage mothers are born premature or with health problems.

Increasing Understanding 4.7

Identify one advantage and one disadvantage of home instruction for teenage mothers. Do the same for in-school programs.

Efforts to deal with the problem of teenage pregnancy focus on programs that encourage mothers to complete their education through home instruction or programs where they bring their babies to school and receive child-care education along with regular classes. Despite these efforts, the majority of teen mothers drop out of school.

Sexually transmitted diseases. Unfortunately, many sexually active teenagers fail to protect themselves from sexually transmitted diseases, such as herpes, genital warts, syphilis, and gonorrhea. AIDS (Acquired Immune Deficiency Syndrome), which can be transmitted through sexual activity, has made the problem more urgent and deadly.

Teen pregnancies force students to mature too rapidly, diverting attention from their own personal development.

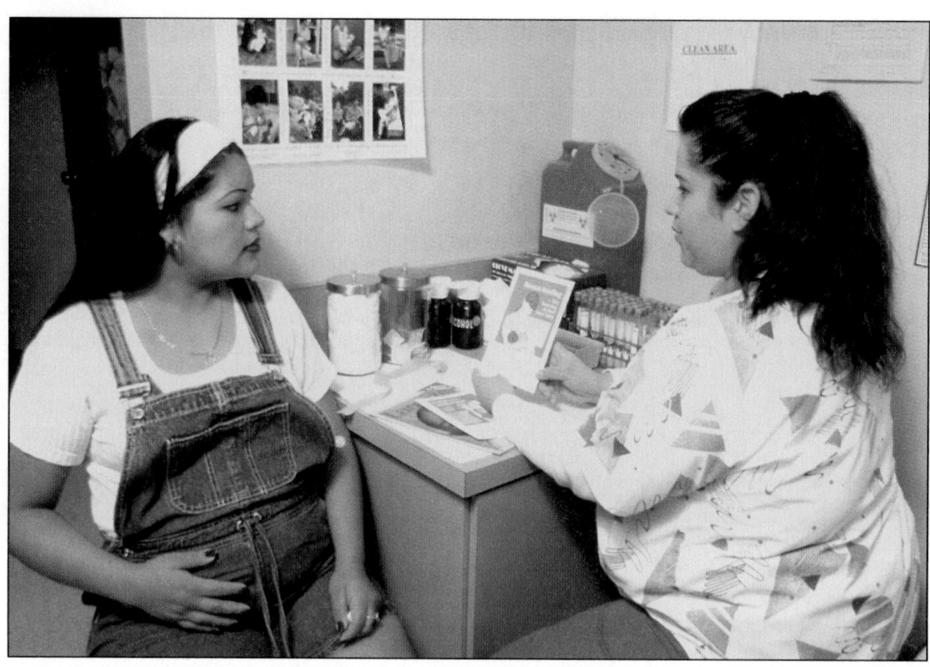

While over 50 percent of teenagers 15 to 19 years old report being sexually active and 19 percent of these teenagers have had four or more sex partners (Kann et al., 1993), only 27 percent of sexually active females and 47% of sexually active males reported using condoms, the only reliable defense, other than abstinence, against sexually transmitted diseases (Stevens-Smith & Remley, 1994). The House Select Committee on Children, Youth and Family estimates that 40,000 teens each year contract HIV, the virus that causes AIDS. While it was first believed that AIDS was confined to homosexual men and intravenous drug users, research indicates that 8 percent of HIV/AIDS cases stem from heterosexual intercourse (Center for Disease Control and Prevention, 1996).

Increasing Understanding 4.8

What could teachers do on the first day of class to minimize peer sexual harassment? Throughout the school year?

Homosexuality. Experts estimate that between 5 and 10 percent of our students are homosexual. Gay and lesbian students commonly face rejection, which leads to feelings of alienation and depression. As a result, drug use among homosexual youth is much higher than in the heterosexual population (Sears, 1991). Further, while homosexual students account for only 5 to 10 percent of the student population, they commit 30 percent of youth suicides each year (Gibson, 1989).

While the problem has no easy solution, teachers can do much to shape attitudes towards homosexual students (Shakeshaft et al., 1997). They can define appropriate behavior and maintain "zero tolerance" for harassment. Schools and classrooms must be emotionally safe places for *all* students.

Sex education. In response to teenagers' increasing sexuality, many school districts have instituted some form of sex education. The form and content that this takes varies from state to state and community to community. At issue here are two major questions: 1) What is the proper role of the family versus the schools in sex education, and 2) what specific content ought to go into these programs?

Polls show that the majority of parents favor some type of sex education, and courts have upheld school districts' right to offer sex education courses (Fischer, Schimmel, &

Figure 4.4 **Student Drug and Alcohol Use**

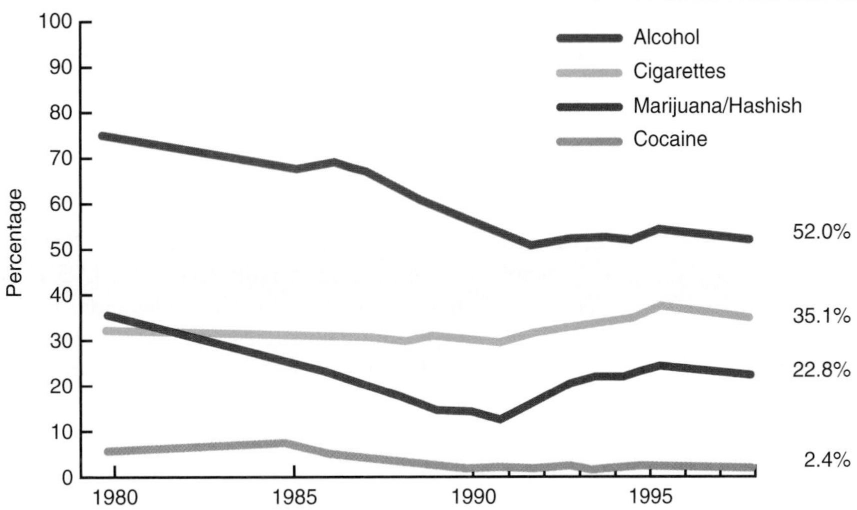

Percentage of High School Seniors Reporting Use in the Previous 30 Days

Source: From Institute for Social Research, (1998). *Monitoring the future.* Ann Arbor, MI: University of Michigan. Reprinted by permission.

Increasing Understanding 4.9

Identify at least two different kinds of background knowledge teachers must have in order to effectively teach about sexuality. (Hint: Recall the different kinds of professional knowledge discussed in Chapter 1.)

Kelly, 1999). Parents who object are free to take their children out of the programs. You'll read more about different curricular approaches to sex education in Chapter 10.

Increasing Use of Alcohol and Other Drugs After a 20-year period of decline, teenage use of alcohol and other drugs has been on the rise in recent years (see Figure 4.4). In a recent study of high school seniors, 51 percent reported using alcohol, 21 percent reported using marijuana, and 2 percent reported using cocaine in the last 30-day period (U.S. Department of Education, 1996). This pattern of drug use starts early, with 21 percent of 8th graders, 33 percent of 10th graders, and 39 percent of 12th graders reporting drug or alcohol use in the last year (Institute for Social Research, 1998). Research indicates that 10.5 million U.S. youth ages 12 to 20 use alcohol, and 4.1 million youth ages 12 to 17 smoke (Coles, 1999b). Between 1992 and 1996, the daily use of cigarettes increased for 8th, 10th, and 12th graders, and the percentage of students in each grade level who reported illicit drug use increased substantially (Federal Interagency Forum on Child and Family Statistics, 1997). Alcohol and drug use are often associated with other risk factors such as poverty, low SES, family instability, and academic problems at school.

For information on this problem from the federal Substance Abuse and Mental Health Services, go to the Web Links Module in Chapter 4 on the Companion Website at **http://www.prenhall.com/kauchak.**

Despite the stereotyped belief that drug use is primarily an inner-city problem, research reveals that drug-use problems are actually most acute in rural areas (Coles, 2000). Rural teens are more likely to use a variety of drugs, ranging from cocaine to amphetamines to alcohol.

Critics contend that a major reason for teenage use of alcohol and other drugs is the mixed messages society sends about them. The media, and particularly teenage pop culture, often glorify alcohol and other drugs, implying that they are not only acceptable but preferred ways of dealing with problems like stress, loneliness, or depression. Unfortunately, as

Increasing Understanding 4.10

Identify two specific ways in which alcohol or other drug use interferes with learning.

teenagers become drug dependent they not only place themselves at risk for other problems like suicide, health risks, and automobile accidents, but they also fail to develop healthy coping mechanisms for life's problems (Berk, 1997). Dependence on drugs can also reinforce alienation, encouraging students to drop out of school life.

Efforts to curtail drug use include programs that teach students facts about drugs as well as programs that help them learn how to make their own decisions, understand and avoid peer pressure, and work to develop self-esteem. Probably best known is the Drug Abuse Resistance Education (DARE) program that started in California and spread across the country. Research on these programs is mixed, however, and evidence suggests that concerted, long-term efforts are needed (Portner, 1993).

Similar criticisms have been directed at the U.S. Department of Education's Safe and Drug-Free Schools program, which provides more than $500 million annually to local school districts with virtually no strings attached. A review of the program found that taxpayer dollars paid for a variety of questionable strategies including motivational speakers, puppet shows, dunking booths, magicians, clowns, and tickets to Disneyland. Even though two federal reports were highly critical of the program and the Congressional Budget Office recommended eliminating it, Congress continues to fund it. This is an example of the problems involved in "throwing" money at educational problems. The need is there, the intent is good, but the implementation is lacking.

Other research suggests that intense, coordinated efforts can curtail teenage smoking (Portner, 1999b). The state of Florida combined an aggressive anti-smoking advertising campaign, increased law enforcement efforts aimed at minors, and a 50-cents-per package increase in the price of cigarettes. Cigarette use among middle schoolers dropped 19 percent; smoking declined 8 percent among high schoolers. Despite these results, the Florida legislature, under pressure from tobacco lobbies, cut funding for this program from $70 million to $45 million.

Increasing Crime and Violence

Case STUDY

For the past few months, Juan and his mother have been in hiding, the entire time he has attended Lafayette Elementary. His 29-year-old mother has been in gangs since she was twelve, and her sons, including Juan, grew up believing that at some point they would gain membership for themselves, and in gaining membership would enjoy status and achieve a measure of safety for themselves and their families. One bloody evening, however, crushed her and Juan's world-view, leaving behind a fearful, small boy and a mother overwhelmed with regret. Looking at his hands, Juan quietly revealed what had happened; it's a story he doesn't like to share: "My uncle was murdered in front of my house with guns." He worries about dying. "They were guys, they were wearing ski masks with beanies on their heads. The [killer], he looked at me and pointed the gun at me and pointed it back to my uncle and shot it. That is when I grabbed both of my cousins, his little kids, and I threw them on the ground and jumped on top of them." "You acted like a hero," I said, more than a little surprised by the tale. Proudly: "I did good for protecting my family." He continued: "It was supposed to be a drive-by [shooting], that is where they are in a car and they just roll down the windows and shoot at people. They were supposed to do a drive-by at some gangsters, and they . . . just shot when [my uncle] was outside with his girlfriend. The girl, his girlfriend, just got shot in the leg. Now she has a metal thingy at her knee and down her leg that connects to her foot." Juan was traumatized, and in the story I found an answer to the principal's question posed before we spoke, "If you can gain any insight into why Juan is so angry, I'd appreciate it" (Bullough, 1999, pp. 22–23).

■ ■ ■

Safety is a basic need for all individuals. Unfortunately, one in four students reports some kind of violence-related problem in their schools (Louis Harris & Associates, 1996), and 40 violent school-related deaths occurred during the 1997–1998 school year (Portner, 1999a). An average of 14 children die each day from gunfire in the United States—approximately one every 100 minutes (Children's Defense Fund, 1999). The problem of school violence came to national attention with the Columbine, Colorado, tragedy where two students went on a rampage, gunning down 13 students before killing themselves.

Parents, taxpayers, and educators rate school safety the highest on a list of concerns about school quality (Olson, 1999). The cost of school crime and vandalism is staggering, more than $200 million a year, according to some estimates (Geiger, 1993).

Theft is most common, constituting 62 percent of all crimes against students, and nearly 5 percent of teachers reported theft crimes (U.S. Department of Education, 1998). In addition, about 4 out of every 1,000 teachers were victims of violent crime at school. Approximately 3 percent of high school seniors reported carrying a gun to school at least once during the previous 4-week period, and during the 1996–1997 school year, more than 5,000 students were expelled for possession or use of a firearm (U.S. Department of Education, 1998).

Increasing Understanding 4.11

Why might student concerns about safety and violence peak at the eighth-grade level? What implications does this have for middle schools? For middle school teachers?

Up-to-date information on national efforts to curb violence in schools can be found in the *Web Links* Module of Chapter 4 in the Companion Website at **http://www.prenhall.com/kauchak.**

Student concerns about safety and violence are highest at the eighth-grade level and decline as students get older. Urban students (33 percent) are more likely to report serious problems with violence than suburban students (22 percent) or rural students (18 percent), and concerns about violence are greatest in high-poverty areas (Louis Harris & Associates, 1996).

School violence is often associated with gangs, but the proportion of young people actually joining gangs is small. The Justice Department estimates that the number of youth gang members numbers is only 250,000 out of the 47 million U.S. youths ages 12 to 25 (Stepp, 1996).

School Violence and the Teacher As a teacher, you will be asked to deal with the problems of aggressive students and the possibility of violence. Involving parents is a good first step (Brophy, 1996; Powell et al., 2001). The vast majority of parents (88 percent) want to be notified immediately if school problems occur (Harris, Kagay, & Ross, 1987). In addition, school counselors and psychologists, social workers, and principals are all trained to deal with these problems and can provide advice and assistance. Experienced teachers can also provide a wealth of information about how they've handled similar problems. You won't have to face persistent or serious problems of violence or aggression alone, and as you continue with your teacher-preparation program, you'll be taught specific skills for dealing with classroom discipline.

Increasing Understanding 4.12

Parents consistently rate discipline and safety among their top concerns about schools (Rose & Gallup, 1998). Given what you've read in this section, are these concerns justified? Defend your position with information taken from this section.

While violence and aggression may seem frightening, they should be put into perspective. Though they are possibilities, the majority of your day-to-day teaching problems will be issues of student cooperation and motivation. Most problems can be prevented, others can be dealt with quickly, and some require individual attention. We all hear about students carrying guns to school and incidents of assault on teachers in the news. However, considering the huge numbers of students that pass through schools each day, these incidents remain very infrequent.

Increasing Suicide The suicide rate among adolescents has tripled in the last 30 years and is now the third leading cause of teen death, after accidents and homicide. Each year about 5,000 youths take their own lives, 7 percent of adolescents report attempting

Teaching in an Era of Reform

EFFORTS TO MAKE OUR SCHOOLS SAFER

Many types of reform exist. Because of the enormous publicity generated by school shooting incidents around the country, some reform efforts focus on making our schools safer places to learn and work. These efforts fall into three general categories: schoolwide security efforts, zero-tolerance programs, and school uniforms.

Schoolwide Security Programs

Schoolwide security programs are designed to make schools safe havens for teaching and learning (Bushweller, 1998). Many schools are adopting comprehensive security measures, such as having visitors sign in (96 percent of schools), closing campuses during lunch (80 percent of schools), and controlling access to school buildings (53 percent of schools). Some schools are adding more rigid policies, such as hallway police, student photo ID badges, transparent book bags, handheld metal detectors, and breath analyzers to check for alcohol. Students are being warned to avoid jokes about violence and are being given hotline numbers to anonymously report any indications that a classmate could turn violent. Many schools are also making discipline more strict, creating peer buddy systems and adult mentorship programs, and teaching conflict-resolution skills (Bender & McLaughlin, 1997; Sauter, 1995).

Zero-Tolerance Programs

Zero-tolerance programs that *punish offenses, such as school disruptions, drugs, and weapons, with automatic suspensions* are becoming increasingly popular across the nation (Skiba & Peterson, 1999).

As a result, the annual U.S. suspension rate went from 3.7 percent to 6.9 percent between 1974 and 1998, an 86 percent increase (Johnston, 2000a). The most common reasons students are expelled include bringing firearms to school (94 percent of schools), other weapons (91 percent), possessing drugs (88 percent), alcohol (87 percent), or tobacco (79 percent), and committing acts of violence (79 percent). During the 1996–1997 school year, 6,093 students were expelled for bringing weapons to school. The majority of the expulsions occurred in high schools (56 percent), though middle schools and junior highs (34 percent) and elementary schools (9 percent) also used expulsion as a disciplinary measure (Bushweller, 1998).

School Uniforms

A growing number of schools are requiring students to wear uniforms. Proponents claim that gang clothing and designer sports clothes contribute to violence, fights, and overall delinquency. In addition, clothes serve as a visual reminder of the economic disparities between students. Long Beach School District in California started the school uniform trend, and about 20 percent of the nation's school districts, including Chicago, Miami, and Phoenix, allow individual schools to require uniforms (Portner, 1999a).

Putting Reform into Perspective

The need for safe schools is obvious, and the premise behind zero-tolerance programs—that students who seriously disrupt the learning environment for the majority of the school population should be removed—is intuitively sensible. Students can't learn when they're worried about either their physical or emotional well-being. Not surprisingly, because of the publicity generated by incidents of school violence, both parents and other taxpayers rank school safety as the most important characteristic of an effective school (Olson, 1999).

In addition, the results of the Long Beach experiment with school uniforms are impressive. After the uniform policy was implemented, school crime dropped by 76 percent, assaults declined by 85 percent, weapons offenses dropped by 83 percent, and attendance figures rose. Proponents argue that these results are due to students being required to wear uniforms.

However, zero-tolerance programs have problems. Because they don't discriminate between major and minor disruptions, they sometimes target trivial and innocent transgressions. For example, one 5-year-old child was suspended for finding a razor blade at his bus stop and showing it to his teacher, and in another case, a 6-year-old child was suspended for kissing one of his classmates (Skiba & Peterson, 1999).

In addition, when expulsion occurs, only 56 percent of students are sent to an alternative placement; the remainder are sent home to fend for themselves, making the likelihood of truancy and crime even greater. One student describes the problem in this way:

Schoolwide security programs attempt to make schools safe places to learn.

▪ ▪ ▪

When they suspend you, you get in more trouble, 'cause you're out in the street. . . . And that's what happened to me once. I got into trouble one day 'cause there was a party, and they arrested everybody in that party. . . . I got in trouble more than I get in trouble at school, because I got arrested and everything (Skiba & Peterson, 1999, p. 376).

▪ ▪ ▪

Expelled students typically fall farther behind, experience increased social difficulties, and sometimes never return to complete school (Barr & Parrett, 2001).

Other critics point to the disproportionate number of minorities affected by these programs (Johnston, 2000a). African American students made up 17 percent of all U.S. students in the 1998–1999 school year but accounted for 33 percent of all students who were suspended, whereas White students made up 63 percent of enrollments and 50 percent of all suspensions. Explanations for these uneven rates range from higher rates of poverty to inexperienced teachers, crowded classrooms, and academically sterile learning environments.

School leadership is significant in implementing effective zero-tolerance policies (Johnston, 2000a). For instance, one middle school in Dade County, Florida, had an expulsion rate of 34 percent, whereas another school that serves basically the same student population had an expulsion rate of only 2.8 percent. Students at the second school who were involved in a fight, for example, were given alternative punishments such as in-school suspensions or work assignments (such as cleaning the cafeteria) instead of being suspended.

Finally, critics of school uniforms point to research indicating that school uniforms have no direct result on behavioral problems or attendance (Brunsma & Rockquemoro, 1999). Instead, they argue, the positive effects are due to greater parental involvement in the school and a visible and public symbol of commitment to school improvement and reform.

As with all reforms, efforts to increase school safety are neither totally positive or negative. Unquestionably, schools must be safe. How this is accomplished remains controversial. Despite difficulties, zero-tolerance programs are, in all likelihood, here to stay, and experimentation with school uniforms is likely to continue. As a professional, you need to be as knowledgeable as possible about these issues, so you're in a position to make informed contributions to the decision-making process.

You Take a Position

Now it's your turn to take a position on the issues discussed in this section. Go to the *Education Week* Website at **http://www.edweek.com,** find "search" on the first page, and type in one of the following three search terms: *school security, zero tolerance*, or *school uniforms*. Locate a minimum of three articles on one of these topics and do the following:

1. Identify the title, author, and date of each article, and then write a one-paragraph summary of each article.
2. Determine if a pattern exists in the articles. (Each article—or even two of the three—suggesting that school uniforms are a good idea would be a pattern, for example.)
3. Take one of the two following positions:
   - The pattern suggested in the articles, if implemented, *is* likely to improve education.
   - The pattern suggested in the articles *is not* likely to improve education.

Document your position with information taken from the articles and your study of the text (this chapter and any other chapter of the text).

To answer these questions online, go to the Take a Position Module in Chapter 4 of the Companion Website.

Schools and teachers exert a powerful influence on developing resilience in their students.

Effective Teachers for Students Placed At-Risk Well-run and academically focused schools are important, but alone, they aren't sufficient. Professional teachers who are highly skilled and sensitive are critical (Waxman, Huang, Anderson, & Weinstein, 1997). In Chapter 1 we said that professionals are skilled in making decisions in ill-defined situations. This ability is essential in working with students placed at-risk because their needs and personal sensitivities make them particularly vulnerable to failure, personal slights, indicators of favoritism, and questions about the relevance of school.

What makes a teacher effective with students placed at-risk? How can teachers help students develop resilience and make connections between their lives and the classroom? Let's have students tell us. First, a ninth-grader offers this view:

▪ ▪ ▪

Well it's like you're family, you know. Like regular days like at home, we argue sometimes, and then it's like we're all brothers and sisters and the teachers are like our guardians or something.

And the teachers really get on you until they try to make you think of what's in the future and all that. It's good. I mean it makes you think, you know, if every school was like that I don't think there would be a lot of people that would drop out (Greenleaf, 1995, p. 2).

▪ ▪ ▪

An interview with other high school students offers additional perspectives:

▪ ▪ ▪

Melinda: I act differently in his [Appleby's] class—I guess because of the type of teacher he is. He cuts up and stuff. . . . He is himself—he acts natural—not tryin' to be what somebody wants him to be . . . he makes sure that nobody makes fun of anybody if they mess up when they read out loud.

Bernard: [I like him] just by the way he talk, he were good to you . . . he don't be afraid to tell you how he feels—he don't talk mean to you, he just speak right to you . . . some teachers only likes the smart people—and Coach Appleby don't do that.

LaVonne: Appleby's fun, he helps you when you feel bad, he'll talk to you. Appleby's got his own style, he makes his own self . . . he's not a brag . . . he get(s) into it—what

MAKING THE GRADE

This ABC News video segment profiles Kathy Morgan, a guidance counselor at All Hallows School, an all-boys school in the inner-city South Bronx. When Kathy first arrived at the school in 1997, less than 20 percent of the graduates went on to college. Through Kathy's and other teachers' concerted efforts, nearly 100 percent of graduating seniors now go on to college.

Think about This

1. In what ways would the students at All Hallows School be considered at-risk?
2. In what ways did the personnel at All Hallows school attempt to make their students resilient?
3. Based on research examining resilience, in what ways was All Hallows School effective for students placed at-risk?
4. All Hallows School is a private, religiously oriented all-boys school. What successful elements of the school's program could be implemented in co-ed, public schools?

To answer these questions online and receive immediate feedback, go to the Video Perspectives Module in Chapter 4 of the Companion Website.

> they [the students] like. Appleby always has this funny grin. . . . He's funny, he tells jokes, laughs with the class. He makes me want to work, he makes me want to give and do something. . . . He show me that I can do it (Dillon, 1989, pp. 241–242).

■ ■ ■

Alienation from school is a problem for students placed at-risk (Dillon, 1989; Goodenow, 1992a). Boredom, lack of involvement, and feelings that they are unwelcome keep them on the fringe, prevent them from participating in school experiences, and lower motivation. When bright spots appear, they are usually the result of teachers who care about these students as people and as learners.

How do teachers communicate this caring? First, they make a special effort to know all of their students. One teacher advised,

■ ■ ■

> I think with children one of the things you have to do first is to get to know them. Even with those you find a little bit hard to like at first, you have to find something that you really appreciate about that child so that you can really teach [him or her], because if you don't you're not going to get any place (Darling-Hammond, 1998, p. 80).

■ ■ ■

Another teacher noted,

■ ■ ■

> Individual kid's needs, awarenesses, and differences are part of understanding the whole teaching process. Whether you have a kid sitting in the front row because he has a visual problem and you have to have an auditory contact, a kid back there who doesn't speak English, a kid who has parents who are breaking up, a kid over here who has just been in a fight with somebody outside the classroom, or a kid who has physical handicaps, it all depends on the situation. . . . There are all types of problems and, of course, the more you know, it puts you in a better situation (Darling-Hammond, 1998, p. 81).

■ ■ ■

Knowing your students will help you relate to them as people as well as help you adapt instruction to their special needs.

A study examining the practices of teachers working with urban junior high students placed at-risk helps us understand differences between teachers who are more and less effective in working with youth placed at-risk. The study used the terms *high impact* and *low impact* to describe these differences (Kramer-Schlosser, 1992). **High-impact teachers** *create caring, personal learning environments and assume responsibility for their students' progress*. They talk with students, find out about their families, and share their own lives. They maintain high expectations, use questioning to involve students in lessons, and emphasize success and mastery of content. They motivate students through personal contacts and attempts to link school to students' lives.

Low-impact teachers, in contrast, *are more authoritarian, distancing themselves from students and placing primary responsibility for learning on them*. They view instructional help as "babying the student" or "holding the student's hand." Instruction is teacher-directed and lecture-oriented, and primary responsibility for motivation is the student's.

Students placed at-risk think of low-impact teachers as adversaries who are to be avoided if possible and tolerated if not. In contrast, these students seek out high-impact teachers, both in class and out. Caring, communication, and ". . . relationships with teachers were related to marginal students' behaviors and attitudes. Marginal students reported losing interest in learning when teachers distanced themselves" (Kramer-Schlosser, 1992, p. 138). Other studies have found effective teachers for students placed at-risk to be approachable, pleasant, easy to relate to, accepting, concerned, caring, and sensitive to the needs of students (Sanders & Jordan, 1997). Caring, personalized learning environments are important for all students; for students placed at-risk, they are essential. But beyond the human element, what else can teachers do?

Increasing Understanding 4.17

What are some concrete things that teachers of at-risk students can do to demonstrate that they care?

Case STUDY

As students entered the classroom after recess, they saw a review assignment on the chalkboard. Teacher Dena Hines took roll, and the students got out their books and started on the assignment. Five minutes later, Dena began teaching with a brief review of the previous day's lesson. Since the students were able to answer her questions quickly and correctly, she felt that the class knew the content and was ready to move on.

As she introduced two-column subtraction, she explained the new idea and gave each student bundles of 10 popsicle sticks bound together with rubber bands. She then guided the students through the steps by having them take the bundles apart to illustrate the process; Dena asked many questions as she went along. She also used questioning to help students link the manipulatives—the popsicle sticks—to the numerals she wrote on the board. Then she had students solve problems on their own mini-chalkboards and hold them up so she could check their solutions. Whenever mistakes occurred, she stopped, explained the errors, and helped students correct them.

When 90 percent of the class was solving the problems correctly, Dena started the students on additional practice problems, which they checked in pairs when they were done. As they worked, she helped those still having difficulty, moving around the room to respond to pairs who disagreed with each other or had questions.

■ ■ ■

How should teachers adapt their instruction to meet the needs of students placed at-risk? The overall suggestion is to offer more structure and support, as Dena did, while still challenging students and emphasizing concrete and real-world applications. In a study involving 140 classrooms, researchers found that achievement in reading and math was enhanced by teachers who emphasized challenge, application, problem solving, and use of student ideas and solutions (Knapp, Shields, & Turnbull, 1995).

Caring teachers with high expectations for success help students placed at-risk succeed in school.

Effective instruction: structure and support. Teachers of students placed at-risk don't need to teach in fundamentally different ways; instead, they need to apply effective strategies more systematically. They should provide enough instructional support to ensure success while at the same time teaching students strategies that allow them to take control of their own learning. Effective practices for students placed at-risk include the following (Gladney & Green, 1997; Wang et al., 1995):

- High expectations.
- Emphasis on student responsibility.
- Frequent feedback and high success rates.
- Interactive teaching with frequent questions.
- Increased structure and support through clear teacher explanations and modeling.

High expectations for student success are a key to the effectiveness of these strategies. But how is this accomplished? One student recalls a former teacher:

▪ ▪ ▪

My sixth-grade teacher was a coach. She could yell, scream, cajole, and nag with the best of them. But we knew that the constant pushing was for our benefit. "You know you can do better," was her favorite phrase. We laughed about her repeating it so often. On the playground and in our neighborhoods we would tease each other when we were not successful at stickball or double Dutch. "You know you can do better," we would sing and quickly dissolve into laughter. Funny, the sound of her voice repeating that phrase haunted me as a college student, as a graduate student, and as a university professional: "You know you can do better!" (Ladson-Billings, 1994, p. 25).

▪ ▪ ▪

Through her daily interactions with students, this teacher was able to instill in them the feeling that they truly could do better.

Increasing Understanding 4.18

Which of these characteristics of effective instruction would be most effective in promoting student resilience? Why?

Reflect on This

INVOLVING STUDENTS

You're a first-year English teacher at Roosevelt High School, an urban school in the Midwest. The year hasn't been easy, but you seem to be turning the corner in most classes—except for one. Your first-period class, composed mostly of low achievers, continues to struggle. The course overview describes the class as an introduction to the mechanics of writing: grammar, punctuation, and basic writing skills. At the encouragement of your department chair, you use the text that is assigned, which stresses basic skills through exercises and worksheets. After months of student complaints, you decide to throw out the text and involve your students in writing projects. The first assignment, "Suggestions for a Better Roosevelt High School," is a disaster. Students don't know where to start, and the few assignments that are handed in are discouragingly poor. You regroup and begin by teaching pre-writing skills like brainstorming, note-taking, and outlining. The next assignment is better, but when you try to have students critique each others' work in groups, the class degenerates into chaos. Most students sit back and talk about the upcoming football game and what they are going to do that weekend. The few that focus on the assignment have difficulty hearing each others' comments.

1. What were the advantages and disadvantages of using the textbook originally?
2. Why are you having such difficulties in involving the students in writing? What could you have done differently?
3. Why did you encounter problems in involving students in small-group work?
4. What would you do now?

To answer these questions online and receive immediate feedback, go to the Reflect on This *Module in Chapter 4 of the Companion Website.*

The Changing Role of Teachers

Working with today's students requires redefined roles for teachers. Traditionally, teachers' efforts were limited to their work in classrooms, and their focus was on academics. Today's student population requires teachers to think more broadly and to consider their students' overall emotional and physical development in addition to academic growth.

Increasingly, schools are being asked to safeguard children's well-being. They're required to report suspected cases of child abuse and neglect. Many provide free breakfasts and lunches for the children of poverty. Effective schools are islands of safety and security in an often chaotic and sometimes dangerous world. Teachers often play a crucial role in ensuring that all of children's needs—physical, social, emotional, and intellectual—are being addressed.

Teachers' instructional roles are also changing. In an ideal world, students come to school motivated and prepared to learn. Some students do, while others do not; in those cases, teachers are being asked to promote motivation and student involvement in addition to helping students understand the topics they're teaching. Stagnant teaching strategies, such as lecturing, that place students in passive listening roles won't work. Many students simply stop listening, and some put their heads down on their desks, making no pretense of paying attention.

Teachers are also being asked to make personal contact with students—not as "buddies," but rather as concerned caregivers committed to the total well-being of students. Expert professionals have always taken a personal interest in their students, but this dimension of teaching has become more important as many students come to our schools feeling like they're unwelcome. Teachers play an essential role in creating schools that are student-friendly along with classrooms that are warm and caring.

Tomorrow's teachers are also being asked to move outside the classroom. Effective outreach programs encourage parents to become actively involved in their child's education (Hoover-Dempsey, & Sandler, 1997; Shumow & Harris, 1998), and teachers are an integral part of these programs. Working with parents and other people in the community is now an integral part of teachers' jobs. Working with tomorrow's students will be more difficult and more challenging. It can also be more rewarding.

SUMMARY

A Changing Society
Society is changing in a number of ways, and these changes have important implications for schools. Traditional family configurations have evolved into alternative patterns that include single parent and extended families. The majority of mothers now work, raising concerns about child care and latchkey children. Poverty presents a number of challenges, ranging from hunger to homelessness.

Teenagers themselves are also changing. They are becoming sexually active at an earlier age, placing themselves at risk for pregnancy and sexually transmitted diseases. The use of alcohol and other drugs, violence, suicide, and child abuse all present challenges to youth as well as the teachers who work with them.

Students Placed At-Risk
Students placed at-risk face a number of challenges to school success. Community-based approaches to working with students placed at risk actively involve parents in designing and implementing educational programs. Effective schools for students placed at-risk create a safe, orderly learning environment in which academic goals are foremost. Studies of successful or resilient children suggest that caring home and school environments with supportive, understanding adults can help these students withstand societal challenges. Effective teachers for students placed at-risk combine interpersonal contacts with instructional structure and support. In working with at-risk students, teachers are advised to combine challenge with this support.

IMPORTANT CONCEPTS

students placed at-risk
high-impact teachers
latchkey children
low-impact teachers
middle class
poverty
resilient students
socioeconomic status (SES)
underclass
upper class
zero-tolerance programs

DISCUSSION QUESTIONS

1. How would your role as a teacher change if you worked in an upper-SES suburb? A lower-SES part of a city?
2. How would your actual instruction change if you worked in an upper-SES suburb? A lower-SES part of a city?
3. What role should schools play in dealing with teenage sexuality?
4. What role should schools play in dealing with drug and alcohol abuse?
5. What strengths do students placed at-risk bring to the classroom? How can teachers take advantage of these strengths?
6. What will be the biggest challenges in working with the parents of students placed at-risk?

VIDEO DISCUSSION QUESTIONS

The following discussion question refers to video segments found on the Companion Website. To answer this question online, view the accompanying video, and receive immediate feedback to your answer, go to the Video Discussion Module in Chapter 4 of the Companion Website at **http://www.prenhall.com/kauchak.**

1. Theodore Sizer is the director of the Coalition for Effective Schools, which attempts to reform high schools. A major challenge facing high-school reform is helping students placed at-risk develop resiliency. From Sizer's perspective, what is the most important thing that schools can do to develop resiliency in students? How do these suggestions compare to information given in this chapter?

GOING INTO SCHOOLS

1. Ask a teacher to identify a student who is at-risk for school failure. Arrange to interview the student.
   a. Get to know the student as a human being. (What does the student like to do when not in school—hobbies, music, sports, friends, activities, favorite foods, etc.) Does the student work? Does he or she like the job? What does the student want to do after graduating? Does he or she intend to graduate? If not, why not?
   b. What does the student like about school? Dislike? How could schools be changed to make them better?
   c. What does the student like about this class? Dislike? How could the class be changed to make it more pleasant? To make it a better learning environment?
   d. What is the student's favorite subject? Least favorite? Why?
   e. Which kinds of teachers does the student like? Dislike? What advice does the student have for you as a new teacher?
   f. How does the student learn the best? What do teachers do to help him or her learn? Interfere with learning?
   g. What motivates the student in school? Out of school? How important are grades? In which classes does the student work the hardest? Why?

   Summarize these responses into a profile of the student. What do the student's responses suggest about teaching students placed at-risk?
2. Interview a teacher who works with students who are placed at-risk. Ask the following questions:
   a. How are at-risk students similar to and different from other students?
   b. What strengths do at-risk students bring to the classroom?
   c. How do you adapt your teaching to meet the needs of at-risk students?
   d. What successful strategies do you use in working with the parents of at-risk students?
   e. What are the rewards and challenges of working with at-risk students?

   How do the teacher's responses compare with research in this chapter? What do these responses suggest about teaching students placed at-risk?
3. Interview a counselor at a school that has significant numbers of students placed at-risk. Ask the following questions:
   a. What proportion of the students in the school are considered at-risk? How does the school identify them?
   b. What special programs within the school are designed for these students?
   c. What types of outreach activities does the school have for connecting with the community?
   d. What kinds of different roles do teachers play in this school?

   How effective is this school in addressing the needs of students placed at-risk? Based on the information in this chapter, how might this school be changed to better address these needs?
4. Identify a classroom with a high number of students placed at-risk. Observe a lesson in that class and analyze it in terms of the following:

a. Emotional tone (for example, supportive and warm)
b. Student–teacher interactions
c. Teacher expectations
d. Interactive teaching (for example, questions, groupwork)
e. Frequency of feedback

Analyze the interaction in terms of the suggestions made in this chapter and make suggestions for changes.

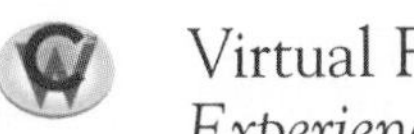

Virtual Field *Experience*

If you would like to participate in a Virtual Field Experience, go to the *Field Experience* Module in Chapter 4 of the Companion Website.

ONLINE PORTFOLIO ACTIVITIES

To complete these activities online, go to the *Portfolio Activities* Module in Chapter 4 of the Companion Website to submit your response.

Portfolio Activity 4.1

Investigating Chapter I Programs and Students

INTASC Principle 3: ***Adapting Instruction***

Locate the Websites for your state's Office of Education or for several local school districts. (Local school districts' phone numbers can be found under "Schools" in the commercial White Pages at the back of a phone book. From there you can get Website addresses.) Click on the module that has information on Title I programs and answer the following questions:

1. Which districts or schools offer the largest number of Chapter I programs?
2. What kinds of students (that is, students from which cultural minority groups) are found in these programs?
3. What is the curriculum in these programs?
4. What is instruction like in these programs?

Based on this information, what are some ways that you can prepare yourself to teach in schools that have high percentages of Title I students?

Portfolio Activity 4.2

School Safety and Security

INTASC Principle 5: ***Motivation and Management***

This activity is designed to familiarize you with school safety and security procedures in your area. Locate the Websites of several local school districts. Click on "Student Conduct Policies and Procedures" and read how each district handles discipline and safety issues. How are the procedures similar and different? How would they affect your life as a teacher?

Portfolio Activity 4.3

Managing Difficult Students

INTASC Principle 5: ***Motivation and Management***

This portfolio activity is designed to help you begin developing a coherent philosophy and strategies for dealing with difficult or hard to manage students. Locate a book on classroom management that discusses the problems of dealing with difficult students. We recommend Brophy (1996) and Powell et al. (2001), but there are many other excellent choices. Based on the information that you read, describe effective management practices for difficult students, and how teachers can deal with this problem.

PART 3

Foundations

Religion was a major reason the Pilgrims came to America and a major force in shaping early schools.

industry, resourcefulness, punctuality, and thrift. According to the Puritans, education was important because it made people more righteous.

The Puritans' views shaped the schools they created. Children were seen as savage and primitive, requiring education (religion) to become civilized and God-fearing. Play was viewed as idleness, children's talk was seen as prattle, and corporal punishment was commonly used to ensure conformity. Students were beaten with switches, forced to kneel on hard pebbles, and made to wear heavy wooden yokes as punishment for unacceptable behavior. It's easy to see why "Idle minds are the Devil's workshop," and "Spare the rod and spoil the child" were principles of Puritan education.

Religion also influenced curriculum and instruction. Reading, writing, arithmetic, and religion ("the four Rs") made up the curriculum. Children were taught to read with books like the *New England Primer,* which taught the alphabet through rhymes such as:

> A—In Adam's Fall
> We Sinned All
> B—. . . Their life to Mend
> This Book Attend.

Instruction focused on memorization and recitation; children were expected to sit quietly for long periods of time, and expressing opinions and asking questions were discouraged.

Paradoxically, a landmark piece of legislation, the Massachusetts Act of 1647, arose from this grim educational landscape. Also known as the **Old Deluder Satan Act,** *this law intended to create scripture-literate citizens to thwart Satan's trickery.* It required every town of 50 or more households to hire a teacher of reading and writing. The historical significance of this act for education is difficult to overstate, because it provided the legal foundation for public support of education. This idea—that the public good was enhanced by government-sponsored efforts at public education—was born and became one of the major cornerstones of American education.

Increasing Understanding 5.2

From what you've seen on television and read about in the media, are the differences between schools in different parts of the United States today greater or less than they were in colonial times? Explain your answer.

Table 5.1 Changes in Educational Thought in Europe

Thinker	Educational Views
John Amos Comenius (1592–1670) Czech philosopher	Questioned the effectiveness of memorization and recitation, emphasizing instead the need to base teaching on children's interests and needs.
John Locke (1632–1704) English philosopher	Emphasized the importance of first-hand experiences in helping children learn about the world.
Jean Jacques Rousseau (1712–1778) French philosopher	Viewed children as innately good and argued that teachers should provide children with opportunities for exploration and experimentation.
Johann Pestalozzi (1746–1827) Swiss philosopher	Criticized authoritarian educational practices that stifled students' playfulness and natural curiosity and recommended that teachers use concrete experiences to help students learn.

European Crosscurrents As we've seen, American colonists brought many ideas from Europe, such as the view that education should be reserved for wealthy White males. Also, since schooling existed for religious purposes or for preparing the wealthy to be leaders, few attempts were made to relate the curriculum to the average person's practical needs or the long-term needs of a growing nation. As we saw, teaching methods emphasized passive learning in the form of memorization and recitation.

Increasing Understanding 5.3

How would these philosophers have reacted to the New England schools? What changes would they have recommended?

Forces of change were altering education in Europe, however, and these ideas slowly made their way across the Atlantic. Some of the prominent persons and their thinking are outlined in Table 5.1.

As we see in Table 5.1, the ideas came from different places, but all involved a more practical, humane, and child-centered view of education. These philosophers are important because they planted the seeds of educational change that would alter the way students were taught in the United States.

The Colonial Legacy

The colonial period shaped American education in at least three ways. First, with few exceptions, poor Whites, females, and minorities such as Native Americans and African Americans were excluded from schools (Spring, 1997). William Berkeley, the aristocratic governor of Virginia, supported this exclusion and in 1671 railed against both free public education and access to books: "I thank God, *there are no free schools nor printing*, and I hope we shall not have them these hundred years, for *learning* has brought disobedience, and heresy, and sects into the world, and *printing* has divulged them, and libels against the best government" (Pulliam & Van Patten, 1999, p. 56). European ideas of class structures and privilege did not die easily in the new America. Given attitudes such as Berkeley expressed, it's easy to see why equality of educational opportunity wasn't realized until the mid-20th century, and some present-day critics argue that today's schools are still racist and sexist (Spring, 1997).

Second, and on the positive side, seeds were planted for the public support for education (the Old Deluder Satan Act) and local control of schools during this period. These two ideas have become important foundations for our present educational system.

Third, and perhaps most significantly, the colonial period helps us understand why religion continues to be an important factor in education. With the constitutional principle mandating separation of church and state, we can also see why religious controversies exist.

Reflect *on* This

INVOLVING ALL STUDENTS

You're in the middle of your student teaching in an urban middle school math classroom on the West Coast. Classroom management is now less stressful, though your students still test you from time to time. They recognize their limits and realize that you're in charge.

Now you're focusing on your instruction and are trying to design lessons that involve all students. When you first started your student teaching, you noticed that Mr. Gibbs, your directing teacher, taught efficient, almost drill-like lessons that proceeded smoothly. But you also noticed that 90 percent of his questions were answered by a handful of students, mostly White boys. Girls and cultural minorities sat quietly, some seeming to pay attention, others not.

When you mentioned this to Mr. Gibbs, he replied, "I know some of the kids don't participate, but they like it that way. I've tried calling on them, but it makes them nervous." Realizing that you seemed skeptical, he continued, "Go ahead and try something different if you want, but don't be discouraged if it doesn't work."

You try different ideas, but the results are mixed. You call on students up and down the rows, but those in the uninvolved rows quickly drift off. You try pulling students' names out of a jar at random, placing the names of the students you've already called in a different jar to ensure that everyone participates. You can't tell who likes it less: the shy students who don't want to participate, the embarrassed ones who don't know the answers, or the previous stars who either chomp at the bit to answer or sit back bored at the slower pace. You're not sure what to do.

1. What are the advantages and disadvantages of trying to call on all students during lessons?
2. What should a teacher do if a student doesn't know the answer? What should a teacher do if the student doesn't want to participate?
3. What responsibilities does a teacher have in attempting to actively involve all students—girls, underachievers, cultural minorities—in lessons? Do these efforts have any negative consequences for more verbally aggressive students?
4. What would you do if you were the student teacher described in this case?

To answer these questions online and receive immediate feedback, go to the Reflect on This *Module in Chapter 5 of the Companion Website.*

and then Japanese immigration in 1924. Perhaps the darkest page in Asian American history came during World War II, when more than 100,000 Japanese Americans were forced out of their homes near the Pacific coast and into internment camps in barren areas of the West.

Like other minority groups, Asian Americans experienced discrimination. For example, in 1906 San Francisco established segregated schools for Asian Americans. Instruction was in English, which resulted in problems similar to those Hispanics encountered. A federal court decision in the case *Lau v. Nichols* (1974) changed this, ruling that students who find their educational experience "wholly incomprehensible" must be taught in their first language if that language is not English.

As a group, Asian Americans have fared better than other cultural minority groups in the U.S. educational system. In 1994 Asian American students had the highest average SAT scores of any group in the country (U.S. Department of Education, 1996), and the proportion of Asian Americans in colleges and universities is higher than that of the general population. This success has led some educators to label this group "the model minority," but more recent immigrants from Southeast Asian countries like Cambodia, Laos, and Vietnam have experienced greater challenges in the U.S. educational system.

The Search for Equality: Where Are We Now?

As we said at the beginning of this section, two concepts—assimilation and separate but equal—have been central to the education of minorities in the United States. Separate but equal has been banned by the courts, but where does assimilation now stand?

Assimilation has always required that ethnic groups sacrifice a portion of their cultural identity to become "American." At the extreme this process has been called a "melting pot" in which the diverse cultures of America blend into a uniform and homogeneous society. This extreme has never occurred, as evidenced in the present day diversity of religions in the United States and holidays such as Kwanza, St. Patrick's Day, and the Jewish and Muslim religious holidays.

Increasing Understanding 5.19

Describe a "melting pot" approach to teaching American history. Describe a multi-flavored salad approach.

In educational circles a multi-flavored salad has replaced the melting pot as the metaphor; different ethnic and cultural groups contribute unique tastes and perspectives. The extent to which Americans should share common values and beliefs is still controversial, with some arguing for greater uniformity (Schlesinger, 1992) and others advocating an America built around diversity and shared values (Takaki, 1993).

The federal government's role in the education of cultural minorities remains poorly defined. In the past, federal courts have played a major role in desegregation, but in recent times they have been reluctant to impose busing and other legal mechanisms to achieve integration (Hendrie, 1998a, 1998b). The same is true in the legislative branch; senators and members of the House of Representatives can't decide what role the federal government should play in the quest for equity and equality (Hoff, 1998). We examine this changing federal role in education in the next section.

THE MODERN ERA: SCHOOLS AS INSTRUMENTS FOR NATIONAL PURPOSE AND SOCIAL CHANGE

The Modern Era in education began at about the end of World War II and continues to the present. It is characterized by an increased emphasis on education, which is now viewed as the key to both individual success and the progress of the nation. Given this perspective, it isn't surprising to see the federal government more actively involved in education than it was in the past. This increased involvement occurred in at least three areas:

- The government's response to the Cold War.
- The government's War on Poverty and search for the "great society."
- The government's role in equity issues.

Let's look at these areas.

The Cold War: Enlisting America's Schools

We commonly think of the Cold War as a stalemate with the Soviet Union, with ever more powerful weapons being stockpiled on both sides. It was also significant in education's history.

The Russian launching of the satellite Sputnik in 1957 was the key event of the period. Believing we were losing the technology war, our government responded by authorizing a five-fold increase in the funding of The National Science Foundation, which had

Increasing Understanding 5.20

Why were educational efforts during the Cold War focused on science, math, and foreign languages?

been created in 1950 to support research and improve science education. Congress also passed the National Defense Education Act (NDEA) in 1958, which was designed to enhance the security of the nation by improving instruction in math, science, and foreign language. The NDEA provided funds for teacher training, new equipment, and the establishment of centers for research and dissemination of new teaching methods. During this period, Admiral Rickover, the father of the American nuclear navy, called education "our first line of defense."

The War on Poverty and the Great Society

During the 1960s, leaders began to realize that, despite the economic boom following World War II, many Americans were living in poverty. America was becoming a nation of "haves" and "have nots," and the problem was exacerbated by an economy that required ever-increasing skills in its workers.

For the unfortunate, a cycle of poverty began with inadequate education, which decreased employment opportunities, leading to a poorer quality of life that resulted in lowered achievement in the next generation. To break this cycle and create a "great society" in which all could participate and benefit, President Lyndon Johnson, in his 1964 State of the Union address, stated that ". . . this administration today, here and now declares unconditional war on poverty in America."

Emphasis on education was a major thrust of the **War on Poverty,** *a general term for federal programs designed to eradicate poverty during the 1960s*. During this period, the central government's involvement increased significantly. Initiatives included the following:

- Increased federal funding. Federal funds for K–12 education went from $900 million (4.4 percent of the total educational budget) in 1964 (prior to LBJ's initiatives) to $3 billion (8.8 percent of the total educational budget) by 1968.
- The development of the Job Corps. Modeled after the Civilian Conservation Corps of the 1930s, the Job Corps created rural and urban vocational training centers, which helped young people learn marketable skills while working on government projects.
- The creation of the Department of Education in 1979. Originally part of the Department of Health, Education and Welfare, education was considered so important that it was elevated to a cabinet-level position during the Carter administration.
- Support for Learners with Exceptionalities. In Chapter 3 you saw that the federal government passed Public Law 94-142, the Individuals with Disabilities Education Act (IDEA) in 1975. In 1976–1977, just after the law's passage, the nation educated about 3.3 million children with exceptionalities; presently, schools serve over 6 million children with exceptionalities, an increase of nearly 82 percent (Sack, 2000a).
- The creation of national compensatory education programs. Let's look at them in more detail.

Increasing Understanding 5.21

How was the "war on poverty" similar to other educational efforts aimed at minorities? How was it different?

Compensatory Education Programs **Compensatory education programs** are *government attempts to create more equal educational opportunities for disadvantaged youth*. These programs provide supplementary instruction and attempt to prevent learning problems before they occur. The two programs that are best known are Head Start and Title I.

Head Start. Part of the Economic Opportunity Act of 1964, **Head Start** is *a federal compensatory preschool education program designed to help 3- and 4-year-old disadvantaged students enter school ready to learn*. It has two goals: to stimulate the development and academic achievement of low income preschoolers, and to educate and involve parents in the edu-

Compensatory education programs like Title I and Head Start created improved educational opportunities for disadvantaged youth.

cation of their children. In 1997, over 94,000 children were involved in the program with a budget of nearly 5 billion dollars (U.S. Department of Education, 1999). It has served almost 17 million children since its inception.

The Head Start curriculum focuses on basic skills such as counting, naming colors, and pre-reading skills, as well as social skills such as taking turns and following directions. Parenting goals focus on helping parents develop their children's literacy skills by encouraging parents to read and talk to their children and provide experiences (like trips to zoos, libraries, and museums) that increase their readiness for school.

Evaluations of Head Start programs have found them to be uneven in quality; some programs have resulted in positive outcomes, while others have had little impact on children's readiness to learn. In general, Head Start 4 year olds perform better than comparable 4 year olds who haven't participated in the program, and almost 90 percent of parents are very satisfied with their children's experiences (U.S. Department of Health and Human Services, 1997). In the better Head Start programs, like the Perry Preschool Program in Ypsilanti, Michigan, researchers found long-term positive effects including fewer special-education placements, higher numbers of high school graduates, and lower crime and teen-pregnancy rates (Cohen, 1993). However, not all Head Start programs have been as successful, with poor program quality the most likely reason.

Title I. **Title I** is *a federal compensatory education program targeting low-income students in elementary and secondary schools.* Between 1965 and 1999, Title I spent over 120 billion dollars and reached almost all of our nation's schools. Presently funded at 8 billion dollars per year, Title I serves 11 million low-income children in 45,000 schools. While considerable, this figure represents only 3 percent of total expenditures for elementary and secondary education, and only about 50 percent of eligible students receive Title I help (Educational Excellence for All Children Act, 1999; Jennings, 1999). Two-thirds of the money goes to elementary schools. Fifteen percent of the highest poverty schools receive

Teaching *in an* Era *of* Reform

REDEFINING THE FEDERAL ROLE

Reforms result from various sources, such as professional organizations, states, and local districts. One of the most powerful sources of reform is the federal government. As we've seen, during the 20th century, the federal government increased its role in influencing education. Initiating or encouraging reforms are major ways it exerts this influence.

The federal government has influenced national reforms in three primary ways:

- Setting standards
- Testing.
- Financial incentives.

Setting Standards

A logical place for the federal government to start influencing education is through the use of standards, which provide common goals for educational efforts. One prominent example occurred in 1989, when President Bush and the governors of the 50 states participated in an Education Summit and created a list of eight National Education Goals, called The Goals 2000: Education America Act, which were later funded by Congress. The major goals of this act are found in Table 5.3.

The provisions of this act continue to influence educational policy across the country. We discuss the effects of Goals 2000 on curriculum in more detail in Chapter 10.

Testing

Begun in 1970, the National Assessment of Educational Progress (NAEP) testing program was designed to provide an objective, external measure of how students in the United States were performing (Hoff, 2000b). Students in fourth, eighth, and twelfth grades were originally tested in the areas of math, science, and reading; writing, art, and civics were added later. Because of conservative concerns about undue federal influence, this testing was voluntary (about 40 of the 50 states chose to participate), and only group scores were reported. In 1990 state-by-state comparisons were published, which gave some indication of how well different states were doing.

Financial Incentives

If national goals are worth pursuing, and tests can measure progress towards these goals, rewarding states that make significant progress towards these goals is a logical step. This is exactly what then President Clinton and current President George W. Bush recommended during the presidential campaign in 2000. President Clinton proposed tying $50 million in rewards to states that showed improvement and closed the gap between high and low achievers on the NAEP (Hoff, 2000b).

Putting Reform into Perspective

Goals 2000 provides worthy ideals to which the country can aspire. Who would oppose, for example, the idea that all children starting school should be ready to learn, or that high school graduation rates should meet or exceed 90 percent? However, the goals—or more accurately, the ideas about setting national goals—have been controversial with both political conservatives and liberals, although for different reasons. As Chester Finn, former Assistant Secretary of Education under President Reagan, observed, "Republicans oppose any proposal with the word 'national' in it; Democrats oppose anything with the word 'standards' in it" (Doyle, 1999, p. 56).

National testing is also controversial. On one hand, knowing how our students are doing and how states compare to each other seems sensible. How can we improve

Congress responded with the Civil Rights Act of 1964, which prohibited discrimination against students on the basis of race, color, or national origin in all institutions receiving federal funds. The federal government now had a mechanism to both encourage and enforce integration efforts.

Equity for Women Historically, women have been underserved by our nation's schools. As we saw at the beginning of the chapter, in the early periods of our history, women were

Table 5.3 **Major Provisions of the Goals 2000 Act**

By the year 2000:

- All children in America will start school ready to learn.
- The high school graduation rate will increase to 90 percent.
- Students will master challenging subject matter in all the disciplines.
- The nation's teaching force will have access to high-quality professional development.
- American students will be first in the world in math and science.
- All adult Americans will possess the skills to compete in a global economy.
- Schools will be safe places to learn.
- Parental participation will increase.

our education systems if we don't know how much our students are learning? On the other hand, critics argue that testing leads to "teaching to the test," which narrows the curriculum and detracts from an overall education. One critic of the NAEP testing program commented, "What gets tested must be taught. [With national testing] we're one step shy of a national curriculum and we're moving fast in the direction" (Hoff, 2000a, p. 29).

Financial incentives also make sense intuitively. Why shouldn't teachers and schools be rewarded for increasing the amount their students learn? However, critics charge that such incentives will further encourage teachers to teach to the tests, and states and districts will align their curricula with the content being tested—in essence, creating a de facto national curriculum.

How will these trends influence your life as a teacher? There is little doubt that in the near future the federal government will become more active in the educational arena. For example, both major parties in the 2000 presidential election identified education as a major campaign theme, unlike in the past where Republicans called for diminished federal influence. Despite backlash from a number of sources, including conservatives, school districts, states, and teachers themselves, the emphasis on standards and testing is likely to continue into the foreseeable future (Bradley, 2000b), and the federal government will certainly play a significant role in the process.

You Take a Position

Now it's your turn to take a position on the issues discussed in this section. Go to the *Education Week* Website at **http://www.edweek.com**, find "search" on the first page, and type in one of the following search terms: *Goals 2000* or *NAEP*. Locate a minimum of three articles on one of these topics and then do the following:

1. Identify the title, author, and date of each article and write a one-paragraph summary of each.
2. Identify a pattern in the articles. (Each article—or even two of the three—suggesting that the National Assessment of Educational Progress [NAEP] be abolished would be a pattern, for example.)
3. After identifying the pattern, take one of the two following positions:
   - The pattern suggested in the articles, if implemented, *is* likely to improve education.
   - The pattern suggested in the articles *is not* likely to improve education.

State your position in writing and document your position with information taken from the articles and your study of the text (use this chapter and any other chapter of the text).

To answer these questions online, go to the Take a Position *Module in Chapter 5 of the Companion Website.*

generally excluded from education, but over time they caught up and actually passed male enrollments (Willingham & Cole, 1997).

Critics charge, however, that numbers don't eliminate discrimination and that differential treatment in schools contributes to the statistics we saw at the beginning of this section, such as girls being only half as likely as boys to pursue college careers in the physical and computer sciences, and women making up only 8 percent of the nation's engineers.

National tests have become a controversial issue in the reform movement.

Congress became involved in gender equity issues by passing **Title IX** in 1972. The purpose of this federal legislation was to eliminate gender bias in the schools. It states:

No person in the United States shall, on the basis of sex, be excluded from participation in, be denied benefits of, or be subjected to discrimination under any education program or activity receiving federal financial assistance.

Increasing Understanding 5.23

How does the concept of separate but equal relate to education for women and students with exceptionalities?

The largest impact of this bill has been in physical education and sports, where female participation in high school athletics has increased from 295,000 in 1970 to more than 2.7 million presently (White, 1999). However, this figure is still below the 3.8 million figure for boys, and in most schools women's teams still do not receive comparable funding, facilities, equipment, publicity, travel budgets, or practice opportunities.

What are the outcomes of this federal intervention? With respect to integration, progress is uncertain. For example, in the South in 1988, 43.5 percent of African American students attended integrated schools, up from virtually none in 1954. However, by 1996 the figure had shrunk back to 34.7 percent (Hendrie, 1999). In the North, segregated housing patterns led to segregated schools. This problem was exacerbated in urban areas by "white flight" to the suburbs. For example, the African American student population in Detroit schools increased from 71 percent in 1975 to 94 percent in 1996 (Kunen, 1996). At the end of the 20th century, one-third of African American students attended schools where the enrollment was over 90 percent minority.

Various strategies have been proposed to remedy the problem of segregation in schools, including compensatory education, school boundary realignments, and mandatory busing. **Magnet schools,** *which attempt to attract African American and White students to schools through quality instruction or innovative programs,* have also been tried. Magnet schools have been used in a number of large cities including Boston, Dallas, Houston, Minneapolis, and San Diego; there are more than 2,600 magnet schools in 230 districts, serving 1.2 million students (Black, 1996; Viadero, 1999).

The results are mixed. For example, in spite of strong governmental support (739 million dollars for experimentation with magnet programs), magnet schools are not always meeting their original intent. For instance, they tend to attract the best minority students, robbing students attending non-magnet schools of role models. In addition, social-class differences between wealthier and poorer students within schools work to minimize true integration and the development of cohesive learning communities.

Civil rights and equity for women continue to be highly controversial. Some minority leaders and women's groups argue that progress for cultural minorities and women has been too slow and that the government should do more. On the other hand, conservative leaders—both African American and White—argue that civil rights have gone too far; they charge that women and minorities are receiving inappropriately preferential treatment (reverse discrimination). The issue is likely to continue in the future as critics on both sides become increasingly vocal and polar in their positions.

The Changing Role of Teachers

You've now completed this chapter and have seen the historical patterns that have emerged. But what implications do these patterns have for your future? Let's think about them.

First, educational goals are becoming more complex and controversial. Early in our history, schools were satisfied with teachers who could teach "the three Rs" and instill some religion in their students. Today's teachers are faced with more complex goals and more variety in the curriculum. Teachers are expected to use more sophisticated teaching methods, utilize technology, teach higher order and critical thinking, help students become effective problem solvers, effectively manage group work, make learning relevant, and motivate reluctant learners.

The importance of education will increase as technology advances and international economic competition increases. Advances in technology have changed both our personal lives and the U.S. economy. At one time, a strong back and willingness to work were the major prerequisites for employment in America. Today however, less than 3 percent of the population makes its living on farms, and industries like auto and steel manufacturing employ a declining percentage of the workforce. People who are well-educated, understand technology, and can adapt to change are needed in the future. The growing importance of education is clear. Schools and teachers will face increasing pressures to ensure that all students possess an adequate education.

Second, teachers of the future will be working with student populations that are ever more diverse. They will be expected to respond to the needs, motivations, and sensitivities of students with different cultural and experiential backgrounds.

Third, teachers and schools are being increasingly asked to respond to societal problems. This can be seen in areas such as working with the children of poverty, identifying incidents of child abuse, helping learners cope with violence and anger, and a host of other problems. Teachers no longer simply teach; they counsel, diagnose, keep records, and confer with parents, among other activities.

Finally, this chapter reminds us that all teachers contribute to the moral and character development of their students. Sometimes this occurs implicitly through teachers' interactions with students, the rules they establish, and the way they enforce them. Other times teachers explicitly focus on moral issues, whether they involve an altercation on the playground or the interpretation of an historical event like the Vietnam War or the Civil Rights movement. As you prepare to become a teacher, you need to think about your views of morality and how those views will influence your students.

SUMMARY

The Colonial Period

Religion played a central role in colonial education. The first place public funds were used to support education was in colonial New England. Despite humanistic influences from Europe, colonial education was influenced by negative views of children and learning.

The Early National Period

During the early national period, the framers of the Constitution made two important decisions. One was to separate religion from government. The other was to place the primary responsibility for funding and governing education in the hands of state and local governments.

The Common School Movement

During the years leading up to the Civil War, the foundations of universal access to tax supported schools were set. State departments of education were established to govern schools, and normal schools were built to advance the idea of professional training for teachers.

The Evolution of the American High School

The history of the comprehensive American high school began with the Latin Grammar School, a colonial college preparatory institution that focused on the classics. Benjamin Franklin's Academy introduced the idea of a practical curriculum. The English High School targeted non-college students and was supported by public funds. The comprehensive American high school evolved as a compromise out of a tug of war between committee reports that advocated either academic or applied orientations. Current middle schools started as more traditional junior highs that began in the early 1900s.

The Progressive Era

During the Progressive Era, educators re-examined goals and methods. Emphasis on teacher-centered academics was replaced by a more student-centered approach to democratic problem solving. A conservative reaction to life-adjustment courses signaled the end of this movement.

The Search for Equality in American Education

The education of minorities in the United States, aimed at assimilation, attempted to be separate but equal, but generally failed. Native American education efforts attempted to assimilate students through boarding schools. African American education had a long history of separate but unequal that was challenged in the Supreme Court in 1954. Bilingual education has been a central controversy for Hispanic and Asian American education.

The Modern Era

During the Modern Era, the federal government took a more active role in education. During the Cold War with Russia, the federal government spent large amounts of money improving math, science, and foreign language education. The federal government also used courts and federal spending to battle poverty and inequalities in the schools.

IMPORTANT CONCEPTS

academies
assimilation
Brown v. Board of Education of Topeka
character education
common school movement
compensatory education programs
comprehensive high school
English classical school
English high school
faculty psychology

Head Start
junior high schools
Latin grammar school
magnet schools
middle schools
normal schools
Old Deluder Satan Act
progressive education
separate but equal
separation of church and state
Title I
Title IX
vouchers
war on poverty

DISCUSSION QUESTIONS

1. What is the proper relationship between education and religion? Is the connection between religion and education likely to get closer or farther apart over the next 10 years? Why do you think so?
2. Is the concept of *choice,* such as the use of school vouchers, likely to increase or decrease in the future? Why do you think so? Will choice positively or negatively influence education?
3. What is your position on bilingual education? Should it be generally banned as it has been in California, or did California make a mistake? Explain your position.
4. How would you attempt to solve the problems of Native American education?
5. Do you believe that racial discrimination remains a major problem for society? What could or should schools do to alleviate this problem?
6. Would our educational system be better if control were at the national level instead of the local and state levels? Why or why not?

GOING INTO SCHOOLS

1. Interview a teacher who has been teaching for more than 20 years and ask him or her to describe educational changes in the following areas:
   a. Emphasis on character or moral education and religion in the schools
   b. Diversity of students and implications for teaching
   c. Gender equity efforts
   d. Federal programs and their effects on the schools

   Analyze these responses in terms of the content in this chapter. Specifically, have the experiences of this teacher been similar to or different from national trends?
2. Interview a Title I teacher about the program he or she teaches in and explore the following areas:
   a. Which student populations are served?
   b. Describe the curriculum and explain who determines it.
   c. How does the Title I curriculum articulate with or connect with the regular curriculum?
   d. What instructional strategies are used and why?
   e. What suggestions does the teacher have for improving the program?

   Analyze these responses, decide how effective Title I has been in the war on poverty, and make suggestions for making it more effective.
3. Examine two textbooks for the same class (for example, social studies or literature). One should be a recent one and the other should be at least 20 years old. (These textbooks can be obtained from your college's curriculum library, a district's curriculum library, or the state's curriculum library.)
   a. How does the content of the two textbooks differ?
   b. What changes can you find in terms of the books' treatments or coverage of women?

   c. What changes can you find in terms of the books' treatments or coverage of minorities?
   d. What do these changes suggest about changing priorities in education?
4. Interview a junior high or middle school teacher about ways that the school attempts to meet the needs of developing adolescents in terms of the following:
   a. Teaming by teachers
   b. Modifications in the curriculum
   c. Interactive teaching strategies like cooperative learning or problem-based learning
   d. Extracurricular activities

   Analyze these responses in terms of the reasons that middle schools were created.
5. Interview a high school teacher about the success of the school in creating a comprehensive high school. The following questions might guide your interview:
   a. Are there different tracks or programs in the school?
   b. What percentage of students are in each track, and what are these students like?
   c. How is the curriculum different for each track?
   d. How is instruction different for each track?
   e. How much do students from different tracks interact? What does the school do to encourage this?

   Analyze these responses in terms of the successes and challenges facing comprehensive high schools.

Virtual Field *Experience*

If you would like to participate in a Virtual Field Experience, go to the *Field Experience* Module in Chapter 5 of the Companion Web site.

ONLINE PORTFOLIO ACTIVITIES

To complete these activities online, go to the *Portfolio Activities* Module in Chapter 5 of the Companion Website and submit your response.

Portfolio Activity 5.1

Character Education

INTASC Principle 2: *Learning and Human Development*

The purpose of this activity is to help you begin thinking about the role of moral or character education in your teaching. Research different views on character education and take a personal position on the issue. (You'll find additional information on the topic in Chapter 10.) In this position statement, make sure you include the following:

1. Your definition of character education.
2. The proper role that religion, parents, and other nonschool institutions should play in character education.
3. What teachers can or should do in this regard.

Portfolio Activity 5.2

Progressive Education

INTASC Principle 4: *Strategies*

The purpose of this activity is to help you understand the important role that the progressive education movement played in American education. Research the progressive education movement in America and write a personal evaluation of the movement.

(You'll find additional information and resources on the topic in Chapter 6.) In your evaluation address the following issues or questions:

1. What was progressive education?
2. What were its strengths and weaknesses?
3. What positive aspects of it would you include in your teaching?
4. How is it related to the present movement in instruction of constructivism (see Chapter 11)?

Portfolio Activity 5.3

Ability Grouping and Tracking

INTASC Principle 3: *Adapting Instruction*
INTASC Principle 7: *Planning*

The purpose of this activity is to help you consider the proper role of grouping and tracking in education. Ability grouping and tracking are found in many schools. Investigate the research on ability grouping and answer the following questions:

1. What are the advantages and disadvantages of these practices in general as well as at the specific level at which you'll teach?
2. What can teachers do to minimize the potential negative effects of these practices? You'll find additional information on the topic in Chapters 3 and 7.

CHAPTER

6 Educational Philosophy

The Intellectual Foundations of American Education

Philosophy often seems rather remote and disconnected from everyday life, but this isn't at all the case. We each have a "philosophy of life;" for many people, this philosophy is tacit and not clearly defined, but for others it is well-articulated. Our philosophy is the set of principles we have chosen to live by; it's what guides us in our daily actions.

As with individuals, professions and professionals have philosophies that guide their practice. This is the topic for this chapter, as we try to answer the following questions:

- What is philosophy?
- What topics do students of philosophy study?
- How do traditional philosophies influence the process of learning to teach?
- What are the most prominent philosophies of education, and what implications do they have for education?
- How do you begin to form your own philosophy of education?

Let's begin the process by looking in on a conversation between two teachers.

Case STUDY

"What's happening?" Brad Norman asked Allie Skinner as he walked into the lounge during the lunch period.

"Working on this quiz," Allie mumbled, glancing up at him.

"You sure do test the heck out of your kids, don't you? Every time I come in here you're either writing a quiz or scoring one, or recording grades, or something."

"Well, it isn't that I love tests so much, but . . . well, you know what I think . . . ."

"Yeah, yeah, I know," Brad replied, waving his hand. "If you don't challenge them, they don't learn. . . . I guess I'm just more interested in trying to motivate them. . . ."

"Wait a minute," Allie interrupted. "I'm as interested in motivation as you are; it's just that I have some different views about how you get there."

"I know you think that *pushing* the kids. . . ." Brad began again.

"High expectations," Allie interrupted with a wry smile.

"Whatever," Brad shrugged. "I know you think that having *high expectations,"* he continued, rolling his eyes at the words, "is important, but I don't see how testing and all that stuff relates to motivation."

"Do you want to hear about it?" Allie nodded. "Might be boring."

"Sure, but keep it brief," Brad smiled.

"Well, this is what I believe . . . and you've got to be true to what you believe, I think, or you just blow back and forth like a leaf in the wind. I've given all this a lot of thought, and this is the best I've been able to come up with so far. I mean, I'll change my mind when I get some evidence that I'm wrong."

"You were going to keep it brief."

"Yeah, yeah, . . . well . . . anyway, I know kids have changed over the last however many years. They don't come to school with the same sort of desire to learn as they once did. Now, I do still believe that kids want to learn, or maybe more specifically, they want to believe they did learn something when they're finished with a topic, or class, or year of school, or whatever. On the other hand, they're not intrinsically motivated, and by that I mean, I don't think they're motivated to study stuff for it's own sake. I think they're often extrinsically motivated, motivated to study as a means to some end, like a good grade, or recognition from their classmates, or compliments from the teacher or something like that.

"Now, I was reading in one of my journals awhile back, and the authors were talking about the link between achievement and self-esteem, and it really made sense. I thought about what they said, and I do believe that kids feel good when they learn something, particularly if it's challenging. I also think that the more they know about a topic, the better they like it. For example, wouldn't you agree that an expert in some area, like a person who really understands literature, or poetry, or physics, is more motivated in that area than a novice, a person who doesn't know much about literature?"

"Look at yourself; you're really into surfing the Internet; you talk about it all the time. The better you've gotten at it, the more you like it, and the more you want to do it."

"Yeah, probably . . . I guess so," Brad shrugged.

"So, my goal is to get them to learn as much as possible about everything, like I mean the topics I'm teaching. The more they learn, the more intrinsically motivated they're going to be, and they're going to be motivated because they're getting good at the topic, and they're acquiring expertise about it."

"Now, there's real, practical stuff out there that they need to know, and there's only one way they're gonna learn it. . . . That's practice and experience. So, I've got to get them to study and practice. One way of doing that is to give them a lot of quizzes. They study for the quizzes, they get lots of feedback, and they tell me they learn a lot. Ultimately they like it, and further, their self-esteem improves, and it improves because they've learned a lot. That's the way it works. It's a win–win all the way around. . . . That's how I think the world works. I'm getting paid to help kids learn. If I don't do my very best to make that happen, I'm not earning my salary."

"Some of what you're saying makes sense," Brad acknowledged. "However, your view is a bit narrow for me. First, I think kids would be intrinsically motivated if school wasn't so boring. How motivated would you be if you had to sit and listen to dry teachers drone on all day, every day?"

"I like the idea of kids knowing stuff too, but school involves more than that. Where in your scheme do kids learn to solve problems, and make choices and wise decisions? A head full of facts may be great if your goal in life is to be good at quiz shows, like "Who Wants to Be a Millionaire?" or "Jeopardy," but the person who really succeeds is the one who continues to learn and is able to adapt to changes in the world by solving the large and small problems they encounter. So, the only way they're going to get good at making decisions is to be put in situations where they're forced to make decisions. They need lots of experience in making decisions and solving problems. That's what life's all about.

"Plus, thinking about doing my job, it would be a heck of a lot easier to just make the kids cram some stuff in their heads, but I would be doing them, their parents, and ultimately our whole society a disservice if I didn't bite the bullet and prepare them for life outside of school."

"And, as long as I'm at it," Brad continued, holding up a hand to prevent Allie from interrupting, "exactly what is real? You said '. . . there's real, practical stuff out there that they need to know.' For instance, let's say that, based on this conversation, you conclude that I'm naive and idealistic. On the other hand, I conclude that I'm actually more practical than you are, because I think schooling should help kids learn to make wise decisions and be adaptable, which requires learning activities where they're forced to make decisions. What is the reality? Am I naive, or am I practical? Who's to say? Reality is in fact this. To you, I'm naive, and you will operate based on that belief. To me I'm not. So, reality is what we perceive it to be, and there's no objective source *out there* to decide which view is the 'right one.' "

"Aw, c'mon," Allie countered. "Sure I acknowledge your point, but look at that oak tree outside the window. You can perceive it to be anything you want, but it's still an oak. And, it doesn't matter what anybody thinks, two plus two is four, not three, not five, not anything in between."

"Plus, I'm not talking about a '. . . head full of facts.' Knowing stuff means that they understand it well enough so they can apply it to whatever situation comes up. For instance, you want them to make wise decisions. They can't make a *wise* decision if they don't know anything."

Just then the bell rang, announcing the end of their planning period and signaling the transition to the next class. Allie and Brad left, agreeing to disagree and promising (or threatening) to continue the discussion later.

■ ■ ■

Let's stop now and consider Brad and Allie's conversation. They were discussing ideas at the heart of learning and teaching, and they obviously disagreed on several of them. However, both had given a good deal of thought to what is important in teaching and why it's important. The result was a philosophy of education that guided their work. This is what our chapter is about.

Increasing Understanding 6.2

A woman is shopping for a new car. In making her decision, she places primary emphasis on cars' mileage ratings, their repair records, and evaluations from organizations such as the American Automobile Association. Is her "way of knowing" primarily the scientific method, intuition, or authority? Explain.

practice." She argued that *the way learners come to know* the ideas they learn is through practice and experience.

Allie was making an epistemological argument. **Epistemology** *deals with the question of how we come to know what we know.* A variety of ways of knowing exist. The scientific method, in which principles are tested with observable facts, is one. Intuition, authority, and even divine revelation are others.

Constructivism, a prominent learning theory, raises interesting epistemological questions. Constructivism argues that, instead of behaving like tape recorders, which reproduce words and music in their original form, people "construct" understanding that makes sense to them. For example, many people have "constructed" the idea that we're closer to the sun in summer (in the northern hemisphere) because it's warmer in summer than in winter, when in reality we're actually farther away from the sun in summer. In thinking this way, people draw analogies between proximity to a candle or a bonfire and the sun's distance to the earth (Mayer, 1998). The way we have come to understand why summer is warmer than winter is to construct ideas that make sense to us.

Epistemology is important for teachers because it suggests the teaching methods that they will use. If teachers believe in constructivism, for example, they provide a variety of experiences for learners and lead discussions that will help them construct valid understandings of the way the world works. In contrast, if we believe that authority is the most important way of knowing, we're likely to lecture and expect students to reproduce on tests what we've told them.

Increasing Understanding 6.3

With respect to epistemology, are Allie and Brad's views quite similar or are they quite different? Explain, citing evidence taken directly from the case study to support your position.

Metaphysics While epistemology examines *how* we know, **metaphysics**—or **ontology**—*considers* what *we know* (Osborne, 1996). Metaphysics considers questions of reality, and ultimately, what is real. With respect to metaphysics, Allie and Brad are far apart. Allie argued, "Now, there's real, practical stuff out there that they need to know . . ." but Brad countered, ". . . reality is what we perceive it to be, and there's no objective source *out there* to decide which view is the 'right one'." Allie believes a reality independent of our perception exists, but Brad believes that perception and reality are inextricably intertwined.

Metaphysics has implications both for the way we teach and for the goals we establish. For instance, since Allie believes in a reality independent of people's perceptions, her goal is for students to understand that reality. In contrast, since Brad believes less strongly in an objective reality, his goals more strongly emphasize students learning to critically examine their own thinking. The teaching methods both Allie and Brad will use will be those that best help students reach these goals.

Increasing Understanding 6.4

Character educators see learners as unsocialized and in need of moral discipline. In contrast, moral educators see learners as undeveloped, needing stimulation to construct more mature moral views. Are these contrasting positions more closely related to metaphysics or to epistemology? Explain.

Axiology **Axiology** *considers values and ethics;* axiological issues are now prominent in American education. Because of current problems, such as drug abuse, teen pregnancy, and juvenile violence and crime, educators generally agree that some form of moral education is needed in schools, although they disagree on the form it should take (Wynne, 1997). One view, labeled **character education** *argues that values, such as honesty and citizenship, should be emphasized, taught, and rewarded* (Doyle, 1997). A contrasting view, called **moral education,** *emphasizes the development of students' moral reasoning and doesn't establish a preset list of values that learners should acquire* (Kohn, 1997). But regardless of which view they favor, all educators believe that the development of moral thinking and moral behavior are important goals for schools.

Let's look again at Allie and Brad's conversation. Allie argued, "I'm getting paid to help kids learn. If I don't do my very best to make that happen, I'm not earning my salary." Brad retorted, ". . . it would be a heck of a lot easier to just make the kids cram some stuff in their heads, but I would be doing them, their parents, and ultimately our whole socie-

ty a disservice if I didn't bite the bullet and prepare them for life outside of school." Both teachers argued that they wouldn't be behaving ethically if they weren't true to their beliefs about what is important. Though they were probably unaware of it, this part of their conversation was concerned with axiology.

Logic Let's look again at some of Allie's thinking. While not in these exact words, it could be described in the following sequence. She suggested that:

"The more people learn, the more intrinsically motivated they become."
"You [Brad] have learned a lot about the Internet."
"You want to surf the Internet more now than ever before. [You're more intrinsically motivated.]"

Logic is *the process of deriving valid conclusions from basic principles*, and Allie was illustrating a form of logic called *deductive reasoning*. Deductive reasoning begins with a proposition, called a major premise, which can be a principle or generalization such as "The more people learn, the more intrinsically motivated they are." The major premise is followed by a fact, called a minor premise, such as "You have learned a lot about the Internet." A deductive reasoning sequence is completed with a conclusion that follows from the two premises. In Allie's case the conclusion was an explanation for why Brad spent time surfing the Internet.

Inductive reasoning is the counterpart to deductive reasoning. For instance, when students see that a rock and paper clip hit the floor at the same time if they're dropped simultaneously, they conclude that objects fall at the same rate regardless of weight (if air resistance is negligible). Based on the specific instances (the rock and the paper clip), the students make a general conclusion about falling objects.

Increasing Understanding 6.5

You're being asked to respond to margin questions, such as this one. We have concluded that questions such as these will increase your understanding of this book. Identify a major premise and a minor premise on which this conclusion could be based.

Logic helps both teachers and learners examine the validity of their thinking. For instance, in social studies we try to help students see that if we stereotype a specific cultural group based on the behavior or appearance of a few members of the group, we're using faulty inductive reasoning. Similarly, many controversies in education and other aspects of life exist because proponents and critics disagree on the validity of conclusions, which are the products of deductive reasoning. For instance, critics of character education conclude that it emphasizes indoctrination (Kohn, 1997). This conclusion is based on the premise that a system based on rewards indoctrinates rather than teaches (a major premise), and character education utilizes rewards (a minor premise). Proponents of character education disagree with both the major premise and the conclusion.

TRADITIONAL SCHOOLS OF PHILOSOPHY

Throughout history, philosophers worked to systematically describe how the world works, that is, they've tried to answer questions about reality and what is real (metaphysics), how we know (epistemology), what is good and valuable (axiology), and whether or not our thinking is clear and accurate (logic). Many of these efforts have resulted in cohesive philosophies. Four of them are considered by many to be the traditional philosophies that undergird most educational decisions (Jacobsen, 1999). They are:

- Idealism
- Realism
- Pragmatism
- Existentialism

We turn to them now.

Idealism

Let's look once more at Allie and Brad's conversation. Brad argued, ". . . let's say that, based on this conversation, you conclude that I'm naive and idealistic. On the other hand, I conclude that I'm actually more practical than you are . . . . What is the reality? Am I naive, or am I practical? . . . To you, I'm naive, and you will operate based on that belief. To me I'm not. So, reality is what we perceive it to be, and there's no objective source *out there* to decide which view is the 'right one'."

Brad argued that ideas are the ultimate reality, which is a basic principle of idealism. Idealism is the oldest of the Western philosophies, having originated with the great Greek philosopher, Plato. **Idealism** *is the belief that, since the physical world is constantly changing, ideas are the only reliable form of reality.*

Increasing Understanding 6.6

Would idealists support the scientific method, or would they be critical of it? Explain. To which of the four branches of philosophy is this question most closely related? Explain.

■ ■ ■

Plato was born at the height of Greek civilization into an aristocratic family in Athens (his birth date is estimated to be about 428 B.C.). Along with Socrates (his teacher and mentor) and Aristotle, Plato was one of the three philosophers of ancient Greece that laid the philosophical foundations of Western culture.

Plato wrote in the form of imaginary dialogues between Socrates and his students. Plato's goal in writing the dialogues was to faithfully represent Socrates' thinking; in the dialogues, Socrates questioned his students' beliefs and assumptions about truth, beauty, and other philosophical topics. His questioning, as illustrated in the dialogues, led to the modern concept of the *Socratic Method* or *Socratic Questioning.*

■ ■ ■

Since, for idealists, ultimate reality exists in the world of ideas, teaching and learning should focus on these ideas. A curriculum based on idealism emphasizes mathematics because of its logic, precision, and abstraction. It also emphasizes great works of literature, art, and music because of their enduring contributions. The thinking of great men and women in history would be studied because of the ideas they offered.

Idealism emphasizes great works of literature, music, and art, which contain powerful ideas from important contributors to our culture.

Teachers have a critical role for idealists. Learners are unlikely to understand enduring ideas without support and guidance. Teachers provide this guidance by helping students become more precise and logical thinkers and by helping them understand the ideas that have existed throughout history. For example, an English teacher might have students read Melville's *Moby Dick* because it emphasizes the conflict between good and evil, an enduring idea. Younger children might study White's *Charlotte's Web* because it deals with a moral dilemma, another time-honored concept.

Idealism has been criticized as elitist and overemphasizing cold, rational ideas at the expense of emotions, feelings, and the personal side of people. It is elitist because the ideas chosen for analysis often come from a small, wealthy, and privileged part of the population. It is considered coldly cognitive because it emphasizes the rational and logical over other dimensions of human experience.

Realism

In contrast with idealism, which argues that ideas are the ultimate reality, **realism** *holds that the features of the universe exist whether or not a human being is there to perceive them.* Realism is also an ancient philosophy, Aristotle being one of its original developers. Allie's argument, ". . . look at that oak tree outside the window. You can perceive it to be anything you want, but it's still an oak. And, it doesn't matter what anybody thinks, two plus two is four, not three, not five, not anything in between." This argument is consistent with realism. Realists argue that there are important ideas and facts that must be understood, and they can only be understood by studying the material world. Realists emphasize science and technology and strongly endorse the scientific method. They argue that ignorance of information about diet, disease, and natural disasters, for example, has caused much of the suffering in human history, and the accumulation of knowledge in areas like science and medicine has improved the quality of life for many people.

■ ■ ■

Aristotle was born in 384 B.C. and studied at Plato's Academy. A great thinker and teacher, he is believed to have participated in the education of Alexander the Great, one of the greatest military leaders in history.

Aristotle studied and wrote about an amazing array of topics ranging from logic, philosophy, and ethics to physics, biology, psychology, and politics. Deductive reasoning and the scientific method were both influenced by his thinking.

■ ■ ■

Critics who argue that American education is in decline because the curriculum has been "dumbed down" with too many superfluous courses and too much emphasis on "self-esteem" are expressing views consistent with realism. A curriculum consistent with realism emphasizes essentials, such as math, science, reading, and writing, because they are tools to help us understand our world. The periodic national focus and refocus on basic skills is also consistent with this view.

Teachers working within the philosophy of realism emphasize observation, experimentation, and critical reasoning. Their goals are for learners to think clearly and understand the material world. They tend to de-emphasize formal emphasis on feelings and other personal factors, arguing that positive feelings and the improvement of self-esteem are an outgrowth of knowledge and understanding.

As with idealism, critics of realism argue that it is inappropriately narrow in its failing to take the whole person—the physical, emotional, and social in addition to the intellectual domain—into account in the learning process.

Pragmatists attempt to connect subject-matter content to children's interests.

Pragmatism

Though it has ancient roots, pragmatism is considered a modern—even American—philosophy, with John Dewey being one of its primary proponents. (Chapter 5 contains a section on John Dewey's involvement in the progressive education movement.) Dewey (1902, 1906, 1923, 1938) wrote extensively on education, and his work has arguably had more impact on American education than has any other body of literature. His ideas continue to be actively debated by educators today (for example, Prawat, 1998; Proefriedt, 1999).

▪ ▪ ▪

John Dewey (1859–1952) is one of the most important American philosophers in history. Educated in his native Vermont and at Johns Hopkins University, Dewey enjoyed a long career as an educator, psychologist, and philosopher. He initiated the progressive laboratory school at the University of Chicago, where his reforms in methods of education were put into practice. As a result, *progressivism,* a prominent educational philosophy, is associated with his work.

▪ ▪ ▪

Increasing Understanding 6.7

Based on the conversation in our opening case study, would Allie or Brad's views be more closely related to pragmatism? Cite evidence from the case to support your contention.

Pragmatism *shares some views with realism, but is less rigid. It rejects the idea of absolute, unchanging truth. Instead, truth is what works, hence the term* pragmatism. For example, our primitive ancestors needed and ate a diet high in fat because it might be a long time between meals, and they were very active as hunter–gatherers. Now, we have a problem. Our evolved selves still enjoy, even crave, fat, but we no longer need as much because we've become sedentary. Historically, truth was that fat was important and healthy; now truth is that fat is less important and too much is unhealthy. A high-fat diet no longer "works."

For pragmatists, *experience* is a key idea. As we've gathered experiences with respect to diet, for example, we've observed the consequences of those experiences and have adapted (or are trying to adapt) accordingly.

This example illustrates the pragmatists' contention that truth isn't an abstract idea, nor is it simply a material aspect of the world. Rather, it represents the interaction between the individual and the environment. Further, truth is personal and relative. For example, some people need more fat in their diet than do others.

Because truth changes, individuals need methods for dealing with these changes. As a result, teachers adhering to pragmatism place the processes involved in learning on an equal plane with content. Direct experiences and problem solving are emphasized. Information needed to solve problems comes from many sources, so studying content areas in isolation isn't effective or practical; interdisciplinary education that focuses on using various academic disciplines to analyze and solve problems is more "pragmatic."

Critics of pragmatism contend that it undervalues essential knowledge. Pragmatism, with it's educational counterpart, *progressivism*, has been blamed by conservative critics for the decline in performance by American students compared to students in other industrialized countries. Critics further contend that pragmatism too strongly emphasizes student interests at the expense of essential knowledge (Ravitch, 2000).

Defenders of pragmatism, and particularly Dewey's work, argue that the critics are either misrepresenting Dewey or don't understand him. "He saw clearly that to ask, 'Which is more important: the interests of the child or the knowledge of subject-matter?' was to ask a very dumb question indeed. The teacher's task, for Dewey, was to create an interaction between the child's interest and the funded knowledge of the adult world . . ." (Proefriedt, 1999, p. 28). Pragmatism doesn't de-emphasize the importance of knowledge; instead, it attempts to connect it to children's interests.

Existentialism

Compared to idealism, realism, and pragmatism, existentialism is quite radical. **Existentialism** is *a philosophical view suggesting that humanity isn't part of an orderly universe; rather, individuals create their own existence in their own unique way.* Influenced by the horrors of World War II, existentialist writers, such as Jean-Paul Sartre, have a pessimistic view of humanity, seeing it as essentially meaningless on a small, isolated planet in an uncertain universe where nothing is determined. If nothing is determined, people have total freedom, freedom to take advantage of others, promote racial strife, or cause conflicts. However, we're also free to promote peace and harmony. With total freedom comes total responsibility. Unwise choices can't be blamed on God's will, other people, or prior experiences.

▪ ▪ ▪

Jean-Paul Sartre (1905–1980) was educated in Paris and Göttingen, Germany. He participated actively in the French resistance to German occupation in World War II, and the experience of the war, combined with his study of earlier existentialist writers, strongly influenced his thinking. He wrote philosophy, fiction, and political treatises, becoming one of the most respected leaders in post-war French culture.

▪ ▪ ▪

Existentialism makes a contribution to education because it places primary emphasis on the individual, and in doing so, it reminds us that we don't teach math, science, reading, and writing; rather, we teach people, and the people we teach are at the core of learning.

Existentialists would have us change our attitudes about education. Education isn't something a student is filled with and measured; education is an individual's search for personal understanding. Existentialist educators decry tracking, measurement, and standardization, arguing that these practices detract from individuals' opportunities for growth. Schools, they suggest, should be places where students are free to engage in activities because these activities are interesting to them and help students define who they are.

Whereas science and technology are important for realists and pragmatists, an existentialist curriculum would place more emphasis on the humanities, because the humanities

Table 6.1 **The Traditional Schools of Philosophy**

	Idealism	Realism	Pragmatism	Existentialism
Metaphysics	Reality is the world of unchanging ideas.	Reality is the physical world.	Reality is the interaction of the individual and the environment.	Reality is the subjective interpretation of the physical world.
Epistemology	Knowing is the personal rethinking of universal ideas.	Knowing is observing and understanding natural laws.	Knowing is the result of experience based on the scientific method.	Knowing is making personal choice.
Axiology	Values are absolute based on enduring ideas.	Values are absolute based on natural law.	Values are relative.	Values are chosen by the individual.
Educational Implications	Curricula focus on content that emphasizes time-honored ideas.	Curricula focus on content that emphasizes natural laws.	Curricula and instruction focus on problem solving and the scientific method.	Instruction emphasizes discussion designed to increase individual self-awareness.

examine human existence, relationships between people, and tragedy as well as triumph. An existentialist teacher, for example, might have students read Albee's *Who's Afraid of Virginia Woolf* to consider why a couple remains together when all they seem to do is develop greater and greater ways of hurting each other.

On a more positive note, existentialism has influenced the thinking of humanistic educators such as Carl Rogers (1967) and Abraham Maslow (1968, 1970), who advocate a learner-centered and non-directive approach to education. Empathy is an important teacher characteristic, and teachers, they argue, should care for their students unconditionally, helping students feel like worthy individuals. Teachers should be students, and students should be teachers. Current emphases on communities of learners, in which teachers and students work together to accomplish learning goals, are consistent with this view.

Critics of existentialism remind us that we all live in a social world, which, whether we like it or not, has rules; total freedom is impossible. However, even critics acknowledge the existentialist position emphasizing that personal freedom carries with it personal responsibility.

Each of the traditional philosophies has implications for teaching. An English teacher whose personal philosophy is grounded in idealism, for example, might have her students read Hugo's *Les Miserables* because it examines the issue of morality, which is a time-honored topic. Class discussions would examine historical considerations of morality. Another teacher, whose philosophical leanings are existentialist, would orient class discussions more strongly toward students' personal conceptions of morality. The topic is the same, but the teachers' goals are different because of the influence of philosophy.

Differences among these traditional philosophies are summarized in Table 6.1.

EXPLORING DIVERSITY: PHILOSOPHY AND CULTURAL MINORITIES

To this point in the chapter, the philosophies we've examined have been "Western," meaning their origins are European or American. Two principles undergird this Western orientation. The first is the preeminence of the individual, such as an individual's search for truth in

Alternate philosophies remind teachers of the need to view each child as an individual with unique needs and interests.

both idealism and realism, the interaction of the individual with the environment for pragmatism, and an individual's search for a meaningful life for an existentialist.

The second is rational thought and respect for objectivity, science, and the scientific method. Realism and pragmatism, in particular, emphasize science as a way of knowing.

Some philosophers criticize these emphases, citing examples such as the fact that technology dominates our lives, Americans are working more hours per week than they ever have in the past, and they're chronically sleep deprived.

In contrast to Western emphasis on individuality and rationality, some philosophies, such as those embedded in certain Native American cultures, use the shared folklore of elders and knowledge that comes from the heart as their sources of wisdom (Morton, 1988). Because of Native Americans' long history of living in harmony with the land, their philosophies also place emphasis on ecological as well as interpersonal harmony. The emphasis on harmony and cooperation results in valuing individual achievement primarily as it contributes to a group's overall well-being. Competition and individual displays of achievement are frowned upon. Understanding these differences can help explain why Navajo students, for example, are sometimes reluctant to participate in the competitive verbal give-and-take of fast-paced questioning sessions that require individuals to demonstrate how much they know (Villegas, 1991; Tharp, 1989).

Similarly, for some African cultures, feelings and personal relationships are equally or more important ways of knowing than are science and rational thought (Nieto, 1996). Art and music are important means of expression and seeking knowledge. As we look at the history of African Americans, this helps us understand why music was such a prominent part of their lives during slavery, why African Americans have made such a strong contribution to modern and impressionistic art, and why African influences can be seen in much of contemporary music in Europe and the Americas.

Many Asians also value harmony—harmony with nature, life, family, and society. The emphasis on harmony leads to reverence for elders, respect for authority, and adherence to traditions. Because harmony is so important, being polite is highly valued, and feelings and

Critics of education and proponents of essentialism periodically write newspaper editorials sounding the alarm about American students' ignorance of the world around them, their inability to communicate either orally or in writing, and their lack of ability to do rudimentary math (American Council of Trustees and Alumni, 2000; Ravitch, 2000). These views are consistent with **essentialism,** which is *the belief that a critical core of information exists that all people should possess*. For essentialists, schools should emphasize basic skills and academic subjects, and students should be expected to master these subjects. The reasons for these emphases and standards are to ensure a literate and skilled workforce in a technological society. Essentialists are concerned about a general "dumbing down" of the curriculum, they decry social promotion of students, and they are wary of student-centered curriculum and instruction.

Many of the reform efforts over the last 20 or more years can be traced to essentialist views. The widely publicized *A Nation At Risk* (National Commission on Excellence in Education, 1983), which recommended that all high school students master core requirements in five "basics"—English, math, science, social studies, and computer science—is one example.

Increasing Understanding 6.10

"High stakes" testing, in which students are required to pass standardized tests before they're allowed to graduate from high school, is being emphasized today. Would essentialists react negatively or positively to this trend? Explain.

Essentialist philosophy is also found in teacher-education programs. The popularity of books such as *Knowledge Base for the Beginning Teacher* (Reynolds, 1989) and the fact that aspiring teachers are required to take a specified sequence of courses and to demonstrate mastery of essential teaching skills reflect the belief that a core of knowledge exists that all pre-service teachers should master.

Essentialism and perennialism share the view that knowledge and understanding are preeminent, and both are wary of the emphasis on learner-centered education and the focus on learner self-esteem. Essentialists differ from perennialists, however, in perennialists' emphasis on universal truths through the study of classical literature. Essentialists, instead, emphasize knowledge and skills that are useful in today's world. From an essentialist perspective, the sequence of courses you're required to take and the competencies or skills you are asked to master in your teacher-preparation program exist because educational leaders believe that they will help you become a better teacher in today's world.

The essentialist curriculum is more likely to change than is the perennialist curriculum. For instance, as our society becomes increasingly diverse, teacher-preparation programs place greater and greater emphasis on learning to work effectively with learners from diverse backgrounds. This is in response to the increasing diversity of our students as well as a growing recognition of the influence of diversity on learning. This means you will likely take a course in multicultural education, or topics in multicultural education will be included in several of your courses. This emphasis wouldn't have existed 20 years ago. The same is true for technology; most teacher-education programs now have some type of technology component. Whether arrived at implicitly or consciously, these shifts in emphasis reflect essentialist thinking.

Progressivism

Think for a moment about some of the practices we are seeing emphasized in education today. For instance, we encounter "learner-centered curricula," which emphasizes learners' interests and needs (Lambert & McCombs, 1998). We also see hands-on learning activities, particularly in science, where children work with batteries, bulbs, magnets, plants, soil, and a variety of other materials. Learners are asked to write about their own experiences in language arts, and math emphasizes problem solving and learning concepts through hands-on manipulatives. Learners collaborating as they work with these materials and solving these problems is also emphasized. Teachers don't simply deliver information; they guide learners and facilitate the learning process.

These practices are philosophically rooted in progressivism, an educational philosophy grounded in pragmatism. As we saw earlier, for pragmatists, reality is what works. **Progressivism** *emphasizes curriculum that focuses on real-world problem solving and individual development*. As Brad argued in our beginning case study, ". . . the person who really succeeds is the one who continues to learn and is able to adapt to changes in the world by solving the large and small problems they encounter," and "They need lots of experience in making decisions and solving problems. That's what life's all about." These are views consistent with progressivism.

In our discussion of epistemology, we briefly examined constructivism, a view of learning asserting that students don't record understanding; rather, they construct it based on their experiences and background knowledge. Constructivism is consistent with progressivism and its precursor, pragmatism. All three emphasize concrete experiences, real-world tasks, and the central role of the individual in determining reality and promoting learning. As you analyze learning in educational psychology, you will undoubtedly study constructivism in detail. As you do, remember that it's rooted in pragmatism and progressivism.

Progressivism is controversial. As we saw in our discussion of pragmatism, critics contend that the pendulum has swung too far in the direction of children's interests and self-esteem at the expense of knowledge and understanding (Ravitch, 2000). Some of these criticisms are justified and reflect misapplications of Dewey's ideas. For example, progressives complained that schools organized subject matter in a detached manner, alien to the interests and abilities of young children. But these same progressives made no sustained effort to develop or understand alternate ways of organizing knowledge so that it would be more accessible or useable to the learner. They recognized the shortcomings of assigning the learner to a passive, receptive role, but too often substituted for it a set of educationally purposeless activities (Proefriedt, 1999, p. 28). Both progressivism and its precursor, pragmatism—when properly interpreted—suggest that effective education isn't a matter of process *or* content; it is process *and* content.

Postmodernism

During the 1960s, the United States went through major cultural upheavals. The Vietnam War was a concrete marker, and its unpopularity caused skepticism about authority and leadership. Other movements, such as civil rights for minorities, feminism, and gay and lesbian crusades, encouraged critiques of American culture, society, and education. Postmodern philosophy emerged among these critiques.

Postmodernism contends that *many of the institutions in our society, including schools, are used by those in power to control and marginalize those who lack power.* The powerful are typically White males, and those marginalized (lacking power) are unskilled workers, women, and cultural minorities. Postmodernists argue that K–12 and university curricula are racist, sexist, and imperialist. As an example of this, postmodernists point to the continued curricular emphasis on the study of Shakespeare. Shakespeare, a White European male, figures prominently in most high school literature programs. Emphasis on Shakespeare and other White male authors has resulted in little room left for literature written by women, minorities, or people from other cultures. Since White males make curricular decisions, marginalizing those without power continues unabated.

Increasing Understanding 6.11

Of the traditional philosophies—idealism, realism, pragmatism, and existentialism—which would be most acceptable to postmodernists? Explain.

Reflect on This

EDUCATIONAL PHILOSOPHY IN THE CLASSROOM

You're an American history teacher and you want your students to do more than simply memorize their way through the information you're teaching. You want them to develop their critical-thinking skills, learn to solve problems, make informed decisions, and get involved in lessons.

This turns out to be a daunting task, however. The students seem to want you to describe every required detail in assignments, and when you call on students who don't have their hands raised, the most common response is, "I didn't have my hand up," or "I don't know." In other cases, they say, "C'mon, just tell us what you want us to know," and "Why do we have to learn this stuff?"

1. To which educational philosophy are your goals most closely aligned? To which are they least aligned?
2. Using one of these educational philosophies how might you respond to students when they ask, "Why do we have to learn this stuff?"
3. Should you "force" students to be involved if they're reluctant to participate? How might you involve reluctant students in lessons?
4. How would you handle the situation just described?

To answer these questions online and receive immediate feedback, go to the Reflect on This *Module in Chapter 6 of the Companion Website.*

Postmodern philosophy raises questions about culture and gender bias in our schools.

A postmodern curriculum would reverse these trends. Literature written by feminist and minority authors would be elevated to a position as prominent or more prominent than traditional literature. Further, traditional literature would be critically examined to see how it has historically shaped our notions of differences, such as race and gender. Issues such as the use of power, personal and group identities, cultural politics, and social

Table 6.2 Characteristics of the Educational Philosophies

	Perennialism	Essentialism	Progressivism	Postmodernism
Traditional Philosophy Most Closely Related	Idealism, Realism	Idealism, Realism	Pragmatism	Existentialism
Educational Goals	Train the intellect; moral development.	Acquire basic skills; acquire knowledge needed to function in today's world.	Acquire ability to function in the real world; develop problem-solving skills.	Critically examine today's institutions; elevate the status of marginalized people (women and cultural minorities).
Curriculum	Emphasis on enduring ideas.	Emphasis on basic skills.	Emphasis on problem solving and skills needed in today's world.	Emphasis on the works of marginalized people.
Role of the Teacher	Deliver clear lectures; increase student understanding with critical questions.	Deliver clear lectures; increase student understanding with critical questions.	Guide learning with questioning; develop and guide practical problem-solving activities.	Facilitate discussions that involve clarifying issues.
Teaching Methods	Lecture; questioning; coaching in intellectual thinking.	Lecture; practice and feedback; questioning.	Problem-based learning; cooperative learning; guided discovery.	Discussion; role play; simulation; personal research.
Learning Environment	High structure; high levels of time on task.	High structure; high levels of time on task.	Collaborative; self-regulated; democratic.	Community-oriented; self-regulated.
Assessment	Frequent objective and essay tests.	Frequent objective, essay, and performance tests.	Continuous feedback; informal monitoring of student progress.	Collaborative between teacher and student; emphasis on the exposure of hidden assumptions.

Increasing Understanding 6.12

Throughout this text, you've been asked to respond to margin questions such as this one. The fact that these questions exist and the types of questions being asked best reflect which of the educational philosophies? Explain.

criticism would enjoy prominent positions. Historical events would be examined from the perspective of power, status, and marginalized people's struggles in those contexts. For instance, Columbus's discovery of the New World has been presented historically as a critical point in European expansion and colonization, and the beginning of modern history in North and South America. Postmodernism would recognize that fact but would emphasize the brutalization of Native Americans by the Spaniards, the ravaging of the indigenous people by diseases such as smallpox (for which they had no natural immunities), their enslavement, and the fact that conquering and colonization were two major goals for explorers.

Postmodernism has sparked hot debate. As postmodernists have risen to positions of power in some universities, for example, the study of Shakespeare has been eliminated from the curriculum in favor of feminist and minority authors. This has caused outrage among perennialist or essentialist thinkers. They argue that postmodernism has resulted in the abandonment of schools as places for intellectual pursuits, contending instead that schools are being used for political purposes. They contend further that postmodernism is as control-oriented as traditional philosophies and institutions; it merely wants to establish controls more to its followers' liking (Ozmon & Craver, 1995).

Classroom applications of the educational philosophies are summarized in Table 6.2.

Teaching 
in an Era *of* Reform

THE ESSENTIAL-KNOWLEDGE DEBATE

Among the criticisms of American education and American students, lack of knowledge about our country and our world is being increasingly voiced. Editorial headlines such as "Historical illiteracy is plaguing many in high schools and colleges" are appearing with greater frequency. Authors then cite facts such as the following: Only 1 in 3 college seniors randomly chosen from 55 top-rated colleges and universities identified George Washington as the American general at Yorktown, and only 22 percent identified the Gettysburg address as the source of the statement "Government of the people, by the people, for the people" (American Council of Trustees and Alumni, 2000). In another survey, only 42 percent of college seniors placed the Civil War in the correct half century, and most adult Americans couldn't find the Persian Gulf on a map (Bertman, 2000). The situation is no better in math. For example, one study asked U.S. fifth graders to solve the problem $45 \times 26 = ?$; only 54 percent were successful (Stigler and Stevenson, 1990).

In response to these criticisms, reformers argue that American students lack the essential knowledge needed to function effectively in today's world. This has resulted in standards—statements about what students should know and what skills they should have—being written in virtually all content areas. E. D. Hirsch (1987), who wrote the controversial but widely read *Cultural Literacy: What Every American Needs to Know,* further illustrates this essentialist position. Hirsch identified a vast list of facts, concepts, and people that he believed all citizens should know in order to function effectively in American society. Since then, he has produced a series of edited paperbacks for parents and teachers that make up what he calls "The Core Knowledge" curriculum. Hirsch has developed products such as *What Your Third Grader Needs to Know: Fundamentals of a Good Third-grade Education (the Core Knowledge Series)* (1994), and *What Your Sixth Grader Needs to Know: Fundamentals of a Good Sixth-grade Education (the Core Knowledge Series)* (1995). Similar titles exist for each of the grade levels from kindergarten through sixth grade.

The content Hirsch advocates is quite sophisticated. For instance, *What Your Sixth Grader Needs to Know* has a section on American civilization that encourages students to understand the country's affairs within the context of global current events; a selection from Maya Angelou's *I Know Why the Caged Bird Sings;* speeches by John F. Kennedy and Martin Luther King, Jr.; plus sections on genetics and biographical portraits of pioneering scientists. Essentialists, as illustrated by Hirsch's work, argue that learners need to know much more than basic skills like reading, writing, and rudimentary math.

Putting Reform into Perspective

Reformers make a valid point, and our country's leaders are alarmed. In response to the American Council of Trustees and Alumni report (2000), members of Congress were so concerned that a resolution was introduced warning that lack of historical knowledge is dangerous for our country's future.

In addition, research on learning indicates that background knowledge is crucial for developing understanding of new content (Bruning, Schraw, & Ronning, 1999; Eggen & Kauchak, 2001). All new learning depends on and builds on what learners already know. For instance, to understand the relationships among people's growing distrust of authority, the civil rights movement, and the Vietnam War, people must know that each began in the 1960s. Similarly, to understand the problems of sub-Saharan Africa, we must also understand European colonialism as well as the geography and climate of this vast area. Knowledge builds on knowledge, and when knowledge is lacking, learning suffers.

Citizens agree that knowledge is important and that our young people lack it. Hirsch's "Core Knowledge" series is popular with both parents and teachers, and many reviewers have responded positively to it. Criticisms that the series focuses on rote memory rather than understanding have gone largely unnoticed or have been sharply refuted.

However, is teaching an increasing number of facts really the way to make students more culturally aware? Public-school students already take several American history courses during their school years (at least one during middle school and another in high school, plus smatterings during their elementary years). But they apparently retain little of the content, as indicated by the survey results cited earlier. So the issue is more complex than simply requiring more content and courses. Students apparently aren't learning from the courses they do take, so essentialism as normative philosophy doesn't provide a complete answer.

The issue is further complicated by an examination of goals. As we said earlier in this section, essentialists argue

The essential-knowledge debate raises important questions about curriculum—what is taught in schools—as well as instruction.

that American students lack the "essential" knowledge needed to function effectively in today's world. However, research indicates that personal motivation and the ability to use strategies to acquire knowledge are better predictors of later success than is the accumulation of knowledge (McCaslin & Good, 1996). "It is the affective and motivational characteristics of workers that our employers worry most about. They depend on employees to show up on time, to get along with others, to care about doing well on the job. . . . They do not find the technical ability of the workforce to be a problem for them" (Berliner, 1992; pp. 33–34).

In essence, does increased knowledge make people happier and more productive workers? Motivational research suggests that increasing learner readiness and eagerness to learn should be the primary goals of schools, not acquiring a vast storehouse of inert knowledge. This position is more consistent with pragmatism and progressivism than with essentialism.

Finally, the question of what knowledge is "essential" is critical. For example, Hirsch (1987) identifies information such as "Who was Spiro Agnew?" and "What is a carnivore?" as essential. Why is this information more important than knowing, for instance, who Cesar Chavez was or what macrobiotic means? (Marzano, Kendall, & Gaddy, 1999). Further, the sheer amount of knowledge called for by standards is overwhelming. Nearly 14,000 benchmarks in 14 subject-matter areas have been written, resulting in "far too many standards and not enough time in the day or year to teach them all" (Marzano et al., 1999, p. 68).

Unquestionably, a dilemma exists. You will be asked to help students reach standards, but you won't have time to accomplish the goal. This will mean that you will have to make decisions that make your job more complex and demanding, not simpler. As more experts question the effectiveness of the "high-stakes" testing of essential knowledge (for example, Linn, 2000), the pendulum is likely to swing back to some extent. How far it will go is anyone's guess.

You Take a Position

Now it's your turn to take a position on the issues discussed in this section. Go to the *Education Week* Website at **http://www.edweek.com**, find "search" on the first page, and type in one of the following two search terms: *essential knowledge* or *basic skills*. Locate a minimum of three articles on one of these topics and then do the following:

1. Identify the title, author, and date of each article and then write a one-paragraph summary of each.
2. Identify a pattern in the articles. (Each article—or even two of the three—suggesting that school districts are increasing their emphasis on basic skills would be a pattern, for example.)
3. After identifying the pattern, take one of the two following positions:
   - The pattern suggested in the articles, if implemented, *is* likely to improve education.
   - The pattern suggested in the articles *is not* likely to improve education.

State your position in writing, and document your position with information taken from the articles.

To answer these questions online, go to the Take a Position *Module in Chapter 6 of the Companion Website.*

Table 6.3 **An Analysis of Allie's Philosophy of Education**

Belief Statement	Component of Her Philosophy
"They [kids] don't come to school with the same . . . desire to learn as they once did."	"They may not be too crazy about it initially. . . ."
"They want to believe they did learn something when they're finished with a topic, or class. . . ."	"Kids basically want to learn."
"They're not intrinsically motivated."	"Some of them might be in it mostly for grades to start with."
"[Kids] feel good when they learned something, particularly if it's challenging."	"If the kids understand the stuff, they'll like it, and the better they'll feel about themselves." "I want them to know why, how they know, and what would happen when conditions change."
"The more they know about a topic, the better they like it."	"The more they learn about the topics, the better they like what they study. Relevance isn't as critical to the kids' motivation as understanding and success are."
"There's real, practical stuff out there that they need to know, and there's only one way they're gonna learn it. . . . That's practice and experience."	"We're going to have class discussions, do homework, go over it, have quizzes, and go over them."

I know that I can get them to learn. We're going to have class discussions, do homework, go over it, have quizzes, and go over them. If I do my job, they'll learn.

■ ■ ■

What you've just read is a succinct description of Allie's philosophy of education. It is clear, well-articulated, and consistent with her beliefs. The relationships between her beliefs and the components of her philosophy are outlined in Table 6.3.

Because her philosophy is clear and well-articulated, it can effectively guide her thinking as she defines her goals and designs learning activities and assessments. Her philosophy helps her ensure that her goals, learning activities, and assessments are consistent with each other. While you may or may not agree with her goals or the rationale for them, the fact that she's clear in her thinking increases the likelihood that her students will reach the goals, and she will be more likely to make conscious choices to change and improve her teaching when evidence and her thinking indicate that change is needed.

Increasing Understanding 6.14

Look again at Brad's thinking, as indicated by his conversation with Allie. Based on this information, describe what you believe is his philosophy of education. Explain how the philosophy is based on his beliefs.

You now have the following information:

- The description of Allie's philosophy.
- Your own description of Brad's philosophy, based on your response to "Increasing Understanding 6.14."
- Your analysis of your own beliefs.

Using this information, you're now ready to compile your ideas into a normative philosophy that will guide your thinking and actions.

We said earlier that your philosophy will likely incorporate elements of the different philosophies we've discussed. We see this in Allie's thinking. Her view that an objective reality exists, independent of the world of ideas, is consistent with realism; from essentialism, she drew the belief that a body of important information exists that all students need to know in order to function effectively in today's world; and her concerns for her students' personal needs, emotions, and self-esteem most closely relate to existentialism.

Dialoguing with other professionals can help beginning teachers shape their own developing personal philosophy of education.

Looking Through

Classroom Windows

EXAMINING PHILOSOPHIES OF EDUCATION

Having examined both traditional and educational philosophies, as well as considering your own, you now have the opportunity to analyze the philosophies of two different teachers. To complete this activity, do the following:

- View the video episode containing two different classroom lessons titled, "Examining Philosophies of Education."
- Read the written transcripts of the two lessons and answer the following questions online by going to the *Classroom Windows* Module in Chapter 6 of the Companion Website at **http://www.prenhall.com/kauchak**. Go to the Web site and follow the directions on your screen.
- Answer the questions that follow:

1. Which of the traditional philosophies is most nearly reflected in Judy's teaching? Explain.
2. Which of the traditional philosophies is most nearly reflected in Bob's teaching? Explain.
3. Which of the educational philosophies is most nearly reflected in Judy's teaching? Explain.
4. Which of the educational philosophies is most nearly reflected in Bob's teaching? Explain.
5. Which teacher, Judy or Bob, most clearly reflects your own personal philosophy of education? Explain.

To answer these questions online and receive immediate feedback, go to the Looking through Classroom Windows *Module in Chapter 6 of the Companion Website.*

The Changing Role of Teachers

The philosophies presented in this chapter have different implications for teachers. For example, perennialism and essentialism suggest that teachers should be knowledgeable in the topics they teach and able to help students learn this information. Progressivism also implies that teachers should be skilled in guiding learning, but it more strongly emphasizes the process of learning than do the first two. Postmodernism focuses on a critical examination of the traditions that have existed in education and in society at large.

Research on the way people learn continually expands, school environments are becoming increasingly complex, and our student populations are the most diverse in our history. For example, estimates suggest that during the next 20 years, dramatic increases in the percentage of Hispanic, African American, Asian American (including Pacific Islanders), and Native American students will occur in the school population (Young & Smith, 1999). These factors suggest that teaching will become more sophisticated and more demanding in the future than it has ever been in the past. In addition, teachers experience pressure from administrators, standardized tests, and mandated curricula to target their teaching toward basic skills. Everyone agrees that all students should leave school knowing how to read, write, and do math, but views differ about how much emphasis should be placed on these basic skills. Should they be the core of the curriculum? Should we teach basic skills first and then use them to teach other content, or should they be integrated into units where students use them in writing and problem solving? How important are other goals, such as learning to work with others and understanding how the world around us works?

A clear philosophy of teaching and learning provides a basis for answering these and other difficult educational questions. In an increasingly complex world, it is essential that teachers develop coherent philosophies of education to guide them as they attempt to do what is best for the students they teach.

In constructing your personal philosophy, you will combine traditional and educational philosophies in the same way.

Hopefully, this chapter has provided you with the background needed to begin this journey and has caused you to think about teaching in a different way. At this point, you won't have all the answers needed to decide what education should be and how you can help make it that way. But if you are now able to begin asking some important questions, then our goal for the chapter has been fulfilled. Good luck.

SUMMARY

Philosophy and Philosophy of Education

Philosophy is a search for wisdom. In forming a philosophy, a professional teacher searches for the wisdom to maximize learning for all students.

Philosophy provides a framework for thinking, and it guides professional practice. Although it overlaps with theory, philosophy differs from theory in that we try to explain events and behavior, as they are, on the basis of theories, whereas philosophies go further to suggest the way events and behaviors ought to be.

Traditional Schools of Philosophy

Idealism, realism, pragmatist, and existentialism are often called the traditional philosophies. Their views of reality, ways of knowing, and what is valuable and good often differ considerably.

Each has implications for teaching and learning. Idealists would create a curriculum focusing on absolute and time-honored ideas. Realists would also emphasize absolutes, but in contrast with the thinking of idealists, these absolutes would focus on natural laws. Pragmatists see the world in relative terms, and they would emphasize experience and practical understanding, validated by the scientific method. Existentialists would take a more extreme position, with the curriculum emphasizing personal awareness, freedom, and responsibility.

Philosophies of Education
The educational philosophies—perennialism, progressivism, essentialism, and postmodernism—are rooted in the traditional philosophies. Perennialism, as with idealism and realism, focuses on time-honored absolutes. Progressivism, rooted in pragmatism, views goals as dynamic and emphasizes that learning should be experience-based and relevant to students' lives. Postmodernism sees schools and other institutions in need of restructuring, with marginalized people and their works elevated to more prominent positions in the content of schooling.

Developing as a Professional: Forming a Personal Philosophy
When professionals form philosophies, they first identify their beliefs and then examine those beliefs to determine if they're valid. Once a coherent system of beliefs is identified, the beliefs are compiled into an internally consistent view of what the goals of the profession ought to be and what they can do to promote those outcomes. In education, this means that professionals consider what kinds of learning should take place, what conditions will best promote that learning, and what they can do to create those conditions.

IMPORTANT CONCEPTS

axiology
character education
epistemology
essentialism
existentialism
idealism
logic
metaphysics
moral education
normative philosophy
ontology
perennialism
philosophy
philosophy of education
postmodernism
pragmatism
progressivism
realism
theory

DISCUSSION QUESTIONS

1. Philosophy has four basic areas: epistemology, ontology, axiology, and logic. Which of these is most useful for teachers? Least useful?
2. Technology is becoming increasingly important in society as well as in education. Which of the four philosophies of education—perennialism, progressivism, essentialism, or postmodernism—is most compatible with applications of technology in education? Least compatible?
3. Our students are becoming increasingly diverse. How well do the different philosophies of education address issues of student diversity?
4. Which philosophy of education has the most support in the geographic area in which you plan to teach? What evidence do you have for your conclusion?
5. Of the different philosophies discussed in this chapter, which is most valuable in framing issues for preschool children? Middle school students? High school

students? Does one particular philosophy fit with a content area that you will be teaching?

6. Public school teachers rated the following educational goals in the following order of importance (U.S. Department of Education, 1993):

Goal	*Rank*
Building literacy skills	1
Promoting personal growth	2
Promoting good work habits and self-discipline	3
Encouraging academic excellence	4
Promoting occupational or vocational skills	5

What do these rankings tell us about teachers' philosophical positions?

GOING INTO SCHOOLS

1. Interview a teacher and ask the following questions:
   a. What are your most important goals for your students?
   b. What do you emphasize the most in your curriculum?
   c. What do you think is your major role as a teacher?
   d. What is the primary teaching method that you use? Why do you use it?
   e. What are your major classroom-management goals? How do you implement them?
   f. How do you assess student learning?

   Based on the teacher's responses, which of the educational philosophies is most nearly reflected in his or her teaching? If possible, share your analysis with the teacher and discuss your conclusions.
2. Observe a lesson at a grade level or in a content area in which you plan to teach. Describe the teacher's classroom and lesson with respect to the following:
   a. Arrangement of desks: How are the desks arranged?
   b. Explaining versus questioning: Does the teacher primarily lecture and explain, or does the teacher ask a large number of questions?
   c. Student motivation: Does the teacher provide a rationale at the beginning of the lesson that explains why the lesson is important?
   d. Use of examples: Does the teacher use examples, or is the information presented primarily in verbal form?
   e. Classroom order: Are the students orderly and attentive during the lesson? How does the teacher attempt to accomplish this?
   f. Assessment: How does the teacher measure student understanding?

   What do these indicators suggest about the teacher's educational philosophy? If possible, share your analysis with the teacher and discuss your conclusions.
3. Locate a social studies or literature text for a level at which you'll be teaching (for example, elementary or high school). Examine how the text treats the relative contributions of males versus females, minorities versus non-minorities. Does the inclusion of topics or literary selections suggest a perennialist or postmodern philosophy? Defend your answer with specific examples from the text.
4. Locate the teacher's edition of a textbook for a subject or grade level that you'll be teaching. (Every book series comes with a teacher's edition that contains suggestions for how to teach the subject.) These can be obtained from a teacher, in a school-district curriculum library, or in the curriculum library at your college or university.

Read the introduction to the text and identify elements of the following educational philosophies: perennialsm, progressivism, essentialism, and postmodernism. How well does the text match your own developing educational philosophy?

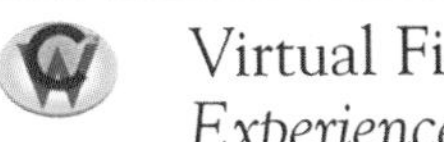

If you would like to participate in a Virtual Field Experience, go to the *Field Experience* Module in Chapter 6 of the Companion Website.

ONLINE PORTFOLIO ACTIVITIES

To complete these activities online, go to the *Portfolio Activities* Module in Chapter 6 of the Companion Website and submit your response.

Portfolio Activity 6.1

Describing Your Philosophy of Education

INTASC Principle 9: *Commitment*
The purpose of this activity is to assist you in developing your philosophy of education. List your beliefs with respect to learning, learners, and teaching. Then, based on the list, write a two-page description of your philosophy of education as it presently exists.

Portfolio Activity 6.2

Assessing Your Philosophy of Education

INTASC Principle 9: *Commitment*
The purpose of this activity is to assist you in developing your own philosophy of education. To assess your developing philosophy of education, respond to the following statements and then answer the questions that follow. Use the following scale in making your responses:

1 = Strongly disagree
2 = Disagree
3 = Neither agree nor disagree
4 = Agree
5 = Strongly agree

1. Schools should emphasize important knowledge more than students' personal interests. 1 2 3 4 5
2. Teachers should emphasize interdisciplinary subject matter that encourages project-oriented, democratic classrooms. 1 2 3 4 5
3. Schools should emphasize the search for personal meaning more than a fixed body of subject matter. 1 2 3 4 5
4. The primary aim of education is to develop a person's intellectual capacity. 1 2 3 4 5
5. Schools should emphasize basic skills more than humanistic ideals. 1 2 3 4 5
6. Teachers should guide student learning rather than lecture and disseminate information. 1 2 3 4 5
7. The best teachers encourage personal responses and develop critical awareness in their students. 1 2 3 4 5

8. The goals of education should be similar for everyone; all students should understand the important literature, mathematics, and science of Western civilization.	1 2 3 4 5
9. The purpose of schools is to ensure practical preparation for life and work more than personal development.	1 2 3 4 5
10. Curriculum should emerge from students' needs and interests; it *should not* be prescribed in advance.	1 2 3 4 5
11. The best education emphasizes the great works in the arts and humanities.	1 2 3 4 5
12. It is more important for teachers to involve students in activities that analyze and criticize society than to accumulate a lot of information.	1 2 3 4 5
13. Education should enhance personal growth through problem solving in the present more than emphasizing preparation for a distant future.	1 2 3 4 5
14. Human nature's most distinctive quality is the ability to reason; therefore, the intellect should be the focus of education.	1 2 3 4 5
15. Schools often perpetuate racism and sexism that is camouflaged as traditional values.	1 2 3 4 5
16. Teachers should help students learn a common core of knowledge, *not* experiment with their own views about curricula.	1 2 3 4 5

Source: Adapted from Leahy (1995).

Now add up your responses in the appropriate boxes (Strongly disagree = 1; Disagree = 2; Neither agree nor disagree = 3; Agree = 4; Strongly agree = 5).

Perennialism:

Item #4 ____ + #8 ____ + #11 ____ + #14 ____ = ____

Progressivism:

Item #2 ____ + #6 ____ + #10 ____ + #13 ____ = ____

Essentialism:

Item #1 ____ + #5 ____ + # 9 ____ + #16 ____ = ____

Postmodernism:

Item #3 ____ + #7 ____ + #12 ____ + #15 ____ = ____

1. Do you think the survey results accurately reflect your philosophy of education? Why?
2. How are the results from this survey similar to and different from your philosophy of education as you described it in Portfolio Activity 6.1?
3. Why do you think the differences exist?
4. Now, using your scores as the basis, summarize what this survey suggests about your developing philosophy of education.

Portfolio Activity 6.3

Assessing an Instructor's Philosophy of Education

INTASC Principle 9: *Commitment*

The purpose of this activity is to help you see how educational philosophies influence teaching practices. Think about an instructor in one of your classes. Based on your observations of the instructor and the way he or she teaches, describe in one page what you believe to be the instructor's philosophy of education.

After you've completed the description, share it with the instructor. Ask if he or she believes that the description is accurate, and if not, to explain why it isn't.

Case STUDY

"Wow, noon. I need to get going," Chris Lucio said to his colleague April Jackson as he jumped up from the couch in the teacher's lounge, finishing the last bite of his lunch. "My kids will be chomping at the bit trying to get into the room."

Chris hurriedly left the lounge, stopped by the main office to take a quick look in his box to check for notes, phone messages, and mail, and then walked across the courtyard to his building.

Chris is a seventh-grade geography teacher at Lakeside Junior High, one of three junior high schools in Orange Park, a suburb of a large eastern city. Originally a middle school, the 30-year-old Lakeside campus is composed of four main buildings surrounding a center courtyard. A gymnasium and fine arts building, built 10 years ago when Lakeside became a junior high school, sit outside the main buildings, and baseball, softball, and soccer fields, together with tennis courts, complete the campus. The administrative building houses the principal's and other administrators' offices, the cafeteria, which—with a stage on one end—doubles as an auditorium, and the media center and computer lab holding 30 computers. Classrooms are in the other three buildings.

Architectural designs for schools vary, and the Lakeside campus is somewhat atypical. Commonly, schools are housed within a single building that has different wings, or they're in squares or rectangles that enclose courtyards.

"Okay everyone, the bell is going to ring in a couple minutes . . . find your seats quickly," Chris calls out, unlocking the door to his room.

"Mr. Lucio, can I go to the bathroom?" Armondo asks as he stands by the open door.

"Hurry, you don't want to be tardy," Chris responds with a smile.

"This split lunch is a pain," Chris thinks, as the last of the students slide into their seats. It takes me 10 minutes to get the kids settled down after lunch, so we're always wasting time.

"On the other hand, I better not complain. I have a great schedule . . . one prep . . . three advanced and two standard classes. . . . It doesn't get much better than that."

"Are you going to come to our track meet this afternoon?" Devon, another of Chris's students, asks as he enters the room. "We're going to kick butt on Ridgeview."

"Wouldn't miss it," Chris smiles back as he thinks, "Yikes, I almost forgot. . . I promised Joe and Karen [the boys' and girls' track coaches] that I'd be a timer for the 100 and 200."

"What time does it start?" Chris asks Devon.

"Right after school; 4 o'clock, I think."

The split lunch that Chris complains about shapes the schedule at Lakeside. It rotates from day to day and can be seen in the schedule below.

Time	Period				
	Monday	Tuesday	Wednesday	Thursday	Friday
9:20–10:05	1	6	5	4	2
10:10–11:00	2	1	6	5	4
11:05–11:30 A	3	3	3	3	3
11:35–12:05 B					
12:10–12:40 C					
12:45–1:35	4	2	1	6	5
1:40–2:30	5	4	2	1	6
2:35–3:25	6	5	4	2	1

The rationale for the rotating schedule is the belief that students are most alert in the morning and least alert late in the day. If sixth period were always from 2:35–3:25, for example, students in that class would be at a learning disadvantage.

Lakeside's schedule has third period split for lunch, giving the students about a half hour to eat and relax. One-third of the students eat during A lunch, another third during B lunch, and the last third during C lunch. Third period doesn't rotate; school officials chose to keep it this way for the sake of simplicity. Chris and his third period class eat during B lunch.

"The schedule is fine . . . other than the split lunch," Chris shrugs when asked about it. "Once the kids got used to it, it was no big deal."

■ ■ ■

WHAT IS A SCHOOL?

Increasing Understanding 7.1

Would a *family* be considered a social institution? Why?
To answer this question online and receive immediate feedback, go to the *Increasing Understanding* Module in Chapter 7 of the Companion Website at **http://www.prenhall.com/kauchak.**

We've all gone to school; in fact, if you're in your mid-twenties or younger, you've spent more than half of your life in school. But exactly what is a school, and what does it mean to teach and learn in one? We consider these questions in this section.

The notion of *school* has different meanings. At a simple level, it is a physical place—a building or set of buildings. At another level, it is a place students go to learn. For example, churches have vacation Bible *school*, and we've all heard of students being home *schooled*.

At a third level, school is a **social institution,** which is *an organization with established structures and rules designed to promote certain goals*. Schools are social institutions, and promoting both students' growth and development and the well-being of a country and its citizens are its goals.

A number of social institutions exist in all societies. Churches or religions are social institutions, as are governments. They are organizations intended to make society a better place in which to live.

Using the idea of schools as social institutions as a frame of reference, this chapter looks at the way schools are organized. Some ways of organizing them are better than others, and these differences influence how much students learn and how well they develop. These differences will also influence your life as a teacher. That's why you're studying this topic.

A school is intended to operate as a relatively independent unit within a **school district,** which is *an administrative unit within a geographical area given the responsibility for education within its borders*. A school district may encompass an entire county, or large counties may be divided into more than one district.

School districts vary in a number of ways, including size and clientele. For example, Dade County, Florida, is a large district with a student population that is predominantly comprised of cultural minorities (over 83 percent), whereas Minot, North Dakota, is a small district with few minorities (U.S. Department of Education, 1996). In some districts, the majority of students are eligible for free lunch, and in other, wealthier districts, virtually none of the students are.

You will study school districts, how they're organized, and how they're governed in detail in Chapter 8. What is important now is to remember that individual schools are part of a larger organizational framework called a district. To learn more about school districts where you might want to teach, access the *Web Links* Module of the Companion Website at **http://www.prenhall.com/kauchak.**

Let's turn now to the organization of individual schools.

THE ORGANIZATION OF SCHOOLS

Think about the schools you attended as a student or schools you've visited as part of your teacher-preparation program. If the organization was typical for American schools, you first went to an elementary school, which began with kindergarten, or even pre-kindergarten,

The central office is a school's nerve center; the office staff plays an important role in greeting guests and assisting both teachers and students.

followed by first grade, second grade, and so on. You then went to a middle school or junior high school, and finally to a high school.

Let's look at the way these schools are organized, and why they're organized this way. In looking at this organization, we'll examine:

- Personnel
- The physical plant
- Curriculum organization

Personnel

No school is any better than the people who work there. This includes all the people—the administrators, the support staff, and the teachers. Each has a role in making a school an effective social institution.

Administrators and Support Staff All schools—elementary, middle, junior high, and high schools—have **administrators,** *individuals who are responsible for the day-to-day operation of the school.* The administrators include a **principal,** *the individual given the ultimate responsibility for the school's operation,* and probably an assistant principal or vice principal (or both) who supports the principal in his or her work. Lakeside, for example, has a vice principal and two assistant principals. The vice principal's responsibilities include scheduling, collecting student records (such as grades) from teachers, keeping master records for the school, and maintaining communication with district-level administrators and parents. One of the assistant principals manages the physical plant; responsibilities may include distributing lockers to students, coordinating the duties of the custodial staff, and overseeing all maintenance and construction. The other assistant principal is in charge of discipline (including referrals as well as in-school and out-of-school suspension of students), ordering and distributing textbooks to department heads, and maintaining in-service records for teachers.

Depending on the size of the school and the organization of the school district, schools may also have school counselors, school psychologists, and health-care providers, such as school nurses. Their roles will be determined by the school's and district's size and organization. Lakeside, for example, has two full-time guidance counselors and a school psychologist that it shares with other schools. The guidance counselors schedule and coordinate the statewide assessment tests and provide a variety of information about course offerings and future options for students. The school psychologist administers individualized intelligence tests, which are used for making decisions about placing students into programs for the gifted and talented or for students with learning disabilities. The school psychologist also provides individual counseling for students having emotional problems and makes recommendations for further mental-health assistance.

Increasing Understanding 7.2

What is the most likely reason that school policies are so rigid with respect to administering any form of medication?

The school also has a full-time, licensed practical nurse. She maintains all student health records, is trained in administering CPR, supervises medical evacuations, and disseminates all medications to students. Students at Lakeside are forbidden from taking even an over-the-counter pain killer, such as an Advil, on their own, and teachers may not give students any form of medication.

In addition, all schools have support staff, which may include the following:

- Secretaries and receptionists, who greet visitors when they come to the school.
- Administrative and instructional support staff, who complete paperwork for the principal and other administrators, duplicate tests and handouts for teachers, and maintain payroll records and other functions.
- Media center specialists, who handle books and different forms of technology.
- Physical plant staff, such as janitors who clean the rooms and buildings and cafeteria workers who prepare school lunches.

Increasing Understanding 7.3

School organizations are more complex than they were in the past. Think about your study of Chapters 3 and 4 and explain why this is likely the case.

Curriculum Specialists Many elementary schools have teachers who specialize in a particular area, such as technology, art, or music; these teachers coordinate their efforts with classroom teachers. For example, schedules are coordinated so that all students can visit a computer center, where the technology specialist works with them for a certain amount of time each day or each week.

Why are we presenting this information? In other words, what difference does it make if you know about the other personnel working in your school and what their roles are?

Here's why. A school is a social institution whose organization is complex, and all the people working in it must contribute to making the school run smoothly. As a teacher, your ability to work with the other personnel in the school will influence how effective you and the school can be. For example, if you have a student who is so unruly that you can't work with him or her in your classroom, you need the support of the assistant principal and/or school psychologist to help you deal with the problem. Although you will probably teach in your classroom without any other adult, your effectiveness in the school will depend on your ability to work with a number of different people.

In addition, a common adage suggests that you can tell a great deal about the social and emotional climate in a school by observing the way a school receptionist greets students and visitors when they enter the school or main office. You also help set the tone for a supportive climate in the way you treat support staff and how important you make them feel. Teachers who request—instead of demand—services, such as having a test duplicated, make support staff realize that they're contributing to the overall functioning of the school. All the personnel in a school working together for the benefit of students is the most important factor in making effective schools what they are.

Teachers' responsibilities extend beyond their classrooms and include ensuring that the total school facility is a safe and productive place to learn.

The Physical Plant

Schools typically have classrooms, hallways that allow students to move from one room to another, a central administrative office, and one or more large rooms, such as auditoriums, gymnasiums, music rooms, and cafeterias. The physical organization of schools has often been criticized for its box-like structure, with hall upon hall of separate "cells." Critics contend that this structure leads to isolation between teachers and fragmentation in the curriculum. When teachers retreat into their classrooms and close their doors, no one else may know what goes on in there.

In elementary schools, space is available for staff parking, playgrounds, and a driveway used for dropping off and picking up students. Junior high and high schools will have playing fields for football, baseball, softball, and soccer, some will have swimming pools, and high schools will have parking spaces available for students who drive their own cars to school. (Some middle schools, because of a philosophical opposition to competition, may not have gymnasiums or other facilities that support competitive activities.)

Increasing Understanding 7.4

Strong efforts are being made in many areas to eliminate the use of portables or temporaries. Identify at least two reasons why this would be the case.

School enrollments often increase so rapidly that physical plants can't keep up. As a result, many schools have "temporaries," individual buildings on the perimeter of school campuses that provide additional classroom space.

What does the physical arrangement of a school mean for you as a teacher? It means at least two things. First, when you're in your classroom and shut the door (as many teachers do), you're essentially on your own. For example, you may be responsible for 20 to 30 second graders all day, every day. A similar situation exists for middle and secondary teachers. You'll be in the confines of your classroom, where you'll be responsible for the education and safety of five or six different classes of eighth graders or eleventh graders, again, essentially on your own.

However, your responsibility isn't limited to your classroom. If you teach in an elementary school, you'll also be responsible for escorting your students from your room to the cafeteria and back, or from your classroom to the media center and back. If you're a middle or secondary teacher, you'll be expected to monitor students as they move through the hallways and attend assemblies in the auditorium. You may also sell tickets at football games, attend track meets, and go to band concerts. Though your primary responsibilities will be to the students in the classroom, you will also be expected to contribute to the governance and running of the school. All these responsibilities result from the ways schools are organized.

Curriculum Organization

We said earlier in the chapter that schools are social institutions, organizations whose purpose is to help young people grow and develop and prepare them to function effectively in today's (and tomorrow's) world. To function effectively in today's technologically oriented and fast-changing world, students' need to acquire essential knowledge and skills. The task for educators is to organize the **curriculum**—*what teachers teach and what students learn*—in a way that maximizes students' opportunities to master the material and to grow and develop.

How do schools organize the curriculum to accomplish this? As an example, let's consider the following goals:

- Students will be able to recognize the letters of the alphabet.
- Students will be able to read and understand sentences such as "Antonio and Carol worked together on their art project."
- Students will be able to simplify the expression $9 + 4(7 - 3)/2$.
- Students will be able to determine how far a ball has traveled after falling freely for 3 seconds (assuming air resistance is negligible).

These goals, which are part of an overall school curriculum, provide direction for teachers as they consider what to teach.

Historically, educators have decided that the most efficient way of helping students reach these goals is to classify what teachers teach according to different grade levels and ages of students. For instance, a child in kindergarten is expected to reach the first goal, third graders the second, seventh graders in pre-algebra the third, and high school juniors taking physics, the fourth.

School Organization and the Curriculum What is the most effective way to group teachers and students in order to help students learn the content of the curriculum? For instance, does it make sense to have 6 year olds in the same building and walking the same hallways as 17 year olds? Safety, as well as seemingly mundane concerns like the height of drinking fountains and toilets, suggests no.

In general, most school systems are organized into three levels—elementary schools for younger children, middle or junior high schools for young adolescents, and high schools for later adolescents. Despite this general agreement about the three levels, as a teacher you may encounter any number of organizational patterns when you teach. Table 7.1 outlines some of these variations. Other forms of organization exist, of course, but the ones you see in Table 7.1 are the most common.

What do educators use as the basis for making decisions about organizing schools? For example, why do middle schools typically include grades 6, 7, and 8, or grades 7 and 8? Two factors are most common: the developmental characteristics of students as well as economics and politics.

Developmental Characteristics of Students **Development** refers to *the physical changes in children as well as changes in the way they think and relate to their peers that result from maturation and experience*. For example, fifth graders are typically bigger, stronger, and more coordinated than first graders; they are physically more *developed*. Similarly, typical fifth graders think differently than do first graders. When shown the following drawing,

Table 7.1 Common Ways to Organize Schools

School Level	Grade Ranges
Elementary School	K–3 K–5 K–6
Middle School	5–8 6–8 7–8
Junior High School	7–8 7–9 8–9
High School	9–12 10–12

typical first graders conclude that Block A is heavier than Block B, because their thinking tends to focus on size—the most obvious aspect of the balance and blocks. Fifth graders, on the other hand, are more likely to realize that the blocks have the same weight, because they recognize that the balance is balanced (level). Their thinking is more *developed*.

Increasing Understanding 7.5

In Chapter 5, we learned that organizing elementary schools into grade levels occurred during the common school movement, which began about 1830. What was the rationale at that time for organizing elementary schools this way?

Differences in social development also exist. For example, when faced with a disagreement about who in a group gets to report on which topic, a fifth grader is more likely to step back, recognize the others' perspectives, and compromise. Socially, fifth graders are more capable of considering where a classmate is "coming from," whereas first graders tend to be more self-centered in their thinking. These differences in social development provide teachers with opportunities to use teaching strategies, such as certain forms of cooperative learning, with older children that might be less effective with younger, less socially developed students.

Similar differences can be found between fifth graders and tenth or eleventh graders. Physically, the older students are young men and women, many think quite abstractly, and they are socially skilled. These developmental differences lead to important differences in the ways schools are organized. For example, students in elementary schools are typically assigned to one teacher who looks after the cognitive, social, and emotional growth of the students. As students mature and their abilities to learn on their own and fend for themselves develop, they are assigned to a number of teachers who also serve as subject-matter specialists.

Economics and Politics Economics and politics are also factors that influence decisions about school organization. As an example, let's look again at Chris's school, Lakeside Junior High School.

When Lakeside was planned over 30 years ago, the middle school movement was gathering momentum. (We discuss middle schools in the next section.) Mary Zellner, who was to be Lakeside's first principal, was an outspoken proponent of middle schools, and she was a respected leader in district politics. Because of her influence, Lakeside was built according to middle school philosophy, part of which de-emphasized competition between students. As a result, the school didn't have competitive athletics, which was the reason the school didn't originally have a gymnasium.

Problems then arose. Orange Park High School, the only high school in the district at the time, became overcrowded because of rapid population growth in the city. District officials solved the problem temporarily by moving sixth graders back to the elementary schools. (The elementary schools were able to absorb them because the students could be distributed among the eight elementary schools in the district.) The middle schools were then converted to junior high schools that housed grades 7, 8, and 9.

Increasing Understanding 7.6

Are organizational decisions based on the developmental characteristics of students more likely to occur in suburban or inner-city schools? Explain why this is likely the case.

The move was also hailed by high school coaches, who claimed that Orange Park High was at a disadvantage because potential athletes came to them without the athletic experiences students attending competing schools enjoyed. These pressures occur nationwide; presently 80 percent of middle-level schools in the United States offer organized competitive sports (Swain, McEwin & Irvin, 1998).

The decision to change the organizational structure was based primarily on economics (with some additional political pressure from high school coaches); it had little to do with the developmental needs of students. Unfortunately, decisions like this are quite common in education.

Let's keep these factors in mind as we look at schools in more depth. We begin by looking at early-childhood programs and elementary schools, and then turn to schools for older students, including high schools, junior highs, and middle schools.

EARLY-CHILDHOOD PROGRAMS

Most of you reading this book probably attended kindergarten, and some of you may have even gone to pre-kindergarten. However, one of your authors, educated in a small town in a predominantly rural area, attended neither, because they weren't offered there at the time.

Early-childhood education is *a catch-all term encompassing a range of educational programs for young children including infant intervention and enrichment programs, preschools, public and private pre-kindergartens and kindergartens, and federally funded Project Head Start.* Early childhood education is a mid-20th-century development in this country, although its philosophical roots go back 250 years. The French philosopher Rousseau suggested:

> Do not treat the child to discourses which he cannot understand. No descriptions, no eloquence, no figures of speech. . . . In general, let us never substitute the sign for the thing, except when it is impossible for us to show the thing. . . . Things! Things! I shall never tire of saying that we ascribe too much importance to words (Compayre, 1888).

In saying "Things! Things!" Rousseau was arguing that young children need to play and work with concrete objects rather than being taught with abstract words. This idea is consistent with the need for concrete experiences that the famous developmental psychologist Jean Piaget (1952, 1970) emphasized, and it is at the core of developmentally appropriate kindergarten and early-childhood education.

Developmental programs *accommodate children's developmental differences by allowing children to acquire skills and abilities at their own pace through direct experiences.* Visitors in a developmental classroom are likely to see learning centers around the room that have activities for the children. For instance, one might have a tub of water and items that the

Self-contained elementary schools attempt to meet young students' developmental needs.

children test to see if they sink or float. Another might have a series of big books with pictures and large-print words. A third might have a series of blocks that children use to construct towers and other structures. Instead of traditional teacher-centered instruction, the teacher's role is to provide experiences for children and encourage exploration.

For more information about different early childhood education programs, visit the Website of the National Association for the Education of Young Children (NAEYC), the largest professional association for early-children education. This Website can be found in the *Web Links* Module in Chapter 7 of the Companion Website at **http://www.prenhall.com/kauchak.**

The need for learning-related experiences early in life is increasingly recognized (Ball, 1992; Hartnett & Gelman, 1998), and the benefits of early intervention programs are long-lasting. In a follow-up study of a program emphasizing language skills for pre-K and kindergarten children, researchers found that participants in their 20s had higher test scores in reading and math and were far more likely to attend college than peers who had not participated in the program (Jacobson, 2000b).

A more ambitious program in North Carolina provided nutritional help and social services to children from birth, as well as parenting lessons and a language-oriented preschool program (Jacobson, 1999). Follow-up studies revealed that participants scored higher on intelligence and achievement tests, were twice as likely to attend post-secondary education, and delayed having children by 2 years versus non-program counterparts. Early-childhood education programs pay off, not only in terms of immediate school success but also later in life. In recognition of this, a number of states, including New York and Georgia, are moving towards making preschool accessible to all students (Jacobson, 2000c).

By the mid 1990s, fewer than half of all 5 year olds in the United States were attending full-time programs (U.S. Department of Education, 1996), but this is rapidly changing, with much greater emphasis now being placed on early intervention programs. As full-time pre-K programs become increasingly common, job opportunities in these areas will grow. For more information about this and other early intervention programs, go to the *Web Links* Module in Chapter 7 of the Companion Website at **http://www.prenhall.com/kauchak.**

Table 7.2 **Schedules for Two Elementary School Teachers**

A First-Grade Schedule		A Third-Grade Schedule	
8:30 A.M.	School begins	8:30 A.M.	School begins
8:30–8:45	Morning announcements	8:30–9:15	Independent work (practice previous day's math)
8:45–10:30	Language arts (including reading and writing)	9:15–10:20	Language arts (including reading and writing)
10:30–11:20	Math	10:20–10:45	Snack/independent reading
11:20–11:50	Lunch	10:45–11:15	P.E.
11:50–12:20	Read story	11:15–12:15	Language arts/social studies/science
12:20–1:15	Center time (practice on language arts and math)	12:15–12:45	Lunch
1:15–1:45	P.E.	12:45–2:00	Math
1:45–2:30	Social studies/science	2:00–2:30	Spelling/catch up on material not covered earlier
2:30–2:45	Class meeting	2:30–2:45	Read story
2:45–3:00	Call buses/dismissal	2:45–3:00	Clean up/prepare for dismissal

ELEMENTARY SCHOOLS

To begin our examination of elementary schools, let's look at the schedules of two elementary teachers and see how they relate to the organization of elementary schools. The schedules are outlined in Table 7.2. Examine them and see what you notice.

Some observations might include the following:

- Both teachers are responsible for all the content areas, such as reading, language arts, math, science, and social studies.
- Their schedules are quite different. Although both teach young children, Sharon, the first-grade teacher, begins with language arts, while Susie, the third-grade teacher, begins by having the children practice their previous day's math.
- The amount of time they allocate to each of the content areas is a personal decision. Susie, for example, devotes 50 minutes to math, whereas Sharon teaches math for 75 minutes.

In addition, both teachers noted that these schedules were approximate and often changed depending on their perception of students' needs and the day of the week. For example, if students were having trouble with a math topic, they might devote more time to math on a given day. (S. Mittelstadt, personal communication, January 22, 1999; S. Van Horn, personal communication, January 21, 1999).

If you observe in elementary classrooms, you're likely to see schedules that vary somewhat from the ones in Table 7.2. This individual teacher freedom and autonomy is characteristic of elementary school organization.

Why are elementary schools organized this way? First, recall the history of elementary schools: typically, a single teacher has been responsible for all of the content areas. We also saw in Chapter 5 that until about the mid-1800s, elementary schools weren't even organized into grade levels; in fact, a single teacher was responsible for all grade levels and content areas in many rural, one-room schools. As you can see, history has influenced the way elementary schools are organized.

Developmental characteristics of the students also influence elementary schools' organization. We saw earlier that young children look, think, and interact with their peers in ways that are different from older students. Educational leaders have historically believed that young children need the stability of one teacher and a single classroom to function most effectively in school. Schools can be frightening places for little children; self-contained classrooms provide emotional security for young learners. Further, simply moving from room to room, as middle and secondary students do, can be difficult for young children. Imagine a first grader going to room 101 for math, room 108 for language arts, and so on. A rotating schedule, such as Lakeside's, would be even more confusing.

Increasing Understanding 7.7

In both Sharon's and Susie's schedules, shown in Table 7.2, reading, language arts, and math are strongly emphasized. On which of the educational philosophies that you studied in Chapter 6 is this emphasis most likely based?

This thinking has been questioned by other educators. For example, expecting one teacher to be knowledgeable enough to effectively teach reading, language arts, math, science, and social studies is asking almost the impossible. As a result, some content areas—frequently science, social studies, art, and music—are de-emphasized by teachers who feel uncomfortable teaching in these areas. So educators, teachers, and parents face a dilemma. Is the social and emotional well-being of students more important than content? Historically, the answer has been "Yes."

HIGH SCHOOLS, JUNIOR HIGH SCHOOLS, AND MIDDLE SCHOOLS

To see differences between elementary schools and middle, junior high, and high schools, we only need to compare Chris's experiences (in the chapter opening case) to Susie's and Sharon's. We saw that elementary teachers typically teach all the content areas and set their own schedules. Also, they are responsible for monitoring their students outside the classroom, such as walking with them to the cafeteria.

In contrast, Chris taught only geography, and he (along with all the other teachers in his school) followed a specific, predetermined schedule. The lengths of the periods were uniform for all the content areas, and the beginnings and endings were signaled by a bell. Also, Chris was not responsible for monitoring his students as they moved from place to place on the Lakeside campus, but he was involved in extracurricular activities (like the track meet) that are part of middle schools, junior highs, and high schools.

Increasing Understanding 7.8

Think again about your study of Chapter 5. Identify three reasons that educational leaders decided that all students—college-bound and non-college-bound—should take the same curriculum.

Why are these upper levels organized this way? To answer this question, let's think back to our definition of schools and remember that they're social institutions—organizations whose purpose is to further the development of children and the welfare of society. Recall from Chapter 5 that views about the role of education have changed over time. For instance, in colonial times, people felt that society would most benefit from having students learn to read and understand the Bible. Much later (near the end of the 19th century), educators felt that society would benefit most by having both college-bound and non-college-bound students take the same curriculum, believing that mental discipline was a primary function of education. Also, schools were reorganized to accommodate the large influx of immigrants, with the goal of helping them assimilate into American society.

As educational thinking continued to change, leaders felt that society needed citizens well-schooled in a variety of practical topics. This emphasis on subject-matter mastery resulted in the departmentalization found in the junior high schools and the high schools that you most likely attended. Let's look at the organization of these schools, starting with high schools.

The Comprehensive High School

Most of you probably attended a **comprehensive high school,** *one designed to meet the needs of all students*. In attempting to do this, most high schools are organized into tracks (Oakes, 1992, 1995). College-bound students study in a college-preparatory track, which

Extracurricular activities provide valuable learning opportunities in areas not typically tapped by traditional classrooms.

allows them to take courses designed to get them ready for college-level work. It might include **advanced placement classes** in English, history, chemistry, or biology; *these courses allow students to earn college credit while still in high school, making college less time-consuming and expensive*. A general track composed of "standard" classes is designed for students of average ability who may or may not go on to college. Students in this track may take some vocational courses, such as word processing or woodworking, designed to provide them with practical skills they can use immediately after graduating, either at home or on a job. A vocational track specifically targets students not going to college, preparing them for careers in areas like automobile repair or technology.

Extracurricular activities such as band, chorus, and athletics like basketball, swimming, soccer, and tennis are also available. These options are intended to help all students develop intellectually, socially, and personally. Educational leaders believe that the more fully developed students are when they leave high school, the better equipped they will be to succeed in college or immediately contribute to society.

Criticisms of the Comprehensive High School Can a comprehensive high school be all things to all students? Critics say no and focus on two factors: tracking and size.

One of the paradoxes of the comprehensive high school is that different tracks, designed to present quality alternatives, often produce exactly the opposite. Research indicates that instead of providing freedom and choice, tracking segregates students, often leaving many with substandard educational experiences (Oakes, 1992, 1995). Lower-ability, minority, and low-SES students are often steered into vocational or lower-level tracks, where the curriculum is less challenging and instruction is often poor. Instead of effectively preparing students for the world of work, lower tracks often segregate students from their college-bound peers and communicate that challenge and deep understanding are not for them.

A second criticism of high schools relates to size and the impersonal nature of life in many large high schools. As schools become larger, they also can become more impersonal and bureaucratic. One study compared large American high schools to shopping malls in which students mill around looking for entertainment and educational bargains (Powell, Farrar, & Cohen, 1985). Like smart shoppers, the brighter students (or their parents) know what they want and quickly find the more challenging, college-preparatory courses. Lower achievers get lost in the shuffle, spending time but not receiving a quality education.

Concrete suggestions to address these problems came from former President Bill Clinton's Secretary of Education, Richard W. Riley (Sack, 1999). He suggested that high schools should do the following:

- Create schools-within-schools to make them smaller and more personal.
- Turn homeroom periods into student-advisory periods where students can get to know teachers and discuss events relevant to their lives.
- Allow students to keep the same counselor for the entire four years.

Interestingly, these suggestions are similar to ones offered to make junior high schools and middle schools more user-friendly.

Junior High Schools

In Chapter 5, we saw that schools in the early 20th century were organized into eight elementary and four high school grades. This 8–4 organization changed when emphasis shifted away from basic skills, such as reading and math, and moved toward the more intensive study of content, like history, literature, and science. In-depth study of content areas required teachers to be subject-matter experts. In addition, a growing recognition of the unique needs of early adolescents was being realized. The result was the development of the "junior" high school.

Most junior high schools today have a variety of offerings—although not as comprehensive as those in high schools—and they include competitive athletics and other extracurricular activities. Though initially designed to help students make the transition between elementary and high schools, they are in every sense of the word "junior" high schools; this is the environment in which Chris is teaching.

Middle Schools

Think back to the friends you knew when you were in the sixth, seventh, or eighth grades. Some of the girls were young women, fully developed physically and emotionally, while others were still little girls. Some boys needed to shave, whereas others looked like fifth graders. Many of the boys and girls were becoming more and more attracted to each other, and others were kind of attracted to the other sex but didn't know why. This is the transitional period of early adolescence.

Because of the rapid physical, emotional, and intellectual changes that early adolescents experience, it is a unique period in their development. Other than infancy, at no time in a person's life is change so rapid or profound. As a result, many educators believe that schools should be organized to meet the unique needs of students during this time in their lives.

The result of this thinking, and the fact that junior high schools weren't meeting early adolescents' needs, led to the formation of **middle schools,** *schools specifically designed to meet the needs of early adolescents and help them make the transition from elementary to high schools*. What does teaching in a middle school "look" like? Let's look at an example.

Case STUDY

Robin West is an eighth-grade teacher in an inner-city middle school. She teaches physical science, and she and her team members have a common planning period. They teach the same group of students and often spend their planning period discussing the students and the topics each is teaching. A number of their students are not native English speakers, and the teachers' discussions often center on what can be done to help students with language problems. In addition, Robin has four students with learning disabilities in her classroom. The teachers try to integrate topics across as many of the four areas as often as possible.

"Can you help me out with anything on graphing?" Mary, the math teacher, asked the others one Monday. "The kids just see graphs as some meaningless lines. I explain the heck out of them, but it doesn't seem to help all that much."

"I know what I can do," Robin offered, after thinking for a few seconds. "I'll do some simple demonstrations and then have them link the demonstration to a graph. . . . Here, look," and she dropped her pen. She then drew a sketch (shown below) on a piece of paper.

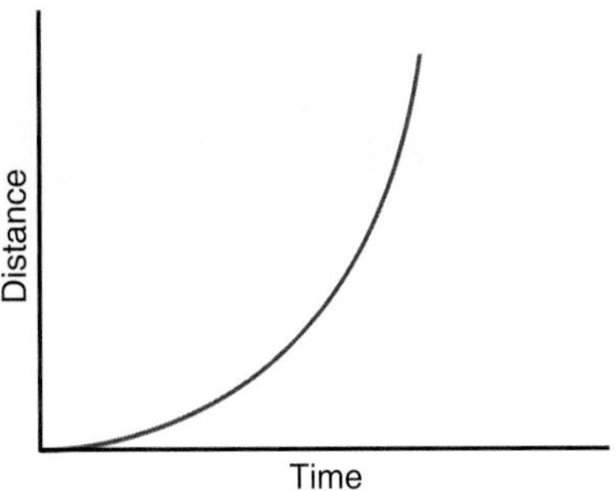

"The graph represents the distance–time relationship when the pen falls," she went on. "Time is on the horizontal axis and distance is on the vertical axis. . . . I'll do this with the kids, and you can refer to what I did when you do your work on graphs," she added, nodding to Mary.

"Great. Thanks. . . . When will you do it?"

"We're between units now, so I can do it tomorrow. . . . Then you and I can talk about it after school for a few minutes, and I'll let you know how it went. . . . By the way, how is Lorraine Williams doing in math?"

"Not good," Mary responded. "In fact, I was going to ask you all about her. She hasn't been turning in her homework, and she seems only 'half there' in class."

"Same thing in history," Keith added. "We'd better see what's going on. . . . I'll call her parents tonight."

■ ■ ■

In this short scenario, we see several middle school adaptations. They include:

- Organizing teachers and students into interdisciplinary teams. For example, a team could be composed of math, science, English, and social studies teachers who all have the same students and work together to coordinate topics.
- Creating and maintaining long-term teacher–student relationships with attention to emotional development. Many middle schools implement an "advisor–advisee" period, in which the homeroom teacher meets with students each day to discuss a variety of non-academic topics. Through these advisory periods, teachers get to know students on an individual basis and can more carefully track their academic progress.
- Interactive teaching strategies. Teachers are encouraged to move away from the lecture-dominated instruction, so common in high schools, and toward instruction based on interactive questioning and student involvement. In addition, greater emphasis is placed on study strategies, such as note-taking and time management.
- Eliminating activities that emphasize developmental differences, such as competitive sports. Instead, everyone is invited to participate in intramural sports and clubs.

When done well, these characteristics have a very positive influence on students. For instance, interdisciplinary teams allow teachers to efficiently plan for the integration of

Teaching 

in an Era *of* Reform

GRADE RETENTION

One basic principle on which the organization of U.S. schools is based is that children progress from grade to grade as they grow older. This makes sense. As children grow and develop, they are exposed to increasingly complex ideas and tasks. However, this natural progression from grade to grade is being challenged by increased interest in **grade retention,** which is *the process of making students repeat a grade if they don't meet certain criteria.*

An important plank in the reform movement is the elimination of "social promotions" through increased use of grade retention for students who fail to achieve at prescribed levels. In a State of the Union address, then President Clinton proclaimed, "No child should graduate from high school with a diploma he or she can't read. We do our children no favors when we allow them to pass from grade to grade without mastering the material" (Quoted in Gordon, 1999, p. 42).

Grade retention is not new, but its popularity as a reform tool is growing. In the past, 5 to 7 percent of public school children (about two children in every classroom) were retained each year (Shepard & Smith, 1990). This figure is likely to grow as a number of states, such as Texas and Louisiana, and several large school districts, including New York, Los Angeles, and Chicago, are either considering or have implemented systems in which students must pass a test to progress to the next grade (Robelen, 2000; White, 1999).

The magnitude of the issue is illustrated in Louisiana, where all fourth and eighth graders must pass a test to progress to the next grade level (Robelen, 2000). In 1999 about 38,000 students, or about one-third of the students taking the test, failed. Those students will be offered summer school and a second chance to pass. Those not passing will repeat fourth or eighth grade.

Putting Reform into Perspective

The concept of grade retention seems logical. For example, allowing students to move from the fourth to the fifth grade when they haven't mastered the content and skills expected of typical fourth graders isn't intuitively sensible. It is also logical to conclude that these students are even less likely to succeed in the fifth grade if they're passed without the necessary understanding and skills. Advocates of grade retention claim that spending a second year in a grade gives learners a second chance to master the content and sends the message that schoolwork is important.

The concepts *social promotion* and *grade retention* are also concrete and easy to understand. As a result politicians, knowing that quality education is important to voters, use the notion of grade retention as a campaign "sound bite" in favor of educational quality to appeal to voters.

topics across different content areas, as Robin and Mary did with math and science. In addition, when teachers have the same students, they are able to more carefully monitor students' progress, as the team did with Lorraine.

The middle school philosophy also applies to extracurricular activities. One middle school in Plainfield, Indiana, encouraged its students to participate, with the following results. Well over half of the 900 students are involved in some sort of extracurricular activity: 350 in band, 325 in choir, 107 in cheerleading, 100 in basketball, and 85 in cross country (Hill, 1999). How did the school accommodate these numbers? Creatively. For example, they broke the cheerleaders into teams assigned to different sports and made room for basketball players by having two teams and opportunities for within-school sports. The results are encouraging. Students are happy with increased opportunities for participation, and a full trophy case attests to the school's ability to produce excellent athletic and musical programs.

Forming relationships helps students adjust to an atmosphere that is less personal than their elementary schools were, and eliminating competitive sports downplays competition, encourages all to participate in sports, and minimizes the advantages early maturing students have over their later developing classmates.

However, research consistently reveals that grade retention doesn't achieve advocates' claims. Students retained in a grade tend to perform lower on subsequent achievement tests than their nonretained counterparts, and they're also more likely to later drop out of school (Hauser, 1999; Shepard & Smith, 1990). Dropouts are five times more likely to have repeated a grade than are students who complete high school, and the probability of dropping out for students who repeat two grades is nearly 100 percent. Minorities and low-SES children are much more likely to be retained than their White, wealthier counterparts. This fact has sparked a lawsuit challenging the state of Texas' pass-or-don't-graduate policy (Zehr, 1999).

Research also indicates that grade retention causes emotional problems. In one study, children rated the prospect of repeating a grade as more stressful than "wetting in class" or being caught stealing. Going blind or losing a parent were the only two life events that children said would be more stressful than being retained (Shepard & Smith, 1990). The psychological effects of grade retention are especially acute for adolescents, where physical size differences and peer awareness exacerbate the problem.

Finally, alternatives to social promotion exist. Before- and after-school programs, summer-school programs with reduced class sizes, instructional aides who work with target children, and peer tutoring are all possibilities. Each is less expensive than spending thousands of dollars to have children repeat what they have already experienced, and the likelihood of students meeting standards is greater than it is by having them repeat grades (Hauser, 1999; Shepard & Smith, 1990). When grade retention does occur, it is important to provide help targeted at specific areas where problems exist.

Increasing Understanding 7.10

We see that research consistently indicates that grade retention is harmful to students. Explain why grade retention is so popular in spite of this research. Also explain how this issue is related to teacher professionalism.

You Take a Position

Now it's your turn to take a position on the issue discussed in this section. Go to the *Education Week* Website at **http://www.edweek.com,** find "search" on the first page, and type in one of the following two search terms: *grade retention* or *social promotion*. Locate a minimum of three articles on one of these topics and then do the following:

1. Identify the title, author, and date of each article and then write a one-paragraph summary of each.
2. Identify a pattern in the articles. (Each article—or even two of the three—suggesting that experts believe that social promotion should be eliminated would be a pattern, for example.)
3. After identifying the pattern, take one of the two following positions:
   - The pattern suggested in the articles, if implemented, *is likely* to improve education.
   - The pattern suggested in the articles *is not likely* to improve education.

State your position in writing, and document your position with information taken from the articles.

To answer these questions online, go to the Take a Position Module in Chapter 7 of the companion Website.

Increasing Understanding 7.9

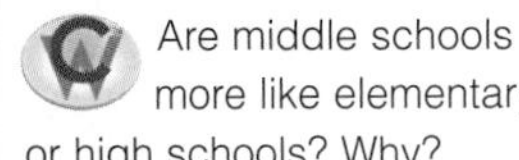

Are middle schools more like elementary or high schools? Why?

Interactive teaching strategies actively involve students in learning activities that can also develop their thinking and social interaction skills. Research indicates that motivation often drops during the early adolescent years; some researchers believe that this drop is due to increased use of teaching strategies like lectures that place students in passive roles (Pintrich & Schunk, 1996; Stipek, 1998).

The number of middle schools continues to increase compared to junior high schools. For instance, in 1968 about 7,200 schools called themselves junior high schools, but by 1996 the number had dropped to about 1,000 (Viadero, 1996). However, critics suggest that many middle schools, rather than implementing the intended adaptations we saw earlier, still largely resemble the junior high schools they were intended to replace (Bailey, 1997).

WHAT IS AN EFFECTIVE SCHOOL?

You're either planning to teach or are thinking about teaching; this is the reason you're taking this course. As you consider job offers from different schools, some important questions you'll want to ask are, How good is this school? Will it be a good school to work in?

Think about the schools you attended, and think about Chris's school. How good were they? What does the term "good" mean? How do you know if a school is good? We try to answer these questions in this section.

While people typically refer to schools as good or not so good, as in "Lakeside is a very *good* junior high school," researchers use the term "effective" instead. An **effective school** is *one in which learning for all students is maximized.* In simple terms, we think of an effective school as one that promotes learning. But what makes a school effective in promoting student learning? Let's see what research has to say.

Research on Effective Schools

Research has identified several characteristics of schools that promote learning. They are outlined in Figure 7.1 and discussed in the sections that follow.

School Organization and Climate This chapter focuses on school organization; the way schools are organized has a significant effect on learning. One important dimension of this organization is size.

School size. Are small schools better than big ones? Is the reverse true? As it turns out, the relationship between size and quality isn't simple or direct. Schools must be large enough to provide the varied curricular offerings needed to help students learn as much as possible, but not so large that students get lost. Research suggests that the ideal size for a high school is between 600 and 900 students. This conclusion is based on research that examined nearly 10,000 students in 789 public, Catholic, and private schools (Lee, 2000).

Increasing Understanding 7.11

Explain why size more strongly influences low-SES students than it does high-SES students. Think about the characteristics of students placed at-risk that were discussed in Chapter 4.

School size affects low- and high-SES students differently, with size more strongly influencing learning for low-SES students than for high-SES students. In other words, while 600–900 students is the ideal school size for all students (that is, both high- and low-SES students learn more in schools of this size), the reduction in learning in very large or very small high schools is greater for low-SES than it is for high-SES students. The only schools not fitting this pattern are elite private schools that enroll students with similar backgrounds and have the money to provide extensive resources, such as well-equipped science and computer labs.

Unfortunately, a disproportionate number of low-SES students attend either very small or very large high schools. Examples include small rural schools in sparsely populated states, such as Wyoming or Montana, and large, urban schools in major cities like New York or Los Angeles.

How does school size influence student learning? Researchers suggest that school size may affect learning *indirectly*. For example, a very large school doesn't directly *cause* students to learn less than they would in a more ideally sized school; rather, size influences

Figure 7.1 **Characteristics of Effective Schools**

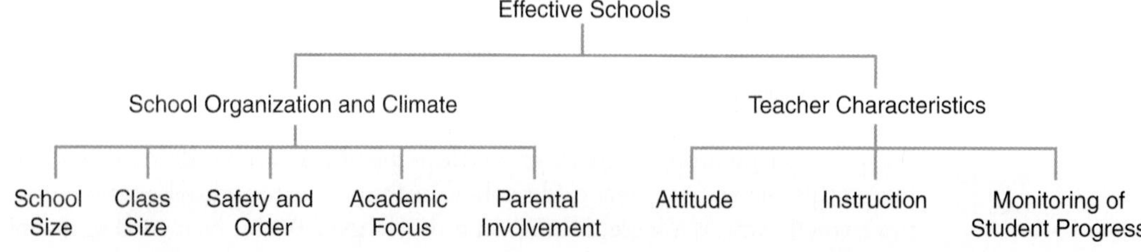

One essential characteristic of an effective school is hallways that are safe and orderly.

other factors (Lee, 2000). As schools becomes larger, it becomes more difficult to create learning communities in which students feel safe to learn and develop. Huge schools tend to depersonalize education, making it harder for teachers and students to know each other and work together.

One solution to the size problem is to create schools within schools, smaller learning communities where both teachers and students feel more comfortable. For example, Creekland Middle School in Georgia has more than 3,100 students, many more than experts recommend for any school, much less a middle school (Jacobson, 2000a). To address this issue, Creekland is divided into five learning communities, each with its own assistant principal, school counselor, and faculty. Students are assigned to one of these communities for the 3 years they attend the middle school, and faculty make a special effort to integrate students into their community.

Class size. In addition to school size, what are some other factors that contribute to an effective school? One of these is class size. Does the number of students in a class influence how much the students learn? This issue is somewhat controversial, with some critics arguing either that class size doesn't matter or that reducing class size isn't worth the cost required to hire extra teachers and provide space and resources.

Research counters these critics' positions. A consistent body of evidence indicates that reducing class size does indeed increase learning for all students; the effects are particularly pronounced in the lower grades and for students in inner-city schools (Robinson, 1990; Rouse, 1997; Wenglinsky, 1997).

Reductions in class size can have both short- and long-term positive effects (Viadero, 1999). In Tennessee, where class sizes were reduced from 25 to 15 students, researchers found immediate gains in reading and math scores. Follow-up studies revealed that the positive effects lasted through twelfth grade. Students in the smaller class dropped out of school less frequently, took more challenging courses, and were more likely to attend college than their counterparts in larger classes. These positive effects were especially strong for African American students.

School safety and order. In a national survey asking students to identify serious problems in their school, 45 percent identified fighting, 54 percent targeted bullying, and 38 percent pointed to stealing. When nine- to eleven-year-old students were asked whether noisy students disrupting class, cheating, and stealing were problems at their school, overwhelming majorities (88 percent, 66 percent, and 51 percent, respectively) said yes (Boyer, 1995). Schools, which should be sheltered communities for learning, often serve as mirrors for the problems of society.

The need for safe and orderly schools is supported by both research and theory. Researchers have described effective schools as places of trust, order, cooperation, and high morale (Rutter, Maughn, Mortimore, Ouston, & Smith, 1979). Students need to feel emotionally safe in schools for learning to occur (Alexander & Murphy, 1998).

Theories of learner development, which we briefly discussed earlier in the chapter, suggest that the need for order is innate (Piaget 1952, 1970). In other words, people are born with a desire to live in an orderly rather than chaotic world. In addition, the psychologist Abraham Maslow (1968), who described a hierarchy of human needs, argued that only the need for survival is more basic in people than the need for safety. Studies of classroom management also confirm the need for order; orderly classrooms promote both learning and student motivation (Purkey & Smith, 1983; Radd, 1998; Wang, Haertel, & Walberg, 1993).

Academic focus. To effective schools, the primary mission of schooling is to promote learning. This mission is clear to the teachers in the school, with the tone being set by the school principal and other administrators. An array of clubs, sports, and other extracurricular offerings exists and is important, but this doesn't take precedence over learning. In effective schools, classes are not canceled so students can attend sporting events, and class time isn't used for club meetings.

One study investigating the effects of academic focus on learning concluded, "Students learn more in schools that set high standards for academic performance, that use their instructional time wisely, and that use student learning as a criterion for making decisions" (Lee & Smith, 1999). Schools with an academic focus are probably more positive places to work because both students and teachers feel that learning is occurring. Look for signs that academic focus is present when you interview for a teaching position at different schools.

Parental involvement. No matter how well they're organized, schools won't be effective if parents aren't involved in their children's education. Learning is a cooperative venture; teachers, students, and parents are in it together.

Research indicates that students benefit from home–school cooperation in a number of ways (Cameron & Lee, 1997; López & Scribner, 1999):

- When parents are involved, students achieve more, regardless of socioeconomic status, ethnic/racial background, or the parents' education level. The more extensive the parent involvement, the higher the student achievement.
- When parents are involved in their children's education, those students have higher grades and test scores, better attendance, and complete homework more consistently.
- When parents are involved, students exhibit more positive attitudes and behavior.
- Educators hold higher expectations for students whose parents collaborate with teachers. They also hold higher opinions of those parents.
- Students' alcohol use, violence, and antisocial behaviors decrease as parent involvement increases.

Effective schools develop mechanisms to allow parents and teachers to work together.

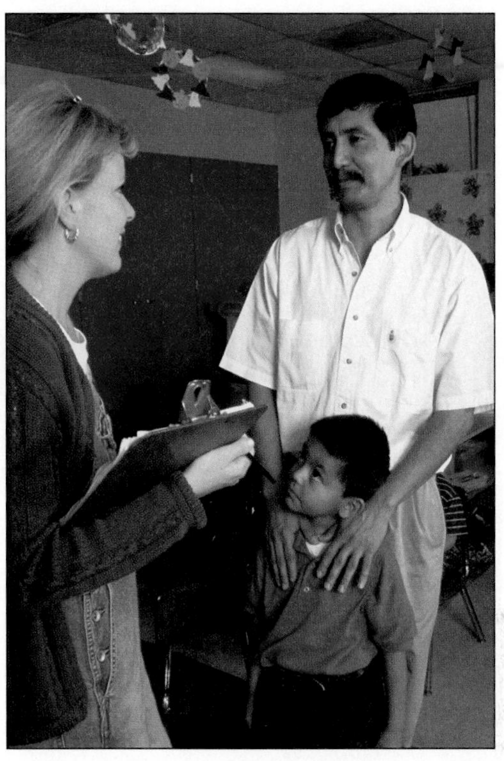

These outcomes likely result from parents' increased participation in school activities, their more positive attitudes about schooling, and teachers' increased understanding of their students' home environments (Weinstein & Mignano, 1993).

Parental involvement is so important that the National PTA has established *National Standards for Parent/Family Involvement Programs* (National PTA, 1998). These standards are outlined in Table 7.3. To learn more about the *National Standards for Parent/Family Involvement Programs* and suggestions for involving parents in their children's education, go to the *Web Links* Module in Chapter 7 of the Companion Website at **http://www.prenhall.com/kauchak.**

Increasing Understanding 7.12

Earlier we saw that a disproportionate number of low-SES students tends to be enrolled in large schools. Is the involvement of low-SES parents likely to be greater than the involvement of high-SES parents? Explain. (Hint: Think about the influence of SES on learning that was discussed in Chapter 4.)

Teacher Characteristics

In the last section, we saw how school size, safety and order, school focus, and parental involvement influence a school's effectiveness and the amount that students learn.

Teachers are also central to a school's effectiveness. Crucial teacher characteristics include:

- Teachers' attitudes.
- The way teachers teach.
- The extent to which student progress is monitored.

Teacher Attitudes. It is difficult to overstate the impact of teachers' attitudes on the way they teach and the amount students learn. One of the most important teacher attitudes is a concept called **personal teaching efficacy,** which is *teachers' beliefs that they can promote learning in all students regardless of their backgrounds* (Bruning, Shraw, & Ronning, 1999). The most significant characteristic of teachers who are high in personal teaching efficacy is that they take responsibility for the success or failure of their own instruction

Table 7.3 **National Standards for Parent/Family Involvement Programs**

Standard	Description
I. Communicating	Communication between home and school is regular, two-way, and meaningful.
II. Parenting	Parenting skills are promoted and supported.
III. Student Learning	Parents play an integral role in assisting student learning.
IV. Volunteering	Parents are welcome in the school, and their support and assistance are sought.
V. School Decision Making and Advocacy	Parents are full partners in the decisions that affect children and families.
VI. Collaborating with Community	Community resources are used to strengthen schools, families, and student learning.

Source: From National Parent Teacher Association (1998). *National standards for Parent/Family Involvement Programs.* Chicago: Author. Reprinted by permission.

WHAT MAKES A SCHOOL GREAT? PARENTAL INVOLVEMENT

This ABC News video segment focuses on Walton High School in Atlanta, a model school for parental involvement. The benefits of parental involvement are explored from both a parent and school perspective. Reporter Thomas Toch also describes characteristics of an effective school and explains how and why parents should get involved in their children's education.

Think about This

1. What are the major benefits of increased parental involvement in education?
2. What are the essential characteristics of an effective school, and how do they influence learning?
3. Which of these characteristics of an effective school will be most important to you as a first-year teacher?

To answer these questions online and receive immediate feedback, go to the Video Perspectives Module in Chapter 7 of the Companion Website.

(Lee, 2000). In other words, if students aren't learning as much as they should be, rather than blaming students' lack of intelligence, poor home environments, uncooperative administrators, or some other cause, high-efficacy teachers conclude that they could be doing a better job teaching, and they look for ways to increase student learning.

Let's look at an example.

"What are you doing with those cake pans?" Jim Barton asked his wife, Shirley, a fifth-grade teacher, as he saw her hard at work constructing some cardboard cake pans.

"What do you think?" she grinned at him. "Do they look like cake?" she asked, holding up rectangular cardboard pieces drawn to resemble two cakes cut into pieces, with the pieces intended to be used to illustrate fractions.

"Actually, they almost do," he responded.

"My students didn't score as well as I would have liked on the fractions part of the Stanford Achievement Test last year, and I promised myself that they were going to do better this year."

"But you said the students aren't as sharp this year."

"That doesn't matter. I'm pushing them harder. I think I could have done a better job last year, so I swore I was really going to be ready for them this time."

Jim walked back into the living room with a smile on his face, mumbling something about thinking that teachers who have taught for 11 years were supposed to burn out (Eggen & Kauchak, 2001, p. 463).

■ ■ ■

Shirley is a high-efficacy teacher; she accepts responsibility for the amount her students learn, and she is increasing her efforts to be sure that increased learning occurs.

High-efficacy teachers create high-efficacy schools. Let's look at how learning is influenced in **high-collective-efficacy schools**, *schools in which most of the teachers are high in personal teaching efficacy*. Figure 7.2 provides some insight (Lee, 2000).

Three findings in Figure 7.2 are important. First, all students—high, middle, and low SES—learn more in high-collective-efficacy schools than they do in schools where collective efficacy is lower. This, in itself, isn't surprising; it makes sense that the more teachers strive for student learning, the more students will learn. Second, and more important, low-SES students in high-collective-efficacy schools have achievement gains nearly as high as high-SES students in low-collective-efficacy schools. Third, differences in achievement gains among low-, middle-, and high-SES students in high-collective-efficacy schools are smaller than they are in low-collective-efficacy schools (Lee, 2000). In other words, high-collective-efficacy schools help reduce achievement differences between groups of students who typically benefit quite differently from schooling.

How do high-efficacy teachers and high-collective-efficacy schools accomplish these results? A number of factors contribute, but two are essential: interactive instruction and continuous monitoring of student progress.

Interactive Instruction. Imagine that you're walking through the hallways of a school and the classroom doors are open. As you walk by each classroom, you glance inside. Can you determine anything about the effectiveness of the school from a simple glance? The answer is yes. If the prevailing pattern is one in which the teachers are asking large numbers of questions, and students are involved in discussions, the likelihood that the school is effective increases. In contrast, if what you see is teachers primarily lecturing, or students spending

Figure 7.2 **Achievement Gains in High-Collective-Efficacy Schools versus Low-Collective-Efficacy Schools**

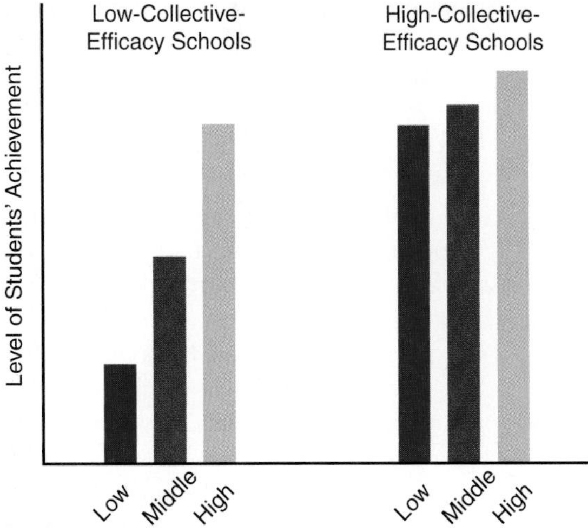

Source: From Lee, V. (2000). Using hierarchical linear modeling to study social contexts: The case of school effects. *Educational Psychologist, 35,* 125–141. Reprinted by permission.

most of their time working alone and doing seatwork, the school is less likely to be effective. This is admittedly simplistic—many additional factors influence how much students learn—but interaction between teacher and students as well as students with each other are essential ingredients for learning (Gladney & Green, 1997; Wang, Haertel, & Walberg, 1995).

Not only is interactive teaching essential for learning, it is also important for motivation (Pintrich & Schunk, 1996). In a study where students were asked to rate different methods of learning, teacher lectures and memorization were rated lowest (Boyer, 1995). In another study, middle school students rated hands-on science and independent research projects as their most memorable schoolwork (Wasserstein, 1995). Effective schools provide opportunities for students to become actively involved in their learning.

Teachers high in personal teaching efficacy—who believe that they can make a difference in student learning—are more likely to promote high levels of teacher–student interaction than their low-efficacy counterparts. "Such teachers view teaching and learning as an interactive process with students cast as active participants, rather than as a one-way flow of information" (Lee, 2000, p. 135).

Increasing Understanding 7.13

Do high-SES students need interactive instruction more than low-SES students, or vice versa? Explain, using the information from Figure 7.2 as the basis for your answer.

Continuous Monitoring of Student Progress. A second instructional factor that contributes to schools' effectiveness is the extent to which teachers frequently assess learning and provide students with feedback. Teachers in effective schools collect a great deal of information about students' learning progress. These teachers give frequent quizzes and tests, the assessments measure more than a recall of facts, the teachers return the assessments shortly after they're given, and the test items are thoroughly discussed (Brookhart, 1997; Dochy & McDowell, 1997; Tuckman, 1998). In addition, teachers regularly collect work samples from students and carefully monitor student understanding in class discussions.

Increasing Understanding 7.14

Look again at the characteristics of effective schools and effective teachers for students placed at-risk. (See pages 127 and 128 in Chapter 4.) Those characteristics are very similar to the characteristics of effective schools we've discussed here. Explain why this is case.

Parents' and Other Taxpayers' Perceptions of Effective Schools

How do parents and other taxpayers view effective schools? What is the basis for their perceptions? What do they most commonly look for in judging a school? Let's take a look.

The results of research examining parents' and other taxpayers' perceptions of effective schools are not surprising. As would be expected, they react most strongly to factors that are concrete and observable. For example, as a result of highly publicized incidents of school violence, school safety is a primary concern; in fact, both parents and other taxpayers rank it as the most essential characteristic of an effective school (Olson, 1999).

A second important characteristic is qualified teachers. Again, this isn't surprising, since teachers represent schools and are the people who work most directly with parents' sons and daughters.

A third measure of a schools' effectiveness is standardized test scores. In the absence of other, more concrete indices of school effectiveness, parents look to standardized test scores to tell them how their children are doing as well as how the school is performing. Forty-eight of the 50 states regularly test their students, and 36 states publish annual report cards on individual schools. "In short, parents and taxpayers view school safety and the presence of qualified teachers as two essential ingredients of education. Once those basic conditions are met, they want results" (Olson, 1999, p. 34).

These results are consistent with the characteristics of effective schools discussed earlier. For instance, we saw school safety on both lists. School size has been discussed in the popular press, but it hasn't received the publicity of characteristics like teacher qualifications and test scores. Other factors, such as personal teaching efficacy, interactive instruction, and monitoring of student progress are more complex, making them harder for people outside the profession to understand.

Reflect on This

WORKING TO CHANGE THE SCHOOL ORGANIZATION

You've been offered a job at Henderson Middle School, an inner-city school in a medium-sized city. Henderson boasts some of the most successful basketball and football teams in the city, and it is a primary feeder school for Raines High School, a city football power. The coaches of the two schools closely coordinate the development of the schools' athletes.

Henderson's students typically score quite low on standardized achievement tests, and the school's administrative staff is working to change the school organization. They want to create teams in which a history, English, math, and science teacher all have the same group of students along with a common planning period. They've also gotten a grant to support in-service activities designed to help teachers move away from using lectures as the primary method of teaching and toward more student involvement and integration of topics between different content areas. "We want to see standardized test scores going up, and we want to see more kids on the honor roll. These kids are going to have to compete when they get to high school, and now is the time for them to learn how. These kids—all of them—can learn; all we have to do is believe it, and we can make it happen," urges Adam Argalas, the school principal.

1. To what extent is Henderson consistent with the characteristics of middle schools?
2. In what area (or areas) is Henderson inconsistent with the characteristics of middle schools?
3. Based on the information presented, is Henderson likely to be a relatively effective or ineffective school? How do you know?
4. Would you accept a job at Henderson? Why?

To respond to these questions online and receive immediate feedback, go to the Reflect on This Module in Chapter 7 of the Companion Website.

Tracking can result in the segregation of cultural minorities into low-level classes where instruction tends to be less challenging.

Exploring Diversity

Considering Multiple Perspectives

SCHOOL ORGANIZATION AND THE ACHIEVEMENT OF CULTURAL MINORITIES

Emphasis on higher standards and increased accountability is perhaps the most prominent reform that exists in education today. However, all change has unintended outcomes, and one that is important in this case is a widening gap in the achievement of cultural minorities—particularly African American and Hispanic students—compared to their White and Asian counterparts (Hoff, 2000). Between 1970, when the National Assessment of Educational Progress first began systematically measuring American students' achievement, and 1980, African American and Hispanic students made great strides in narrowing the gulf that had separated them from their White peers. However, this progress ground to a halt in the late 1980s, and since then, the gap has either remained constant or widened (Jencks & Phillips, 1998).

A number of explanations have been offered for the differences in achievement, including poverty, peer pressure, and parental values. None seems adequate, however, and research examining these explanations is either lacking or inconsistent (Viadero, 2000).

However, consistent research does exist regarding two aspects of school organization that were discussed earlier in the chapter: tracking and class size. Let's look at them.

Cultural Minorities and Tracking

We saw that comprehensive high schools have been criticized for the practice of tracking, because evidence indicates that educational experiences on lower-level tracks are often substandard (Oakes, 1992, 1995). This evidence is particularly relevant for cultural minorities because they tend to be underrepresented in higher-level tracks, that is, a disproportionate number are found in low-achieving classes. The problem is exacerbated by the fact that minority students tend not to enroll in more demanding classes (Jencks & Phillips, 1998). Table 7.4 outlines some of these differences (Viadero, 2000).

Tracking and minority achievement have a form of negative synergy, that is, student achievement in low-level classes is reduced compared to the achievement of students of comparable ability in high-level classes. And because decisions about tracking are based on students' records of past achievement, the negative relationship between achievement and tracking is magnified. School

Class-size reduction can be an effective tool to increase achievement.

Table 7.4 **Correlation between Taking Advanced High-School Courses and Graduating from College**

Race/Ethnicity	High School Graduates Who Have Completed Algebra 2 and Geometry (%)	Freshmen at Four-Year Colleges Who Graduate within Six Years (%)
Asian American	55.5	65
White	53.1	59
Hispanic American	41.9	46
Native American	35.7	37
African American	35	40

Source: From Viadero, D. (2000). Lags in minority achievement defy traditional explanations. *Education Week, XIX* (28), 1–21. Reprinted by permission.

leaders haven't been able to identify a satisfactory approach to solving this problem.

Cultural Minorities and Class Size

The relationship between class size and minority achievement is more encouraging. Earlier we saw that research supports the contention that student achievement is higher in smaller classes. This research is important, because the effects of reducing class size are greater for cultural minorities than for their White peers (Gewertz, 2000; Robinson, 1990).

Two studies are particularly significant. First, an assessment of a major class-size-reduction project in Tennessee revealed the following (Illig, 1996):

- Children in small classes (about 15 students per class) consistently outperformed children in larger classes.
- Inner-city children (about 97 percent of whom were minorities) closed some of the achievement gap between themselves and nonminority children.
- Children in small classes outperformed children in larger classes, even when teachers in the large classes had support from aides.

In the second study, a four-year experiment with class-size reduction in Wisconsin, researchers found that the achievement gap between minorities and nonminorities shrank by 19 percent in smaller classes, whereas in regular classrooms it grew by 58 percent (Molnar, Percy, Smith, & Zahorik, 1998). The results of the class-size reduction experiment were so compelling that the Wisconsin legislature planned to spend $59 million beginning in 2000 to expand the program to 400 schools (Gewertz, 2000).

However, as with all initiatives, simply reducing class size won't automatically increase achievement. If the other characteristics of an effective school don't exist, reducing the number of students in classes, by itself, won't increase achievement. Narrowing the achievement gap requires the systematic implementation of all the effective school characteristics.

The Changing Role of Teachers

What implications will the patterns described in this chapter have for you as a teacher? At least three are likely.

First, accountability is here to stay. You will be expected to prepare students for high-stakes tests and to balance "teaching to the test" with a well-rounded instructional program. For instance, you will be required to integrate goals and the content in textbooks with the content measured on the tests. Your students will be expected to perform well on the tests, and you'll be held accountable for ensuring that they do. Your salary may even be partially tied to the results, as occurs in some states, such as Texas (Boser, 2000).

Second, you may be expected to spend more time teaching. The school year may start earlier and end later, and you may be asked to teach summer school. You could be involved in a year-round school. As far back as the early 1990s, more than 1.5 million students in over 2,000 schools were on year-round programs (Harp, 1993). This number is likely to increase in the future. In 1999, about half of the nation's big-city systems offered remedial summer programs (White & Johnston, 1999). The New York City School District had over 300,000 students attending summer school in 2000, two-thirds for remedial work and one-third for enrichment programs (Johnston, 2000). For teachers looking for ways to augment their 9-month salary, this is good news. (The New York City program alone required 16,000 teachers.) But teachers who want the freedom of a summer vacation may feel pressured to work during these extra months.

You will need more expertise than has been expected of teachers in the past. For example, you might find yourself teaching in a block schedule, so lecture will be even less

1. Dr. Urie Triesman is a professor of mathematics at the University of Texas at Austin and director of the Charles A. Dana Center for Math and Science Education. His work focuses on school reform and the ways that schools can be helped to improve. He believes principals are essential to effective schools. What does Dr. Triesman believe is the single most important thing that principals can do within a school to promote learning? Do you agree with him?
2. Theodore Sizer is the director of the Coalition for Effective Schools, which attempts to reform high schools. From his perspective, what are some arguments against grouping students together by age? How practical do you think the alternatives are?
3. Dr. John Goodlad is professor emeritus and co-director of the Center for Renewal at the University of Washington and president of the Independent Institute for Educational Inquiry. How does Dr. Goodlad believe that students suffer psychologically from grade retention? What alternatives are there to grade retention? Which of these do you think are most effective?

GOING INTO SCHOOLS

1. Go to an elementary school and either a middle, junior high, or high school. Interview a teacher at each school. Ask the teacher to describe the school administration and support staff and to explain the duties of each person. This might include some or all of the following (as well as others):
   - Vice principal
   - Assistant principal
   - Dean
   - School psychologist
   - Guidance counselor
   - School nurse
   - Media-center director
   - Curriculum specialists (such as a technology specialist)

   In addition, ask each teacher how the school is organized and how the organization of the school could be improved so that all students would learn more. Report your results in a paper comparing the two types of schools.
2. Visit the type of school in which you plan to teach. How does the receptionist greet you? Is she pleasant and cordial, or cool and businesslike? As you're standing in the school reception area, watch the receptionist. How does she treat students when they come into the area? Again, is she pleasant and cordial, or cool and businesslike? What does this tell you about the school from a student's perspective? From a teacher's perspective?
3. Visit a school and stand in a hallway as students are moving to or from lunch, or from one class to another. Describe the behavior of the students and the teachers as students are making these transitions. In particular, look for the following:
   - How orderly is the movement? Do students move quickly and with a minimum of apparent confusion?
   - Are teachers monitoring the students' movement? What are the teachers saying? Is the general tone of the teachers' comments and directives pleasant and cordial or harsh and critical?
   - Do students move into classrooms in an orderly way? Are they in their seats and waiting when instruction is scheduled to begin?

   What does this information tell you about this school as a learning environment?
4. Interview a teacher; place special emphasis on questions about the teacher's students. You might include some or all of the following questions:

- How capable of learning are the teacher's students?
- What are their lives like at home?
- Can you overcome home problems if they exist? Why?
- What could be done to organize the school so that learning could be increased for all students?
- What is the toughest part of your job?
- What is the easiest part of your job?
- What is the most distasteful part of your job?
- What is the most pleasant or rewarding part of your job?

What do the teacher's responses tell you about teaching in a school like this?

5. Observe the class of the teacher you interviewed. Look for the following:
   - The number of questions the teacher asks. Does he or she ask large numbers of questions or is most of the instructional time spent lecturing?
   - How much of the teacher's time is spent in instruction (explaining and lecturing or question and answer)?
   - How much time do students spend doing seatwork?
   - How much time do students spend in nonlearning activities, such as visiting with each other or moving around the room?

   On the basis of your observations, decide how well the organization of this classroom promotes learning.

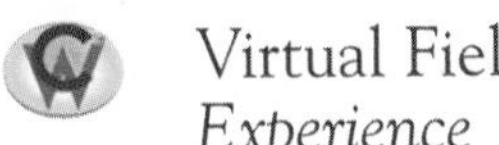

If you would like to participate in a Virtual Field Experience, go to the *Field Experience* Module in Chapter 7 of the Companion Website.

ONLINE PORTFOLIO ACTIVITIES

To complete these activities online, go to the *Portfolio Activities* Module in Chapter 7 of the Companion Website to submit your responses.

Portfolio Activity 7.1

Involving Students with Diverse Backgrounds

INTASC Principle 4: *Strategies*

The purpose of this activity is to help you begin thinking about how to adapt your instruction for all students. Suppose about half of your students are cultural minorities. Describe specifically what you would do to be certain that all of your students are as involved in your learning activities as possible.

Portfolio Activity 7.2

Effective Schools

INTASC Principle 5: *Motivation and Management*

The purpose of this activity is to encourage you to think about what an effective school would look like from your personal perspective. Based upon the information in this chapter, write a two-page description of an effective school at the level in which you plan to teach. In the paper, explain how this organization would influence your life as a teacher.

Portfolio Activity 7.3

Involving Parents

INTASC Principle 10: *Partnership*

Write a two-page description of your philosophy regarding parental involvement in their children's education. Include in the description a minimum of four suggestions for involving parents.

duplication of administrative staff. For example, one medium-sized district with a superintendent and district staff of ten people is more efficient than two small districts that require a superintendent and a staff of six to eight people each.

Which is better, bigger or smaller? From a teacher's perspective, there are advantages and disadvantages to both. Small districts are less bureaucratic and easier to influence, but they typically lack resources and instructional support staff. For example, Carla's committee functioned in a larger district. As Carla's committee worked on the elementary math curriculum, they had assistance from a district math coordinator, a testing specialist, and various technology experts who helped the committee evaluate the claims of different commercial math programs. These people would not exist in a very small district.

Large districts also have problems. They tend to be hierarchical and bureaucratic, and getting anything done can take a long time. Teachers sometimes feel like nameless, faceless cogs in a large, impersonal organization. Instead of the face-to-face contacts that can make things happen quickly in smaller districts, decision making is placed in the hands of large and sometimes contentious committees. From a teacher's perspective, the ideal district is an administrative structure that is supportive and responsive but also leaves teachers alone to do what they love most—working with students.

Increasing Understanding 8.3

From a beginning teacher's perspective, what might be some advantages and disadvantages of starting in a large district? A small district?

Every school district has a local school board, a superintendent, and a central staff. These are the people who make the district-level decisions about teaching and learning in their districts. Let's see how they will influence your life as a teacher.

The Local School Board **Local school boards,** *groups of elected lay citizens, are responsible for setting policies that determine how districts operate.* Because local school boards are responsible for many important decisions affecting your life as a teacher, you should understand what they do and who is on them. With respect to governance, what are the functions of school boards? Who are the members of these boards? How are school board members selected?

Functions of school boards. School boards have five major functions. They are outlined in Figure 8.2 and discussed in the paragraphs that follow.

Perhaps the most important (and contentious) school board function involves the district budget. School boards are responsible for raising money through taxes and disbursing funds to the schools within the district. They also make decisions about various district services, such as providing buses and maintaining lunch programs. School boards directly influence teachers by making decisions about salary increases and the benefits teachers receive. Teachers are also affected by board decisions because the district budget influences class size and the amount of instructional materials that will be available.

Wrestling with each year's budget occupies more than one quarter of a school board's time and energy; it's a continual process that begins in the fall and ends in the spring (Odden et al., 1995).

Figure 8.2 **Functions of Local School Boards**

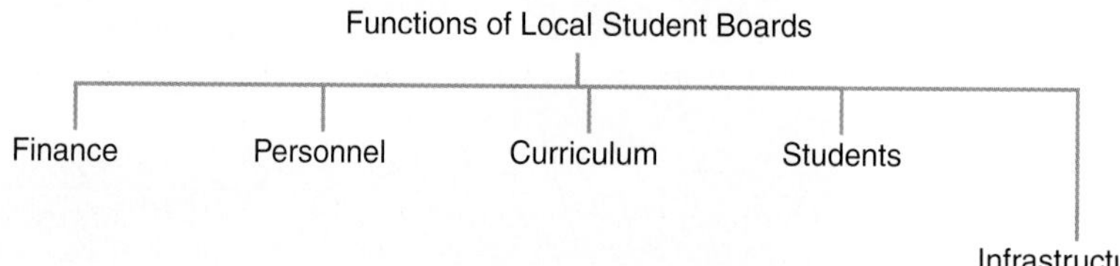

Closely aligned with financial decisions are personnel responsibilities. School boards are legally responsible for hiring and firing all school personnel, including teachers, principals, janitors, and school bus drivers. Your teaching contract will be offered by a school board that has the legal authority to hire and fire teachers.

The **curriculum**—*what is taught in the district's schools*—is a third area of school board jurisdiction. School boards are responsible for fleshing out and implementing the general guidelines developed by states. In virtually all districts, teachers are consulted about the curriculum; in the better ones, they are directly involved in decisions about curriculum. For example, Carla, as a spokesperson for her committee, was directly involved in deciding which math curriculum the district would adopt.

Decisions that impact students are also made by school boards. They set attendance, dress, grooming, conduct, and discipline standards for their districts. For example, the issue of school uniforms has been debated at district, state, and national levels, but the decision is ultimately made (sometimes after contentious debate) by local school boards.

School boards also determine extracurricular policies. Some districts have instituted minimal grade levels for participation in sports, a policy critics contend doubly punishes struggling student athletes by failing them in the classroom and not allowing them to participate in extracurricular activities. Supporters of no-pass/no-play policies argue that it improves motivation to learn by providing incentives for academic success (White, 1997). As another example, the question of what to do with gay and lesbian clubs that want equal status with other school-sponsored organizations has also generated controversy at school board meetings. When controversial issues such as these are on the school board meeting agenda, attendance usually rises, with different citizens' groups attending in attempts to influence board decisions.

Increasing Understanding 8.4

From a teacher's perspective, which of the school board functions is likely to be most important? Least? Explain.

On a less controversial note, school boards are also responsible for making sure that school buildings and school buses are well-maintained and safe. This is the function of the boards that focuses on infrastructure.

Not surprisingly, student achievement has been school board members' number one concern in recent years, followed by budget issues and increasing enrollment pressures (Vital Education, 1998). Interestingly, student achievement wasn't even listed in the top ten school board members' concerns as recently as the late 1980s. Reform efforts and the national trend toward greater school accountability have strongly impacted the ways that school boards operate.

Membership and selection of school boards. Who serves on school boards, and how do they get there? Most (90 percent or more) school boards are elected, with the remainder being appointed by large city mayors or city councils (Leadership, 1994). School board elections can be controversial for two reasons. First, the voter turnout for most school board elections is embarrassingly low; often as few as 5 to 10 percent of eligible voters decide school board membership. Critics contend that such low voter turnout results in school boards that don't represent the citizens in the district. The second controversy involves the question of whether school board elections should be at-large or limited to specific areas within a city. In a limited-area election, for example, only citizens who reside in a specific part of the city are allowed to vote for candidates who represent that area. At-large elections tend to favor wealthier, White majority candidates who either have more money to run an election campaign or benefit from White majority voting pools. Area-specific elections provide greater opportunities for minority candidates to represent local, ethnic minority neighborhoods.

Increasing Understanding 8.5

How is the membership of state and district boards similar? How is the selection of members for state and district boards different?

Who serves on these boards? The typical school board member tends to be male, White, older, and wealthy, although these figures are gradually changing in some areas. For example, in 1987, 61 percent of board members were male and 94 percent were

Property taxes are the most common way of financing schools and can result in funding disparities between districts.

Increasing Understanding 8.12

Based on past trends, predict changes in local, state, and federal funding of education. Explain your prediction.

contrast, 20th century leaders saw a direct connection between education and the country's political and economic well-being. Because quality schools and a well-educated workforce were national concerns, supporters of greater federal involvement argued that the federal government's role in education should increase. Similarly, states began to recognize the importance of education in attracting high-tech industries and high-paying jobs. This insight, plus efforts to equalize funding within states, has led to an increasing state role in educational funding.

Let's look now at how funds are raised at these levels, and how they make their way to classrooms.

Local Funding As we saw in our discussion of school governance, financing education at the local level is the responsibility of local school boards. That's why Carla made her presentation to her school board. One of the implications of her presentation was the need for increased funding. At the local level, most funding for schools (76 percent) comes from property taxes that are determined by the value of property in the school district (U.S. Advisory Commission on Intergovernmental Relations, 1994). Other local revenue sources include income taxes, fees for building permits, traffic fines, and user fees charged to groups that hold meetings on school facilities. In 11 states, more than 98 percent of local school revenues come from property taxes. In collecting property taxes, local authorities first assess the value of a property and then tax the owners a small percentage of the property's value (usually less than 1 percent).

Increasing Understanding 8.13

Of the local options to property taxes—income taxes, fees for building permits, traffic fines, and user fees charged to groups that hold meetings on school facilities—which option is most fair to older taxpayers? Least fair? Explain.

The property-tax-based method of funding education has disadvantages, the most glaring of which is inequities between property resources in different districts (Arnold, 1998; Rothstein, 1998). Wealthier cities or districts have a higher tax base, so they're able to collect (and spend) more money for their schools. Poorer rural and inner-city school districts find themselves on the opposite end of this continuum, with a lower tax base resulting in lower revenues. Property taxes also place an unfair burden on older taxpayers, whose homes may have increased in value, while their ability to pay taxes has remained constant or decreased. In addition, many older taxpayers resist these charges because they no longer have children in school and don't see the immediate benefit of increased spending for school taxes.

The property-tax method of financing schools also has a political disadvantage. Unlike a sales tax, which taxpayers pay in small, continual, and essentially unnoticed increments, announcements for property taxes are conspicuous, arriving once a year along with a comparison to the previous year. Therefore, they are visible targets for taxpayer dissatisfaction. This causes problems when school boards, like Carla's, ask their taxpayers for increased funding. This dissatisfaction reached a head in California in 1978 when voters passed an initiative called Proposition 13, which limited property taxes in the state. By the 1990s, 45 other states had passed similar measures (McAdams, 1994). The effect on educational funding was chilling. Schools and school districts had less money to spend and had to fight harder when requesting new funds.

State Revenue Sources The second largest source of educational funding comes from the states. In 1992, state governments spent $121 billion on elementary and secondary education, roughly 20 percent of total state expenditures (Nelson, 1999). State sales taxes represent the largest source of state income, contributing about one third of all state revenues (U.S. Advisory Commission on Intergovernmental Relations, 1994). Sales taxes are regressive, however, meaning they take proportionally more from lower-income families who spend a larger portion of their income on necessities, such as food, clothing, and housing. Progressive states provide some relief by excluding food from items that are taxed. Personal income tax accounts for another third of state revenues. The remaining third comes from other sources, such as taxes on liquor and tobacco, oil and mining, and corporate incomes.

Increasing Understanding 8.14

Liquor and tobacco taxes are often called "sin taxes" because they target commodities that either pose health risks or are viewed as socially unacceptable by a portion of the population. What are the advantages and disadvantages of "sin taxes"?

Recently, state lotteries and gambling have also become sources of revenue, but education is often the victim of a zero-sum shell game in which increased funding from lottery monies, for example, are balanced by decreasing monies from other sources, such as sales taxes. In addition, research indicates that the poor and uneducated are more apt to participate in these gambling ventures. The long-term viability of gambling revenues for education is uncertain and highly controversial.

Federal Funding for Education The third, smallest, and most controversial source of educational funding is the federal government. As we saw earlier, federal funding for education was virtually nonexistent prior to 1920 but increased over time to its present level of about 7 percent. Proponents of a greater federal role in education believe that education is absolutely essential for the country's continued progress in the 21st century and that the federal government should continue to exert leadership (and funds) in this area. Critics warn of increased federal control over what they believe should be a local responsibility. In addition, conservatives also argue against the expansion of what they consider to be an already bloated federal bureaucracy. For these critics, less is better when it comes to federal funding, both in terms of efficiency and local control. Conservative critics also contend that local funding makes schools more efficient and responsive to local needs and wishes.

Although the actual percentage of money spent by the federal government on education has been small, the impact has been considerable; this is due in large part to the use of **categorical grants,** *money targeted for specific groups and designated purposes*. Head Start, aimed at preschoolers, Title I, targeted at economically disadvantaged youth, and the Bilingual Education Act of 1972 are examples of categorical aid programs targeting specific needs or populations (We discuss these programs in greater detail in Chapter 3.) Because the funds must be used for specific purposes, categorical grants have strongly influenced local education practices.

During the 1980s, categorical funds were replaced by **block grants,** which *provide states and districts with funds with few federal restrictions*. Begun during the conservative Reagan

Disparities in property tax revenues can result in dramatic differences in fundings for schools that are quite close geographically.

did just the opposite, ruling that the U.S. Constitution does not guarantee citizens a right to an education. However, the Court did point out that funding inequities may violate state constitutions, many of which *do* guarantee citizens a right to an education.

Increasing Understanding 8.17

Explain why the California and Texas court cases ended up in different court systems.

This sent the issue back to state courts, and other state suits followed, resulting in 32 cases in all. Of these, 13 were ruled in favor of the plaintiffs, and 19 were lost (Fischer et al., 1999). When rulings favored the plaintiffs, researchers found that inequities were reduced by almost 14 percent (Nelson, 1999).

An important reason for differences in state rulings has to do with the wording of state constitutions, some of which are quite specific in guaranteeing "equal education for all" while others vaguely specify that educational opportunity should be "ample" or "efficient."

The problem of funding inequalities is complicated by the fact that not all districts in a state have the same needs (Odden & Clune, 1998; Wenglinsky, 1998). Some have a higher proportion of low-income children, non-native English speakers, or children who need special-education services. Each of these special populations requires extra resources. Reformers are calling for funding formulas that go beyond simply equalizing dollars; they want plans that meet the needs of all students. These proposed reforms will be expensive and controversial, as many parents from wealthier districts object to having their local taxes used to fund distant schools across the state. In addition, the problems involved in attempting to quantify educational needs in terms of dollars and cents is complex and messy.

Site-based Decision Making

Carla made her proposal to her school board, which will ultimately decide which math series to use. Her recommendation came from a committee composed of other teachers in the district whose ideas and opinions were solicited and considered. Concerned parents, whose children would use the new series, were also at the meeting; they were able to ask questions and influence the decision. This appears to be democracy in action, but is it?

Critics of this top-down, district-level governance contend that too many important educational decisions are being made by people removed from the schools. They contend that school board members from across town may not know what is best for a particular school. **Site-based decision making** is *a movement towards placing more responsibility for governance at the school level.* Proponents of site-based decision making believe that the people most affected by educational decisions—teachers, parents, and even students—ought to be more directly involved in those decisions (Sarason, 1997). In addition to being more democratic, site-based decision making ought to result in better-run schools with an increased likelihood of improvement. People who help make decisions are more likely to buy into them and want to see them succeed.

Increasing Understanding 8.18

Explain why teachers in large, urban districts might feel more strongly than those in suburban districts about teacher input into educational decisions.

Both parents and teachers desire a greater say in educational issues. National polls show that the public in general, and parents in particular, overwhelmingly support the idea of parental involvement, and that parents should play a major role in shaping their children's education (Johnson, 1994). In one national poll, a majority of respondents said that parents, teachers, and students had too little input in decisions affecting the local public schools (Rose & Gallup, 2000). Teachers also want more say in how their schools are run. More than half of all teachers surveyed nationally, and two-thirds of teachers in large urban districts, expressed a desire for greater say in school governance issues (Louis Harris, 1993).

Site-based decision making usually exists in one of two forms. The most common is increased community participation in advisory committees, which are composed of parents, teachers, community members, and sometimes students. School boards and building administrators maintain legal control over schools, with the advisory committees providing input in areas as school goals and priorities, curriculum and extracurricular activities, and selection and evaluation of teachers and administrators.

A more radical form of site-based decision making, which results in greater decentralization, involves actual community control of educational decisions through an elected council. When this occurs, the district school board shares decision-making power with these councils in areas such as curriculum, budgets, and the recruitment and retention of principals and teachers. Experiments in several large cities have raised thorny questions about who should serve on these community councils as well as whether decentralized decision making results in better schools for children (Walberg & Niemiec, 1994).

Site-based decision making is appealing from a professional perspective. Professional educators should have a substantial say in how learning and teaching occur in their schools. However, site-based decision making creates dilemmas for teachers. One dilemma concerns time and effort. Teachers join the profession to work with students, and the increased time and effort required by extended committee work often drain teachers' energies away from their teaching. For example, is the effort Carla spent on the textbook selection process worth it, or would students be better served if she had been able to devote more of her time to teaching? If decisions such as these are made at the school level, will this increase duplication of effort in the district? These questions don't have easy answers.

School Choice

The freedom to choose is a central American value. Americans can choose how they make a living and where and how they live. Shouldn't they also have a choice in the kind of schools their children attend? As they are presently organized, schools tend to be bureaucratic and centralized, and the schools that students attend are determined by the neighborhoods in which they live. In the name of efficiency, we've created a governance and finance system that begins in state capitals, runs through local district offices, and culminates in schools that are amazingly similar in form and function. Walk into most schools across the country and you'll experience the same basic, box-like architecture with teachers teaching basically the same way (Cuban, 1984; Goodlad, 1984).

Critics decry this uniformity. At one level, it violates America's passion for individuality. We are a nation of 50 states with unique individuals and distinctive subcultures; our schools ought to reflect this diversity. In addition, experimentation and innovation have been central to our nation's progress. Conformity discourages innovation. From an

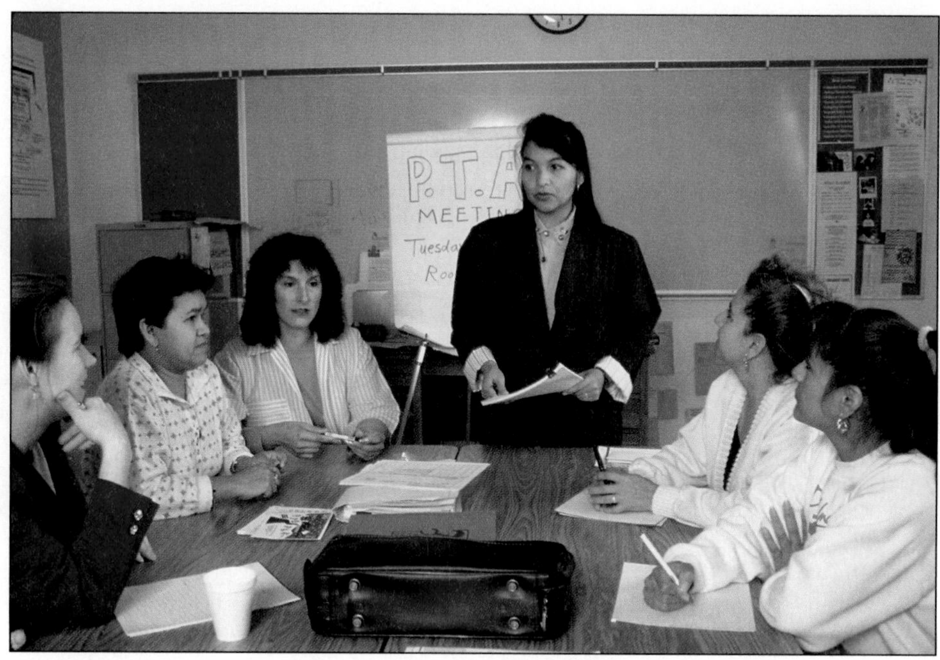

Site-based decision making actively involves parents and teachers in the running of their schools.

economic perspective, critics contend that the present system represents a monopoly that forces parents to send their children to neighborhood public schools (Goldhaber, 1999). They believe that alternatives would result in healthy competition, which would ultimately result in better schools. Critics also argue that the public school system has become bloated, bureaucratic, and unresponsive to individual citizens' needs. In response to these criticisms, reformers call for choice.

What does *choice* mean? Theoretically, parents already have choices, because the schools their children attend will be determined by the neighborhoods in which they choose to live. One of the major factors parents use in choosing a neighborhood is the quality of schools that serve the area. And if parents don't like the schools in their neighborhood, they can always send their children to private schools, something that 11 percent of parents currently do (Newman, 1998). In addition, through open-enrollment programs, districts typically allow parents who believe their local schools are sub-par to send their children across town to better schools. Although this requires greater time and expense, parents still have choices.

But choice advocates point out that many poor, minority, and inner-city parents don't have the resources to vote with their wallets or their cars. They can neither afford to move to better neighborhoods with better schools nor send their children to private schools. In addition, critics contend that some school districts are so bad that other schools in the district don't really provide viable alternatives. These parents deserve the right to choose just as much as their more wealthy counterparts.

But how can parents be provided with options? The concept of school choice has resulted in two educational innovations: charter schools and vouchers.

Charter Schools Charter schools attempt to create alternatives to existing public school offerings; parents who don't like the school choices available to them are given the right to create their own alternative or specialty schools. Some school districts already have alternative schools, which are designed to meet the needs of students who can't successfully function in regular schools and classrooms (such as children with serious behavior or emotional problems). **Charter schools** *are alternative schools that are independently* *operated but publicly funded*. To create a charter school, teachers or community members first develop a plan that includes curriculum, staffing, and budget. This plan or "charter" must then be accepted by the local school board and state office of education and serves as a contract with the state. Charter schools are similar to other alternative schools in that they target special populations; they differ from other alternative schools in that they are independently administered public schools and generally subject to less regulatory control from a district's central administration (Goldhaber, 1999).

The charter-school movement began in Minnesota in 1991 when the legislature approved the creation of eight teacher-created and operated outcome-based schools. (An outcome-based school makes curricular and instructional decisions based upon student performance on specified assessments.). Since that time, 35 additional states and the District of Columbia have passed charter-school legislation, resulting in more than 1,700 schools that educate more than 350,000 students (Bowman, 2000; Gresham, Hess, Maranto, & Milliman, 2000). Arizona is a leader in this area, having appropriated $600 million to fund over 350 charter schools; other states such as California, Texas, and Michigan are also experimenting with the idea. The federal government has committed $145 million per year to encourage experimentation with charter schools.

Increasing Understanding 8.19

Identify one similarity and one difference between charter schools and the schools we've discussed up to this point in the chapter.

The focus and purpose of different charter schools vary dramatically (Toch, 1998). Some are designed by inner-city community leaders to meet the needs of urban youth. One school in Michigan focuses on developing students' African heritage through language instruction, literature, and the arts. Other schools attract parents who want a return to the basics, while some schools focus on the arts.

A disturbing trend in the charter-school movement is the entrance of for-profit companies into the arena. Cutting corners to save money, many of these schools offer substandard educational experiences to their students. One researcher discovered the following:

■ ■ ■

Many of the charters' teachers are low-paid neophytes; as a result, staff turnover is high. Labs and libraries are rare. Even basic classroom supplies are often lacking. The kindergarten teacher at Eco-Tech Agricultural Charter School in Chandler, Ariz., for example, appeared to have little more than paper and pencils available for her students. And there are plenty of charter schools housed in buildings few would deem conducive to learning: Teachers at the West Michigan Academy of Environmental Sciences spent more than a year teaching 300 students at picnic tables and old desks in the Stadium Arena in Grand Rapids, briefly vacating the building for a knife-and-gun show (Toch, 1998, p. 40).

■ ■ ■

These problems illustrate one of the dilemmas with charter schools: how to encourage innovation and alternatives while ensuring quality.

The issue of quality surfaced in the state of Texas, a national leader in the charter-school movement. Near the end of 2000, a panel of state lawmakers recommended a moratorium on new charter schools, citing poor student performance, financial troubles, and unexpected closures (Associated Press, 2000). In 1999 there were 193 charter schools in Texas, and the state spent $218 million on them. However, only 59 percent of charter-school students passed a state skills exam in the 1998–1999 school year compared with the state average of 78.4 percent. In reviewing existing charter schools, the state education agency gave an "unacceptable" rating to nearly one-fourth of the 103 schools it studied. In addition, seven charter schools in the state closed because of problems ranging from declining enrollments to financial mismanagement to embezzlement. A major advantage of charter schools—freedom from bureaucratic oversight—also seems to be a major weakness of this reform.

Vouchers Vouchers are another approach to school choice. In essence, a **voucher** *is a piece of paper or check that parents can use to purchase educational services*. The basic idea

School choice in the form of vouchers and state tax credit can provide opportunities for minorities to choose the schools they want.

private and religious schools of their choice (Walsh, 1998). Proponents designed the program to provide inner-city students with alternatives to what they believed was a seriously flawed public-education system. The heaviest opposition has come from those who oppose the religious school option. In a 4 to 2 ruling, the Wisconsin Supreme Court did not find the law unconstitutional, and the U.S. Supreme Court refused to hear an appeal, giving the voucher program a temporary green light. However, experts expect additional legal challenges to the Ohio and Florida voucher systems (Walsh, 2000).

The outcomes of school choice are uncertain. Some research suggests that providing students with choice can lead to small achievement gains (Bowman, 2000a, 2000b; Goldhaber, 1999). Explanations offered for these gains include better instruction, a curriculum emphasizing academics, and greater parental involvement. In addition, parents provided with choice are clearly more satisfied with the schools their children attend (Goldhaber, 1999). However, questions about the effects of choice on school diversity are continually raised as we saw in the Exploring Diversity box on page 265.

SUMMARY

Governance: How are Schools Regulated and Run?

The responsibility for governing schools in the United States is given to the states by the U.S. Constitution. Within each state, the governor and state legislature are aided by the state office of education in regulating school functions.

Local control of education, a uniquely American idea, occurs through local school districts. Each district is governed by a local school board, containing lay people from the community and administered by a district superintendent. The superintendent is responsible for running the district office as well as overseeing the operations of the individual schools within the district. At the school level, the principal plays a major role in shaping the instructional agenda for each school.

Districts are part of a larger governance structure in each state that is determined by the state constitution. Within this structure, the state governor and legislature provide leadership through bills and initiatives. The overall responsibility for governing the state goes to the state board of education. Assisting this board is the state superintendent or commissioner, who is assisted by and responsible for the state office of education.

School Finance: How are Schools Funded?

Schools are funded from three different sources. Almost one-half of school funds come from local sources, which typically use property taxes to collect revenues. States provide another major source of funding; typically this is done through state income taxes and special taxes. The third source of school funding comes from the federal government.

Most education monies (60 percent) go to instructional services, which primarily target teacher salaries. Large variations in the amounts that different states invest for education are accounted for by different capacities to pay as well as by differences in the cost of living.

Emerging Issues in School Governance and Finance

Controversies over inequities in school finance have focused on differences within rather than between states. A large number of court cases has caused states to reexamine funding formulas and resulted in increased state funding and decreased local funding. Current approaches to funding equity go beyond absolute dollar amounts to include student and district needs.

Site-based decision making has emerged as a major trend in governance reform. In site-based decision making, both parents and teachers play a greater role in curricular and instructional decisions.

School choice in the form of charter schools and vouchers provides parents with greater control over their children's education. Charter schools, created by interested teachers and parents, attempt to target their efforts to specific educational goals or patrons. Vouchers, essentially tickets for educational services, allow parents to shop around for schools that fit their needs.

IMPORTANT CONCEPTS

block grants
categorical grants
charter schools
curriculum
local school boards
school district
school principal
site-based decision making
state board of education
state office of education
state tax-credit plans
superintendent
voucher

DISCUSSION QUESTIONS

1. Should legislation be passed to make local school boards mirror the populations they serve? (For example, if 25 percent of the population is Hispanic, should one-fourth of the school board be Hispanic?) What advantages and disadvantages are there to this approach to equitable representation? What alternatives might be better?
2. Would teachers make good school board members? Should a certain number or percentage of school board positions be reserved for teachers? Why?
3. Should the percentage of male and female principals reflect the gender composition of the teachers at that level? Why?
4. Should school districts in a state be funded equally? What are the advantages and disadvantages to this approach to educational funding? Should we fund all school districts in the United States equally? What are the advantages and disadvantages to this approach to educational funding?
5. Will school choice be a positive or negative development in education? Why?
6. Should vouchers be made available to private religious schools? Why?

CHAPTER 9

School Law

Ethical and Legal Influences on Teaching

At this point in your preparation to become a teacher, legal issues may seem distant, unrelated to your work, and perhaps not very interesting. Imagine, however, that you're an elementary teacher and are called to the main office to talk with a parent. Can you leave your class unsupervised? Or you're a high school teacher and you read a poem that strikes you as a powerful and moving commentary on love. Do you dare share it with your students without the approval of their parents? Perhaps you're a science teacher, and you've discovered a program on the Internet that you would like to use in your classes. Can you legally download and duplicate the information?

The answers to these questions are influenced by legal decisions. Our purpose in writing this chapter is to help you understand how legal issues can influence your life as a teacher. In this chapter, we try to answer the following questions:

- How do the law and ethics influence teacher professionalism?
- How is the U.S. legal system organized?
- What are teachers' legal rights and responsibilities?
- What legal issues are involved with religion in the schools?
- What are students' rights and responsibilities?

Let's begin by looking at two teachers struggling with legal and ethical issues.

Jason Taylor is a science teacher in a suburban school in the Pacific Northwest. The town in which he teaches is considering an open-space initiative that will limit urban growth. Environmentalists support the law because they believe it will help to preserve local farms and wildlife habitat in the area; businesses in the town oppose it because of its potential to curtail economic growth. Jason talks about the initiative in class, explaining how it will help the environment. At the end of his presentation, he mentions that he is the head of a local action committee and that interested students can receive extra credit for passing out fliers after school.

Some parents complain to the principal, claiming that school time shouldn't be devoted to political activity. When the principal calls in Jason to talk about the problem, Jason is adamant about his right to involve students in local politics, claiming that civic awareness and action should be part of every course that is taught. Unconvinced, the principal points out that Jason was hired to teach science, not social studies, and warns that persisting on this path could cause Jason to lose his job. What should Jason do?

■ ■ ■

Sasha Brown looks at the two folders in front of her and frowns. Her job is to recommend one of two students from her school for a prestigious science and math scholarship to the state university. Although the decision will ultimately be made by a committee that she'll be on, she knows that her recommendation will carry a lot of weight because she is chair of the math department.

One of the candidates is Brandon, a bright, conscientious student who always scores at the top of his class. The son of a local engineer, he has a good grasp of mathematical concepts. Sonia, the other candidate, is probably not as strong conceptually, but often solves problems in creative and innovative ways. She's also a female—and a female hasn't won this award in its 6-year history. In addition, Sasha knows that Sonia comes from a single-parent family and really needs the scholarship. Knowing this does not make the selection process any easier.

■ ■ ■

What would you do in these situations? What personal values would you use to resolve these dilemmas? What external guidelines exist to guide you? How does all this relate to teacher professionalism?

LAWS, ETHICS, AND TEACHER PROFESSIONAL DECISION MAKING

As you've learned from other chapters, professionalism is a theme of this book. We've said throughout that professionals are responsible for making decisions in ill-defined situations, they have the autonomy to do so, and they base their decisions on a thorough understanding of their professional literature.

There are several important dimensions of this literature. For example, teachers must understand the content they're expected to teach. They must also know how to represent it in ways that make sense to students, and they must understand the intellectual, emotional, and social makeup of their students.

They must also understand the legal and ethical guidelines influencing their profession, what their professional limitations are, and why professional decision making is so important. This chapter examines the law and how it influences teaching. But before we do that, let's put legal aspects of teaching in a larger perspective.

The Law and Its Limitations

You are a teacher in a middle school, and you see a fight between two students on the playground. What must you do? First, you can't ignore the fight, because you're responsible for the safety of the children; in fact, parents have the right to sue a teacher if they can demonstrate that the teacher failed to protect students from injury, a problem called *negligence*. However, should you physically break up the fight, or can you simply report it to the administration? The law is vague on this and other specific legal issues.

Laws regulate the rights and responsibilities of teachers, but they only partially guide our professional decision making. This is true for two reasons. First, laws are purposely general so that they can apply to a variety of specific situations. We saw this illustrated in the example involving a playground altercation; Jason's dilemma at the beginning of the chapter is another case. The law *generally* protects teachers' rights to freedom of speech, but does it protect teachers' rights to campaign politically in their classrooms and deal with issues that may not be part of the assigned curriculum? Unfortunately, the answers to these questions are not explicitly spelled out in laws; therefore, professional decision making is required.

A second limitation of laws is that they've been passed in response to problems in the past, so they aren't necessarily able to provide specific guidelines for future decisions. For example, what are the rights of students and teachers who have AIDS? (We examine this issue later in the chapter.) Technology is another issue. (We devote Chapter 12 to this topic.) It is changing the way we teach, but what kinds of materials can we legally borrow from the Internet? What are the legal limitations to software use in schools? What can be legally copied? Experts are wrestling with these issues, and preliminary guidelines have appeared, but educators must often make decisions based on their knowledge of the law and their professional judgment. We see again why professional knowledge is so important.

Increasing Understanding 9.1

Think back to your study of Chapter 6, which examined philosophical issues and education. How does the section you're reading now relate to your study of that chapter? Explain specifically.

To answer this question online and receive immediate feedback, go to the *Increasing Understanding* Module in Chapter 9 of the Companion Website at **http://www.prenhall.com/kauchak.**

Ethical Dimensions of Teaching

The law tells teachers what they can do (rights) and what they must do (responsibilities). However, laws don't tell teachers what they *should* do. This is where ethics, which examines values and appropriate conduct, is so important. **Ethics** *provides a set of principles that can be used to decide whether or not acts are right or wrong.*

Professional ethics *are moral principles adopted by a group to provide guidelines for conduct* (Corey, Corey, & Callahan, 1993). For example, the Hippocratic oath, which says that physicians will do their best to benefit their patients (with both curative methods and kindness), to tell the truth, and to maintain patients' confidences, is a code that guides the medical profession. Other professions have similar ethical codes, which are designed to both guide practitioners and protect clients.

We were first introduced to the National Education Association's (NEA) Code of Ethics in Chapter 1 when we discussed teacher professionalism. This code provides teachers with potential guidance in ambiguous professional dilemmas such as we found at the beginning of this chapter. As with the law, however, codes of ethics are limited; they only provide general guidelines for professional behavior. Let's look again at Jason's dilemma to see why this is so. Item 2 within the NEA Code of Ethics states, ". . . the educator shall not unreasonably deny the student access to varying points of view." Has Jason been balanced and fair in presenting both sides of the environmental and political issue? A code of ethics isn't, and never can be, specific enough to provide a definitive answer. Jason must answer the question for himself based on his personal philosophy of education, and within it, his personal code of ethics.

Sasha's dilemma also illustrates the limitations of this code. Item 6 in the NEA Code cautions us not to discriminate on the basis of race, color, creed, or sex, but does it specifically tell us what to do with Sonia? Based strictly on academics, Brandon appears to be the better candidate. However, Sonia's need along with the good that might result from other females seeing a girl receive recognition in math (a traditionally male-dominated area of the curriculum), might influence the decision.

Increasing Understanding 9.2

Earlier we said that laws are limited because they are *general* and *reactive,* that is, written in reaction to problems in the past. Which of these two limitations also applies to professional codes of ethics?

In response to these complexities, teachers are often admonished to "treat all students equally." However, even encouraging teachers to treat all students alike isn't as simple as it appears. Sensitive teachers purposefully call on shy students to involve them in lessons, strategically avoid calling on assertive students who tend to dominate discussions, and give students who have difficulty with English more time to answer questions and finish tests. These teachers treat specific students differently depending on their individual needs; their decisions involve issues of fairness and professional ethics.

These examples illustrate why your personal philosophy of education is important. We saw in Chapter 6 that a philosophy of education provides a framework for thinking about educational issues and guides professional practice. Your personal philosophy will guide you as you make decisions about what is important, what is fair, and why. Since the law and professional codes of ethics can only provide general guidelines, developing a personal philosophy is critical in helping you make the specific decisions that you must make every teaching day.

Having briefly examined the law, ethics, and their limitations, now let's look at the American legal system in more detail.

THE U.S. LEGAL SYSTEM

Laws regulating schools and teachers are part of a larger, complex legal system that exists at three interconnected levels: federal, state, and local. This system attempts to use peoples' rights and responsibilities to each other as the basis for defining fairness.

Federal Influences

At the national level, the Constitution is the law of the land. It doesn't provide specific educational guidance, but it has influenced education in two forms: amendments and laws.

Constitutional Amendments Think about the following questions:

- As a teacher, how much freedom do you have in selecting topics to teach? Are you limited in what books and articles you can ask your students to read?
- Can you publicly criticize the administrators and school board members for whom you work?
- How much freedom do students have in running their school newspapers and yearbooks?

The First Amendment to the Constitution guarantees all citizens the right of freedom of speech, but where do you draw the line with respect to the preceding questions? You certainly can't have your students read *Playboy* magazine, but how about *Catcher in the Rye*, a classic American coming-of-age novel with explicit sexual references? Similar uncertainties exist with respect to the second and third questions.

Professional ethics provide broad guidelines for teachers as they make decisions in complex situations.

The Fourth Amendment protects citizens from unreasonable searches and seizures. To what extent does this amendment protect teachers and students? For instance:

- Can school officials search students' backpacks and purses when they're on school property?
- Are students' lockers considered to be personal property or can they be searched if school officials suspect they contain drugs or weapons?

The Fourth Amendment provides general guidelines about search and seizure but doesn't specifically answer these two questions.

The Fourteenth Amendment states that ". . . nor shall any State deprive any person of life, liberty, or property without due process of law." What does "due process" mean in the context of schools? For example:

- Can teachers be fired without a formal hearing?
- Can students be expelled from class without formal proceedings?
- How long can a student be suspended from school, and what kinds of deliberations need to precede such a suspension?

Increasing Understanding 9.3

Which amendment is relevant to Jason's situation at the beginning of this chapter? Why?

Again, the Constitution provides general guidelines about due process, but the specifics are left for teachers and other educators to decide. These examples further illustrate why an understanding of legal issues is so important for beginning teachers.

Federal Laws Through the laws it passes, Congress exerts federal influence on education. The Civil Rights Act of 1964 states: "No person in the United States shall on the ground of race, color, or national origin, be excluded from participation in or be denied the benefits of, or be subjected to discrimination under any program or activity receiving federal financial assistance." This law was influential in ending segregation in schools

required textbooks are often identified. Within this general framework, teachers are free to teach topics as they see fit. Sometimes these topics and methods are controversial and may result in a teacher being disciplined or dismissed.

In considering issues of academic freedom, the courts consider the following:

- The teacher's goal in discussing a topic or using a method.
- The age of the students involved.
- The relevance of the materials to the course.
- The quality or general acceptance of the questioned material or methods.
- The existence of policies related to the issue.

Increasing Understanding 9.4

One of the criteria used by the courts is the age of the students involved. How might this criteria influence the case involving taboo words; that is, would the verdict have been different if the class were in a middle school or an elementary school? Why?

In applying these principles to the teacher using the "Learnball" format, the courts upheld the district's dismissal. The court based its decision on the fact that this teaching strategy was not widely accepted, and the teacher had been warned repeatedly by the administration to stop using it.

The case of the high school English teacher resulted in the opposite outcome. The teacher's job was reinstated because the court upheld the importance of two kinds of academic freedom: the "substantive" right to use a teaching method that serves a "demonstrated" purpose, and the procedural right not to be discharged for the use of a teaching method not prohibited by clear regulations. The teacher's goal was for his students to understand taboo words and how they influenced literature, a topic that fell under the broad umbrella of the English curriculum. Had this not been the case, the outcome would probably have been different, as it might have been if the teacher had been clearly warned about using this strategy.

When considering controversial topics, teachers should try to decide if they fall within the scope of the assigned curriculum. When discussing controversial topics or using potentially controversial teaching methods, teachers should have a clear educational goal in mind and be able to defend it if objections arise. Academic freedom protects knowledgeable, well-intentioned teachers working within their assigned responsibilities. As a beginning teacher, if you're uncertain about an issue that could involve academic freedom, check with your principal or other school administrator.

Copyright Laws

As teachers, we want to share the most up-to-date information with our students. This can involve copying information from newspapers, magazines, books, and even television programs. Unfortunately, our desire to bring this information into the classroom can violate copyright laws (Murray, 1994).

Copyright laws *are federal laws designed to protect the intellectual property of authors, including printed matter, videos, and computer software.* Just as patents protect the intellectual work of inventors, copyright laws protect the intellectual work of writers, songwriters, and filmmakers. To balance the rights of authors with the legitimate needs of teachers and learners, federal guidelines have been developed.

Fair-use guidelines *specify limitations in the use of print, video, and software materials.* Teachers may do the following:

- Make a single copy of a book chapter, newspaper or magazine article, short story, essay, or poem for planning purposes.
- Copy short works (less than 250 words for poetry; less than 1,000 words for prose) for use in the classroom.

Copyright laws provide guidelines for teachers when they use technology in their teaching.

However, teachers may not create class anthologies by copying material from several sources or charge students more than it cost to make the copies. In addition, pages from workbooks or other consumable materials may not be copied.

Videotapes and software pose unique challenges. They too were created by and belong to someone, and fair-use guidelines also apply to them. For example, teachers may tape a television program, but they must use it within 10 days of taping; they may show it again for reinforcement but must erase the tape after 45 days. One copy, and no more, of computer software may be made for a "backup." Materials on the Internet may not be copied unless specific permission is given or unless the document is published by the federal government.

These guidelines do restrict teachers, but the restrictions are not usually a major handicap. Teachers may want to share the principle of fair use with students to help them understand its purpose and the ways that copyright laws help protect people.

Increasing Understanding 9.5

Would a suit concerning a copyright violation be brought to a state court or a federal court? Why?

Teacher Liability

■ ■ ■

An elementary teacher on playground duty mingles with students, watching them as they run around. After the teacher passes one group of students, a boy picks up and throws a rock that hits another boy in the eye, causing serious injury. The injured boy's parents sue the teacher for negligence (*Fagen v. Summers,* 1972).

■ ■ ■

A teacher takes a group of first graders on a school-sponsored field trip to the Oregon coast. The teacher has four of the students stand on a log for a photo. A big wave rolls in, causing the log to roll, seriously injuring one of the children. The parents sue the teacher for negligence (*Morris v. Douglas County School District,* 1965).

■ ■ ■

come in and talk any time if something is bothering you. . . even if it's just a little thing." As she gets up to leave, you see that she moves rather stiffly.

"Anita, are you sure you're okay?"

"I fell the other day."

"But, how did you hurt your back?"

Anita's expression suggests that a fall wasn't the cause.

"Did someone hurt you, Anita?" you ask firmly.

"Please, please. . . you can't tell anyone," she blurts out.

■ ■ ■

What are your responsibilities in this situation? She begged you to say nothing. Do you honor her request?

The answer is no. All 50 states and the District of Columbia have laws requiring educators to report suspected child abuse (Fischer et al., 1999). In addition, teachers are protected from legal action if they act in "good faith" and "without malice." Teachers suspecting child abuse should report the matter immediately to either school counselors or administrators.

Teachers' Private Lives

Case STUDY

Gary Hansen had lived with the same male roommate for several years. They were often seen shopping together in the local community, and they even went to social events together. Students and other faculty "talked," but Gary ignored the hints that he was homosexual until the principal called him into his office, confronted him with the charge, and threatened dismissal.

■ ■ ■

Mary Evans had been in Chicago for over 8 years and didn't mind the long commute from the suburbs because it gave her an opportunity to "clear her head." She had been living with her boyfriend for several years, and everything seemed fine until one day she discovered she was pregnant. After lengthy discussions with her partner, she decided to keep the baby but not get married. When her pregnancy became noticeable, her principal called her in. She affirmed that she wasn't married and didn't intend to be. He asked for her resignation, suggesting she was a poor role model for her students.

■ ■ ■

An individual's right to "life, liberty, and the pursuit of happiness" is one of our country's founding principles. What happens, however, when teachers' lifestyles conflict with those of the community in which they work? Are teachers' private lives really "private," or can teachers be dismissed for what they do in their free time?

In answering these questions, the courts have relied upon a definition of teaching that is broader than classroom instruction. Teachers do more than help students understand English and history, for example; they also serve as role models for students. This results in greater scrutiny than most citizens receive. Other professionals, such as attorneys or physicians, might be able to lead lifestyles at odds with community values, but teachers might not. What *are* teachers' rights with respect to their private lives?

Teachers have a right to their own private lives but must meet community standards of acceptable conduct.

Unfortunately, clear answers in this area don't exist. Morality and what constitutes a good role model is contextual. For example, in the 1800s, teachers' contracts required them to do the following:

- Abstain from marriage.
- Be home between the hours of 8:00 P.M. and 6:00 A.M. unless attending school functions.
- Wear dresses no more than two inches above the ankle.

More recently, pregnant teachers were required (even if married) to take a leave of absence once their condition became noticeable. Obviously, views of morality change. As one California Supreme Court noted, "Today's morals may be tomorrow's ancient and absurd customs" (Fischer et al., 1999, p. 296).

Moral standards also vary among communities. What is acceptable in large cities may not be acceptable in the suburbs or in rural areas. Cities also provide a measure of anonymity, and notoriety is one of the criteria courts use to decide if a teacher's private activities damage their credibility as role models. For example, many young people are choosing to live together as an alternative to marriage. This lifestyle is less noticeable in a large city than in smaller communities.

Where does this leave teachers? Generalizations such as "Consider the community in which you live and teach" provide some guidance, as do representative court cases. Unfortunately, the law isn't clear with respect to the specifics of teachers' private behavior.

The issue of homosexuality illustrates how schools can become legal battlegrounds for people's differing beliefs. Some people believe that homosexuality is morally wrong, whereas others believe that it is either an inherited condition or a personal choice and has

Teaching in an Era of Reform

EMERGING LEGAL ISSUES

The reform movement is having a profound effect on the educational landscape, requiring both educators and the public to rethink fundamental questions about education. It's not surprising, then, that educational reform is also raising legal issues. They overlap in at least two important areas:

- Teacher licensure.
- Teacher tenure.

Licensure

As you saw earlier in the chapter, tests are increasingly being used to determine who will be eligible for teacher certification. Historically, testing has been limited to entry-level applicants, but this is now changing.

For example, lawmakers from North Carolina passed the ABCs of Public Education Law in 1996, which mandated that teachers in the state's lowest performing schools be required to take a test of general knowledge (Bradley, 1999b). Those who failed the test three times would be dismissed.

The law was highly controversial. In fact, after the North Carolina Association of Educators threatened to sue and other critics argued that the tests would make it difficult to recruit teachers for low-income schools, the state backed off.

A similar reform strategy was proposed in Massachusetts. Governor Paul Cellucci proposed that teachers of low-performing math students be required to take a test measuring their understanding of math content (Bradley, 2000). He further proposed that the results be made public but that no disciplinary actions for teachers be taken. The implementation of this proposed policy is still to be determined by the state's board of education.

Tenure

Reformers are also attacking tenure, suggesting that it protects incompetent teachers and arguing that it is virtually impossible to remove a tenured teacher, regardless of competence. One study of 30 school districts found that only .15 percent of teachers believed to be incompetent were either dismissed or persuaded to resign (Bradley, 1999a). This is only slightly more than one-tenth of 1 percent, and superintendents in these districts estimated that the percentage of tenured teachers who should be dismissed for poor performance is significantly higher.

In 1997 lawmakers in Oregon eliminated tenure for teachers, replacing it with 2-year contracts (Bradley, 1999a). Whether or not other states follow remains to be seen.

Putting Reform into Perspective

Reformers' attempts to improve the performance of students by upgrading the quality of their teachers make

no relevance to schools. When the issue has gone to courts, they have generally ruled in favor of homosexual teachers. In a landmark California case, a teacher named Marc Morrison engaged in a brief homosexual relationship with another teacher. About a year later, the other teacher reported the relationship to Morrison's superintendent, who reported it to the state board of education. The state board revoked his teaching credentials, arguing that state law required teachers to be models of good conduct and that homosexual behavior is inconsistent with the moral standards of the people of California (*Morrison v. State Board of Education*, 1969).

The California Supreme Court disagreed. The court concluded that "immoral" was so broad that it could be interpreted in a number of ways, and no evidence existed indicating that Morrison's behavior adversely affected his teaching effectiveness.

However, in other cases involving criminal or public sexual behavior (for example, soliciting sex in a park), courts have ruled against teachers (Fischer et al., 1999). **Notoriety,** *the extent to which the teacher's behavior becomes known and controversial,* is a key element in these cases.

The case involving the unwed mother further illustrates the murkiness of school law. A case in Nebraska in 1976 resulted in an unwed mother being fired because the school board

Increasing Understanding 9.7

A teacher became involved in her city's gay rights movement, passing out leaflets at demonstrations and making speeches. Her school district warned her and then fired her for her activity. What legal issues would be involved here?

intuitive sense. We can't teach what we don't know and, without question, teachers must understand the content they're teaching. Perhaps more than any other professionals, teachers need a broad background of general knowledge that will help them guide and inspire the students they teach.

Similarly, some of the reformers' points with respect to tenure are valid. Dismissal of a tenured teacher is time-consuming and expensive—one California district took 8 years and spent over $300,000 in legal fees to dismiss one tenured teacher (Richardson, 1995). Districts typically respond to the issue by moving incompetent teachers from school to school instead of taking them out of classrooms.

However, while the use of tests to ensure teacher quality has been upheld in courts (Melnick & Pullin, 2000), critics argue that student performance depends on many factors besides teachers' knowledge, the most powerful being the students' own background knowledge and motivation (Kohn, 2000). Critics contend that more effective ways to measure competence exist, direct observation being one. Watching a teacher actually work with students in teaching-learning activities, while admittedly more time-consuming and labor intensive, provides a better indication of teacher competence than a paper and pencil test. However, politicians who pass teacher-testing laws often don't understand this.

The issue of tenure is also complex. It was created to protect teachers from political or personal pressure, and it continues to serve that function. Those who support tenure contend that teachers need protection from the potential abuse of power that can exist if a principal or other district leader has a vendetta against a teacher for unprofessional reasons. But does tenure sometimes protect incompetent teachers? Unfortunately, sometimes the answer is yes.

You Take a Position

Now it's your turn to take a position on the issues discussed in this section. Go to the *Education Week* Website at **http://www.edweek.com,** find "search" on the first page, and type in one of the following two search terms: *teacher licensure* or *teacher tenure*. Locate a minimum of three articles on one of these topics and do the following:

1. Identify the title, author, and date of each article and then write a one-paragraph summary of each.
2. Identify a pattern in the articles. (Each article—or even two of the three—suggesting that teacher tenure be abolished would be a pattern, for example.)
3. After identifying the pattern, take one of the two following positions:
   - The pattern suggested in the articles, if implemented, *is* likely to improve education.
   - The pattern suggested in the articles *is not* likely to improve education.

State your position in writing and document your position with information taken from the articles and your study of the text. (You may use this chapter and any other chapter of the text.)

To answer these questions online, go to the Take a Position Module in Chapter 9 of the Companion Website.

claimed there was ". . . a rational connection between the plaintiff's pregnancy out of wedlock and the school board's interest in conserving marital values" (*Brown v. Bathhe*, 1976). In other cases, however, courts have ruled in favor of pregnant unwed teachers, including one in Ohio who became pregnant via artificial insemination (Fischer et al., 1999).

While the law is ambiguous with respect to teachers' private sexual lives, it is clear regarding sexual relations with students. Teachers are in a position of authority and trust, and any breach of this trust will result in dismissal. When teachers take sexual advantage of their students, they violate both legal and ethical standards.

Issues of morality and teachers as role models influence other areas as well. Drug offenses, excessive drinking, driving under the influence of alcohol, felony arrests, and even a misdemeanor, such as shoplifting, can result in dismissal (Fischer et al., 1999). The message is clear: teachers are legally and ethically responsible for being good role models.

Teachers with AIDS AIDS is a special issue with respect to teachers' rights, and the courts have generally used the principle of nondiscrimination towards AIDS-infected people as a legal principle to guide decisions. The legal foundation for this principle was

DANGEROUS HALLWAYS

This ABC News video segment describes an incident of school harassment that led to the filing of a lawsuit against a school district. Two seventh-grade girls named Christina and Jessica discuss the harassment they encountered at the hands of four older students. Their parents took the problem to the assistant principal, the superintendent of schools, and finally the school board. Despite death threats and verbal and physical abuse, the older girls were never punished, and Christina and Jessica's parents were advised to homeschool their children.

Think about This

1. Schools are responsible for ensuring the safety of its students. Was the school district negligent with respect to ensuring the girls' safety in this situation? Explain.
2. What other course of action might the school and district have pursued to solve this problem?
3. What would you have done had your child been harassed as these girls were?

To answer these questions online and receive immediate feedback, go to the Video Perspectives Module in Chapter 9 of the Companion Website.

established in 1987 in a case involving an Arkansas teacher with tuberculosis (*School Board of Nassau County v. Arline*, 1987). The courts' dilemma involved weighing the rights of the individual against the public's concern about the possible spread of disease. In ruling in favor of the teacher, the court considered the disease a handicap and protected the teacher from discrimination because of it.

This decision set a precedent for a California case involving a teacher with AIDS who had been removed from the classroom and reassigned to administrative duties (*Chalk v. U.S. District Court Cent. Dist. of California*, 1988). The court ruled in favor of the teacher, using medical opinion to argue that the AIDS-infected teacher's rights to employment outweighed the minor risk of communicating the disease to the children.

RELIGION AND THE LAW

Religion provides a fertile ground for helping us understand how conflicting views of education can result in legal challenges. The role of religion in schools is controversial, and teachers and administrators are often caught in the crossfire.

We know from our study of Chapter 5 that the Constitution provides for the principle of *separation of church and state*. The **establishment clause** of the First Amendment *prohibits the establishment of a national religion*, and the **free exercise clause** (freedom of speech) of this amendment *prohibits the government from interfering with individuals' rights to hold and freely practice religion*. Given the central role of religion in many people's lives, the issue of religion in schools has become legally contentious. Some of the questions that have arisen include:

- Can students and teachers pray in schools?
- Can religion be included in the school curriculum?
- Can religious clubs have access to public school facilities?

We answer these questions in the sections that follow.

Although the Constitution forbids the establishment of any particular religion in schools, a number of complex issues make this a controversial topic.

Prayer in Schools

In the past, prayer and scripture reading were common in many, if not most, schools. In fact, they were required by law in some states. Pennsylvania passed legislation in 1959 that required daily Bible reading in the schools (but exempted children whose parents did not want them to participate). The law was challenged, and the U. S. Supreme Court ruled that it violated the First Amendment's establishment clause (*Abington School District v. Schempp*, 1963). Nondenominational or generic prayers designed to skirt the issue of promoting a specific religion have also been outlawed. In a New York case, the Supreme Court also held that generic prayers violated the establishment clause of the First Amendment (*Engle v. Vitale*, 1962). Neither schools nor teachers can officially encourage student prayer; it is permissible when student initiated and when it doesn't interfere with other students or the functioning of the school (Walsh, 1999).

The law also forbids the use of religious symbols in schools. For example, the courts ruled that a 2-by-3 foot portrait of Jesus Christ displayed in the hallway next to the principal's office was unconstitutional (Fischer et al., 1999).

In a similar way, the U.S. Supreme Court struck down a Kentucky law requiring that the Ten Commandments be posted in school classrooms (*Stone v. Graham*, 1980). To circumvent the law, some Kentucky educators and legislators are advocating posting the Ten Commandments next to the Bill of Rights and the Magna Carta as important cultural or historical documents (Gehring, 1999a). The constitutionality of this strategy is uncertain at this time.

Increasing Understanding 9.8

Which aspect of the First Amendment—establishment or free exercise—would relate to the case involving the portrait of Jesus Christ? Why?

These cases illustrate a legal trend; prayer and religious symbols are not allowed in public schools because they violate the principle of separation of church and state. In addition to the law, the principle of separation of church and state also acknowledges learner diversity. Our students—Christians, Jews, Muslims, Buddhists, Hindus, and others—belong to many different religions. Imposing a particular form of prayer or religion on all children can be both illegal and unethical, because it can exclude children on the basis of religion.

Although the courts have been clear about denying prayer as a regular part of schools' opening ceremonies, the issue of prayer at graduation and other school activities is less clear. In a landmark case, a high school principal asked a clergyman to provide the graduation invocation and also suggested the content of the prayer. This was ruled a violation of separation of church and state by the U.S. Supreme Court (*Lee v. Weismann*, 1992). The school's involvement in the prayer was the key point; whether or not the court would have banned the prayer if it had been initiated by students or parents is uncertain.

In a recent decision, the Supreme Court voted 6 to 3 against student-led prayers at football games in Texas (Walsh, 2000). Central to the Court's decision was the conclusion that students would perceive the pre-game prayer as "stamped with the school's seal of approval," thus violating the principle of separation of church and state.

Religious Clubs and Organizations

While organized prayer in schools is illegal, extracurricular religious clubs meeting on school grounds may be legal. For example, a student in Omaha, Nebraska requested permission to meet with her Bible study group before school. Officials refused, concerned about the possibility of undesirable groups such as the Ku Klux Klan using the case as precedent. The U.S. Supreme Court ruled in the student's favor, stating that schools must allow religious, philosophical, and political groups to use school facilities on the same basis as other extracurricular organizations (*Board of Education of the Westside Community School v. Mergens*, 1990). The fact that the club was not school sponsored or initiated was central to the court's argument.

In a related case, the Supreme Court recently approved the use of federally funded computers and library books for Catholic schools in Louisiana (Walsh, 2000). The principle of separation of church and state will likely be revisited in future educational court cases.

Religion and the Curriculum

■ ■ ■

A high school biology teacher prefaces his presentation on evolution with a warning, stating that it is only a "theory" and that many theories have been proven wrong in the past. He encourages students to keep an open mind and offers creationism, or the Biblical version of the origin of the world, as an alternate theory. As part of his presentation, he holds up a pamphlet, published by a religious organization, that refutes evolution and argues that creationism provides a more valid explanation. He offers the pamphlets to any interested students.

■ ■ ■

Where does religion fit in the school curriculum? Can a well-intentioned teacher use his classroom to promote religion? Given court decisions on school prayer, simplistic answers might be no or never. But considering the enormous influence that religion has had on human history—art and literature being two important examples—the issue becomes more complex.

Evolution is one point of tension. Concern over this issue dates back to the famous 1925 "Scopes Monkey Trial," where a high school teacher (Scopes) was prosecuted for violating a Tennessee state law that made it illegal to teach "any theory which denies the story of the Divine Creation of man as taught in the Bible and to teach instead that man is descended from a lower order of animals." Scopes argued that the law violated his academic freedom, contending that the theory of evolution had scientific merit and should be shared with his high school biology students. Scopes was found guilty of violating the state law and fined $100, but the decision was later reversed on a technicality.

Since then, several states have attempted to use legislation to resolve the evolution issue. In the 1960s the Arkansas legislature passed a law banning the teaching of evolution in that state. The U.S. Supreme Court declared the law unconstitutional because it violated the establishment clause of the First Amendment. In 1982, the Louisiana legislature, trying to create a middle ground, passed a Balanced Treatment Act, requiring that evolution and creationism be given equal treatment in the curriculum. The U.S. Supreme Court threw out this law, arguing that instead of being balanced, it was designed to promote a particular religious viewpoint.

In a more recent case, the Kansas State Board of Education voted 6 to 4 to remove most references to evolution from state standards (Keller & Coles, 1999). This decision gave local school boards leeway to exclude or downplay the topic because the state standard determines state testing policies. While the decision did not violate any legal statutes, it was highly criticized, not only in the state, but across the country. Bill Nye, public television's "Science Guy," even joined in the criticism.

The broader issue of religion in the curriculum has also surfaced in several court cases. In one, fundamentalist parents objected to the inclusion of several literature stories in the curriculum including *The Wizard of Oz*, *Rumpelstiltskin*, and *Macbeth*, arguing that these materials exposed children to feminism, witchcraft, pacifism, and vegetarianism. A lower court supported the parents, but a higher federal court reversed the decision, asserting that accommodating every parent's religious claims would "leave public education goals in shreds." It supported the right of districts to use religiously controversial materials if they were useful in achieving important educational goals (*Grove v. Mead School District, 1985*). A comparable case in Illinois (*Fleischfresser v. Directors of School District No. 200*, 1994) resulted in a similar outcome. When schools can show that learning materials have a clear purpose, such as exposing students to time-honored literature, parental objections are usually overridden.

Teaching about Religion in Schools

Unfortunately, legal controversies have had a dampening effect on teaching *about* religion in schools. Here we emphasize the difference between teaching *about* different religions and *advocating* a particular one. Religion has had enormous impact on history (for example, the Crusades and New World exploration) as well as on art and literature. Avoiding the study of religion leaves our students in a cultural vacuum that is both inaccurate and potentially dangerous (Nord & Haynes, 1998). But how can we teach about religion without provoking religious controversies?

The U.S. Department of Education wrestled with this problem and developed the following guidelines (U.S. Department of Education, 1995):

- Advocacy of religion by teachers and administrators has no place in public schools.
- Public schools should not interfere with or intrude upon a student's religious beliefs.
- Students may pray in private but cannot do so to a captive audience or compel other students to pray.
- Public schools may teach about the history of religion, comparative religions, the Bible as literature, and the role of religion in the history of the United States and other countries.

Increasing Understanding 9.9

A biology teacher wants his students to know how the Bible is the basis of the theory of creationism. Would this be legally permitted? Why? Under what circumstances wouldn't it?

In addition, the directive reaffirmed students' rights to distribute religious literature and display religious messages on items of clothing, as protected by the First Amendment.

Critics caution that the Bible should not be used as a history textbook, should not be framed and taught strictly from a Christian perspective, and should not be used to promote Christian faith formation and religious values (Gehring, 2000). The First

Students' Rights and Responsibilities

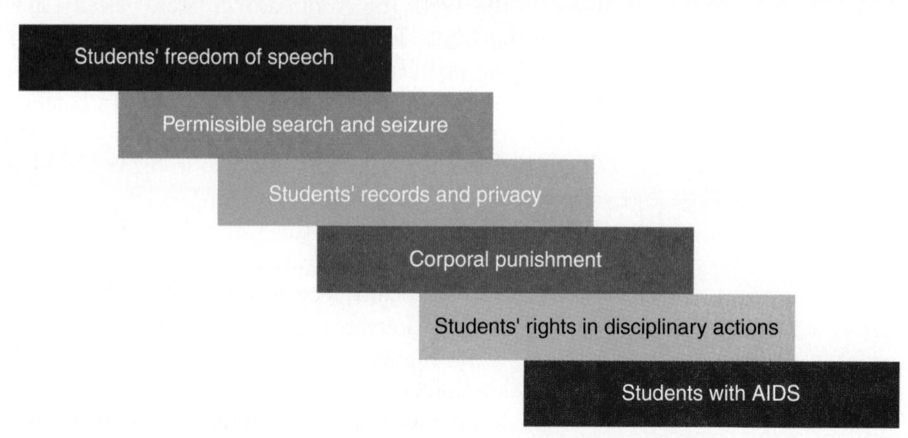

Amendment Center, a national organization promoting free speech, recently published new guidelines "The Bible and Public Schools: A First Amendment Guide" (Gehring, 1999b). The guidelines, endorsed by the National Education Association, the American Federation of Teachers, as well as the National School Boards Association, recommend using secondary sources to provide alternate scholarly perspectives on the Bible as a historical document. These guidelines are available online in the *Web Links* Module of Chapter 9 on the book's Companion Website. These guidelines seem straightforward, but future legal battles over this emotional issue are likely.

STUDENTS' RIGHTS AND RESPONSIBILITIES

As it does for teachers, the law also helps define students' rights and responsibilities. Students' legal rights and responsibilities are important because they provide guidelines for teachers and other educators regarding how students should be treated. They are also important because they provide educational opportunities to teach students about our legal system along with their rights and responsibilities as future adult citizens. These rights and responsibilities are outlined in Figure 9.2 and discussed in the sections that follow.

Students' Freedom of Speech

■ ■ ■

Many parents in an urban middle school are advocating that school uniforms be required. They believe that having students wear uniforms would reduce classroom management problems, discourage gang colors, and minimize social comparisons between wealthy, well-dressed students and less-wealthy students. The school administration has voiced support for the proposal.

The student editors of the school newspaper hear of this proposal and conduct an informal poll of students, which indicates that the majority of students are opposed to uniforms. The editors want to publish these results along with an editorial advocating student choice in what they wear. The principal refuses to let them print the article. What are students' rights in this matter?

■ ■ ■

The law guarantees students' rights to freedom of speech, but students may not disrupt a school's main mission—learning.

As we've repeatedly seen, the First Amendment guarantees American citizens freedom of speech; as teachers, we want our students to understand and appreciate this right as they prepare to be responsible citizens. Do they lose this right when they enter our schools? Yes and no. Yes, they have the right to express themselves in schools, provided doing so doesn't interfere with learning.

The landmark case in this area occurred in the late 1960s during the peak of the controversial Vietnam War. As a protest against the war, three high school students wore black arm bands to school, despite the school's ban on such protests (*Tinker v. Des Moines Community School District*, 1969). The students were suspended and then sued the school district, arguing that the suspensions violated their freedom of speech. The case went all the way to the U.S. Supreme Court, which ruled in favor of the students. The Court ruled that freedom of speech is an essential right for all citizens and that students' freedom of expression should not be curtailed if it isn't disruptive and doesn't interfere with the educational mission of the school.

Students' freedom of speech was tested again in 1986; during a school assembly, a high school student made a student-government nominating speech that contained a graphic and explicit metaphor comparing the candidate to a male sex organ. Not surprisingly, students in the audience hooted, made sexual gestures, and became disruptive. After he was reprimanded, the student sued, claiming his freedom of speech had been curtailed. This case also went to the U.S. Supreme Court, which ruled that "The schools . . . may determine that the essential lessons of civil, mature conduct cannot be conveyed in a school that tolerates lewd, indecent or offensive speech. . . ." (*Bethel School District No. 403 v. Fraser 106*, 1986). The court ruled, in essence, that freedom of speech may be limited if it interferes with learning or with the running of a school.

Increasing Understanding 9.10

How are the two cases involving students' freedom of speech similar? Different?

With respect to freedom of speech, school newspapers pose a special problem. We want students to feel ownership and responsibility for the stories they write and the paper they create. However, school newspapers are an integral part of a school's extracurricular activities

teacher's consent. Also, a teacher's letter of recommendation may remain confidential if students waive their rights to access. To protect teachers in these situations, the Buckley Amendment excludes teachers' private notes, grade books, or correspondence with administrators.

A recent court case involving the Buckley Amendment has implications for classroom practice (Walsh, 2000). A mother in Oklahoma objected to the practice of having her children's papers graded by other students and the results called out in class. She claimed this violated her children's rights to privacy, and a federal circuit court agreed on both counts—student grading and the public disclosure of grades. Consequently, teachers who want to use other parents or students as graders must first seek parental permission. In addition, the court ruling calls into question the practices of publicly displaying graded student work and students passing out corrected or graded assignments and tests.

Increasing Understanding 9.11

You are a high school teacher and receive a letter from a prospective employer of one of your former students. The letter contains a form that asks you to provide, in addition to a letter of recommendation, information about the student's GPA. What are the legal aspects of this request?

Because of the extra effort and paperwork required to put these procedural safeguards into place and because of potential encroachments into teachers' private records, administrators and teachers have mixed feelings about this law. However, while not perfect, the Buckley Amendment has improved parents' access to information as they try to make sound decisions about their children, and it has made school officials more sensitive to parents' needs for that information and the importance of confidentiality.

Corporal Punishment

■ ■ ■

In one Pennsylvania elementary school, a 36-year-old, 6-foot tall, 210-pound school principal paddled a 45-pound first-grade boy four different times during a school day for a total of 60 to 70 swats. After the incident, the boy needed psychological counseling, cried frequently, and had nightmares and trouble sleeping (*Commonwealth of Pennsylvania v. Douglass,* 1991).

The Fayette County Board of Education in Tennessee specifies that any paddles used to discipline students must be:

- not less than ⅜ inch or more than ½ inch thick.
- free of splinters.
- constructed of quality white ash.
- 3 inches wide (except handle) and not more than 15 inches long: grades K–5.
- 3½ inches wide (except handle) and not more than 18 inches long: grades 6–12.

Students can receive a maximum of three swats with this district-approved paddle (Johnston, 1994).

■ ■ ■

Corporal punishment is highly controversial, both because of the legal issues involved and because using physical punishment as a disciplinary tool is questionable. As of 1997, it was prohibited in 27 states and the District of Columbia (Fischer et al., 1999), but in a 1977 landmark case the U.S. Supreme Court ruled that corporal punishment in schools is not a violation of the Eighth Amendment to the Constitution (which prohibits cruel and unusual punishment). The court further ruled that states may authorize corporal punishment without prior hearing and without the prior permission of parents (*Ingram v. Wright*, 1977), which left the door open for the use of corporal punishment in the remaining 23 states. So where does that leave prospective teachers?

In the states where corporal punishment is permitted, legal guidelines suggest teachers may use corporal punishment under the following conditions:

Increasing Understanding 9.12

How would these guidelines apply to the Pennsylvania principal who paddled a first grader?

- The punishment is intended to correct misbehavior.
- Administering the punishment doesn't involve anger or malice.
- The punishment is neither cruel nor excessive and doesn't result in lasting injury.

Teachers considering this disciplinary option, even though it is legal, should ask themselves several questions:

- Is this the best way to teach students about inappropriate behavior?
- Would other options be more effective in encouraging students to consider their behaviors and the effects of those behaviors on others?
- What does corporal punishment teach children about the use of force to solve problems?

Behavioral psychologists, who regularly use reinforcers and punishers to shape student behavior, have this to say about corporal punishment:

> There should never be a need to use physical punishment with a regular classroom population. If there are severe behavior problems that cannot be treated by other response-weakening techniques in conjunction with positive reinforcement, the classroom structure and the teaching procedures should be carefully examined (Jenson, Sloane, & Young, 1988, pp. 110–111).

Their point is a good one; classroom corporal punishment should be used only as a last resort and under extreme conditions.

Students' Rights in Disciplinary Actions

Case STUDY

Jessie Tynes, a sixth-grade teacher, turned around just in time to see Billy punch Jared. "Billy, what did I tell you about keeping your hands to yourself? This school and my classroom have no room for this kind of nonsense! You're out of this class until I meet with your parents. Come with me to the principal's office where you'll sit until we can solve this problem of keeping your hands to yourself."

■ ■ ■

Sean, a high school junior, was walking to his locker when someone reached in from behind to knock his books on the floor. When he turned around, he saw Dave standing behind him with a smirk on his face. Losing his temper, Sean pushed Dave and a scuffle broke out, which was broken up by Mr. Higgins, the vice principal. Both students received 10-day suspensions from school.

■ ■ ■

Increasing Understanding 9.13

What amendment to the Constitution guarantees students due process? (Hint: Under what circumstances are teachers guaranteed due process?)

How are these problems similar? How are they different? What legal guidelines assist educators as they try to deal fairly and effectively with school discipline problems?

Both incidents involve infractions of school rules, but they differ in the severity of the problem and resulting actions. These differences are important when the courts consider *due process*, a central issue when students' rights are involved.

Students have a right to an education, and the courts specify that limiting this right can only occur when due process is followed. However, the courts also acknowledge the rights of schools to discipline students in the day-to-day running of schools.

Suspending Billy from class would be considered an internal affair best resolved by his teacher, his parents, and himself. Unless a suspension lasts longer than 10 days or results in expulsion from school, teachers and administrators are generally free to discipline as they see fit, assuming the punishment is fair and is administered equitably.

Actions that lead to out-of-school suspensions, entry on a student's record, or permanent expulsion require more formalized safeguards. These include the following:

1. A written notice specifying charges and the time and place of a hearing.
2. A description of the procedures to be used, including the nature of evidence and names of witnesses.
3. The right of students to cross-examine and present their own evidence.
4. A written or taped record of the proceedings as well as the findings and recommendations.
5. The right of appeal.

As we can see from this list, the procedures involved in long-term suspensions and expulsions are quite detailed and formal. They exist to safeguard students' rights to an education, an economic necessity in today's modern world. They also consume time and energy, so they are generally used only as a last resort.

Students with AIDS

AIDS, or Acquired Immune Deficiency Syndrome, became a major health and legal issue in the schools in the 1980s. Previously thought to be limited to sexually active gay men and drug users who shared hypodermic needles, AIDS entered the school-age population through contaminated blood transfusions.

Battle lines were quickly drawn. Concerned parents worried that the AIDS virus would be spread in school through either casual contact or the sometimes rough-and-tumble world of children on playgrounds. Parents of children with AIDS wanted their children to have access to an education that was as normal as possible. The courts were soon drawn into the fray.

A landmark and precedent-setting case occurred in St. Petersburg, Florida, in 1987 and involved 7-year-old Randy Ray, a hemophiliac who had contracted AIDS through a blood transfusion. Because of his condition and fears about possible spread of the disease, school officials refused to allow Randy and his two brothers, who also had AIDS, to attend school. His parents first reacted by moving elsewhere, but when that failed to open school doors, they moved back to St. Petersburg and sued the school district.

A U.S. district court ruled that the boys should be allowed to attend school with special safeguards including special attention to the potential hazards of blood spills (*Ray v. School District of DeSoto County,* 1987). Subsequent cases involving other students with AIDS have been similarly resolved, with courts holding that these children are protected from discrimination by the Individuals with Disabilities Act of 1991 as well as Section 504 of the Rehabilitation Act of 1973, which protects otherwise-qualified handicapped individuals from discrimination. Central to the courts' decisions has been the potential negative effects of exclusion on the social and emotional well-being of the child. The courts have been clear in rejecting exclusion as the automatic solution to the problem of dealing with AIDS-infected students; instead, they have required schools to address the specific risk factors involved in each case.

Exploring Diversity

Considering Multiple Perspectives

AFFIRMATIVE ACTION

One outcome of the civil rights movement of the 1960s was **affirmative action,** *a collection of policies and procedures designed to overcome past racial, ethnic, gender, and disability discrimination*. The rationale for affirmative action was that merely outlawing discrimination was not enough; society should take steps to correct past discriminatory practices to ensure racial and gender balance in all aspects of society, including schools.

The legal basis for affirmative action comes from at least three sources. The Fourteenth Amendment to the Constitution guarantees equal protection under the law. Titles VI and VII of the Civil Rights Act of 1964 specifically prohibit discrimination in federally assisted educational programs in terms of race, color, religion, sex, or national origin. The Americans with Disability Act of 1991 extends similar protection to persons with disabilities.

Affirmative action affects schools in two important ways: hiring policies for teachers and admission policies for students. In an attempt to remedy past discriminatory hiring practices, a number of school districts are required under affirmative action guidelines to hire more minority teachers. The courts have generally upheld this practice if affirmative action is deemed necessary to reverse past discriminatory practices (Fischer et al., 1999). However, in past instances where discrimination is not seen as a problem, preferential hiring practices for minorities on criteria other than merit or qualifications are discouraged. For example, because of declining enrollments, a school district in New Jersey was forced to reduce the teaching staff in the business department of a high school by one teacher. Two teachers, one White and one African American, had equal seniority and were considered to be of equal quality. The school board decided to retain the African American teacher, using affirmative action as a rationale. The White teacher sued, claiming she was being discriminated against; federal courts agreed, arguing that minorities had not been underrepresented in the district's teaching force in the past (*Taxman v. Board of Education of Township of Piscataway*, 1996). In essence, for affirmative action to be legal, there must be a logical basis for its use.

Affirmative-action cases such as these have resulted in charges of reverse discrimination, with critics alleging that minorities and women were being given unfair preferential treatment in hiring and admission decisions. One such claim was made in 1974 by Alan Bakke, who was denied admission to medical school, while minority candidates with lower grades and test scores were admitted. The case went all the way to the U.S. Supreme Court, which ruled in a 5 to 4 vote that Bakke should be admitted. However, in making this decision, the Court did not rule out other forms of race-conscious admission procedures (*Regents of the University of California v. Bakke*, 1978).

The issue of affirmative action is likely to remain controversial in the future. Toward the end of the 1990s, voters in California and Washington supported legislation eliminating preferential higher-education admission policies (Dworkin, 1998). In addition, court cases have raised questions about the legality of racial quotas for magnet schools (Dowling-Sendor, 1999). Legal experts in this area conclude, "Whether affirmative action will be mended by government and supported by voters is a question that is likely to continue to challenge schools and colleges during the coming decade" (Fischer et al., 1999, p. 480).

The Changing Role of Teachers

Education exists in a complex social environment. The society in which we live is constantly changing; these changes will affect your life as a professional.

One societal trend is the growing tendency to settle problems in court. As one legal expert observed, "Americans are a litigious people" (Fischer et al., 1999, p. vii). We tend to seek lawyers rather than talk, to sue rather than compromise. The United States has more lawyers per capita than any other country on the planet. Teachers, fearful of this trend, are increasingly seeking protection through professional liability insurance (Portner, 2000).

How should the profession respond to all this? A simplistic response would be to embrace this confrontational approach in solving educational disputes. But this "my lawyer's tougher than your lawyer" approach to problem solving is inadequate for at least two reasons. First, it creates adversarial relationships within the profession. Second, and more importantly, it emphasizes standards of professional behavior that are minimal rather than ideal. Instead of looking to courts and lawyers for professional guidance, teachers should try to improve and enforce their professional code of ethics to make it a guiding light in our legally and morally confusing times.

But where does this leave individual teachers, who can be vulnerable to legal challenges? Teachers need to become "legally literate" with respect to their rights and responsibilities as professional educators (Fischer et al., 1999). Knowing their rights provides them with the authority to do what they know is right and just; knowing their responsibilities better enables them to serve their students effectively.

Becoming legally literate has another positive professional consequence. It will improve teaching. Teachers who understand rights guaranteed by the Constitution can help students understand how these rights apply to them and to their lives in and out of classrooms. Teachers can also help students understand their individual responsibilities. Finally, teachers who clearly understand issues involving freedom of speech, freedom of religion, freedom from unreasonable search and seizure, and due process are more likely to behave democratically in their classrooms.

SUMMARY

Laws, Ethics, and Professional Decision Making

Laws and professional ethics provide guidelines as teachers make professional decisions. Laws specify what teachers must and can do. Codes of ethics provide guidelines for what teachers should do as conscientious and caring professionals.

The U.S. Legal System

The U.S. legal system is a complex web of interconnected bodies. At the federal level, the U.S. Constitution provides broad guidelines for legal issues, and Congress passes laws that impact education. However, most of the direct legal responsibility for running schools belongs to states and local school districts.

Teachers' Rights and Responsibilities

Teachers have rights and responsibilities as professional educators. Licensure provides them with the right to teach; a teaching contract specifies the legal conditions for employment. Most new teachers are hired on probationary status. Once granted tenure, teachers cannot be dismissed without due process.

Teachers' academic freedom is guaranteed by the First Amendment to the Constitution. However, in deciding upon issues of academic freedom, the courts examine the educational relevance of the content or method involved as well as the age of students.

Copyright laws, designed to protect the property rights of authors, provide restrictions on teachers' use of published materials. New educational copyright issues are being raised by the increased use of videotape, television, and Internet technologies.

Liability poses unique challenges to teachers. The courts hold that teachers act *in loco parentis*, and when they fail to protect the children under their charge, they can be sued for negligence. When deciding on issues of liability, the courts take into account the age and developmental level of the student as well as the kinds of risks involved in an activity.

Teachers' private lives are not as private as some would wish. Because they are expected to be role models to students, what teachers do in the hours away from school is often scrutinized and, if illegal, can result in dismissal.

Religion and the Law

Religion provides a legal battleground in the schools. While banning organized prayer in schools, the courts have approved religious clubs and organizations as well as private expressions of students' religious beliefs. While the courts disapprove of religious advocacy, teaching *about* religion is legal when it can be justified educationally.

Students' Rights and Responsibilities

Many of the same issues of rights involving freedom of speech and due process that affect teachers also pertain to students. In addition, students are protected from unreasonable search and seizure by the U.S. Constitution, and their education records are protected by federal legislation called the Buckley Amendment.

IMPORTANT CONCEPTS

academic freedom
affirmative action
Buckley Amendment
copyright laws
establishment clause of the First Amendment
ethics
fair-use guidelines
free exercise clause of the First Amendment
in loco parentis
negligence
notoriety
professional ethics
reduction in force
tenure

DISCUSSION QUESTIONS

1. What are the advantages and disadvantages of teacher tenure? What arguments might there be for a longer period of probation before granting a teacher tenure? A shorter period? Should teachers be reviewed periodically after tenure is granted?
2. What is the proper role of religion in the schools? In what areas of the curriculum should religion enter? Should teachers reveal to students their religious beliefs? What should a teacher do if a student shares his or her religious beliefs with the class?
3. Touching can be a powerful way of expressing caring or concern. Should teachers touch their students? In what way and under what circumstances? How might your answer be influenced by the following factors: the age and gender of the students and the age and gender of the teacher?
4. What should be the place of corporal punishment in schools? How might the following factors influence your response: the age of the student, the type of misbehavior, and the age and gender of the teacher?
5. Should teachers' private lives be placed under more public scrutiny than other professionals' lives (such as doctors or lawyers)? Why?

GOING INTO SCHOOLS

1. Obtain a teacher's contract from a local school district or teacher. Explain how it deals with the following:
   a. probationary period before tenure
   b. tenure
   c. extra teacher responsibilities
   d. due process

   Compare your findings with information from the text.
2. Obtain a school or district's policy handbook. Explain how it deals with the following:
   a. student records and privacy
   b. student freedom of speech
   c. disciplinary guidelines and due process
   d. student lockers and searches for drugs and alcohol

In a paper, describe what you found and discuss the implications for you as a future teacher.

3. Interview a teacher about professional ethics.
   a. Does the teacher have a copy of either the NEA or AFT Code of Ethics? (If not, share the NEA Code of Ethics from Chapter 1.)
   b. How helpful are these guidelines in professional decision making?
   c. What changes would the teacher like to see made in these codes?

   Re-read the NEA Code of Ethics and using the teacher's comments as a sounding board, decide how helpful this code of ethics would be for a beginning teacher.
4. Interview a teacher about the district's policy in terms of reporting child abuse.
   a. Are the policy and procedures clear?
   b. Does the teacher know what his or her rights and responsibilities are in terms of reporting child abuse?
   c. Has the teacher ever had to report child abuse, and if so, what was the outcome?

   In a paper, describe what your responsibilities would be in reporting child abuse. Also, list any unanswered questions you might have about the process.
5. Interview several middle or high school students to find out about their knowledge of legal issues. Ask them what their rights and responsibilities are in terms of:
   a. freedom of speech
   b. student records and privacy
   c. search and seizure
   d. student rights in disciplinary actions.

   What do their responses tell you about their legal literacy? What could you do as a teacher to increase your level of legal literacy?

Virtual Field *Experience*

If you would like to participate in a Virtual Field Experience, go to the *Field Experience* Module in Chapter 9 of the Companion Website.

ONLINE PORTFOLIO ACTIVITIES

To complete these activities online, go to the *Portfolio Activities* Module in Chapter 9 of the Companion Website to submit your response.

Portfolio Activity 9.1

School Law and Professional Ethics

INTASC Principle 10: *Partnership*

Sometimes professional ethics are backed by the law, other times they are not. The purpose of this activity is to acquaint you with connections between the NEA Code of Ethics and legal issues. Reexamine Principle I, Commitment to the Student, in the NEA Code of Ethics in light of the content of this chapter, noting places where the professional ethics overlap with legal issues.

Portfolio Activity 9.2

Deepening Your Knowledge of Legal Issues

INTASC Principle 9: *Professional Commitment*

The purpose of this activity is to encourage you to deepen your understanding of one aspect of school law. Choose a topic from this chapter and research it further. (The book *Teachers and the Law,* (1999) by Fischer, et al., is an excellent source.) In a short paper, describe the issue you've chosen and the implications it might have for you as a teacher.

PART 4

Teaching

Case STUDY

Suzanne Brush, a second-grade teacher at Webster Elementary School, has her students involved in a unit on graphing. After getting her students settled down for math, she began, "I'm planning a party for our class. While I was doing that, a question came to my mind that I thought maybe you could help me solve today. I need to know how I can figure out the class's favorite kind of jelly bean. How could we find out? If you can help me out, raise your hand."

Several students offered suggestions and, after considerable discussion, they finally settled on giving each student several jelly beans and having them indicate which one was their favorite.

"It just so happens," Suzanne smiled, as they decided on the idea, "that I did bring in some jelly beans today, and you'll be able to taste these jelly beans and vote for your favorite flavor."

She then handed out a baggy with seven different-flavored jelly beans in it to each student.

"Okay," she started when everyone was done tasting. "Right now I need your help. . . . Raise your hand, please, if you can tell me what we can do now that we have this information. How can we organize it so that we can look at it as a whole group? Jacinta?"

"See how many people like the same one, and see how many people like other ones," Jacinta responded.

"Okay, can you add to that? . . . Josh?"

"You can write their names down and see how many . . . like black," Josh answered uncertainly.

"That was right in line with what Jacinta said," Suzanne smiled and nodded. "Here's what we're going to do. We have an empty graph up in the front of the room," she continued, moving to the front of the room and displaying the outline of a graph that appeared as follows:

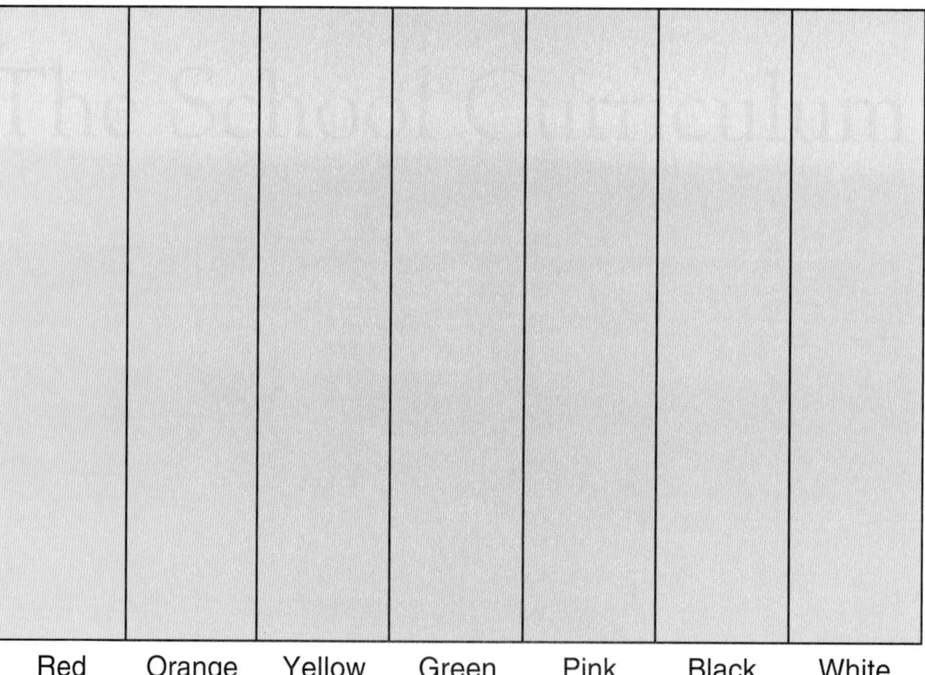

"Yes, Justin," she nodded in response to his raised hand.

"See which ones like red, get the people that like red and write it down; get all the colors like yellow, green, orange, black, yellow, white," he suggested haltingly; Suzanne carefully monitored the attention of the rest of the students while Justin made his suggestion.

"That's a great idea. We're going to do that," Suzanne responded, explaining that she had a series of cut-out cardboard squares that matched the jelly bean colors for the graph. She directed individual students to come to the front of the room and paste the color of square that represented their favorite color on the graph. After all the groups were done, the graph appeared as follows:

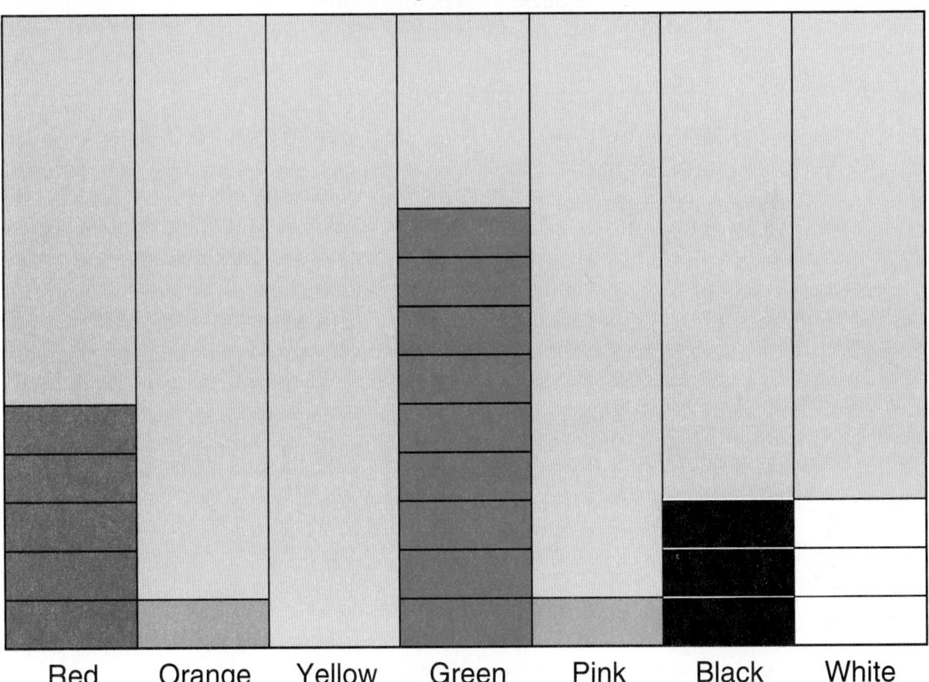

"I need your attention back up here, please," she continued. "We collected the information and organized the information up here on the graph. Now we need to study and analyze the information. I need you to tell me what we know by looking at this graph. Candice, what do we know?" she asked, walking toward the middle of the room.

"People like green," Candice answered.

"Candice said most people like the green jelly beans. . . . Candice, how many people like green?"

"Nine."

"Nine people like green. . . . And how did you find that out? Can you go up there and show us how you read the graph?"

Candice went up to the graph and moved her hand up from the bottom, counting the green squares as she went.

"What else do we know by just looking at the graph? . . . Justin?

"There are three people that like black and three people that like white."

"Three people like black and three people like white," Suzanne repeated, pointing to the black and white columns on the graph. "Let's let Stacey add some more to that."

"No one liked yellow," Stacey answered.

"Nobody picked yellow," Suzanne repeated.

"Okay, what else do we know from looking at the bar graph? . . . Andrew?"

"One took orange."

"Only one person picked orange," Suzanne repeated.

"And one person picked pink. . . . Okay, here we go. . . . How many more people liked green than red?" she asked, changing the direction of the questioning. "How many more people liked the green jelly beans than the red? Look up at the graph. Try to find the information, set up the problem, and then we'll see what you come out with. You have to have a problem set up on your paper."

Suzanne watched as the students looked at the graph and began setting up the problem. She commented, "Quite a few hands, and a few people are still thinking," as she moved across the room. She stopped briefly to offer Carlos some help, continued watching the students as they finished, and then said, "I'm looking for a volunteer to share an answer with us. . . . Dominique? How many more people liked the green jelly beans than the red ones?"

"Nine plus 5 is 14," Dominique answered.

"Dominique says 9 plus 5 is 14. Let's test it out," Suzanne said, asking Dominique to go up to the graph and show the class how she arrived at her answer.

As Dominique went to the front of the room, Suzanne said, "We want to know the difference. . . . How many more people liked green than red, and you say 14 people, . . . 14 more people liked green. Does that work?" Suzanne asked, pointing at the graph.

Dominique looked at the graph for a moment, shrugged her shoulders, grinned sheepishly, and then said, "I mean 9 take away 5."

"She got up here and she changed her mind," Suzanne said with a smile after Dominique responded. "Tell them."

"Nine take away 5 is 4," Dominique said.

"Nine take away 5 is 4," Suzanne continued, "so how many more people liked green than red? . . . Carlos?"

"Four," Carlos responded.

"Four, good, four," Suzanna smiled warmly. "The key was you had to find the difference between the two numbers."

After several more similar problems, she said, "I have one more question, and then we'll switch gears a little bit. How many people participated in this voting? How many people took part or participated in this voting?"

Suzanne watched as the students turned to the graph. "Matt? How many people?" she said as she saw that students were finished and several had their hands raised.

"Twenty-four," Matt answered.

"Twenty-four," Suzanne repeated. "How many people are in the room right now?"

"Uhmm, 24," he answered.

"Is that where you got your answer?" she asked, leaning over him and touching his shoulders. "What was the problem you set up?"

"How many people voted," he answered.

"Matt said 24. Did anyone get a different answer? So we'll compare. . . . I can't call on you if you're jumping up and down," she said as she walked among the students, who were waving their hands energetically.

"Roberto?"

"Twenty-two."

"How many people got 22 for their answer?"

A number of hands went up, and Suzanne asked, "How many people got a different number?" A few students raised their hands.

"How did you solve the problem?" she asked, walking past the table and motioning to Robert. "That's the most important thing."

"Nine plus 5 plus 3 plus 3 plus 1 plus 1 equals 22," he answered quickly.

"Where'd you get all those numbers?"

"There," he said, pointing to the graph.

"He went from the highest to the lowest, added the numbers, and the answer was 22. . . . Matt, why isn't it 24?" Suzanne asked, walking back toward him, smiling.

There's no reply from Matt.

"Raise your hand if you didn't put a square up there," she directed the class, and two students who didn't participate raised their hands. Suzanne explained why the answer wasn't 24.

As time for lunch neared, Suzanne said, "Raise your hand if you can tell me what you learned this morning in math."

"How to bar graph," Jenny responded.

"How to bar graph," Suzanne repeated. "More important, when we set up a problem, what do we have to do to solve the problem. . . . Timmy?"

"Add or subtract."

"Okay, but what do we have to decide *before* we add or subtract?"

"The numbers."

"So, we have to collect the information, and then we have to organize it. We organized it by setting up a bar graph, something that we can look at and talk about and use to decide what we need to do with the information. Then we set up some problems, and we solved them. It's a nice way to look at information and make decisions about certain things," she said as she ended the lesson.

■ ■ ■

WHAT IS CURRICULUM?

To begin this section, let's look back at Suzanne's lesson. She wanted her students to understand that information can be simplified and made more usable by representing it in a graph. She also had her students practice basic arithmetic skills and problem solving by asking questions such as "How many more people liked the green jelly beans than the red?" and then having the students create similar problems.

Suzanne's lesson reflects decisions about both curriculum and instruction. Let's see how they relate to each other.

The Relationship between Curriculum and Instruction

Curriculum has different definitions, ranging from descriptions such as "all the educational experiences students have in school" to "the results of decisions about what content should be taught and what learning experiences students should have." Definitions of curriculum and instruction often overlap, and in some cases curriculum appears to subsume instruction. We will avoid these issues and simply define **curriculum** as *what students learn in school* and **instruction** as *the way they learn the curriculum or the ways in which it is taught*.

Curriculum focuses on learning goals and the reasons the goals have been selected; instruction is the way teachers help students reach the goals. For example, Suzanne wanted

her second graders to understand that graphs help us represent information; that goal indicated a curriculum decision. To reach the goal, she had her students sample a variety of jelly beans, pick their favorite flavor, and represent their preferences on a large graph; that method reflected a decision about instruction. Another option would have been for Suzanne simply to explain why graphs are valuable, give her students some information, and then have them graph it. (We examine instruction and learning in detail in Chapter 11.)

Increasing Understanding 10.1

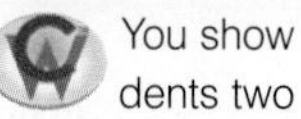

You show your students two short essays on the overhead projector. One effectively makes and defends an argument, and the other does not. Your purpose in doing so is to help your students learn to make and defend an argument in writing. Identify the curriculum decision and the instruction decision in what you did. Describe an alternative to your instructional decision (a different way of helping your students reach the goal).

To answer this question online and receive immediate feedback, go to the *Increasing Understanding* Module in Chapter 10 of the Companion Website.

The Explicit Curriculum

The school curriculum exists in three parts. The first is the explicit curriculum, which is the curriculum found in textbooks, curriculum guides, courses of study, field trips, and other formal educational experiences (Vallance, 1995); Suzanne's lesson on graphing was part of it. The **explicit curriculum** *includes what teachers are expected to teach, what learners are expected to learn, and what schools are held accountable for.* The explicit curriculum at the elementary level is heavily influenced by language arts and math, as we'll see in the next section.

Curriculum in Elementary Schools To begin this section, let's look again at Sharon and Susie's schedules, which you first saw in Chapter 7. As you may recall from that chapter, Sharon is a first-grade teacher and Susie teaches third grade. Their schedules appear in Table 10.1.

We saw in Chapter 7 that both teachers are responsible for all the content areas, such as language arts, math, and science, and the amount of time each teacher devotes to different content areas is a personal decision.

The way elementary schools are organized has an important influence on the curriculum. To see how, take another look at the schedules. Remembering that we're now focusing on what is taught—the curriculum. What do you notice? Some similarities and differences include the following:

- Both teachers strongly emphasize language arts and math. In a 6-hour instructional day (subtracting the half hour for lunch in each case), Sharon devotes 1 hour and 45 minutes to language arts, and Susie spends a minimum of 1 hour and 5 minutes on this subject.

Table 10.1 **Two Elementary Teachers' Schedules**

Sharon's First-Grade Schedule		Susie's Third-Grade Schedule	
8:30 A.M.	School begins	8:30 A.M.	School begins
8:30–8:45	Morning announcements	8:30–9:15	Independent work (practice previous day's language arts and math)
8:45–10:30	Language arts (including reading and writing)	9:15–10:20	Language arts (including reading and writing)
10:30–11:20	Math	10:20–10:45	Snack/independent reading
11:20–11:50	Lunch	10:45–11:15	P.E.
11:50–12:20	Read story	11:15–12:15	Language arts/social studies/science
12:20–1:15	Center time (practice on language arts and math)	12:15–12:45	Lunch
1:15–1:45	P.E.	12:45–2:00	Math
1:45–2:30	Social studies/science	2:00–2:30	Spelling/catch up on material not covered earlier
2:30–2:45	Class meeting	2:30–2:45	Read story
2:45–3:00	Call buses/dismissal	2:45–3:00	Clean up; prepare for dismissal

The elementary curriculum is heavily influenced by language arts and reading.

Increasing Understanding 10.2

How much time does each teacher devote to math? What do these allocations suggest about the relative importance of language arts compared to math?

- Science and social studies receive limited emphasis.
- Art and music don't appear in the schedules; neither do computers, in spite of today's emphasis on technology.

Both teachers reported that they have computers in their classrooms and that their students take turns working with them. Art and music are handled by resource teachers who come into the classrooms on a rotating basis.

Both teachers also reported that when science and social studies are taught, they are usually integrated with language arts; they are seldom taught independently. This is typical of elementary classrooms (S. Mittelstadt, personal communication, January 22, 1999; S. Van Horn, personal communication, January 21, 1999).

If you observe in elementary classrooms, you're likely to see schedules that vary somewhat from the ones in Table 10.1. However, the emphasis on language arts and math and the de-emphasis on science, social studies, and the arts is likely to be similar.

Increasing Understanding 10.3

Think again about "block" scheduling, which you first studied in Chapter 2. (An example of this would be having classes meet for 90–100 minutes a day for half of the school year.) Identify at least two ways in which block scheduling might influence the curriculum.

Curriculum in Middle and Secondary Schools We also saw in Chapter 7 that middle and secondary schools are organized so that the curriculum is much more structured than it is in the elementary schools. When you were in high school, you passed from class to class based on a bell schedule, and periods were commonly 50 or 55 minutes long. When schoolwide activities were held (such as a pep rally before an athletic event), periods were shortened.

As with elementary schools, the organization of middle and secondary schools has important influences on the curriculum. For example, Chris Lucio, the junior high teacher we featured in Chapter 7, teaches *only* geography. Also, all of his periods are the same length—50 minutes. As a result, in a given year geography receives the same curricular emphasis as does language arts (English), math, and all the other content areas. This would not hold true over the course of several years, as geography has to compete with other social studies subjects such as history, government, and economics.

Figure 10.1 **Forces Influencing Curriculum**

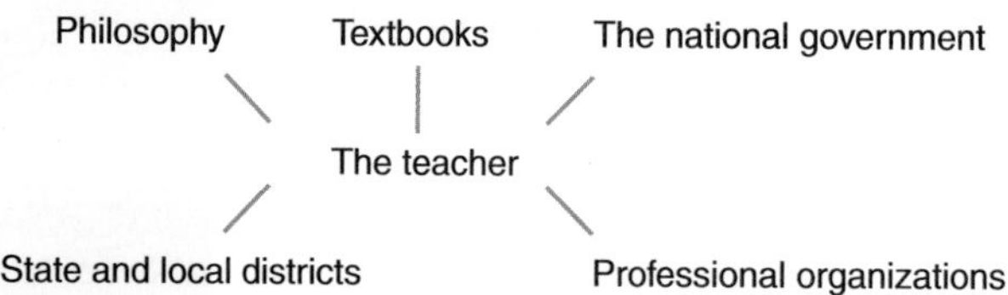

Curriculum and the Professional Teacher

As we've emphasized throughout the book, you're taking this course to introduce you to the world of teaching and to help you understand your crucial role in promoting student learning.

In Chapter 1, we said that professionals are people who use their knowledge and understanding to make decisions in complex and often ill-defined situations. Nowhere will professionalism be more important than in designing the curriculum. While a number of factors influence what is taught and learned, you, the teacher, are at the center of the process (which is why *the teacher* is at the center of Figure 10.1).

We see this illustrated in Suzanne's, Sharon's, and Susie's work. Suzanne emphasized graphing as part of her math curriculum and made a special effort to link the content to students' experiences with a hands-on activity. Because she believes that her students benefit from additional experiences with language, Susie allocates 1 hour and 5 minutes to language arts in the morning, and sometimes teaches additional language arts from 11:15–12:15.

These decisions are the teachers'. No one specifically told Suzanne how much emphasis to place on graphing in her math class. She could have de-emphasized it or even ignored it completely. Also, if Susie chooses to teach science on Monday from 11:15 to 12:15 and additional language arts on Tuesday during the same time, it is her decision—and hers alone—based on her understanding of the content, her students' needs, and her goals. These are professional decisions that only teachers can make.

Increasing Understanding 10.7

Teachers who feel strongly that basic skills are a crucial part of the curriculum are basing their decision most nearly on what educational philosophy? Explain.

Middle and secondary teachers have only slightly less autonomy than elementary teachers have. For example, a beginning algebra teacher might choose to spend a great deal of time on basic skills, such as solving problems like $x + 2x + 3x = 24$, or she might choose to emphasize word problems such as:

▪ ▪ ▪

Greg has some coins in his pocket, Sally has twice as many as Greg, and Juanita has three times as many as Greg. They have 24 coins altogether. How many does each student have?

▪ ▪ ▪

Again, these are professional decisions based on knowledge and understanding—understanding of algebra, understanding how to represent it so students can understand it, and understanding what students need and how they learn. One geography teacher might focus on geography and culture, whereas another might emphasize climate and physical features, such as mountains, rivers, and plains. Similar curricular decisions are made in all the content areas every day.

We've said before that teachers are "alone" as professionals when they shut their classroom doors. Closing the door is symbolic, representing teachers' professional control over what is taught in their classrooms and how it is taught. But external forces, some subtle, others not so subtle, creep into classrooms and influence teachers' curricular decisions. Let's examine some of them.

Increasing Understanding 10.8

Are decisions about curriculum made at the national level, such as by the federal government, or by states and local districts? Why? (Hint: Think about your study of the history of the American educational system in Chapter 5.)

Philosophical Foundations: Sources of Curriculum

We said earlier that curriculum reflects goals and the reasons for teaching them. Because time doesn't allow all possible goals to be taught, decisions have to be made about priorities. For instance, of the following goals, which would you consider to be most important?

- To acquire a thorough understanding of traditional content, such as literature, science, history, and advanced mathematics.
- To develop basic skills such as the ability to read fluently, write effectively, and complete mathematical tasks.
- To develop workplace skills, such as the ability to work with others and solve problems.
- To develop self-esteem and the motivation to be involved in learning for its own sake.

Answers to this question vary and can be controversial. Some educators suggest that the last goal is most important, arguing that intrinsically motivated people will adapt and acquire the skills needed to function effectively in a rapidly changing world. The development of the individual is preeminent in their view. Others favor the third goal, suggesting that society needs people who can solve problems and function well in groups. Still others advocate the first or second goals, asserting that academic skills, knowledge, and understanding are the keys to expertise and the ability to solve today's complex problems.

As we think back to Chapter 6, we see that these arguments come from different philosophical positions, which reflect varying degrees of emphasis on the needs of individuals, our society, or the academic disciplines. In addition, each of these positions also has both strengths and weaknesses, as outlined in Table 10.2.

Many of today's curriculum controversies are rooted in these different philosophical positions. For example, the reform movement has resulted from widespread complaints about young people entering the workforce without the content background, problem-solving abilities, and decision-making skills needed to function effectively in a technological world. Reformers are making an essentialist argument; they're saying that workers lack the basic skills needed to function effectively in today's society.

We see this essentialist position in Sharon and Susie's work with their students. Their schedules reflect their emphasis on language arts, reading, and math, which are all basic skills.

Increasing Understanding 10.9

The emphasis on children's needs is most nearly based on which educational philosophy? Explain.

While essentialism is prominent, the needs of individuals occupy an important place in schools as well. This emphasis is controversial, with critics arguing that the development of self-esteem has lowered standards and decreased achievement (Pintrich & Schunk, 1996). Advocates counter that a major goal of schools should be to give students self-confidence about their ability to learn and that students can't learn if they dislike themselves and the content they're learning.

As a teacher, you will need to think about the students you are teaching, the content, and the time and resources that are available. Based on your understanding of these factors, you then will develop your own philosophy of curriculum. This is not an easy task, but every teacher faces these decisions. Consciously recognizing the task ahead is an important first step in the long professional journey of creating a productive and defensible curriculum for your students.

Having seen how philosophy influences priorities, let's look at some other forces that impact curriculum decisions.

Textbooks

You're a beginning teacher, and you're thinking about what you will teach during the next week. Where will you turn for help? If you're a typical first-year teacher, you will

Table 10.2 Philosophical Foundations of Curriculum

Basis for Curriculum	Dominant Educational Philosophy	Advantages	Disadvantages
Needs of individuals	Progressivism	■ Concern for individuals is placed at the heart of curriculum development. ■ Learner motivation is promoted.	■ Efforts to respond to the special needs of each individual are virtually impossible. ■ Students may not be the best judges of their long-range needs, opting for shallow learning experiences.
Needs of society	Progressivism	■ Students learn to integrate information from a variety of sources. ■ Curriculum is relevant, contributing to learner motivation.	■ Society's needs change rapidly, often making curriculum obsolete. ■ Learners may be steered into career choices too early, limiting long-range opportunities.
Academic disciplines	Essentialism Perennialism	■ Research indicates that expertise and problem-solving ability depend on knowledge.* ■ Schools and teachers are being held accountable, and accountability depends on discipline- based tests.	■ Academic disciplines tend to artificially "compartmentalize" what students learn. ■ Students complain that traditional subjects are irrelevant.

Source: *Bruning, Shraw, & Ronning (1999) *Cognitive Psychology & Instruction* (3rd ed), Upper Saddle River, NJ: Prentice Hall.

Increasing Understanding 10.10

How are educational philosophies reflected in textbooks? For example, what would you expect to see in a math textbook based on essentialism? A math textbook based on progressivism? Explain in each case.

reach for a textbook, the book you'll be using for the content area you're teaching (Bullough, 1989).

For better or worse, textbooks are a fact of teaching life. Research indicates that teachers depend heavily on them; in grades K–8, texts in some form were involved in instruction 95 percent of the time and influenced 90 percent of homework assignments (Venezky, 1992). In some of your university teacher-education classes, you may be encouraged to set textbooks aside or at least not depend heavily on them. If your behavior is consistent with patterns identified by research, you're unlikely to do so (Zahorik, 1991). Some experts believe that textbooks are the most powerful influence on all curriculum decisions (Morrison, 1993).

While textbooks will strongly influence your curriculum decisions, you shouldn't depend on them completely. The following are some reasons why.

- Needs. The topics presented in textbooks may not be consistent with the specific needs of your students, school, or district. Following a textbook too closely then fails to meet these needs as effectively as possible.
- Scope. To appeal to a wide market, textbook publishers include a huge number of topics, more than you can possibly teach in the time available. Therefore, you will need

Despite questions about quality, textbooks exert a powerful influence on the curriculum.

to be selective in the topics you teach. Curriculum experts advise, "Schools [and teachers] should pick out the most important concepts and skills to emphasize so that they can concentrate on the quality of understanding rather than on the quantity of information presented" (Rutherford & Algren, 1990, p. 185).

- Quality. Textbooks are sometimes poorly written, lack adequate examples, or even contain errors of fact. One study of history textbooks found that "Content is thinner and thinner, and what there is, is increasingly deformed by identity politics and group pieties" (Sewall, 2000). One analysis of middle school science texts concluded, "It's a credit to science teachers that their students are learning anything at all" (Bradley, 1999c, p. 5). Similar problems have been found in other areas (Manzo, 2000a). Following a textbook too closely can then lead to shallow understanding or even faulty ideas that detract from learning.

To access up-to-date information about textbook quality, go to the *Web Links* module in Chapter 10 of the Companion Website.

What does this information mean for you as a teacher? As we began this section of the chapter, we said that nowhere in teaching is professionalism more important than in making curriculum decisions. This is particularly true regarding textbooks. It's easy to allow textbooks to make professional decisions for you, such as teaching the next chapter because it's there; unfortunately, this is what many teachers do.

Textbooks can be a valuable resource, and they will certainly influence your curriculum decisions. However, don't be afraid to de-emphasize, or even eliminate, topics and chapters in the text, and include other topics that aren't in it. Curriculum decision making such as this requires understanding, effort, and energy. Teachers report that the process of personal curriculum construction can be one of the most creative and satisfying aspects of teaching (Clandinin & Connelly, 1996).

Professional Organizations

Educators' professional organizations have also influenced curriculum. Unfortunately, the content areas, such as math, science, and social studies, don't speak with a single voice, so examining the curriculum standards generated by the professional organizations can sometimes be confusing. Science is an example. The National Research Council (1996) published the *National Science Education Standards*, and the American Association for the Advancement of Science (1989) also published a list of recommendations. Both lists of standards are designed to achieve the goal of scientific literacy for all students by the time they leave school, but the lists differ in fundamental ways such as emphasis on scientific literacy for all versus a deep understanding of science by a few. Teachers are often left to sort through these issues by themselves.

Instead of looking at all the standards that the various organizations recommend, we will examine a sampling from three areas (social studies, science, and math), examine patterns that appear in them, and then consider what implications they have for you as a teacher.

Social Studies Standards Let's begin by looking at social studies. The National Council for the Social Studies (1994) presents 10 themes—including culture; people, places, and environments; and civic ideals and practices—that form the framework for their standards. The standards and performance expectations are then attached to these themes.

For example, the standard for the culture theme is: "Social studies programs should include experiences that provide for the study of culture and cultural diversity, so that the learner can. . ."; performance expectations then follow the standard. These expectations (for the early, middle, and high school levels, respectively) ask the learner to:

- Give examples of how experiences may be interpreted differently by people from diverse cultural perspectives and frames of reference.
- Explain how information and experiences may be interpreted by people from diverse cultural perspectives and frames of reference.
- Predict how data and experiences may be interpreted by people from diverse cultural perspectives and frames of reference.

Increasing Understanding 10.14

Look again at what is receiving increased emphasis in science. What educational philosophy is best reflected in this increased emphasis? Explain.

We see how the performance expectations build on each other as students progress through the grades. Additional expectations exist for the culture theme, and each of the other themes has its own set of performance expectations as well. To access the themes presented by the National Council for the Social Studies, go to the *Web Links* Module in Chapter 10 of the Companion Website.

Science Standards Standards from science appear in Table 10.5. Rather than themes and expectations, they are presented in the form of "changes in emphasis" as recommended by the National Research Council (1996).

To access Websites for professional organizations, which in most cases will include the organization's standards, go to the *Web Links* Module in Chapter 10 of the Companion Website.

CONTROVERSIES IN CURRICULUM

In your work as a teacher, you will encounter controversies. Many of them will be related to what is taught (or not taught), that is, the curriculum. We examine some of these curricular controversies in this section when we consider the following:

Table 10.5 Examples of Changes in Emphasis in Science

Area	Increased Emphasis	Decreased Emphasis
Facts and concepts	Understanding concepts.	Knowing facts and information.
Curriculum	Selecting and adapting curriculum.	Rigidly following curriculum.
Content coverage	Studying fewer topics in depth.	Covering many topics superficially.
Communication	Discussion and communication between teacher and students and students with each other.	Answering factual questions presented by the teacher.
Teaching practices	Guiding students in active inquiry.	Presenting knowledge through lecture, books, and demonstrations.

- A national curriculum.
- Societal issues: sex and morals education.
- Diversity: cultural minorities and women in the curriculum.

A National Curriculum

In our study of Chapter 5, we saw that by the late 1700s, the federal government had removed itself from a central role in operating schools through the passage of the Tenth Amendment. This gave each state major decision-making power concerning what would be taught in that state's schools. The principle of state control of curriculum has been in place since that time.

Today, this principle is being questioned by some prominent voices who advocate a national curriculum. Some of their reasons for wanting a national curriculum include:

- The high achievement of students in countries such as Germany and Japan, which have national standards and national exams.
- The need for stability and coherence in the curriculum. Our population is highly mobile: 20 percent of Americans relocate every year, and some inner-city schools have a 50 percent turnover rate during the school year (Hirsch, 1996). Teachers working with these students often can't tell what they have or haven't already studied.
- Standards vary significantly from state to state; some states have much lower standards and levels of achievement than do others. A national curriculum would create uniform standards for all.

Opponents of a national curriculum also make compelling arguments. Some are wary of a large federal bureaucracy, which would also weaken local accountability. Others believe that a national curriculum would detract from the positive aspects of our cultural diversity; they feel that our disadvantaged students would be even further disadvantaged by a nationalized curricula that would be unresponsive to individual diversity and needs.

A partial response to these opposing views is a federal strategy that recommends, but does not require, exemplary textbooks. For example, the U.S. Department of Education recently published a list of promising and exemplary math texts, most based on recent National Council of Teachers of Mathematics standards (Viadero, 1999a). Even this approach draws criticism. One critic, a conservative math professor, commented, "This is an abomination. It [the math curriculum] has no business being debated by the federal government. . . ." (Viadero, 1999a, p. 14). Defenders of federal leadership in terms of textbooks compare it to *Consumer Reports*, noting that this publication serves an educational function and that not everyone who reads it is forced to buy the same product.

As you begin your career, you will probably see increased federal influence in the form of goals and standards, such as we saw with *Goals 2000*, but state adoption and compliance

place) forbids dissemination of any positive information about contraception, regardless of whether their students are sexually active or at risk of pregnancy or disease.

Increasing Understanding 10.16

Identify at least two different kinds of background knowledge teachers must have in order to effectively teach about sexuality.

How does the public feel? Overwhelmingly, 93 percent of Americans favor sex education and believe that young people should be given information to protect themselves from unplanned pregnancies and sexually transmitted diseases (Sexuality Information and Education Council of the United States and Advocates for Youth, 1999). It appears that conservatives' positions are at odds with the views of most Americans. David Landry, a nationally recognized expert in this area, observed, "Students aren't receiving accurate, balanced information about how to protect themselves from unplanned pregnancy or disease" (Coles, 1999b, p. 13). This in unfortunate, as the statistics regarding teen pregnancy at the beginning of this section reveal a real student need.

Moral and Character Education The proper place of values and moral education in the curriculum is also controversial. The controversy is less about whether or not it should be taught—most educators agree that it is needed—and more about the form that it should take (Wynne, 1997).

One position, called **character education,** *emphasizes the transmission of moral values, such as honesty and citizenship, and the translation of these values into behavior.* For example, the state of Georgia recently passed a law requiring character education programs to focus on 27 character traits including patriotism, respect for others, courtesy, and compassion (Jacobson, 1999). Instruction in character education emphasizes the study of values, practicing these values both in school and elsewhere, and rewarding displays of these values.

Moral education, by contrast, *is more value-free, emphasizing instead the development of students' moral reasoning.* Moral education uses moral dilemmas and classroom discussions to teach problem solving and to bring about changes in the way learners think with respect to moral issues.

Critics of character education argue that it emphasizes indoctrination instead of education (Kohn, 1997); critics of moral education assert that it has a relativistic view of morals, with no right or wrong answers (Wynne, 1997).

The strength of character education is its willingness to identify and promote core values, such as honesty, caring, and respect for others. Few would argue that these values are inappropriate. However, emphasizing student thinking and decision making is important as well, and this is the focus of the moral education perspective.

For either moral or character education to work, there must be some public consensus about the values included in them. Does such consensus exist? A recent poll suggests that it does (Rose & Gallup, 1999). When asked whether the following values should be taught in public schools, the following percentages of a national sample replied affirmatively: honesty (97 percent), democracy (93 percent), acceptance of people of different races and ethnic backgrounds (93 percent), and caring for friends and family members (90 percent). At the other end of the continuum were acceptance of people with different sexual orientations, that is, homosexuals or bisexuals (55 percent) and acceptance of the right of a woman to choose an abortion (48 percent). In considering which values to promote in their classrooms, teachers should be aware of public attitudes towards these values. This doesn't mean that teachers should avoid discussing controversial topics or values; instead, it suggests being aware of students' current values and beliefs and building upon them. This makes sense both pedagogically as well as politically (Eggen & Kauchak, 2001; Ormrod, 2000).

Service learning. An innovative approach to character education, called **service learning,** *involves students in voluntary social-service projects.* The idea behind service learning is to make students more socially responsible by combining character education with an action component. Service-learning programs can be divided into two main categories:

Service learning attempts to teach values by actively involving students in helping projects.

those that encourage the goal of social change and those that foster the goal of charity (Kahne & Westheimer, 1996). Examples of service-learning programs that focus on social change include environmental-education projects designed to encourage people to recycle and voter-education projects aimed at getting people out to vote. Charity-oriented projects include delivering food to shut-ins and doing volunteer work in hospitals.

The popularity of service-learning programs is growing. In 1984, only 2 percent of high school students were involved; by 1997, nearly one-quarter participated (Blair, 1999). In addition, 83 percent of high schools currently offer community-service opportunities (Westheimer & Kahne, 2000).

A major policy question is whether to make service learning voluntary or required. The state of Maryland requires 75 hours of service before high school graduation; a number of districts in California, Washington, Pennsylvania, and North Carolina have similar requirements (Fischer et al., 1999). However, not all parents agree with the value of service learning; some have legally challenged the requirement. Courts have upheld the legality of these courses, noting that they promote habits of good citizenship and introduce students to the idea of social responsibility.

Unfortunately, some educational leaders believe teacher preparation programs are not doing an adequate job of preparing future teachers for the issues involved in moral and character education (Jacobson, 1999; Ryan & Bohlin, 2000). If this is true, even greater demands will be placed on your professionalism when you take your first job.

Censorship What do the following books have in common?

Of Mice and Men by John Steinbeck
Diary of a Young Girl by Anne Frank
The Adventures of Huckleberry Finn by Mark Twain
To Kill a Mockingbird by Harper Lee
Leaves of Grass by Walt Whitman

Exploring Diversity

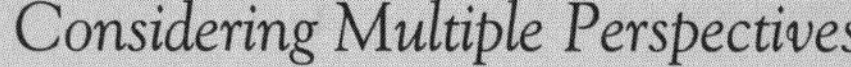

Considering Multiple Perspectives

MINORITIES AND WOMEN IN THE CURRICULUM

A considerable amount of criticism has been directed at the curriculum in American schools because, according to critics, it has failed to adequately represent the contributions of women and cultural minorities. For example, until as recently as the 1960s and 1970s, the majority of the works included in junior high and high school literature books were written by White males, with a few additional contributions by White females. When these books examined authors in depth, the authors chosen were generally White men, such as William Shakespeare, Mark Twain, and Robert Frost.

Recognition of the historical contributions of minorities was similarly lacking. For example, Dr. Charles Drew (1904–1950), an African American, developed the procedure for separating plasma from whole blood. This was an enormous contribution that unquestionably saved many soldiers' lives in World War II. Dr. Charles Norman, (b. 1930), another African American, was the first person to implant an artificial heart in a human. Until recently, most history books ignored contributions such as these.

Increasing Understanding 10.17

On which educational philosophy are the critics' arguments most likely based? Explain.

In response to critics and because of shifts in our society, this has changed. A postage stamp was issued in Drew's honor in 1981, and science fiction writer Isaac Asimov, a friend of Norman's, based his novel *Fantastic Voyage* on work done in Norman's laboratory. History texts have been expanded to include the contributions of women and minorities. Literature books, too, have changed. Many now include works written by minority writers, such as Maya Angelou, Sandra Cisneros, Gary Soto, and Toni Cade Bambara (Probst, Anderson, Brinnin, Leggett, & Irvin, 1997).

The issue is highly controversial, with some critics charging that cultural minorities remain underrepresented in the curriculum (Wong-Fillmore & Meyer, 1996). Content focusing on the contributions of men of northern European descent—often derisively described as a "Eurocentric" curriculum—is perceived as out of balance and irrelevant to minorities. Critics argue that because minorities make up more than one-third of our school chil-

All of these works have, at various times, been targeted for banning in the public school curriculum (People for the American Way, 1991).The language arts area has often served as a battleground for curriculum controversy due to the issue of censorship. **Censorship** occurs in the schools when *the use of certain books in the library or in literature classes is prohibited.*

The controversial and divisive nature of censorship can be seen in a censorship battle that took place in Kanawha County in West Virginia. In the mid-1970s, parents objected to certain language arts books including *The Diary of Anne Frank* as well as works by John Steinbeck and Mark Twain (Manzo, 2000b). Emotions reached crisis level quickly, resulting in death threats to teachers, pipe bombs, and a school boycott. The Ku Klux Klan and John Birch Society got involved, and several local minsters were convicted for their roles in school bombings. Censorship scars are evident even today; recently, district officials who felt censorship pressures ordered health teachers to avoid teaching about the excretory and reproductive systems of the human body. Can you imagine a student asking his health teacher about how the kidneys work and the teacher replying, "We can't talk about that in this class"?

Censorship can also occur with content-area textbooks. For example, a fourth-grade history text used in Utah contained the following passage:

■ ■ ■

People often hurt the land. Automobiles and factories pollute the air. People and factories sometimes dump trash and harmful chemicals into lakes and rivers. These kill birds and

dren (a percentage that is increasing), the curriculum should be further broadened to better reflect their contributions and presence in our society. In addition, critics assert that some time-honored literature, such as Mark Twain's *The Adventures of Huckleberry Finn*, portrays characters in ways that promote racial stereotypes and prejudice.

Some critics argue further that entire curricula should be oriented to specific ethnic groups. For instance, to help African American students understand and appreciate their cultural heritage, proponents of an "Afrocentric" curriculum advocate focusing on the achievements of African cultures, particularly ancient Egypt. Studying the contributions of people with similar ethnicity will increase self-esteem, motivation, and learning, they contend. Afrocentric curricula are currently being experimented with in a number of inner-city school districts (Toch, 1998).

However, these positions have critics of their own. The counter critics question the accuracy and balance of the content and whether the emphasis on differences leads to racial and ethnic separatism (Coughlin, 1996; Ravitch, 1990). They also argue that we've already gone too far in emphasizing cultural differences, resulting in the reduction or elimination of some of the great contributions of literature, such as the study of Shakespeare. Further, they maintain, we are all Americans, and this increased emphasis on diversity has resulted in the failure of students to develop a common cultural heritage and shared national identity (Hirsch, 1987; Schlessinger, 1992).

Increasing Understanding 10.18

Adler (1982) argues for a "core" curriculum that would be composed of great literary works that have endured over the years. Hirsch (1987) argues for studying the great works, but then going beyond them to include the central ideas and knowledge of a culture, resulting in what he calls "cultural literacy." Which of the educational philosophies that we studied in Chapter 6 is most consistent with Adler's argument? Hirsch's argument? Explain in each case.

The role of women in the curriculum is also controversial. Many feminist groups contend that women continue to be both underrepresented and misrepresented in the curriculum; they argue that students read too many books and materials that portray men as doctors, lawyers, and engineers, and women as nurses, teachers, and secretaries. When this occurs, they assert, girls are sent messages about which careers are and are not appropriate for them (American Association of University Women, 1992).

However, a strong and systematic national effort has been made to address the needs of girls and women in today's schools (Riordan, 1996). In fact, some counter critics argue that the emphasis on girls' needs has gone too far. This is the argument made in *The War Against Boys*, the provocative and controversial book written by Christine Hoff Sommers (2000) that we discussed in Chapter 3.

The debate continues, and the controversy is likely to remain in the future.

fish and make the water unsafe for people. Companies cut down forests. They build roads, dams, and cities. They put oil wells and telephone lines on the land. We need these things, but sometimes they look ugly and destroy nature (Egan, 1997, p. B1).

■ ■ ■

This seems pretty innocuous, but one critic contended,

> This book is a blatant attempt by the federal government and environmentalists to try to 'brainwash' our young students into believing their ancestors were petty opportunists having no conscience about the lands for which they had stewardship (Egan, 1997, B3).

Unfortunately, as textbooks become political footballs, their quality diminishes, as text writers aim for blandness and "the middle of the road" at the expense of accuracy or making a point. This is a problem you'll encounter as you attempt to use textbooks to help students learn.

Censorship is interesting because it raises questions with conflicting answers about other important issues in education. One is parental choice and control over their children's education. Shouldn't parents have a say in the books their children read? A second question involves professional autonomy. Shouldn't teachers be free to select books that they feel are important, if not essential, to student development and learning? In considering these opposing views, the courts have usually decided against censorship of books, ruling that schools and teachers have a right to expose students to different ideas and points of view through literature (Fischer et al., 1999). To get additional information about censorship and banned books, go to the *Web Links* Module in Chapter 10 of the Companion Website.

The Changing Role of Teachers

As you've studied this book, you've seen that several of the chapters end with a section titled "The Changing Role of Teachers." What might be less obvious, however, is the theme that runs through these sections, which is, *the teacher's role is now more complex and demanding than it has ever been in the past*. We also stress that the need for teachers to be professional has never been greater. The kinds and amount of professional knowledge teachers must possess are greater than they've ever been. As an example, think about this chapter. Not only must teachers understand the content they are expected to teach, but they're also expected to make decisions about what topics to include, how extensively textbooks should be used, and to what extent district guidelines should be followed. State and district curriculum guides provide support, but they don't substitute for teachers' professional decisions.

The importance of knowledgeable and highly skilled teachers is supported by research linking teacher quality and student achievement (Bradley, 1999d; Darling-Hammond, 1998). Students in high achieving states, like North Dakota, Minnesota, and Iowa, do as well as students in foreign countries with reputations for high achievement, such as Korea and Japan. Those states have rigorous requirements for teacher education and don't allow districts to hire unlicensed teachers. The opposite is true for the lowest achieving states (National Commission on Teaching and America's Future, 1996). You are ultimately the person who controls the curriculum, and you will ultimately determine, to a large extent, how much your students learn.

In addition, teachers will be required to respond to federal and state mandates that influence the curriculum. The trend is toward increased testing and accountability. Taxpayers want to know if their education dollars are being well spent, students will be expected to learn more, and teachers will be expected to ensure that the learning occurs. These mandates create increased curriculum pressures for teachers.

Despite these pressures, this is an exciting time to be a teacher. The level of professionalism in teaching is increasing, teachers are better prepared than they have ever been in the past, and the challenges in the profession have never been greater. Further, a significant percentage of the teaching force will retire within the next 10 years, so opportunities for leadership roles will also increase. Your future as a teacher has never been more challenging, but at the same time it has never been filled with so many opportunities.

SUMMARY

What Is Curriculum?

While defined in a variety of ways, curriculum can be thought of as *what* students learn in schools, and instruction is the way the curriculum is taught. The explicit curriculum is the curriculum found in textbooks and other formal educational experiences, whereas the implicit curriculum is reflected in the climate of the classroom together with its unstated values and priorities.

The formal curriculum is sometimes integrated so that concepts and skills from different disciplines are combined. Integrated curriculum, while somewhat controversial, is common in elementary schools.

Extracurriculum includes learning experiences that extend beyond the core of students' formal studies. Participation in extracurricular activities is correlated with a number of positive outcomes, including achievement and attitudes toward school.

Forces That Influence the Curriculum

The teacher is the most powerful force influencing the curriculum. Ultimately it is the teacher who must decide what is taught and how it will be taught.

A teacher's philosophical orientation, available textbooks, federal mandates, state and local district guidelines, and reform movements sponsored by national committees and professional organizations all influence a teacher's curriculum decisions.

Controversies in Curriculum

Whether or not our country should have a national curriculum is one of the most controversial issues facing American education. Proponents cite the mobility of our population and the achievement of students in other countries with national curricula; opponents fear a large federal bureaucracy, reduction of local accountability, and a decrease in the positive aspects of our cultural diversity.

Sex education, education in morals and values, censorship, and the underrepresentation of women and minorities in the curriculum remain controversial curriculum issues. These issues are likely to remain unresolved in the near future.

The Changing Role of the Teacher

The teacher's role is becoming more complex and demanding, and nowhere is this more true than in the area of curriculum. The decisions teachers will be expected to make in the future include those about curriculum, instruction, and the interpersonal aspects of working with students from diverse backgrounds. Making these decisions requires a knowledgeable and highly skilled professional, one who is comfortable making decisions in ill-defined situations.

IMPORTANT CONCEPTS

censorship
character education
curriculum
explicit curriculum
extracurriculum
implicit curriculum
instruction
integrated curriculum
moral education
outcomes-based education (OBE)
service learning

DISCUSSION QUESTIONS

1. Which has the greater influence on students' learning, curriculum or instruction? Why do you think so?
2. Think back to your own experience in schools and then consider what you've read in this chapter. Which has changed more over time, curriculum or instruction? Why do you think so?
3. Some critics argue that the implicit curriculum has more impact on students' overall education than does the explicit curriculum. Do you agree or disagree with this argument? Defend your position with a concrete example.
4. In periods of financial crises, some schools have reduced their extracurricular offerings. To what extent does this detract from students' overall education? Defend your position with a concrete example.
5. Which of the factors that influence the curriculum do you believe will most influence your teaching? Why do you think so?

VIDEO DISCUSSION QUESTIONS

The following discussion questions refer to video segments found on the Companion Website. To answer these questions online, view the accompanying video, and receive immediate feedback to your answers, go to the *Video Discussion* Module in Chapter 10 of the Companion Website.

1. Theodore Sizer is the director of the Coalition for Effective Schools, which attempts to reform high schools. In his view, what is the most important thing that schools can do to prepare students for college? Where in the curriculum would we find this emphasis, and how could teachers integrate it into their teaching?
2. Theodore Sizer, the director of the Coalition for Effective Schools, recommends a standard, focused curriculum for all students. How could a standard, focused curriculum be used to encourage student critical thinking? What are the advantages and disadvantages of this approach to curriculum?

GOING INTO SCHOOLS

1. Obtain a copy of a teacher's lesson plans for a week. Based on the teacher's plans, what is being emphasized? What is being de-emphasized? What do these lesson plans tell you about the teacher's explicit and implicit curriculum?
2. Examine the teacher's textbook (or textbooks). To what extent do the teacher's lesson plans appear to depend on the textbook(s)? What other resources are the basis for the teacher's plans?
3. Interview a teacher about different forces that shape her curriculum.
   a. Ask her why she emphasizes what she does, and why she de-emphasizes other aspects of her teaching.
   b. How much does she depend on textbooks to determine what she teaches? How much do curriculum guides influence what she teaches? How much does testing influence what she teaches?
   c. Ask her to describe the school's extracurricular program. Find out who participates and why. (For example, Do low-SES students and minorities participate as much as other students?) How important is the extracurricular program, and why does she feel that way?
   d. Ask the teacher to describe her impression of current curriculum reforms. Do they influence what and how she teaches? If so, describe specifically how they are influenced. If not, why not?

   Compare the forces that shape this teacher's curriculum to forces described in this chapter.
4. Interview a teacher about controversial topics in the curriculum. What is her position with respect to the following controversial curricular issues:
   a. Sex education. Should the schools teach sex education, or should it be the responsibility of parents and churches? Why does she feel the way she does?
   b. Morals and values education. Should schools teach morals and values? Is so, how should they be taught?
   c. The underrepresentation of minorities and women in the curriculum. Does she believe minorities and women are underrepresented? If so, how can the problem be solved?

   How does she find out about whether and how these topics should be taught? How much of these decisions are personal ones, and how much guidance or restrictions come from external sources? What implications does all this have for you as a teacher when faced with similar curricular decisions?
5. Observe in a classroom (for an extended period of time if possible).
   a. What rules and procedures guide student behavior? How are they explained or defended?
   b. When the teacher corrects or reprimands a student, what explanation or rationale is given?

c. How does the teacher motivate students? What reasons are given for learning different things?
d. How does the teacher treat students? How do students treat each other?

Based on your observations, what implicit curriculum is being promoted in the classroom? Defend your conclusions with examples taken directly from your observations.

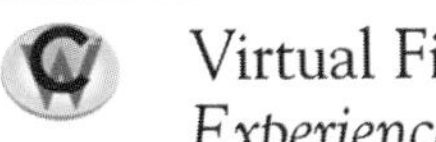

Virtual Field *Experience*

If you would like to participate in a Virtual Field Experience, go to the *Field Experience* Module in Chapter 10 of the Companion Website.

ONLINE PORTFOLIO ACTIVITIES

To complete these activities online, go to the *Portfolio Activities* Module in Chapter 10 of the Companion Website to submit your response.

Portfolio Activity 10.1 **Planning for Instruction**

INTASC Principle 9: *Commitment*

The purpose of this activity is encourage you to think about the topics you will plan to teach.

Write a two-page description of your philosophy of curriculum, or what is important for students to learn in your class. In it, explain specifically how it is consistent with the description of your overall philosophy of education (which you described in Portfolio Activity 6.1).

Portfolio Activity 10.2 **Making Decisions about Curriculum**

INTASC Principle 7: *Planning*

The purpose of this activity is to acquaint you with resources, such as textbooks, that will influence your curricular decisions. Locate a textbook for an area in which you will teach. (If you're a middle school science major, for example, you might select a seventh-grade life science book. If you're an elementary major, you can select from a variety of books.)

Photocopy the table of contents from the book. Then identify several topics that you would delete if you were using the book. Also, identify several topics you might add. Defend your additions and deletions and explain how your changes are consistent with your curriculum philosophy.

Portfolio Activity 10.3 **Using Curriculum Guides for Planning Decisions**

INTASC Principle 8: *Assessment*

The purpose of this activity is to acquaint you with curriculum guides as a planning resource. Analyze either a state or district curriculum guide in one area of the curriculum (or compare two levels).

a. How recent is it?
b. Who constructed it?
c. How is it organized (for example, chronologically, developmentally, topically, and so on)?
d. How do the topics covered compare with a text for this area?
e. How many objectives are listed for a particular course of study?
f. How many objectives per week are implicitly suggested? Is it a realistic number?
g. What types of learning (for example, memory versus higher levels) are targeted?

How helpful would this curriculum guide be for you as a first-year teacher?

CHAPTER

11 Instruction in American Classrooms

The reason you're taking this and other courses in your teacher-preparation program is to help you understand American schools, how they attempt to promote student learning, and what teachers can do to contribute to that process. Over the past 25 years, a continually expanding body of research has provided educators with a great deal of information about relationships between what teachers do and what students learn. Our purpose in writing this chapter is to describe some of these relationships as we try to answer the following questions:

- What kinds of personal characteristics do effective teachers possess?
- How do effective teachers organize their classrooms so students can learn?
- What kinds of instructional strategies do effective teachers use?
- How do effective teachers assess their students?
- On what theories of learning do effective teachers base their instruction?

Let's begin the process by looking at one teacher's classroom and seeing how she works with her students.

Case STUDY

Martina Hernandez is a fifth-grade teacher at Oneida Elementary School, an inner-city school with a largely low-SES student body. Martina is working with her students on the addition of fractions, and begins today's class with a brief review.

"Look at this fraction," she says, writing 3/4 on the board. "What do we call the number on the bottom? . . . Celena?"

"Uh, denominator."

"Good, Celena. And what do we call the number on the top, Carl?"

There's no reply from Carl.

"Ooh, ooh, I know," Tad interjected.

"Tad, I'm glad you know, but let's give Carl a chance. Remember, we agreed that it's important for everyone to participate, and we're going to work hard to avoid blurting out answers."

"Carl, think about this for a second. Remember, it tells us the number of parts in the fraction. It comes from the term *number.*"

". . . Oh yeah, numerator."

"And why do we want to know these terms? . . . Andrea?"

"You said it was . . . so we could talk about the numbers. When we talk about the bottom number, we have something to call it."

"Yes, good Andrea," Martina smiles. "Sure. In this case it's simply for communication. It's much easier for us to call this the 'denominator' than to constantly refer to it as 'the number on the bottom.' Remember, it's very important to understand *why* we want to understand the ideas we study."

"Now, let's look closely at this problem," Martina continues, pointing to the overhead. "It says, 'I drank half a cup of milk with my sandwich, and now I need to add a third of a cup to this recipe. I had one cup of milk in the refrigerator. Do I have enough milk for the recipe?' What should we do first? . . . I want everyone to think real hard now, because you all can do this, and it's important to know how to do problems like this . . . Tanya?"

There's no reply from Tanya.

"First, what does 1/3 mean? Remember when we folded the papers to illustrate fractions?" Martina prompts. She reaches over to her desk, picks up a piece of paper, and folds it so it appears as follows:

"Oh, yes, we had three parts altogether, and we're . . . I'm not sure, like *working* with one of the parts," Tanya responds.

"Excellent, Tanya."

The lesson continues with Martina encouraging her students to see the relationship between the numbers in fractions and different configurations of folded paper.

■ ■ ■

Is Martina a "good teacher?" What specifically did she do to promote learning in her classroom? What could she have done differently to improve her instruction? We try to answer these questions in the next section.

LOOKING IN CLASSROOMS TO DEFINE EFFECTIVE TEACHING

Classrooms are logical places to look for answers to questions about good teaching; a line of inquiry focusing on classroom teaching began when researchers found that students in some teachers' classrooms were learning more than in others. In trying to find reasons for these differences, the researchers analyzed literally thousands of hours of teaching, focusing on teachers in both high- and low-achieving classes. After ensuring that students and resources, such as the availability of technology and textbooks, were comparable, they found that the thinking of the teachers as well as the way the teachers taught were different for the two groups (the high achievers and the lower achievers) (Good & Brophy, 1986, 1997). *A description of these differences resulted in a body of knowledge called the* **teacher effectiveness research.** This research found that the personal characteristics of the teachers were different, their planning was different, and their teaching strategies, classroom management techniques, and assessment strategies were also different. This research is important because it established links between teacher actions and student learning in real-world classroom settings.

The dimensions on which effective and less effective teachers differ are outlined in Figure 11.1.

Personal Characteristics

Think about some of the best teachers you've had. When you do, what is the first thing that comes to mind? If you're typical, you believe that they cared about you as a person, they were committed to your learning, and they were enthusiastic about the topics they taught.

These factors describe effective teachers' personal characteristics, and they provide a foundation that guides their work. In this section we examine four of these attributes:

- Personal teaching efficacy
- Caring
- Modeling and enthusiasm
- Teacher expectations

Personal Teaching Efficacy To what extent can teachers overcome the problems that students bring with them to school? If students lack supportive home environments, can teachers still promote high achievement, or do students' backgrounds overwhelm teachers' efforts? To gain some insight into your beliefs regarding these questions, respond to

Figure 11.1 Dimensions on Which Effective and Less Effective Teachers Differ

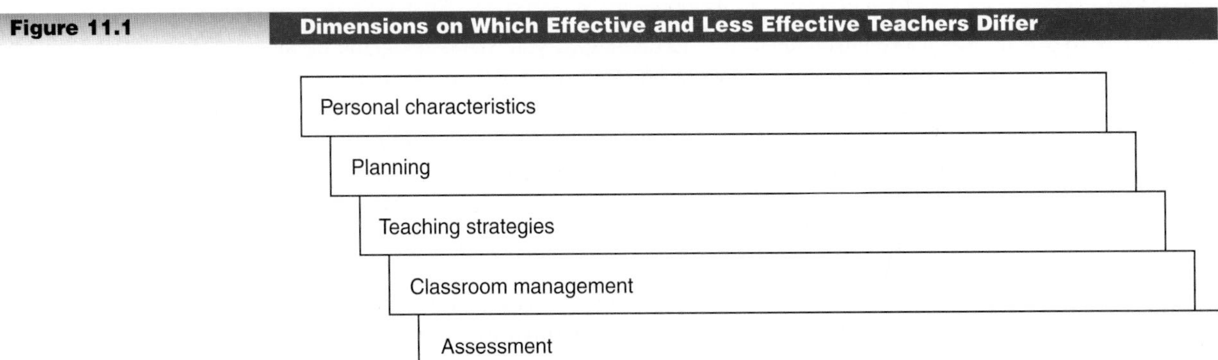

the following statements by circling SA (Strongly agree), A (Agree), U (Undecided), D (Disagree), or SD (Strongly disagree).

1. Students' home environments have a stronger influence on their learning than do teachers.	SA	A	U	D	SD
2. If teachers try hard enough, they will be able to get through to even the most difficult students.	SA	A	U	D	SD
3. If parents' values don't support teaching and learning, teachers can do little to increase student achievement.	SA	A	U	D	SD
4. If students don't remember information from a previous lesson, teachers should know how to increase their retention in the next lesson.	SA	A	U	D	SD

Source: Adapted from "Teacher efficacy: A construct validation," by S. Gibson and M. Dembo, 1984, *Journal of Educational Psychology, 76.*

Increasing Understanding 11.1

Explain why low-efficacy teachers are likely to spend less time on learning activities than high-efficacy teachers.

To answer this question online and receive immediate feedback, go to the *Increasing Understanding* Module in Chapter 11 of the Companion Website at **http://www.prenhall.com/kauchak.**

Researchers asked teachers to respond to statements similar to these, and based on their responses, assessed the teachers' **personal teaching efficacy,** a concept we introduced in our discussion of effective schools in Chapter 7 and defined as *a teacher's belief that he or she can promote learning in all students regardless of their backgrounds* (Bruning, Shraw, & Ronning, 1999). Teachers who are high in personal teaching efficacy take responsibility for the success or failure of their own instruction (Lee, 2000).

When students aren't learning as much as they could, high-efficacy teachers don't blame it on lack of intelligence, poor home environments, uncooperative administrators, or some other external cause. Instead, they redouble their efforts, convinced they can increase student learning. They create classroom climates in which students feel safe and free to express their thinking without fear of embarrassment or ridicule. They emphasize praise rather than criticism, persevere with low achievers, and maximize the time available for instruction. Low-efficacy teachers, in contrast, are less student-centered, spend less time on learning activities, "give up" on low achievers, and are more critical when students fail (Kagan, 1992). High-efficacy teachers also adopt new curriculum materials and change strategies more readily than do low-efficacy teachers (Poole, Okeafor, & Sloan, 1989). Not surprisingly, students taught by high-efficacy teachers learn more than those taught by low-efficacy teachers (Tschannen-Moran, Woolfolk-Hoy, & Hoy, 1998).

Martina displayed several characteristics of a high-efficacy teacher. She had a positive attitude about learning and communicated this attitude to her students. She kept them involved in the lesson through her questioning, encouraged them to think about the reasons for studying the topic, and praised their efforts.

Caring You've made an appointment to meet an instructor about some problems you're having in his class and he shows up 15 minutes late with a mumbled, "I've been so terribly busy lately." As he talks with you, he keeps glancing at his watch, giving you the impression he wants to be somewhere else. In contrast, when you make an appointment and meet with another instructor, he is there at the designated time, and he spends as much time with you as you need. How do you feel in each case?

These simple incidents relate to caring. We all want to be cared about, and advertisers capitalize on that fact with slogans such as, "We care about you after the sale," and "Shop with the people who care."

We saw in Chapter 2 that "caring professional" is one of the many roles of a teacher, and caring is essential for effective teaching. Students can tell when teachers care, all parents want their children to be with caring teachers, and even older university students

Caring, an essential component of effective teaching, connects teachers with students on a human level.

Increasing Understanding 11.2

Identify the single most important indicator of caring that exists. Use this indicator to explain why you are likely to react badly when an instructor arrives 15 minutes late to an appointment.

value instructors who genuinely care about them and their learning. **Caring** refers to *teachers' willingness to invest time in the protection and development of young people* (Chaskin & Rauner, 1995). A growing body of research documents the importance of caring for both student achievement and motivation (Bosworth, 1995; Stipek, 1996). Caring teachers are committed to their students' learning and developing competence. They attempt to do their very best for the people under their charge (Noddings, 1995).

Modeling and Enthusiasm We often hear that "actions speak louder than words," and this statement is especially true for teachers. Teachers are powerful role models for students, and the way they act influences both learning and motivation (Bandura, 1989). **Modeling** simply means *behaving in ways you would like your students to imitate*. For instance, since you want your students to be courteous and respectful to you and each other, you treat them with courtesy and respect. You want them to be diligent and conscientious in their studies, so you demonstrate that you also prepare thoroughly and work hard at your teaching.

Martina modeled patience and understanding with her students in her interactions with them. When Tad attempted to blurt out an answer, Martina patiently reminded him that everyone in the class needs an opportunity to participate. Messages like this, delivered through modeled behaviors, are much more effective than lectures or admonitions.

Your approach to the content you're teaching has similar effects on students. Student interest in a topic is virtually impossible if you make statements such as, "I know this stuff is boring, but we have to learn it," or "This isn't my favorite topic either." In contrast, even the most mundane topic is more palatable to students if you're genuinely interested in it. Teachers who present information enthusiastically increase both student achievement and learners' beliefs about their ability to understand the topics they're studying (Perry, 1985; Perry, Magnusson, Parsonson, & Dickens, 1986). Modeling can make enthusiasm contagious.

thinking, low-level questions are effective. On the other hand, if the goal is to understand the interplay of factors leading up to the Civil War, as was the case in Kathy's lesson, high-level questions are more effective. Teachers' first concerns should be what they are trying to accomplish—their goals—not the level of questions they ask. When goals are clear, appropriate questions follow.

Equitable distribution. Teachers' questioning patterns send powerful messages to students. For example, if girls or minority students are called on less often, are prompted less, or are given less time to answer than boys or nonminorities, they become less involved in lessons, and gradually they stop paying attention to what is going on. In time, they begin to feel less welcome in the class, and may even come to believe that they're not as bright as those who are called on more frequently or given more time to think.

One solution to this dilemma is to *interact with all students—girls, boys, minorities and nonminorities—as equally as possible.* One way of communicating to students that they all are welcome and expected to learn is through **equitable distribution,** *the practice of calling on all students—both volunteers and nonvolunteers—as equally as possible.*

To understand the process of equitable distribution, let's think about Martina's lesson again. In this brief vignette, we see that Martina asked five questions, she directed them to four different students (Celena, Carl, Andrea, and Tanya), and in each case she called on the student by name. The practice of equitable distribution sends a clear message to students that all are expected to participate and all are expected to learn. Students rarely misinterpret the messages, and it doesn't matter what the teachers' or students' cultural backgrounds are.

Think about what this communicates. By treating students equally, the teacher is saying, "I don't care whether you're a boy or girl, minority or nonminority, high-achiever or low achiever—I want you in my classroom. I believe you're capable of learning, and I will do whatever it takes to ensure that you're successful." When this happens, students come to believe that the teacher expects them to participate and learn. Perhaps even more importantly, because the teacher is making this effort, they believe the teacher is genuinely committed to their learning. No message is more positive.

Increasing Understanding 11.4

In this section, we said that effective teachers call on all students as equally as possible, and call on them by name. Predict what less effective teachers do in their classrooms. To what two personal characteristics do these patterns relate? Explain.

Equitable distribution is a powerful tool for promoting both achievement and student motivation. Research indicates that teachers who treat their students as equally as possible have higher achieving students, fewer classroom management problems, and higher attendance rates (Kerman, 1979). Equitable distribution also works at the college level; expectation of being called on results in increased student preparation for class, greater retention of information, and greater confidence in what is learned (McDougall & Granby, 1996).

Presentation of Subject Matter Students study a variety of topics in their classes, such as the rules for forming plural nouns in language arts, equivalent fractions in math, density in science, and culture in social studies. Describing and explaining the topics is the most common method teachers use to help learners understand them (Cuban, 1984; Goodlad, 1984). However, research indicates that simply explaining or telling isn't the most effective way of helping students learn (Brenner et al., 1997; Spiro, Feltovich, Jacobson, & Coulson, 1992; Shulman, 1986). Instead, learners need concrete examples that they can use to develop their understanding. For instance, a science teacher might teach the concept *density* by having students compress cotton balls in a drink cup so they see that the compressed cotton is more compact (dense). She might also drop an ice cube into a cup of water and another into a cup of alcohol. The ice floats on the water but sinks in the alcohol, demonstrating that the ice is less dense than the water but more dense than the alcohol. In language arts, teachers can use actual student writing samples to illustrate principles of good organization, grammar, and punctuation. In social studies, the teacher might prepare descriptions such as the following to illustrate the concept *culture:*

■ ■ ■

Pedro is a boy living in a small Mexican village. Every day he rises early, for he must walk the two miles to his school. He has breakfast of beans and bread made from ground corn, leaves the house, and begins his trek. He likes the walk, for he can wave to his papa toiling daily in the cornfields that provide food and income for the family.

When Pedro comes home from school, he often plays soccer with his friends in the village. After dinner, his mother usually plays songs on a guitar while his papa sings, but this evening she must go to a meeting of the town council, where they are trying to raise money for a new addition to the school. No decisions can be made without the approval of the council.

■ ■ ■

Chu is a young girl living in a fishing village in Japan. She is up early and helps her mother with breakfast for her younger brothers and sisters. Chu loves the rice smothered in a sauce made from raw fish that she often eats in the morning.

Chu skips out the door, bowing to her father as she goes. He is preparing tools to go to the docks, where he will meet his partner for their daily fishing expedition. He has been a fisherman for 30 years. Chu comes home from school, finishes her work, and then goes down the street to play ping pong with the rest of the neighborhood boys and girls. She is the best one in the area. Before bed, Chu listens to stories of the old days told by her grandfather, who lives with them.

■ ■ ■

Increasing Understanding 11.5

Describe the differences in the ways that Judith Thompson and Kathy Johnson represented their subject matter. Explain why Kathy's approach was more effective.

Each example includes a description of foods, recreation, the way the people make a living, and aspects of their home life. These are all characteristics of the concept *culture*. Instead of abstract descriptions, the examples provide students with concrete information about what culture is and how it influences our lives.

The importance of high-quality examples in teaching can't be overstated; effective teachers are able to illustrate topics in ways that are understandable to students, whereas less-effective teachers tend to rely on verbal explanations (Shulman, 1986).

Effective Feedback Have you ever been in a class where you had to wait until the midterm exam to find out how you were doing? Have you handed in assignments and had to wait weeks before they were scored and returned? In both instances, you were left uncertain about your learning progress because of the absence of feedback. **Feedback** *is information about current performance that can be used to increase future learning.* The most effective feedback is immediate, specific, and provides corrective information about how well we're doing.

One of the most effective ways of providing feedback is through our interactions with learners. For instance, let's consider the concept *density* again. Students commonly equate density with weight, concluding that heavy objects are more dense than light objects. When they do, they must be provided with feedback that helps them eliminate this misconception. As an example, let's look at a class where the teacher had students compress cotton in a cup to illustrate density.

Teacher: What can we conclude about the cotton now? (after being compressed)

Student: It's heavier.

Teacher: How does the total amount of cotton we have now compare to the amount before we compressed it?

Student: It's . . . the same.

Teacher: So, if the amount is the same, how does the weight now compare to the weight before?

Student: It must be . . . the same.

Teacher: What is different?

Student: The . . . amount of space it takes up. It's "squished" down.

Teacher: Yes, good. The volume is less, but the weight is the same. Only the density has changed.

This kind of interactive feedback is essential for learning. Merely explaining that the weight is the same is much less effective, because students passively listen to the explanation instead of actively wrestling with their own understanding.

Classroom Management

Case STUDY

The teacher says, "We have a little filmstrip on weather." And she quickly overviews the content of the filmstrip, which is called "The Weather is Poetry." As the teacher arranges the filmstrip in the machine, she says, "Before we start this, we're going to turn out the light, but you can finish your work anyway. We're going to pick it up afterwards." Greg says, "Miss, I can't see to finish." The teacher says, "Yes, you can. Your eyes will adjust." Andrew is yelling, "Lights off, lights off," four times. Finally, the teacher starts the filmstrip, which is a sound filmstrip. Someone turns the lights off. Everyone starts yelling, "I can't see. It's dark in here." The teacher assures everyone that their eyes will adjust. As the film is running, the students talk, move around. Apparently, two of them go outside to work, although the observer did not notice until later. Some move desks. Observer notes that no one can hear the movie. Joe comes in from the hall and stands at the front of the room to watch. The class finally settles a little. About half are watching the film, and half are working on the assignment in the dark. The teacher walks out of the room. And then she walks about the room. She says, "In a few minutes, you're going to see the part about the mud. That's my favorite part. They describe the sound of people walking in the mud." Greg says, "Turn on the lights." The teacher ignores him. During the filmstrip there is a steady exchange of students with restroom passes. Susan comes in, Joe goes out. The teacher goes out. Robert calls after her sarcastically, "You missed the mud" (From Evertson, C., (1982) *Teacher behavior, student achievement and student attitudes: A multi-classroom study.* Presentation at the annual meeting of the American Educational Research Association, Boston. Reprinted by permission.)

■ ■ ■

Classroom management is the number-one concern of beginning teachers (Rose & Gallup, 1999), and this episode helps us understand why. Students learn less in classrooms that are disorderly, and research indicates that disruptive students are an important source of teacher stress (Abel & Sewell, 1999).

Classroom management refers to *teachers' abilities to create and maintain orderly classrooms*. The importance of classroom management in effectively run classrooms is clear. One group of researchers concluded, "Effective classroom management has been shown to increase student engagement, decrease disruptive behaviors, and enhance use of instructional time, all of which results in improved student achievement" (Wang et al., 1993, p. 262). Effective management is one of the key characteristics of an effective school (Purkey & Smith, 1983), and an orderly classroom increases students' motivation to learn (Radd, 1998).

Commonly overlooked in discussions of management and discipline is the role of effective instruction. Effective teaching and classroom management are interdependent.

Classroom management, when done right, not only maintains an orderly learning environment, but also teaches students about their rights and responsibilities in relation to others.

> **Increasing Understanding 11.6**
>
> Based on what you saw in the beginning episode with Martina Hernandez, does she base her management on an obedience model or on a responsibility model? Cite specific evidence from the episode to support your answer.

It's virtually impossible to maintain an orderly classroom in the absence of effective teaching, and effective teaching is impossible when students are disruptive (Doyle, 1986).

We have two goals when we plan for and implement classroom management. The first is to create environments that promote the most learning possible (Morine-Dershimer & Reeve, 1994), and the second is to help students learn to manage and direct their own learning (McCaslin & Good, 1992).

In attempting to accomplish the second goal, the difference between an obedience orientation and a responsibility orientation is important (Curwin & Mendler, 1988). An **obedience model of management** *teaches students to follow rules and obey authority using reward and punishment*. A **responsibility model of management,** by contrast, *teaches students to be responsible for their actions by explaining reasons for rules and applying logical consequences for behavior*. Differences between these orientations are outlined in Table 11.2.

Let's see how one kindergarten teacher, faced with a handful of wet, dripping students, applied logical consequences in her classroom.

Case STUDY

The kindergarten boys found a lovely mud puddle in the playground during recess. They had much fun running and splashing and then came back into the room wet and dripping, and they left muddy footprints all over the room.

Their teacher called them aside for a conference. "Boys, we have two problems here. One is that the classroom is all dirty and it needs to be fixed so that the other children don't get wet and dirty. What can you do to fix it?"

One little boy suggested that they could mop the floor.

"Good idea," said the teacher. "Let's find our custodian, Mrs. Smith, and you can get a mop from her and mop the floor. Now what about our other problem, your dirty clothes?"

"We could call our mothers and ask them to bring us clean clothes!" suggested one boy.

Table 11.2 The Obedience and Responsibility Models of Management

	Obedience Model	Responsibility Model
Goal	Teach students to follow orders.	Teach students to make responsible choices.
Organizing Principle	Obey authority.	Learn from actions and decisions.
Teacher Actions	Punish and reward.	Explain and apply logical consequences.
Student Outcomes	Students learn obedience and conformity.	Students internalize the reasons for rules and learn to self-regulate.

Source: From Curwin, R., & Mendler, A. (1998). *Discipline with dignity.* Alexandria, VA: Association for Supervision and Curriculum Development. Adapted by permission.

"Another good idea," said the teacher. "But what if your mothers are not home?"

This was a tougher problem. Finally, one boy said, "I know, we could borrow some clean clothes from the lost and found box!"

"Good thinking," said the teacher. "And what can we do so that you don't lose so much time from class again?"

"Stay out of mud puddles!" was the reply in unison (McCarthy, 1991, p. 19).

■ ■ ■

By involving students in problem solving about their own behavior, the teacher creatively turned the possibility of discipline into an opportunity for learning.

Effective Assessment

■ ■ ■

A middle school science teacher notices that her students have difficulty applying scientific principles to everyday events. In an attempt to improve this ability, she focuses on everyday problems (for example, why different cubes of wood that are the same size float differently in water), which students have to solve in groups and then discuss as a class. On Fridays, she presents another problem (for example, why two clear liquids of the same volume, when put on a balance, don't have the same mass), and the students have to solve it in groups. As they work, she circulates among them, taking notes that will be used for assessment and feedback.

■ ■ ■

A health teacher reads in a professional journal that the biggest problem people have in applying first aid is not the mechanics per se, but knowing what to do and when. In an attempt to address this problem, the teacher periodically has unannounced "catastrophe" days. Students entering the classroom encounter a catastrophe victim with an unspecified injury. With each victim they must first diagnose the problem and then apply first-aid interventions.

■ ■ ■

As we better understand how people learn and how effective teachers contribute to the process, we see that teaching is much more complex than it appears on the surface. Promoting learning requires much more than simply explaining topics to learners. Students interpret what they hear in an effort to make sense of it, and these interpretations may result in distortions and misunderstandings. As teachers, our goal is to prevent these misconceptions, if possible, and to help learners eliminate them if they occur.

MAINTAINING ORDER IN THE CLASSROOM

You're a first-year, sixth-grade world history teacher in an urban middle school, and you're having a difficult time maintaining order in your classroom. Some of your students talk and whisper while you're lecturing and explaining the information in the text. For example, you're beginning the study of factors leading up to World War I, and you explain that one of the factors was increased nationalism—loyalty to a country's language and culture. As you're explaining, some of the students talk openly to each other; a few even get out of their seats and sharpen pencils in the middle of your presentation. You threaten them with referrals and other punishments, which work briefly, but the disruptions soon recur.

Other students seem listless and make no effort to pay attention; several even put their heads down on the desk during the lesson. You try walking around the room as you talk, and you stand near the inattentive students, but neither strategy works well.

1. Why do you suppose some of the students are disruptive?
2. Why do you believe many of the students are inattentive?
3. Are teachers responsible for making sure that students pay attention in class, or should paying attention be the responsibility of students?
4. What would you do in this situation?

To answer these questions online and receive immediate feedback, go to the Reflect on This Module in Chapter 11 of the Companion Website.

But how will we know if learners have distorted or inaccurate understandings of the topics they're studying? The only way we can find out is through **assessment,** which is *the process of gathering information and making conclusions about student learning*. As we better understand learning, we realize that assessment is much more than simply giving a test after a unit. In fact, to promote clear and deep understanding of the topics students study, assessment must be an integral part of teaching. For instance, Martina was continually assessing her students' understanding of fractions during her lesson. Her efforts to help students understand fractions and her assessment of their understanding were inseparable; she was doing both simultaneously.

Assessment, and the grading that accompanies it, can be challenging for first-year teachers. As one first-year teacher commented:

■ ■ ■

Of all the paperwork, grading is the nitty-gritty of teaching for me. Students take their grade as the bottom line of your class. It is the end-all and be-all of the class. To me, a grade for a class is, or at least should be, a combination of ability, attitude, and effort. Put bluntly: How do you nail a kid who really tried with an F? Or how do you reward a lazy, snotty punk with an A? (Ryan, 1992, p. 4).

■ ■ ■

Another teacher explained:

■ ■ ■

Grading is still kind of a problem with me. . . . I try not to play favorites (even though I have them)—I don't like S's personality . . . I do like J's, isn't it unfair? You want to be easier on someone you like. Or harder on someone you don't. . . . I wouldn't mind taking a class on grading. I think grading could be hit much harder in college . . . I just don't know what to do. . . (Bullough, 1989, p. 66).

■ ■ ■

As you progress through your teacher-education program, you'll learn how to assess students in different ways, including alternative assessments.

Changing Views of Assessment: Alternative Assessments Think about your experiences as a student, and think further about some of the tests you've taken. If your experiences are typical, many were multiple-choice, true-false, or fill-in-the-blank tests. These traditional formats—particularly multiple-choice—have been the mainstay of both classroom assessments and standardized intelligence and achievement tests. In recent years, they've been increasingly criticized (Paris, 1998; Reckase, 1997). In response to these criticisms, the use of **alternative assessments,** or *assessments that directly measure student performance through "real life" tasks* (Wiggins, 1996/97; Worthen, 1993) are being emphasized.

Some examples of alternative assessments include:

- Writing an essay or letter to the editor of the school newspaper.
- Comparing the amounts and percentages saved from different newspaper advertisements.
- Designing menus for a week's worth of balanced meals.
- Designing and conducting an experiment to see which brand of aspirin is likely to be most effective.
- Creating an original piece of watercolor art.
- Giving a speech in support of one side of a controversial topic.

In addition to products, such as the essay, menu, or piece of art, teachers using alternative assessments examine the thinking students do as they create the products. For example, the teacher might interview students to examine their thinking as they design the experiment, organize the essay, or create the art.

The idea of alternative assessment isn't new. Oral exams, exhibits of art work, proficiency testing in language, and hands-on assessments in vocational areas, such as word processing, have been used for years. In recent years, however, concerns about traditional testing, primarily in multiple-choice formats, and the perception that our students aren't performing as well as they should be, has caused more widespread interest in alternative assessment.

Alternative assessments commonly occur in two forms. **Performance assessments** *ask learners to demonstrate their competence in a lifelike situation*. Applying first aid, writing an essay, or giving a speech are all examples of performance assessments because they ask students to demonstrate their knowledge in realistic, lifelike situations.

In a second form of alternative assessment, teachers evaluate **portfolios,** which are *collections of student work that are judged against preset criteria*. Research suggests that over half the teachers in the United States currently use portfolios to assess student learning in some area of learning (Viadero,1999a). You were introduced to portfolios in Chapter 1, you are creating portfolio products related to the content of each chapter, and a detailed discussion of teaching portfolios appears in Chapter 13.

One unique feature of portfolios is that students are actively involved in selecting and evaluating portfolio content. For example, in a language arts class, students might select different pieces that they have written over the course of a year. These writing samples then provide concrete evidence of writing progress for parents, the teacher, and the students themselves. (As you develop your teaching portfolio during your teacher-preparation experience, you'll see similar evidence of growth in your teaching expertise.)

Increasing Understanding 11.7

A geography teacher assesses her students' understanding of longitude and latitude by having them identify the longitudes and latitudes of several cities around the world. Is this a traditional or an alternative assessment? Explain.

Alternative assessments provide opportunities for students to demonstrate their knowledge in active, realistic ways.

USING OUR UNDERSTANDING OF LEARNING TO DEFINE EFFECTIVE TEACHING

Increasing Understanding 11.8

What were Martina Hernandez's goals? Describe specifically what she did to help her students reach these goals.

In the first section of the chapter, we looked at research focusing on teachers: their personal characteristics as well as how they involved students, presented topics, and assessed their students' understanding. We saw that some teachers apply these variables more effectively than do others, and as a result, their students' achievement is higher.

We now turn to important questions such as, How do students learn? and How can we use our understanding of learning to teach more effectively? We saw in Chapter 1 that professional teachers have a great deal of knowledge about learners and learning. The answers to these questions provide some of this knowledge.

Psychology, and particularly educational psychology, attempts to explain how we learn and develop. We examine this body of knowledge in this section.

Behaviorism

You probably recognize the names Pavlov and Skinner. These learning theorists were major figures in **behaviorism,** *a view of learning that—as the name implies—focuses on specific and observable behaviors*.

Behaviorism dominated learning theory and education for the first half of the 20th century. From a behaviorist perspective, **learning** is *a change in observable behavior occurring as the result of experience*. In a behaviorist classroom, learning occurs when students consistently give specific, observable, desired responses to questions. The way they learn to give these responses is determined by reinforcement and punishment. For example, if a teacher asks, "How do you spell *Tennessee?*" and the student responds "T-e-n-n-e-s-s-e-e," the teacher nods and says, "Right!" Spelling *Tennessee* is specific, the teacher can observe (hear) the correct spelling, and the teacher's smile and comment reinforce the student; consequently, the response is strengthened. However, if the student responds, "T-e-n-e-s-s-e-e," the teacher would correct him or her by saying, "Not quite" or "You'd better check your list," decreasing the likelihood that the student will use the incorrect spelling a second time.

According to behaviorism, the goal of instruction is to increase the number, or strength, of correct student responses. Learning is measured by observing changes in behavior, such as seeing that students correctly spell 12 of 20 words on a list on Monday but correctly spell 16 on Wednesday.

When using behaviorism as a guide for planning and conducting instruction, the teacher designs learning activities that require students to produce specific, observable responses to questions and exercises. Then, during lessons, the teacher reinforces desired responses (as we saw when the student spelled *Tennessee* correctly) and punishes undesired ones.

Let's look now at a teacher using behaviorism to structure his instruction.

Case STUDY

Kevin Lageman, an eighth-grade English teacher at Longview Middle school, is working with his students on pronoun cases.

"All right, listen everyone," Kevin begins. "Today, we're going to begin a study of pronoun cases. . . . Everybody turn to page 484 in your text.

"This is important," he continues, "because we want to be able to use good English when we write, and this is one area where people get mixed up. . . . So, when we're finished with our study here, you'll all be able to use pronouns correctly in your writing."

He then displays the following on the overhead:

- Pronouns use the nominative case when they're subjects and predicate nominatives.
- Pronouns use the objective case when they're direct objects, indirect objects, or objects of prepositions.

"Let's review briefly," Kevin continues. "Give me a sentence that has both a direct and indirect object in it. . . . Anyone?"

"Mr. Lageman gives too much homework," Leon offers, to the laughter of the class.

Kevin smiles and writes the sentence on the chalkboard; he then continues, "Okay, Leon. Good sentence, even though it's incorrect. I don't give you *enough* work. . . . What's the subject in the sentence?"

There's no reply from Leon.

"Go ahead, Leon."

"Ahh, . . . *Mr. Lageman."*

"Yes, good. *Mr. Lageman* is the subject," Kevin replies, as he underlines *Mr. Lageman* in the sentence and writes "Subject" above it.

"Now, what's the direct object? . . . Joanne?"

". . . *Homework."*

"All right, good. And what's the indirect object? . . . Anya?"

". . . *Us."*

"Excellent, everybody."

Kevin continues by reviewing predicate nominatives and objects of prepositions.

He then continues, "Now, let's look at a few examples of pronouns up here on the overhead."

He then displays 10 sentences. The following are the first four.

1. Did you get the card from Kelly and (I, me)?
2. Will Antonio and (she, her) run the concession stand?

3. They treat (whoever, whomever) they hire very well.
4. I looked for someone (who, whom) could give me directions to the theater.

"Okay, look at the first one. Which is correct? . . . Omar?"

". . . *Me.*"

"Good, Omar. How about the second one? . . . Lonnie?"

". . . *Her.*"

"Not quite, Lonnie. This one is a little tricky, but it's the nominative case."

Kevin then points up at the overhead and says, "How about the third one. . . . Cheny?"

". . . I don't know. . . . *whomever,* I guess."

"Excellent, Cheny. Indeed, that's correct."

Kevin continues with the rest of the sentences and assigns a page of similar exercises from the students' books as homework.

On Tuesday, Wednesday, and Thursday, Kevin covers the rules for pronoun-antecedent agreement (pronouns must agree with their antecedents in gender and number) and using indefinite pronouns as antecedents for personal pronouns (*anybody, either, each, one, someone*). He then has the students work on examples as he had done before.

On Friday, Kevin gives a test that is composed of 30 sentences: 10 of the sentences deal with case, 10 more with antecedents, and the final 10 with indefinite pronouns.

The following are some items from the test:

For each of the items below, mark A on your answer sheet if the pronoun case is correct in the sentence, and mark B if it is incorrect. If it is incorrect, supply the correct pronoun.

1. Be careful *who* you tell.
2. Will Renee and *I* be in the outfield?
3. My brother and *me* like water skiing.

Increasing Understanding 11.9

Give an example of the use of punishment in Kevin's interaction with his students. Explain why it is an example of punishment.

■ ■ ■

Now let's look at Kevin's lesson and see how it is based on behaviorism. To elicit observable responses, he displayed exercises such as:

1. Did you get the card from Kelly and (I, me)? and then asked, "Okay, look at the first one. Which is correct? . . . Omar?" Omar responded by saying "Me," and Kevin reinforced him by saying, "Good, Omar." Kevin designed the learning activity so that students could give specific, observable responses, which he could reinforce if correct, as he did with Omar.

Learning to provide specific, observable responses is desirable for some forms of fact learning, such as a learner being able to respond, "54" quickly and effortlessly when asked, "What is six times nine?" Behaviorists often view memorization of facts as a foundation or prerequisite for more complex behaviors. For example, knowing multiplication tables helps in solving word problems, and being able to pronounce words quickly and efficiently helps students comprehend when they read (Mayer, 1998; Bruning et al., 1999).

For many other learning goals, however, behaviorism isn't a satisfactory basis for guiding instruction. For instance, being able to write effectively was Kevin's goal for his students, as indicated by his comment, "This [using pronoun cases correctly] is important, because we want to be able to use good English when we write. . . . So, when we're finished with our study here, you'll all be able to use pronouns correctly in your writing."

Teaching 

in an Era *of* Reform

TEACHER-CENTERED VERSUS LEARNER-CENTERED INSTRUCTION

In Chapter 10, we saw that over-emphasis on memorization and drill-and-practice activities resulted in the math reforms emphasized in the 1989 *Curriculum and Evaluation Standards for School Mathematics*. Critics suggested that this changing emphasis left students with inadequate basic skills, so they called for a new wave of reform, reflected in the *Principles and Standards for School Mathematics* (2000). This is a specific example of broad trends in curriculum reform; reforms occur, criticisms of the reform begin, and counter reforms are then offered. Similar issues exist in instruction. We examine these issues in this section.

Historically, teachers have extensively utilized **teacher-centered instruction,** meaning *teachers carefully specify objectives, present the content to be learned, and actively direct learning activities* (Shuell, 1996). For example, a teacher might want her students to solve algebraic equations for the values of *a* and *b*, such as:

$$4a + 6b = 24$$
$$5a - 6b = 3$$

Using a teacher-centered approach, teachers model and explain the solution to the problem and then have students practice, first with their guidance, and then independently. A lecture, in which teachers systematically present carefully organized information, is another example.

Teacher-centered instruction has been criticized as being based on behaviorist views of learning, focusing primarily on low-level objectives at the expense of deep understanding (Marshall, 1992; Stoddart, Connell, Stofflett, & Peck, 1993). The following lesson segment involving a third-grade teacher who is attempting to help her third graders understand place value illustrates these criticisms:

The teacher, based on the directions given in the teacher's manual, begins by putting 45 tally marks on the chalkboard and circles four groups of 10.

Teacher: How many groups of 10 do we have there, boys and girls?

Children: 4.

Teacher: We have 4 groups of 10, and how many left over?

Children: 5.

Teacher: We had 4 tens and how many left over?

Beth: 4 tens.

Sarah: 5.

Teacher: 5. Now, can anybody tell me what number that could be? We have 4 tens and 5 ones. What is that number? Ann?

Ann: (Remains silent)

Teacher: If we have 4 tens and 5 ones, what is that number?

Ann: 9.

Teacher: Look at how many we have there (points to the 4 groups of ten) and 5 ones. If we have 4 tens and 5 ones we have? (slight pause) 45.

Children: 45.

Teacher: Very good (Wood, Cobb, & Yackel, 1992, p. 180).

Unfortunately, getting the students to say "45" didn't really change the way they understood place value in numbers.

Criticisms of teacher-centered instruction led to a wave of reform; this resulted in the development of **learner-centered instruction,** *which encourages teachers to guide learners toward a thorough understanding of the topics they study*, rather than simply explaining content to them. Prominent professional publications that illustrate this emphasis include *How Students Learn: Reforming our Schools Through Learner-Centered Education*, which was published by the American Psychological Association in 1998, and *The Right to Learn*, which was written by Linda Darling-Hammond (a well-known Columbia University educator) and published in 1998.

Discovery learning, where *the teacher identifies a content goal, arranges information so that patterns can be found, and guides students to the goal*, and **cooperative learning,** which *consists of students working together in groups small enough so that everyone can participate in a clearly assigned task* (Cohen, 1994), are prominent examples of learner-centered approaches to instruction. Leslie Nelson used aspects of both in her lesson. First, she displayed the paragraphs on the overhead and then said, "Get together with your partner and see if you can figure out how these passages are similar and different. . . ." Working together capitalizes on cooperative learning, and looking for similarities and differences is characteristic of discovery learning.

Putting Instructional Reform into Perspective

Teacher-centered instruction is criticized because it emphasizes teacher actions rather than student understanding. As the dialogue on place value suggests, Ann, and probably many others, didn't understand place value, and the teacher did little to increase their understanding. Once students' gave the desired response, they were reinforced with "Very good," and the lesson moved on.

Cognitive views of learning emphasize social interaction and the active involvement of learners in hands-on activities.

This pattern of focusing on student verbalization or overt performance at the expense of understanding occurs in many classrooms (Goodlad, 1984; Stodolsky, 1988); seeing that the instruction is teacher-centered, critics place the blame on the approach, suggesting that—in addition to being based on behaviorism—content is delivered primarily through lecture and explanation. Student thinking is minimized, critics assert; they contend "that the most effective learning takes place when students are able to make choices about what they're doing [and] when they're able to play an active role in making sense of ideas" (Kohn, 1999, p. 43).

Defenders of teacher-centered instruction argue that the problem is not with instructional approach; rather, it is with the teacher's inability to implement it effectively. When teacher-centered instruction is done *effectively*, they argue, none of these criticisms is true (Rosenshine, 1997). Expert teacher-centered instruction keeps learners involved, and understanding and thinking are strongly emphasized. Those who defend teacher-centered instruction further argue that some criticisms of teacher-centered instruction are made on political grounds, teacher-centered instruction not being "politically correct or romantically correct" (Rosenshine, 1997, p. 2).

Similar issues exist with learner-centered instruction. Critics suggest that this approach is one more example of widespread "dumbing down" of the curriculum, that learning basic skills is abandoned in favor of fuzzy thinking, and self-esteem is emphasized instead of understanding (Battista, 1999; Schoen, Fey, Hirsch, & Coxford, 1999). As a result, counter reforms have resulted in a pendulum shift back in the direction of teacher-centered instruction (Stein & Carnine, 1999).

However, emphasizing real-world applications, involving students in learning activities, using high-quality examples and representations, and focusing on deep understanding—all principles of learner-centered instruction—are inarguable.

As with most issues involving reform, teacher decision making and professionalism are keys. No strategy—teacher-centered or learner-centered—is more or less effective than the ability of the teacher implementing it. Teacher-centered approaches are more effective for some topics, whereas learner-centered approaches are better for others. Research suggests that most teachers are eclectic, using both teacher-centered and learner-centered strategies to promote student learning (Viadero, 1999a). Your ability to make decisions about which strategy to use in different situations, and your ability to use both strategies effectively, will determine how much your students learn.

You Take a Position

Now it's your turn to take a position on the issue discussed in this section. Go to the *Education Week* Website at **http://www.edweek.com,** find "search" on the first page, and type in one of the following two search terms: *effective teaching* or *effective teachers*. Locate a minimum of three articles on one of these topics and then do the following:

1. Identify the title, author, and date of each article and then write a one-paragraph summary of each.
2. Identify a pattern in the articles. (Each article—or even two of the three—suggesting that students in high-poverty schools have the greatest need for expert teachers, would be a pattern, for example.)
3. After identifying the pattern, take one of the two following positions:
   - The pattern suggested in the articles, if implemented, *is* likely to improve education.
   - The pattern suggested in the articles *is not* likely to improve education.

State your position in writing, and document your position with information taken from the articles.

To answer these questions online, go to the Take a Position Module in Chapter 11 of the Companion Website.

Exploring Diversity

Considering Multiple Perspectives

THE ACHIEVEMENT GAP AND EFFECTIVE TEACHING

In Chapter 7 we saw that a widening gap exists in the achievement of cultural minorities, particularly African American and Hispanic students, and their White and Asian counterparts (Hoff, 2000).We also saw in Chapter 7 that reducing class size is one promising aspect of school organization that can help close the gap. The effective-teaching research has much more to say about narrowing the achievement gap, particularly in the area of effective instruction. For example, in schools where the achievement gap is narrowing, the following exist (Barth et al., 1999; Haycock, 1998; Viadero, 2000b):

- A vision established by the school leadership that all students can and will learn.
- Specific and demanding goals.
- Teaching that actively involves students.
- Regular and thorough assessment of student progress.

These characteristics are consistent with both the research on effective schools that you studied in Chapter 7 and the effective-teaching research and cognitive views of learning discussed earlier in the chapter. A vision that all students can learn relates to *teaching efficacy;* specific and demanding goals are consistent with effective planning and high expectations; and the active involvement of learners is supported by cognitive learning theory. Finally, regular and thorough assessment provides both teachers and learners with feedback about learning progress.

Sound instruction isn't enough, however. One study of inner-city minority high school students found that many effective practices were being implemented (Miller, Leinhardt, & Zigmond, 1988). The schools were adapting at every level, from school policies to classroom instruction, and this adaptation kept students in school. However, researchers also found:

- Lowered expectations for students.
- Lack of emphasis on higher level thinking and problem solving, with an increase in low-level worksheets.
- Student apathy and boredom.

In essence, increased efforts to provide instructional structure and support had resulted in a remedial program that lacked intellectual rigor and excitement.

Several programs have been developed to provide challenge for students. The Accelerated Schools Program builds on student strengths by combining high expectations with an enriched curriculum focusing on a language-based approach in all academic areas (Levin, 1988; Rothman, 1991). The Higher Order Thinking Skills Program (HOTS) focuses on teaching students skills such as inferencing and generalizing to help them realize the importance of critical thinking in learning (Pogrow, 1990).

approach emphasized a deep and thorough understanding of the rules. Not only was her approach more sophisticated and demanding than Kevin's, but it was also likely to result in more student learning. Her instruction was guided by cognitive views of learning; his was based on behaviorism.

The Changing Role of Teachers

Think back to your experiences as a student. If they were typical, you probably spent most of the day listening to your teacher lecture or explain topics to you and then completed a written assignment related to the topic (Goodlad, 1984; Cuban, 1984). At times, you may have spent entire class periods working on a seatwork assignment. Most of the questions the teacher asked, when she asked questions at all, required recall of memorized information. You were expected to work quietly and alone at your desk.

Teaching under these conditions was simpler than it is today (Darling-Hammond, 1998). The teacher's role was more manager of paperwork rather than instructor. Because students spent most of their time listening to the teacher, maintaining an orderly class-

Effective programs for minority students combine challenge with high expectations for success.

Results from both programs have been encouraging. One Accelerated Schools site in San Francisco registered the highest achievement gains on standardized test scores in the city, and spring-to-spring comparisons of achievement gains in one HOTS program showed students were 67 percent above the national average in reading and 123 percent higher in math (Rothman, 1991).

Common to both programs are high expectations, emphasis on enrichment versus remediation, and the teaching of higher-order thinking and learning strategies. These strategies are integrated into the regular curriculum so that students can see their usefulness in different content areas (Means & Knapp, 1991).

This research is encouraging. It suggests that teachers and schools can and do make a difference in student learning. Narrowing the achievement gap obviously isn't easy, and daunting problems remain. The task isn't impossible, however. With sustained effort, that gap can be narrowed.

room was reasonably easy. Teachers' biggest tasks were organizing and explaining the content they were teaching.

What you experienced was essentially *the teacher as technician*. As you recall from Chapter 1, we defined a technician as a person who can apply specific skills in completing a well-defined task, such as an electrician wiring an outlet. Teachers as technicians needed to understand the content they were teaching, and they needed to be skilled lecturers.

As you go out and observe in classrooms, you will likely see many examples of the teacher as a technician. However, this is no longer the ideal. The environment you will enter will be much more demanding; it will require you to be a professional, which means you must be able to apply a broad background of knowledge to make instructional decisions in complex situations. For instance, in addition to organizing the content you plan to teach, you will have to prepare examples and other representations that illustrate the topic in ways that students can understand. Then, instead of lecturing and explaining, you will ask questions that guide your students to their own understanding of the topics.

Preparing meaningful examples is difficult, and asking questions is a very complex process. You must decide, on the spot, what question to ask and whom to call on, while at the same time watching other students to be sure they're paying attention. You prompt students if they're unable to answer, but don't spend so much time with a single student that other students "drift off." These tasks require more than a skilled technician; they require an expert professional.

The diversity of your students will make your teaching even more complex. They will come from a variety of socioeconomic, cultural, and ethnic backgrounds. You'll need to adapt your instruction to students' unique backgrounds and learning styles. The expert professional is able to accommodate these differences to help all the students learn as much as possible.

To join the ranks of these experts, you must be intelligent, hard-working, sensitive, and caring. It is very challenging, but at the same time, one of the most rewarding experiences that exists.

SUMMARY

Looking in Classrooms to Define Effective Teaching

Effective teachers teach differently than their less effective counterparts. They believe they are capable of helping all students learn, they are caring, enthusiastic, and they have high expectations for their students. They actively involve students in learning through questioning; they provide detailed feedback about learning progress; they create orderly and learning focused environments; and they use assessment as a mechanism to further increase learning.

Using Our Understanding of Learning to Define Effective Teaching

Historically, learning was viewed as an increase in specific, observable student behaviors, and learners were seen as passively responding to their environments. This was teaching based on a behaviorist view of learning.

Near the middle of the 20th century, views of learning began to change, and learners were viewed as actively attempting to make sense of their experiences. Learners' background knowledge, interaction between the teacher and students, and the quality of examples and representations that teachers use are all essential in helping learners construct their own understanding of the topics they study.

The Changing Role of the Teacher

In the past, a teacher-as-technician perspective was quite common. Teachers simply organized and delivered content to students who listened passively. Now, the teacher-as-professional is expected to provide meaningful examples and representations, accommodate learner diversity, and maintain classroom order while at the same time actively involving students in learning activities. The teacher-as-professional requires work that is much more complex and demanding than it has ever been in the past.

IMPORTANT CONCEPTS

alternative assessment
assessment
behaviorism
caring
classroom management
cooperative learning

discovery learning
equitable distribution
feedback
goals
instructional alignment
learner-centered instruction
learning (behaviorist)
learning (cognitive)
modeling
obedience model of management
performance assessment
personal teaching efficacy
portfolios
questioning frequency
responsibility model of management
teacher-centered instruction
teacher effectiveness research
wait-time

DISCUSSION QUESTIONS

1. Why is the practice of calling on volunteers to answer a question so prevalent? What are its advantages? What are its disadvantages?
2. Virtually no teacher would suggest that it isn't important to be a good model. Given that belief, why do you suppose some teachers don't model the behaviors they expect their students to imitate?
3. Many teachers lecture instead of guiding their students to their goals using questioning. Why do you think this is the case?
4. Why is the obedience model of management so popular in many schools? What advantages and disadvantages does this perspective hold?
5. What will be the future of alternative assessment? Will it continue to be emphasized, or will emphasis decline in favor or more traditional testing? Why do you think so?

GOING INTO SCHOOLS

1. Interview a teacher about the use of questioning strategies to promote learning. Specifically ask the following:
   a. Why and how does the teacher use questions in class?
   b. How does the teacher decide who to call on?
   c. What does the teacher do if a student is unable to respond?
   d. What is the biggest challenge in using questions to promote learning?
   Compare the teacher's responses to the content of this chapter.
2. Observe a teacher in her classroom before she begins her instruction for the day. As you observe, attempt to answer the following questions:
   a. Before she begins her instruction, how much time does she spend on non-instructional activities, such as taking roll, passing out papers, and gathering materials to be used in the lesson?
   b. How does she conduct her instruction? Does she primarily lecture and explain, or does she ask a number of questions and guide her students to the goal with questioning?
   c. How much time does she spend in instruction, and how much time is spent having the students do seatwork?
   d. How often does she reprimand students for misbehavior? How does she reprimand?

   e. How often does she praise students for desirable behavior or good answers to questions? Count the number of times she praises students.

   On the basis of these observations, decide whether the instruction is based more on behaviorist or cognitive views of learning and teaching.

3. Obtain a copy of a test a teacher has used in reading, language arts, math, science, and social studies (if you're in an elementary school), or get a copy of a test for one of the courses the teacher teaches (if you're in a middle or secondary school). After examining the test, answer the following questions:
   a. What format is used (for example, multiple-choice, true-false, matching, etc.)?
   b. At what level are the items written? (That is, do they require mere recall of information, or do they require the students to apply understanding to new situations?)
   c. Talk with the teacher about his or her goals for the content being assessed. Were the goals and the assessment aligned? (That is, did the assessment measure important goals of instruction?)
4. Interview the teacher about her assessment practices. The following questions can be used to guide the interview.
   a. What does "alternative" or "performance" assessment mean to the teacher?
   b. Does she use alternative assessments in her teaching? If so, how does she use them?
   c. Does she use portfolios? If so, how does she use them?
   d. Examine the contents of a portfolio. What does the teacher include? Ask her how she decides what will be included and what will be left out.

   On the basis of the interview, determine one advantage and one disadvantage of alternative assessment formats.

Virtual Field *Experience*

If you would like to participate in a Virtual Field Experience, go to the *Field Experience* Module in Chapter 11 of the Companion Website.

ONLINE PORTFOLIO ACTIVITIES

To complete these activities online, go to the *Portfolio Activities* Module in Chapter 11 of the Companion Website and submit your response.

Portfolio Activity 11.1 **Planning for Instruction**

INTASC Principle 7: *Planning*

The purpose of this activity is to help you think about the role of planning in effective instruction. Identify a topic and then write two specific goals related to the topic. Explain why the goals are important.

Portfolio Activity 11.2 **Designing Instruction**

INTASC Principle 1: *Knowledge of Subject*

The purpose of this activity is to assist you in thinking about alignment and ways that teachers can link goals to teaching strategies. Describe how you would help students from a variety of backgrounds reach the goals you specified in Portfolio Activity 11.1. Be very specific in your description, and explain how you would accommodate background differences in your students.

Portfolio Activity 11.3 **Assessing Student Understanding**

INTASC Principle 8: *Assessment*
The purpose of this activity is to help you begin thinking about connections between assessment and instruction. Explain specifically how you would measure the extent to which your students reached the goals you described in Portfolio Activity 11.1.

CHAPTER

12 Technology in American Schools

Technology is changing education in the United States in ways that are varied and complex. Most of you probably plan to use technology when you begin teaching, and if you asked 50 teachers whether or not technology enhanced learning, most would probably say yes. However, if you asked the same 50 teachers for a definition of instructional technology, you would probably get nearly that many different answers. Questions about how best to use technology to promote learning are important, but a great deal of disagreement exists in the answers. In this chapter, we present an overview of technology and the way it's used in schools as we try to answer the following questions:

- What is technology?
- How can technology increase learning in our schools?
- What different types of technology are available to teachers as they attempt to help students learn?
- What problems and obstacles are there to greater technology use in our schools?

To begin, let's look at two teachers using technology in their classrooms.

Case STUDY

Latisha Evans, a first-year teacher at Henderson Middle School, ran into one of her colleagues and friends, Carl DeGroot, in the hallway.

"You sure look excited," Carl said with a smile. "What's happening?"

"Wow," Latisha responded, gesturing for emphasis. "They got it today; they really got it. . . . I've been trying to get my classes to understand what we mean by *internal conflict* and it seemed to be just too abstract for them. . . . Plus, they would only half pay attention when I would explain it. . . . So, I wrote up a few little vignettes, like 'Kelly didn't know what to do. She was looking forward to the class trip, but if she went, she wouldn't be able to try out for city soccer league.' Then, I put them together with a PowerPoint presentation and included some pictures of people with pensive looks on their faces and that kind of thing. . . . Neat animation tricks to make each example appear on the screen and then follow it with the pictures. . . . It was the best I've ever done. I think the attention-getting aspects of PowerPoint are what really did it."

■ ■ ■

Peter Adamson, a 5-year veteran at the same school, is highly regarded by the principal, his students, and their parents. When we enter Peter's classroom, it appears chaotic, and we wonder how anyone could consider him a "good" teacher. One group of five students is working on a 4-by-8-foot sheet of heavy paper to be used in a presentation to their classmates. Two other groups of four students are working on different displays, and the seven computers in Peter's room are all being used by pairs of students searching the Internet. The noise level is quite high, giving the impression that there is no order. As we walk around the room, we notice that each group of students is working intently. Peter explains that he had the students organize themselves into pairs—with one group of three, since he has 27 students—and each pair selected one of the original 13 colonies in the United States. Their task was to create a company like the Hudson Bay Trading Company for each colony. He went on to say that pairs could team up and work on two related colonies together if they chose to do so, motioning to the group of five and the two groups of four.

Peter explains that he wanted to try something different in this unit on American history. Instead of simply presenting information to the students and discussing it, he presented the students with a problem—creating a company that could use the resources of the particular colony or colonies. The students then went to work searching for information that would help them solve the problem. They were using the classroom's computers to gather information, and they had to collaboratively make decisions about how to present the information to their classmates. The presentation had to include a description of how their investors could make a profit using the resources of the colony.

■ ■ ■

WHAT IS TECHNOLOGY?

We tend to think of technology as a recent innovation in American education, and we usually link technology to computers. In fact, technology is much broader than this, and it has been used in teaching for nearly as long as schools have existed. For example, teachers in the first schools in our country had children use individual slate boards to practice their "letters and numbers." As the multi-age, one-room school evolved into schools organized into grade levels, the chalkboard became an essential tool for communicating with larger groups of students. These are rudimentary forms of technology.

The invention of electricity revolutionized teaching by allowing teachers to use radio, television, filmstrips, films, and overhead projectors (Trotter, 1999b). Technology further evolved, and teachers now routinely use videotapes, many have access to laser discs, most have at least one computer in their classrooms, and some have sophisticated demonstration equipment, such as Latisha used in her PowerPoint presentation. These are all different forms of technology.

But how is this increasingly vast resource most effectively utilized, and will it make your job simpler and more efficient, or more complex and demanding? We try to answer these questions in this chapter, but before we begin, let's consider the most basic question: What is technology?

Increasing Understanding 12.1

Compare the teacher's role when using technology with a hardware view versus a process view. How do the teacher's and student's roles change? How might you incorporate these two views in your own classroom? What benefits would you expect to gain from either approach?

To answer these questions online and receive immediate feedback, go to the *Increasing Understanding* Module in Chapter 12 of the Companion Website at **http://www.prenhall.com/kauchak.**

Contrasting Views of Technology

In the past 50 years, experts have defined educational technology in two distinct ways: as hardware and as a process (Seels & Richey, 1994; Gentry, 1995). Those holding a hardware view believe that technology increases learning by providing tools, such as overheads, videos, and laser discs, that support and amplify the teacher's message (Lumsdaine, 1964). From a hardware perspective, technology is commonly thought of in terms of machinery gadgets, instruments, devices, and computers (Forcier, 1999). This hardware view is illustrated by historical technologies, such as chalkboards, films, and filmstrips, and more recent technologies like computers and Latisha's PowerPoint presentation.

The hardware view received a major boost in 1957 when the Soviet Union beat the United States into outer space by launching the satellite Sputnik. This shocked the nation and caused people to re-examine our educational system. In response, the Federal Government passed the National Defense Education Act in 1958 that authorized research on media effectiveness and funds for schools to purchase media equipment. The bill provided $70 million a year for these purchases for 1959 to 1962. This money was targeted at technology hardware; if the Soviet Union beat us to outer space using technology, then technology would be the key to improving our schools.

In contrast to a hardware perspective, the process view looks at technology more broadly by considering issues such as using technology to increase student motivation, improving the effectiveness of instructional strategies through technology, and teaching students to use technology as a learning tool. When Peter integrated technology and other learning resources into his instruction to help students learn history, he was viewing instructional technology as a process.

In the hardware view of technology, the different machines serve as teaching aids to transmit information. The hardware view assumes that the teacher is in control of learning and that technology will improve learning by enhancing the communication of the instructional message. In contrast to the hardware view, the process perspective of technology allows learners to use technological learning tools as aids to learning. This approach to technology removes the teacher from directly instructing students, through strategies like lecturing, and allows students to directly interact with a learning system such as a computer.

As experts' thinking has progressed, most have come to see technology as a combination of the two views (Seels & Richey, 1994; Gentry, 1995). **Technology** "*is a combination of the processes and tools involved in addressing educational needs and problems, with an emphasis on applying the most current tools: computers and their related technologies* [italics added]" (Roblyer & Edwards, 2000, p. 6). For instance, while Latisha emphasized her PowerPoint presentation as a tool, her goal was for students to understand the concept *internal conflict*. Developing this understanding is a process. Peter emphasized process by

Figure 12.1 **Classroom Applications of Technology**

Using technology to support instruction

Technology tools

Assistive technology

The Internet

presenting his students with a problem and helping them as they tried to solve it, but the students used the computers as tools as they worked toward their solutions. Remembering that technology is a combination of tools and processes, let's turn now to some specific uses of technology to promote learning.

USING TECHNOLOGY IN THE CLASSROOM

Unquestionably, we now live in a technological society. There is so much cell phone usage, for example, that some states now ban them when people are driving, and cell phones ringing in restaurants have become an etiquette issue. Most homes have computers, and the majority of those have Internet access. Sending e-mails halfway around the world has become nearly routine.

Similarly, technology is increasingly affecting the way teaching and learning occur. In this section, we examine some of those applications. The way these applications are classified is somewhat arbitrary, of course, and there is overlap among them. Keep this in mind as you study the following sections. The different applications are outlined in Figure 12.1.

Using Technology to Support Instruction

One of the most common and important uses of technology in schools is to directly support instruction. When a teacher uses an overhead transparency, videotape, or filmstrip, for example, the technology is a form of support.

As technology has advanced, its capability to effectively support instruction has increased. Let's look at two examples.

■ ■ ■

Sandy Hutton, a fifth-grade teacher, is working on the circulatory system and wants to explain the functions of the heart and blood pressure to her students. Searching the Internet, Sandy found some great pictures of a real heart on the National Institute of Health's Website. She used these pictures in a PowerPoint presentation on the heart, its parts, and the way it works with the lungs and other parts of the body.

■ ■ ■

Steve Davis, who teaches in the room next door to Sandy, has similar goals. He wants his students to understand that the heart is a pump that moves blood through the arteries and veins. As it pumps the blood, it also builds pressure in the arteries and veins. He found a model illustrating how the heart is like a bicycle pump with valves opening and closing. He shared this model with his class and brought in an old bicycle pump to illustrate how valves need to open and shut to create pressure. Then he worked with the school nurse to find several sphygmomanometers (blood-pressure measuring devices) that his stu-

The hardware view of technology emphasizes its capabilities to present information in a clear and organized manner.

dents used to determine their own blood-pressure under different types of activities. As they worked in groups, the students used computers to organize their information into charts and compared their results as a whole group later in the class.

■ ■ ■

What did Sandy and Steve accomplish? In Sandy's case, her PowerPoint presentation helped her students see the parts and function of the heart in a way that was more concrete, detailed, and effective than would have been possible with the textbook alone. She used both the Internet and the presentation capability of technology to support her instruction.

In Steve's case, the bicycle pump acted as a concrete metaphor for the heart's function; that is, it allowed students to develop the idea of the heart as a pump, which helped them understand the heart's function. Then, when students measured their own blood pressures, they could feel both the cuff tightening around their arms and their pulses moving and could see the digital readout of their blood pressures. This strategy helped his students translate an abstract idea, blood pressure, into something concrete that they could feel and see. Steve used technology to support his instruction in a way that was probably even more effective than Sandy's; it helped him provide his students with a hands-on, concrete learning experience. Technology both increased the effectiveness of his teaching and made it more efficient.

These strategies illustrate different ways teachers can use technology to translate abstract ideas for learners into concrete learning experiences. Students can then use these concrete learning experiences to understand and interpret new ideas. When we use PowerPoint, overhead transparencies, videotapes, or even bicycle pumps, we are using technology as a delivery system to communicate ideas to our students. This use of technology, while more sophisticated than chalkboards and overheads, still is embedded in a transmission view of teaching. In a transmission view, a teacher's primary role is to dispense information. While this role is an important one, as evidenced by the popularity of teacher-centered direct instruction, there are other alternative views of technology use.

Steve also used technology as an enabling learning tool. He provided his students with blood pressure equipment and asked them to work in small groups to find patterns in the ways different activities influenced students' blood pressure. To find these patterns, they used a computer to organize the information into charts that allowed them to search for and find patterns. In addition to learning about blood pressure, his students were also learning how to:

- Conduct experiments in a systematic fashion.
- Use a computer to organize information.
- Work productively in small groups.

Technology provided a vehicle for students to learn these important skills by actually using them in their investigations. We'll return to this topic shortly, but first let's look at alternate ways that technology can be used to actively engage students in learning.

Using Software to Deliver Instruction Computers and the software in them have become powerful tools to deliver instruction. As soon as educators began to recognize the potential of computers and other forms of technology to do tasks quickly and systematically, they began to experiment with their capacity to imitate and improve on the functions of human teachers (Roblyer & Edwards, 2000).

Both Sandy and Steve used technology as a form of support, but they remained directly involved in the lessons. As it has advanced, technology's capacity for supporting instruction has increased to the point where it can be used without the teacher's direct involvement. For instance, students practice basic skills, such as knowing multiplication facts like 6 × 9 = 54, using worksheets and flashcards. Educators began to wonder if computers could be used to provide an improved form of practice, and if there were other applications of technology that could enhance teaching. This kind of thinking has led to the development of different kinds of **software**—*programs written in a computer language*—that are used to deliver instruction. We examine four of them in this section, including:

- Drill-and-practice
- Tutorials
- Simulations
- Problem Solving

Drill-and-practice. As an elementary or secondary student, you may have used flashcards to memorize facts like 6 × 9 = 54, foreign language vocabulary, or new concepts in science or health. A friend or relative would show you a card, you would provide the answer, and the other person would go to the next card. After awhile, he or she either grew tired or impatient and left you to study on your own. A computer-based drill-and-practice program is similar to the flashcards you once used, but the computer never grows tired or impatient; it keeps presenting card after card as long as you enter an answer—even if 48 is repeatedly given as the answer to 6 × 9 = ?.

Students use drill-and-practice programs on their own; the teacher isn't directly involved. However, these programs don't substitute for a teacher's expertise, and developers of these programs assume that students have had previous instruction on the ideas behind facts or concepts. For example, math teachers first help students understand the concept of multiplication and want them to know that 6 × 9 is 6 sets of 9 items, or 9 sets of 6 items. In the process, they illustrate these sets with concrete examples. Then, drill-and-practice programs are used to help students practice until they know the facts without having to think about them. This is how technology can support the teacher's instruction.

Computers can be used to provide drill and practice, perform tutorials, and present simulations and problems to students.

Some drill-and-practice software also uses a "gaming" concept to increase students' motivation. For example, rather than just typing in the correct response to 6 × 9 = ?, students might aim a laser blaster at an alien emblazoned with the correct answer.

The best drill-and-practice programs are adaptive, matching the demands of the task to a student's ability. For example, in a program designed to improve knowledge of math facts like 6 × 9 = 54, an adaptive program would begin by pretesting to determine how many of the facts the student already knows. Then, it introduces new facts at a pace that ensures high success rates. When the student fails to answer, or answers incorrectly, the program prompts by providing the answer and then retests that fact.

Because students must be able to recall math facts without thinking about them, the amount of time they are given to answer is shortened as they become more proficient. This also increases motivation by challenging students to become quicker in their responses.

What are the benefits of drill-and-practice programs? First, they provide effective feedback, informing students immediately of what they've mastered and where they need more work. They can also be motivating for students turned off by paper-and-pencil exercises (Roblyer & Edwards, 2000). In addition, they save teachers' time, since teachers don't have to present the information and score the students' responses.

Research indicates that computerized math learning games can be effective tools for teaching math facts (Archer, 1998). Researchers caution, however, that more time on computers does not necessarily equal more learning. More important is the quality of the learning experiences and the extent to which they are linked to the teacher's goals.

Tutorials. In contrast with drill-and-practice software, which focuses on the mastery of isolated facts, **tutorials** are *technology applications designed to deliver an entire integrated instructional sequence similar to a teacher's instruction on the topic*. For example, a tutorial in a high school accounting class on calculating depreciation might first present and explain the formula "annual depreciation = cost/expected life" and then ask, "If an electric pasta machine costs $400 and is expected to last 4 years, what is the annual depreciation?" In response to the answer "$100," the computer would say, "Good," and go on to the next problem or concept. A student who typed $400 might be told, "Sorry, but you're probably not ready to work for H & R Block. $400 is the cost. To find annual depreciation, divide this figure by the expected life (4 years). Please type the correct answer."

Let's look at another tutorial application.

■ ■ ■

Lisa Hoover, a first-grade teacher, has created a number of learning centers in her classroom where her students can work independently. Students can earn "classroom money" for good behavior and finishing assignments, and the money can be used to purchase prizes from the class store. The students who work in the store as clerks must first complete several of the math units, with the last one focusing on giving change. Lisa's students have widely varying backgrounds, and she believes that they shouldn't complete the giving-change unit until they're ready. As a result, she has students who want to take the unit at various times during the fall semester. They often must wait or she must drop some other activity to teach them the rules for calculating and counting change. This past year, Lisa took a technology course where she learned to develop HyperStudio™ stacks. One of the first stacks she developed was a tutorial on giving change. Lisa used pictures of different coins and created a number of scenarios that provided students with practice in giving change. Now, students can complete the unit on giving change anytime they have access to one of the computers in the classroom. In addition, Lisa designed the tutorial so that it would give students any number of problems and help until they have mastered the information. Lisa noticed that students easily mastered the process and were happy about having access to the instruction immediately.

■ ■ ■

Increasing Understanding 12.2

Based on the definition of *hypermedia,* identify one important difference between multimedia, which is a collection of different media forms, and hypermedia.

Tutorials can be simple software, like the accounting example, but they are now more often **hypermedia,** which are *linked forms of technology,* such as Lisa's HyperStudio™ stack on making change. In another case, a hypermedia product on the solar system might include some written material, such as information on Saturn's rings, a laser disc clip, and a video episode. Students view a computer screen that contains **icons,** which are *pictures that act as symbols for some action or item.* To view the laser disc clip, students click on the laser disc icon (a small picture of a laser disc), and the clip is then displayed for them.

Effective tutorials have several positive features. Technology makes the instruction flexible, adaptive, and efficient. For example, Lisa's HyperStudio™ stack was available anytime; the students didn't have to wait until Lisa had free time to teach them. Second, it was adaptive and individualized, providing each student with the amount of practice needed to master the content. Before she prepared her tutorial, Lisa had worked with students individually, but she was frequently interrupted, and she often was unable to tutor students when they were ready to work on the unit. She could have created the same type of instruction with printed worksheets, but the instruction would have been less efficient since Lisa had to interrupt what she was doing to grade and monitor the task. In addition, hypermedia are generally much more motivating for students than worksheets.

Increasing Understanding 12.3

Was the HyperStudio™ stack that Lisa developed to teach her students to make change aimed at rote memorization tasks or a higher level? Explain.

The effectiveness of tutorials depends on the quality of interactions between the technology and the learner. Interactions can range from asking for simple, factual information such as "What color was the ball that Billy found?" to higher level questions that require the student to apply information to new situations like "Who do you think lost the ball?" and "What should Billy do with the lost ball?"

Tutorials have been criticized for focusing too much on rote learning—memorized information—instead of challenging students to think and apply understanding. While this doesn't have to be the case, finding high quality software and hypermedia materials is an obstacle facing teachers who want to integrate tutorials into their classrooms.

Simulations. In addition to using interactive tutorials to teach skills, teachers also use software simulations to bring the real world into the classroom. **Simulations** (or microworlds) are *types of software that model a real or imaginary system in order to help learners understand that system*. They have the great advantage of being able to involve students in complex, realistic learning tasks that are unique and often unavailable in classrooms. A driver's education course, for example, might have students use a driving simulator to experience a near accident designed to help them learn to drive defensively (and avoid the wrath of their driving instructors). The learning is meaningful because it involves students in situations that are both realistic and safe.

As another example, students can use computer software to simulate a frog dissection rather than cutting up an actual frog. While the simulation has the disadvantage of not allowing students the hands-on experience, it has at least three advantages: it is less expensive, since it can be used over and over; it is more flexible, because the frog can be "reassembled;" and the simulation avoids sacrificing a frog for science (Roblyer & Edwards, 2000).

One of the most popular social studies simulations, *Oregon Trail* (and its second generation *Oregon Trail II*, which contains realistic graphics), allows students to travel like the original Oregon Trail pioneers from Independence, Missouri, to Oregon's Willamette Valley (Forcier, 1999). Students shop for supplies within a given budget and make decisions along the way about the pace of travel, food supplies, and health problems. As students proceed, they can interact with Native Americans and other settlers along the way, gaining valuable historical information as they travel to Oregon. A new, networked version allows a number of users to interact simultaneously during their journey.

Other simulations give students a sense of what it would be like to walk on the moon or see how personnel work together in a hospital emergency room. As the quality of software improves, representations will become more sophisticated and simulations more interactive, further increasing learner motivation and understanding.

Problem solving. Computer software can also be used to teach students to solve problems. When we teach problem solving, we want students to get the right answer *and* become better at figuring out how to solve future problems. One of the difficulties in teaching problem solving is how to create and present real-world problems that are not "cut and dried." Problems in textbooks are usually well-defined and routine, the numbers needed to solve the problem (and only those numbers) are included, and even the operation, such as subtraction or multiplication, is often suggested by where the problem is presented (for example, in a chapter on subtraction) (Cognition and Technology Group at Vanderbilt, 1992).

These aren't the kinds of problems people typically face. Real-world problems are often ill-defined, and their solution isn't as routine as the problems students usually encounter in school. Technology can help learners acquire experience with more realistic problems. Let's look at an example.

■ ■ ■

Jasper has just purchased a new boat and is planning to drive it home. The boat consumes 5 gallons of fuel per hour and travels at 8 mph. The gas tank holds 12 gallons of gas. The boat is currently located at mile marker 156. Jasper's home dock is at mile marker 132. There are two gas stations on the way home. One is at mile marker 140.3 and the other is at mile marker 133. They charge $1.109 and $1.25 per gallon, respectively. They don't take credit cards. Jasper started the day with $20. He bought 5 gallons of gas at $1.25 per gallon (not

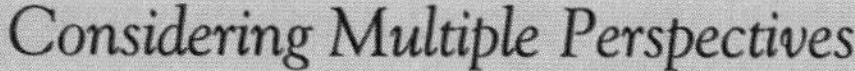

Exploring Diversity

Considering Multiple Perspectives

ASSISTIVE TECHNOLOGY

Jaleena is partially sighted, with a visual acuity of less than 20/80, even after corrective glasses. Despite this disability, she was doing well in her new fourth-grade class. Tera Banks, her teacher, placed her in the front of the room so that she could better see the chalkboard and overhead and assigned several students to work with her on projects. Using a magnifying device, she was able to read most written material, but the computer was giving her special problems. The small letters and punctuation on things like Website addresses made it very difficult for her to learn to use the computer as an information source. Tera worked with the special-education consultant in her district to get a special monitor that magnified content several times. She knew it was working when she saw Jaleena quietly working alone at her computer on the report due next Friday.

As we've said throughout this chapter, technology is changing the ways we teach and the ways students learn. **Assistive technology,** *which includes adaptive tools that help students with disabilities learn and perform better in daily life tasks*, is having a particularly important impact on students with exceptionalities. These adaptive tools include motorized chairs, remote control devices that turn machines on and off through a nod of the head or other muscle action, and machines that amplify sights and sounds. Probably the most widespread contribution of assistive technology is in the area of computer adaptations. For example, some students, such as those who are blind or who have severe physical impairments, cannot interact with a standard computer unless adaptations are made. These adaptations include either alternative input devices or output devices (Lewis & Doorlag, 1999).

Adaptations to Computer Input Devices

To use computers effectively, students must be able to input their words and ideas. This can be difficult if not impossible for those with visual or other physical disabilities that don't allow standard keyboarding.

One adaptation includes devices that enhance the keyboard, such as making it larger and easier to see, arranging the letters alphabetically to make them easier to find, or using pictures for nonreaders. Additional adaptations completely bypass the keyboard. For example, students with physical disabilities that don't allow them to use their hands to input information are able to use switches activated by a body movement, such as a head nod, to interact with the computer. Touch screens allow students to go directly to the monitor screen to indicate their responses.

Adaptations to Output Devices

Adaptations to the standard computer monitor either bypass visual displays or increase their size. Size enhancement can be accomplished by using a special large-screen monitor, such as the one Jaleena used, or by using a magnification device that increases screen size. For students who are blind, speech synthesizers can read words and

Even this very small sample gives us some idea of the variety of information available on the Internet and helps us understand the comment "You can find anything on the Internet." The Internet can also be a powerful teaching tool, providing access to information and allowing links to other learners.

The Internet as a source of information is widely known. However, it's potential to influence communication, social development, and problem solving isn't as commonly examined. We discuss these uses in following sections.

The Internet as a Communication Tool **Electronic mail (e-mail)** is *a message sent via telecommunication from one person to one or more other people*. It has revolutionized communication by allowing people to quickly and efficiently communicate with others virtually anywhere in the world. It also allows the transmission of pictures and other attachments, such as written text, databases, or spreadsheets. With e-mail, for example, an individual can effortlessly send family photos to friends in Germany, Japan, or Kenya. **Chat rooms** are *expanded, collective versions of e-mail*. When one user in a chat room types comments, what he or she types is seen by everyone in the "room" in real time. In this respect,

Assistive technology provides adaptive tools to help students with exceptionalities learn.

translate them into sounds. In addition, special printers can convert words into Braille and Braille into words.

Speech/voice recognition technologies are rapidly developing and can assist students with exceptionalities in several ways (Newby et al., 2000). Speech recognition systems can translate speech into text on the computer screen, bypassing the need for keyboard inputting. These systems can be invaluable for students with physical disabilities that affect hand and finger movement. Other devices translate printed words into speech, allowing nonspeaking students to communicate verbally.

These technologies are important because they prevent disabilities from becoming obstacles to learning. Their importance to students with exceptionalities is likely to increase as technology becomes a more integral part of classroom instruction.

Increasing Understanding 12.6

How can assistive technology be combined with computer-based instruction? With technology as a learning tool? With technology as a communication tool?

Increasing Understanding 12.7

What is one advantage of a chat room over a bulletin board? One disadvantage?

chat rooms are like telephones or CB radios. They're considered the most interactive of all the written communication options. **Bulletin boards** *serve as electronic message centers for a given topic.* They function just like physical bulletin boards; they're a place where messages can be posted and stored. Students can read the comments of others and then leave their own messages.

Because the Internet efficiently connects students to others all over the world, they can share views and perspectives that can promote learning as well as social growth. This kind of access is impossible to obtain in any other way. In some cases, the power, feelings, and emotions elicited in e-mail communications are greater than would be captured in even a face-to-face encounter.

Advantages and disadvantages of Internet communication. As with any educational tool, Internet communication has both advantages and disadvantages (Jehng, 1997; Johnson & Johnson, 1996). In addition to connecting students all over the world, Internet interactions can be more equitable, since extraneous factors such as attractiveness, prestige, and material possessions are eliminated. In addition, communicating on the

TECHNOLOGY IN CLASSROOMS

Having examined different ways that technology can be used to enhance learning in the classroom, you now have the chance to examine a classroom teacher who is using technology with her third-grade students. Suzanne Brush is a third-grade teacher who is teaching her students about bar graphs. To do this, she gave each of her students different flavored jelly beans and asked them to vote for their favorite flavor. After graphing the results, Suzanne taught them how to understand and interpret the graph. As a follow-up activity, she created technology-based learning centers.

To complete this activity, you will need to do the following:

- View the video episode titled "Technology in Classrooms."
- You may want to read the written transcript of the lesson, which is available at **http://www.prenhall.com/kauchak.** Simply go to the Website and follow the directions on your screen.
- Answer the questions that follow:

1. Did Suzanne Brush's use of technology reflect more of a hardware or process view? Explain.
2. How effective was Suzanne's use of technology as a problem-solving tool? What could she have done to make it more effective?
3. In what ways did Suzanne use technology as a support tool to complement her students' learning? How effective were these uses, and what might she have done to increase their effectiveness?
4. How could Suzanne use technology as an assessment tool? What advantages and disadvantages would there be over pencil-and-paper measures?

To answer these questions online and receive immediate feedback, go to the Looking Through Classroom Windows Module in Chapter 12 of the Companion Website.

create an online university capable of teaching as many as 80,000 soldier-students at locations all around the world (Trotter, 2001a). Virtual high school programs are also appearing around the country, providing alternatives to standard attendance at a high school.

ISSUES IN THE USE OF EDUCATIONAL TECHNOLOGY

In earlier sections, we looked at process and hardware views of technology and examined some of the most common applications of technology in schools. But, as with any innovation or reform, important questions remain. What kinds of technology will be available in your first teaching position? How will you use technology in your teaching? What kinds of help and support are you likely to receive? You saw in earlier sections of the chapter that a number of innovative instructional technology applications are now available nationally. In this section we examine two issues related to the use of technology in classrooms: access issues and instructional issues.

Access Issues

One of the most important issues in the use of technology is easy to understand; it is a simple matter of access. If teachers and students don't have access to technology, they can't use it to increase learning.

Computer labs allow schools to cluster computers in one location to teach basic computer literacy skills.

One study of technology use in education across the country concluded that ". . . a critical mass has been reached. More than half the nation's classrooms are connected to the Web, and schools have an average of one instructional computer for every 5.7 students" (Fatemi, 1999, p. 5).

So, in a class of 30 students, the "average" teacher will have something like five computers available. This is a significant improvement from one computer per 19 students in 1992 (Soulé, 2000).

However, when asked to identify major barriers to effective use of technology, 71 percent of teachers and 66 percent of principals targeted "insufficient number of computers" (Jerald & Orlofsky, 1999). Another national teacher survey also named insufficient computer numbers as the major obstacle to greater software and Website utilization (Trotter, 1999a). It is apparent that the question of whether or not teachers and students have adequate access to technology still doesn't have a definitive answer.

The issue of access is even more complex. For example, 84 percent of all fourth graders had computers available in classrooms compared to 47 percent of eighth graders (U.S. Department of Education 1998a). However, 91 percent of eighth graders had computers available in computer labs compared to 79 percent of fourth graders. Overall, 43 percent of school computers are found in labs, and 48 percent are found in classrooms (the remainder are used by teachers, administrators, and school secretaries).

Cost of Technology Cost is a major factor influencing accessibility. As anyone who has tried to buy a computer has discovered, technology is expensive. In the 1997–1998 school year, the United States spent more than $5 billion on technology; this translates into $88 per student (White, 1997b; Gursky, 1999).

The problem doesn't end with the purchase of the computer itself. Experts attempting to describe the overall costs involved with technology use the concept *total cost of ownership* (Soulé, 2000), which includes costs associated with software, maintenance and repairs, system linkages, technical support, and training. Districts hard-pressed by the public to increase the use of technology in their schools often rush out to buy computers but fail to consider the support needed to make the technology effective and efficient. Typical school districts in the United States spend over 50 percent of their budgets on hardware, software, and supplies, allocating only 27 percent to networking, the Internet, and staff development (Jerald & Orlofsky, 1999).

Increasing Understanding 12.9

In the future, would you predict that more school computers will be found in labs or in classrooms? Why? How does your answer relate to process and hardware views of technology?

Cost also influences the question of where to put computers—in classrooms or computer labs. Obviously, it's less expensive to supply one lab with 30 computers than to buy four or five for every classroom in the school. In addition, even with four or five computers, the teacher still must plan carefully to allow all students access to the computer in the course of the day.

Advantages and disadvantages exist in each configuration. Computer labs allow the teacher to present basic computer-literacy skills in a whole-class format, and clustered computers provide opportunities for students to individually practice skills and receive feedback. However, labs are not as effective for integrating technology into the curriculum, which is an important instructional goal.

Federal Support The federal government has responded to the problem of technology funding in at least two ways. The Telecommunications Act of 1996 provided districts with a fund of $2 billion per year to help them provide equal access and "universal service." These funds can be used to provide electronic networking, access to the Internet, high-speed data lines, and pay for telephone charges resulting from technology use.

An innovative but controversial plan would provide tax incentives to businesses that donate their used computers to schools (Soulé, 2000). Advocates claim that computers up to 3 years old, while no longer viable for industry purposes, would be useful in schools. Critics question whether the donated computers can be integrated into existing district networks and fear that they will be used as cheap "stand alones," only able to teach word processing skills.

Instructional Issues

Access to technology is a major issue facing teachers; they can't use what they don't have. Other more subtle issues will affect the ways you use technology in your classroom. In this section, we examine a range of issues related to instruction. They include:

- Instructional goals for the use of technology.
- Quality of available technology.
- Curricular match with instructional goals.
- Curricular pressures.
- Preparation time constraints.
- Internet access.

Instructional Goals for Technology Use Why use technology in your classroom? Let's take a walk down the hallway of a typical elementary school to try and answer this question.

■ ■ ■

In his first-grade class, Chris Carter is working with students on their basic word processing skills, getting them ready to use their computers on creative writing assignments.

Down the hall in Jim Henderson's fourth-grade classroom, several students are working in the back of the room at a program called Math Blasters. Once they answer a certain number of questions correctly, they are allowed to play an arcade-like game as a reward.

In Maria Robles's sixth-grade classroom, students are working in teams on projects, using the Internet to gather information on pollution problems in various parts of the United States. In addition to using Websites on pollution, they also correspond with other students across the country who are working on similar projects, sharing their local data and comparing it with data gathered by others.

■ ■ ■

Your instructional goals will influence the ways in which you use technology. It can perform many wonderful tasks, but using technology that isn't linked to clear and precise goals is questionable and potentially counterproductive.

The International Society for Technology in Education (ISTE) lists the following six technology goals for students (ISTE, 1998):

- To become proficient in basic operations and concepts (for example, word processing and printing).
- To understand the social and ethical issues involved in the use of technology (for example, computer hacking and creating viruses).
- To use technology as a productivity tool (for example, creating an online literary magazine).
- To use technology as a communication tool (for example, interacting with peers across the country).
- To use technology as a research tool (for example, using search engines to locate information about a specific topic on the Internet).
- To use technology for problem solving and decision making (for example, using technology to find the best price for an airline ticket).

Increasing Understanding 12.10

What kind of school computer configuration is most compatible with the goal of computer literacy? Why isn't this configuration compatible with other ISTE goals?

To help teachers integrate these goals into their teaching, ISTE has produced a 373-page guide that contains lesson plans linked to appropriate technologies. The Website address for this publication can be found in the *Weblinks* Module in Chapter 12 of the Companion Website at **http://www.prenhall.com/kauchak**.

Note that only one of these goals is targeted on what used to be called "computer literacy." Initially, when computer technology was first introduced into the schools, **computer literacy,** or *understanding how to operate computers*, was a primary goal. Now, as more and more students come to us with computer skills, the emphasis has shifted to more complex goals.

Despite the shift in emphasis, teachers need to be aware of their students' computer backgrounds and skills. Students can't use computers as a learning tool if they don't have basic computer skills. For example, word processing can be a powerful tool for improving writing skills, but only if students possess the prerequisite processing skills to perform tasks like editing and spell checking (Kellogg & Mueller, 1993).

Quality of Available Software: The Good, the Bad, and the Ugly Quality is an important issue in technology: it affects how easily you can use technology in your classroom and influences how much students learn. The quality of existing educational software is generally rated "good" by teachers, but varies greatly due to at least two factors (Trotter, 1999; Zehr, 1999a). One is the market economy that drives much software production. Companies are in the software business to make money, and quality is secondary to making a profit. A second factor influencing quality is the heavy reliance on outmoded views of learning, resulting in the proliferation of "drill and kill" programs that are nothing more than electronic flashcards.

Teaching in an Era of Reform

TECHNOLOGY: THE GREAT EQUALIZER?

One aspect of reform that is being promoted in this country is greater use of and access to technology. Reformers suggest that technology can be the great equalizer, minimizing learning gaps between the rich and poor, minority and nonminority, and male and female students. Let's see how this reform effort is progressing.

We saw in Chapter 8 that great disparities in educational funding exist between "rich" and "poor" school districts. These disparities result in differences in teachers' salaries, the kinds of buildings and classrooms they teach in, as well as the kinds of resources available to promote learning. They also impact students' access to technology, suggesting a growing "digital divide" between these different groups (National Telecommunications and Information Administration, 1999).

Ethnicity and Computer Use

As we can see in Table 12.2, ethnicity plays a major role in access to and use of computers, especially in home use. For example, at the elementary level, while 54 percent of White students use computers at home, only 21 percent of African American students and 19 percent of Hispanic students use them. Disparities are even greater at the high school level. The disparities in home use are especially troubling because research shows that education is the primary way that children use computers at home (53 percent of students), outdistancing e-mail (32 percent) and games (12 percent) (Trotter, 2000).

Income and Computer Use

Similar disparities occur in terms of technology and parents' incomes. As we can see in Table 12.3, there are huge differences in access to computers for students from families with household incomes ranging from about the poverty level versus those above $75,000. Unfortunately, these differences in computer use occur both at home and at school. Only 16 percent of elementary students from lower income levels used computers at home versus 80 percent of students from higher income levels. The cost of buying, installing, and maintaining computers was identified as the main reason for this disparity. If students are expected to work on computers at home to complete assignments, access is a serious problem.

Increasing Understanding 12.13

Some claim that the data on ethnicity and computer use is related to money or availability. Others claim it is due to technology background knowledge. What data in Table 12.3 suggests the latter argument?

In addition to computer numbers, the quality of available computers is a problem because computer quality influences the kinds of software that can be used, as well as access to the Internet. Schools serving high percentages of cultural minorities and schools located in communities with high poverty rates tend to have older, lower quality computers without CD-ROM capabilities or Pentium or Power Mac processors (Bracey, 1999a).

Table 12.2 Ethnicity and Computer Use

Ethnicity	School Use of Computer Grades 1–8	School Use of Computer Grades 9–12	Home Use of Computer Grades 1–8	Home Use of Computer Grades 9–12
White	61%	84%	72%	54%
African American	21%	72%	73%	21%
Hispanic	22%	68%	63%	19%

Source: Data from U.S. Department of Commerce. (1998). Washington, D.C.

Table 12.3 **Household Income and Computer Use**

Household Income	School Use of Computer		Home Use of Computer	
	Grades 1–8	Grades 9–12	Grades 1–8	Grades 9–12
$15,000 – $20,000	75%	67%	16%	21%
$35,000 – $40,000	80%	70%	44%	46%
$75,000 or more	86%	72%	80%	81%

Source: Data from U.S. Department of Commerce. (1998). Washington, D.C.

Access to the Internet also requires infrastructure and wiring and is influenced by the percentage of economically disadvantaged students in a school. Those schools with the most disadvantaged (71 percent or more) had 17 students per Internet-linked computer versus 10 students per computer for schools with fewer than 11 percent disadvantaged (U.S. Department of Education, 1998a). Overall, in 1999 schools reported that 63 percent of their classrooms were hooked up to the Internet, but this figure fell to 39 percent for the poorest schools. For additional information on Internet access, consult the *Weblinks* Module in Chapter 12 of this book's Companion Website.

Gender Divides

Gender also influences computer access and use. Boys are three times more likely to enroll in computer clubs and summer classes, and only 15 percent of users in cyberspace are female (Hale, 1998). At the Massachusetts Institute of Technology, one of the premier science and technology universities in the country, one-third of its total graduates are women, but only 15 percent of computer science graduates are women, compared to 60 percent in chemistry and 52 percent in biology (Hale, 1998). At the high school level, only 17 percent of students taking the College Board Advanced Placement Test in computer science were women (American Association of University Women, 1998).

These differences in computer access and use are troubling for several reasons. Research suggests that the number and quality of computers influences teachers' use of technology (Trotter, 1999a). When obstacles are too great, teachers tend not to use it, which deprives their students of valuable learning opportunities. From a student's perspective, these statistics raise the question of whether or not all students are being provided with equal opportunities to learn. In the long term, access to computers can influence the kinds of career options available to students. Students are less likely to pursue high-tech careers in areas such as science and engineering if they have inadequate technology backgrounds or have not been introduced to ways that technology is used in these areas.

You Take a Position

Now it's your turn to take a position on the issues discussed in this section. Go to the *Education Week* Website at **http://www.edweek.com,** find "search" on the first page, and type in the following search term: *technology funding*. Locate a minimum of three articles on this topic, and then do the following:

1. Identify the title, author, and date of each article, and then write a one-paragraph summary of each article.
2. Determine if a pattern exists in the articles. (Each article—or even two of the three—suggesting that technology funding is a major obstacle to reform would be a pattern, for example.)
3. Take one of the following two positions:
   - The pattern suggested in the articles, if implemented, *is* likely to improve education.
   - The pattern suggested in the articles *is not* likely to improve education.

State your position in writing, and document it with information taken from the articles and your study of the text. (This chapter and any other chapter of the text may be used.)

To answer these questions online, go to the Take a Position Module in Chapter 12 of the Companion Website.

Issues of computer access have raised questions about technology's ability to act as a great equalizer.

responsibilities, and new teachers should seek guidance from administrators or more experienced peers if questions remain. In all likelihood, the whole area of Internet access will continue to grow in importance as more classrooms use the Internet to access data.

The Changing Role of Teachers

As we've seen, technology is changing not only the way we teach but also the ways students learn. Technology is also changing your role as a teacher, the challenges you'll encounter as you begin your new career, and your professional development as you progress from novice teacher to expert.

For starters, you'll be expected to know about technology and how it can be used to promote student learning. Of the 50 states, 42 currently require teachers to have formalized training in educational applications of computers. Chances are that during your certification program, you'll encounter either a specific course in this area or specialized training on this topic integrated into several methods courses.

Once you acquire a teaching position, you will be given additional assistance to integrate technology into your classroom. The form that this assistance takes will vary, with the most common form of support coming from a full-time technology coordinator (30 percent of schools), followed by a part-time teacher or staff member (27 percent of schools), or a district technology coordinator (20 percent of schools). This assistance is essential; research shows that the more training and help teachers receive, the more likely they are to use technology in their teaching and to use technology to promote problem solving and higher level thinking versus rote memorization (Archer, 1998; Education Week, 1999).

Increasing Understanding 12.14

In terms of the different uses of computers that you have read about in this chapter, what are the advantages and disadvantages of learning about technology in a stand-alone course or integrated into methods courses?

Unfortunately, the major part of each district's technology budget goes to hardware (40 percent), networks (20 percent), software, peripherals, and the Internet (20 percent), with only 16 percent going to service and support, professional development, or computer training (Education Week, 1999). In industry, the rule of thumb is that companies should spend one-third of their technology budget on training and support (Gursky, 1999). By this standard, the percentage allocated to teacher development in this area is clearly inadequate.

In addition, although access to technology has increased rapidly in recent years, the percentage of schools with full-time technology coordinators has increased only 1 percent from 1996 to 1998, and schools in poorer districts are less likely to have such support. One study found that the Chicago Public School System had only six computer technicians—which means that each technician is responsible for 93 schools (Gursky, 1999). One of the major questions you'll want to ask as you interview for a teaching position is what kind of support you can expect in this area. Once you land a job, you'll need to connect with the tech specialist in your school or district to find out what resources are available and how to get help when you need it. Research shows that this help will be a major factor in your use of technology as you begin your career (Strudler et al., 1999).

As you progress from novice to expert in your teaching career, you are likely to move along a competency continuum in terms of technology use (Zehr, 1999a). At the entry or novice level, teachers tend to use technology either as an end in itself or as a reward to students for completing some other instructional task. At the next level, adaptation, teachers use technology to support the existing curriculum or already established instructional strategies. At the highest level, transformation, teachers use technology as a tool to change and improve their teaching, involving students in authentic and challenging tasks. As a novice, you will want to experiment with using technology to transform your teaching during your first years of teaching, but you may only achieve this level after several years of experimentation.

A technological tool to assist you in this area of professional growth is an individualized, self-administered assessment tool that you can access on the Internet. This assessment tool assists teachers in evaluating their technological knowledge in the following five dimensions: core technology skills; curriculum, learning, and assessment; professional practice; classroom and instructional management; and administrative competencies. In assessing themselves, teachers read short descriptions of skill levels in each of the five categories and decide where they stand on the continuum. The designers of this instrument intend it to be used alone or by groups of teachers in a school who are working together to transform their teaching from traditional to more technologically student-centered.

SUMMARY

What Is Technology?

One view of technology looks at it in terms of hardware, such as computers, whereas another view sees technology as an integrative process that completely transforms instruction. Most experts now see technology as a combination of the processes and tools needed to address educational needs.

Using Technology in the Classroom

Technology has many different uses in the classroom. Common classroom uses include the following: drill-and-practice software; tutorials, which provide entire instructional sequences; simulations, that bring difficult-to-illustrate topics into classrooms; and problem-solving episodes, which capture aspects of real-world situations for instructional purposes.

Technology-support tools, such as word processing, databases, spreadsheets, assistive technology, and the Internet, help both teachers and students in the teaching-learning process. Technology can also help teachers design and give tests and maintain student records.

Issues in the Use of Technology
A number of issues face teachers as they attempt to use technology in their teaching. Foremost among these is how computers are organized and distributed in schools. Computer labs are designed to teach computer literacy skills, but they are not optimal for integrating technology into instruction. Funding, availability, and accessibility also influence the ways teachers use technology in their teaching.

Teachers' use of technology is also affected by a number of instructional issues. Experts have identified six major goals for technology use; only one of these targets computer literacy. When using technology, clear goals are essential; technology should match teacher and district goals and relate to existing assessment systems. As teachers attempt to integrate technology into their instruction, they are often faced with curricular pressures and preparation time constraints. In addition, the whole issue of Internet access places the teacher directly in the middle of censorship and student-protection issues.

IMPORTANT CONCEPTS

assistive technology
bulletin boards
chat rooms
computer literacy
databases
distance education
electronic mail (e-mail)
hypermedia
icons
Internet
simulations
software
spreadsheets
technology
tutorials
uniform resource locator (URL)
Websites

DISCUSSION QUESTIONS

1. Which view of technology—hardware or process—is more prevalent in the schools? Why is this the case? What could be done to improve the balance?
2. In what areas of the curriculum is technology, as a way of delivering instruction, most useful? Least useful? Why?
3. What are the advantages and disadvantages of using technology (such as drill-and-practice programs or tutorials) as a learning tool? In what areas and at what levels is this use of technology most effective?
4. Should Internet filtering occur at the national or local level? What are the advantages and disadvantages of each approach?
5. What can teachers do to overcome the digital divide in their own classrooms? What can they do at the school or district level?
6. What is the biggest obstacle to more effective technology use in schools? What can beginning teachers realistically do to address this problem?
7. What are the advantages of using technology to deliver instruction? What are the disadvantages?

GOING INTO SCHOOLS

1. Observe two classrooms that have computers. How are the computers used? Are they used for instruction? If so, are they for remediation, new learning, rewards, or enrich-

ment? Describe these uses in a paper and make suggestions for alternate or improved ways to utilize technology in the classroom.

2. Observe a teacher and students in a classroom with computers and in a lab with computers. How does the teacher's role vary between the two? Are the goals and activities different in the classroom versus in the computer lab? Describe these differences in a summary that examines advantages and disadvantages of each configuration.
3. Visit a school and make an inventory of the various types of media production equipment available for use in the classroom. (Examples include cameras, videotape equipment, lettering equipment, and computer graphics, all of which are typically found in a centralized teacher prep room.) How could these be used to enhance your instruction? Describe at least three concrete ways that you could use different forms of technology in your teaching.
4. Interview a teacher and ask to see the district's Internet filtering policy. Is the policy effective and easy to implement? Are there any gray areas? Are parents active in shaping the policy? What are parents' and administrators' major concerns? In a paper, describe these practices and how filtering policies will influence your teaching.
5. Interview a teacher and ask about the tech support available. Is there a person who performs this function at the school? How easy is it to access help? What professional development activities are available to increase technology skills? Describe these opportunities in a paper.

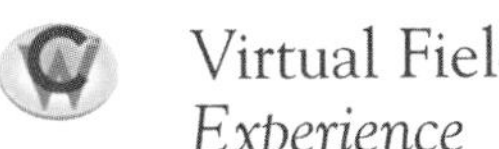

If you would like to participate in a Virtual Field Experience, go to the *Field Experience* Module in Chapter 12 of the Companion Website.

ONLINE PORTFOLIO ACTIVITIES

To complete these activities online, go to the *Portfolio Activities* Module in Chapter 12 of the Companion Website to submit your response.

Portfolio Activity 12.1

Technology and Curriculum

INTASC Principle 7: ***Instructional Planning Skills***

The purpose of this activity is to acquaint you with technology resources in the content area(s) in which you'll be teaching. Decide on a content area (your major or minor if you're leaning toward the secondary level, or one of the content areas taught in the elementary schools) and locate a teacher's edition. What technological teaching tools are available to you in teaching the course? What kinds of hardware and software are needed to use these? What kinds of skills would be required of you to use these? Describe your findings in a paper.

Portfolio Activity 12.2

Technology and Instruction

INTASC Principle 4: ***Instructional Strategies***

The purpose of this activity is to acquaint you with instructional technology resources in terms of Websites on the Internet. Locate a Website in a content area that you are interested in teaching. (Two resources to locate this Website are the September 2000 issue of *Instructor* magazine, which contains 44 "top sites for teachers," and *Quick Guide to the Internet for Education* by E. Provenzo and D. Gotthoffer, which can be found in this text's references.) Locate and explore the Website and then write a two-page paper describing the instructional resources available to teachers.

Portfolio Activity 12.3

Technology and Assessment

INTASC Principle 8: *Assessment*

The purpose of this activity is to familiarize you with the technology resources available in the area of assessment. Research how technology can be used to make assessment more efficient and effective. Two excellent sources are textbooks written by M. Roblyer and J. Edwards (2000), and T. Newby et al. (2000); information on both of these books can be found in this text's references. After reading about the resources available, write a two-page paper describing specifically how technology can help you personally in the assessment process.

PART 5

Careers

CHAPTER

13 Joining the Profession

You're now reading the last chapter of this text. On the surface, it appears that your study is coming to a close, yet it's really just beginning. Our goal in writing this book has been to provide you with information that will help you take the first steps toward becoming a competent and confident professional. The path to teaching expertise is long and difficult, but worthwhile accomplishments are rarely easy.

In this chapter, we hope to take some of the surprises out of your first year of teaching and help you begin the transition from thinking like a student, who wants to do well in a course, to thinking like a teacher, who can make professional decisions in complex situations. To help you in this process, we try to answer the following questions:

- Who are beginning teachers, and what happens to them?
- What do beginning teachers believe, and how do these beliefs influence their behavior?
- What kinds of knowledge must teachers possess, and how does this knowledge influence their teaching?
- How are teachers licensed, and what efforts are being made to increase teacher professionalism?
- What can preservice teachers do to make themselves marketable, and how can they secure their first job?
- How can preservice teachers prepare for their first year of teaching?

My first faculty meeting. Very interesting. Mrs. Zellner [the principal] seems like a really nice person. She went on and on about what a great job the teachers did last year and how test scores were way up compared to the year before. She also extended a special welcome to those of us who are new.

Speaking of new, there sure are a lot of us. I wonder if they're all as scared as I am. I'm not sure what I would have done if Mrs. Landsdorp [the teacher in the room next door] hadn't taken me under her wing. She made me feel a lot better about starting in an inner-city school. So many of the kids come from low-income homes, and English isn't the first language for a lot of them. She said that some of the teachers tend to "write them off" and assume that they can't learn, but that isn't true at all. In fact, a lot of them are quite bright. They just need help and support. She's wonderful. She's sort of gruff, but Andrea [a new friend and second-year teacher] say's she's a softy underneath, and she really loves the kids.

I can't believe how much there is to do—IEPs, progress reports, CPR training, responsibility to look for signs of abuse. When do I teach? I hope I can cut it. (Shelley, a new third-grade teacher, reflecting on her first faculty meeting.)

■ ■ ■

If you choose to teach when you finish your program—and statistics indicate that approximately 60 percent of you will begin teaching immediately after graduating (U.S. Department of Education, 1998e)—you'll join the growing ranks of beginning teachers. Let's take a look at this beginning-teacher population.

CHARACTERISTICS OF BEGINNING TEACHERS

You're a beginning teacher. Who are your colleagues? What does the future hold for you? How do you feel about teaching and the people who are now in the profession? We consider these questions in this section as we examine the following:

- The beginning-teacher population.
- What happens to beginning teachers.
- The beliefs of preservice and beginning teachers.

The Beginning-Teacher Population

As the 20th century came to a close, nearly 2.7 million people taught in K–12 education in this country, with about 400,000 teaching in private schools (Snyder, 1999). However, many of these people will be retiring within the next few years. This, combined with increased immigration into our country, growing school populations, and the demand for smaller classes, leads researchers and policymakers to believe that school districts will need to hire about 200,000 teachers a year over the next decade, for a total of more than 2 million new teachers (Fideler & Haselkorn, 1999).

As we've moved into the new millennium, concerns about the looming teacher shortage have been so prominent that the October 2, 2000, issue of *Newsweek* asked "Who Will Teach Our Kids?" on its front cover and made "Teachers Wanted" its feature article. In the next few years, the teaching profession is going to see many more people like Shelley—that is, new teachers.

What do the Shelley's of the profession look like in comparison to the existing teaching force? They are more likely to be female (79 percent versus 74 percent for the total teaching force), White (91 percent compared to 87 percent), and younger (28 years old

Increasing Understanding 13.1

The minority population of students in this country is increasing significantly. Considering this trend, why do you suppose the teaching population is becoming increasingly White? Also, as opportunities for women have increased in other professions, why is the teaching population becoming increasingly female? Explain in both cases.

To answer this question online and receive immediate feedback, go to the *Increasing Understanding* Module in Chapter 13 of the book's Companion Website at **http://www.prenhall.com/kauchak.**

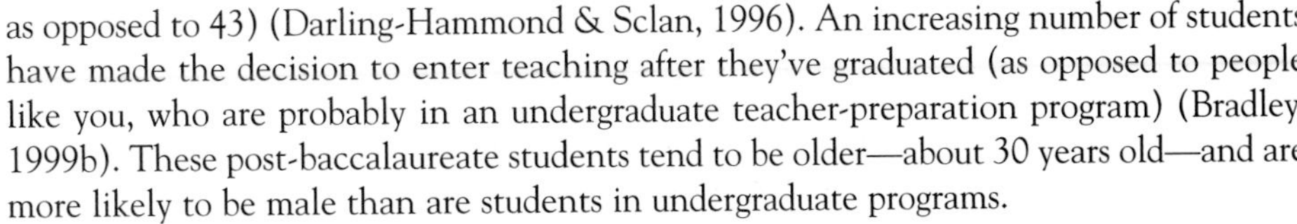

as opposed to 43) (Darling-Hammond & Sclan, 1996). An increasing number of students have made the decision to enter teaching after they've graduated (as opposed to people like you, who are probably in an undergraduate teacher-preparation program) (Bradley, 1999b). These post-baccalaureate students tend to be older—about 30 years old—and are more likely to be male than are students in undergraduate programs.

What Happens to Beginning Teachers?

What happens to beginning teachers after they graduate from a college or university? As we saw earlier, about 60 percent immediately enter teaching, but a significant number drop out in the first few years (U.S. Department of Education, 1998e). The overall attrition rate for teachers—the percentage who leave the profession—is about 6 percent for public schools and about twice that rate for private schools, with low salaries in private schools being a commonly cited reason (Croasmun, Hampton, & Herrmann, 1999).

The number of *new* teachers who leave during their first year is much higher (about 15 percent). In addition, another 15 percent will leave after their second year, and still another 10 percent after their third year (Croasmun, Hampton, & Herrmann, 1999). Shelley's comment—"I'm not sure what I would have done if Mrs. Landsdorp hadn't taken me under her wing"—helps us understand why. Beginning teachers without mentors and support are nearly twice as likely to leave as those who have structured programs designed to help them make the transition from the university environment to the K–12 classroom.

Other reasons for this attrition also exist.

■ ■ ■

Wow! Was I naive. I was tired of sitting in classes, and I wanted so badly to be finished and get out into the "real world." What I never realized was just how cushy being a student was. If I was a little tired, or didn't study enough, I would just coast through class. Now, no coasting. You have to be ready every minute of every day. I've never been so tired in my life. You're in front of kids all day, and then you go home and work all night to get ready for the next day. They have us filling out reports, doing surveys, and everything other than teaching, so I don't get a chance to plan during the day. I can't even make a phone call unless it's during my lunch break or planning period.

And then there's my fourth period. They come in from lunch just wired. It takes me half the period to get them settled down, and that's on a good day.

Sometimes I just need someone to talk to, but we're all so busy. Everybody thinks they're an expert on teaching, because they've been a student. They don't have a clue. Let them try it for two days, and they'd be singing a different tune. (Antonio, a first-year high school English teacher.)

■ ■ ■

Antonio's lament helps us further understand why beginning teachers drop out. The paperwork, his fourth period class, and even a seemingly minor inconvenience like not having access to a phone illustrate negative factors such as (Shoho & Martin, 1999):

- Working conditions, in which teachers spend too much time on nonteaching duties, have too little time for planning, and don't have a moment to themselves.
- Dissatisfaction with student behavior and a disorderly teaching environment.
- Loneliness and alienation.

Increasing Understanding 13.2

Of the factors listed here, which can teachers best control? What might they do to improve the situation with respect to the other factors?

It probably is difficult to believe now, but separation from the support of your professors and other students can be very stressful in the first year of teaching (Bullough, 1989).

Not all is gloom and doom, however.

■ ■ ■

My first lesson with the kids. Chris [her supervising teacher] said I was on my own, sink or swim. I hardly slept last night, but today I feel like celebrating. The kids were so into it. I brought my Styrofoam ball, and I had the kids compare the latitude and longitude lines I had drawn on it and then look at the globe. I thought the first period was supposed to be Chris's lowest, but they did the best. He was impressed.

Now I understand the stuff Dr. Martinez [one of her professors] stressed so much when he was always after us to use concrete examples and question, question, question. I know I have a lot to learn. I thought I could just explain everything to them, but they got confused and drifted off so fast I couldn't believe it. As soon as I started asking questions about the lines on the Styrofoam ball, though, they perked right up. I think I can do this. It was actually a heady experience. (Suzanne, an intern in a seventh-grade geography class.)

■ ■ ■

In Chapter 1, we talked about the rewards in teaching; Suzanne experienced some of those rewards. It is, indeed, a heady experience to see kids understand something new and know that you're the cause of that understanding.

Suzanne's comments also illustrate beliefs typical of preservice and beginning teachers. These beliefs often affect beginning teachers' professional growth. Let's take a look at them.

Beliefs of Beginning Teachers

The course for which this book is used is likely one of the first you'll take in your teacher-preparation program. One of the goals of the course is to help you begin the process of learning to teach.

Research indicates that teachers' beliefs have a strong influence on their teaching and learning to teach (Borko & Putnam, 1996). Our goal in this section is to help you become aware of your beliefs and perhaps dispel some that aren't helpful in your professional growth as a teacher.

To begin, we're asking you to complete a short survey. Using the following scale to guide your responses, circle the number that best represents your beliefs.

5 = Strongly agree
4 = Agree
3 = Agree and disagree
2 = Disagree
1 = Strongly disagree

1. When I begin teaching, I will be a better teacher than most of the teachers now in the field. 1 2 3 4 5
2. As I gain experience in teaching, I expect to become more confident in my ability to help children learn. 1 2 3 4 5
3. The most effective teachers are those able to most clearly explain the content they teach to their students. 1 2 3 4 5
4. I will learn about most of the important aspects of teaching when I get into a classroom. 1 2 3 4 5
5. If I thoroughly understand the content I'm teaching, I'll be able to figure out a way of getting it across to students. 1 2 3 4 5

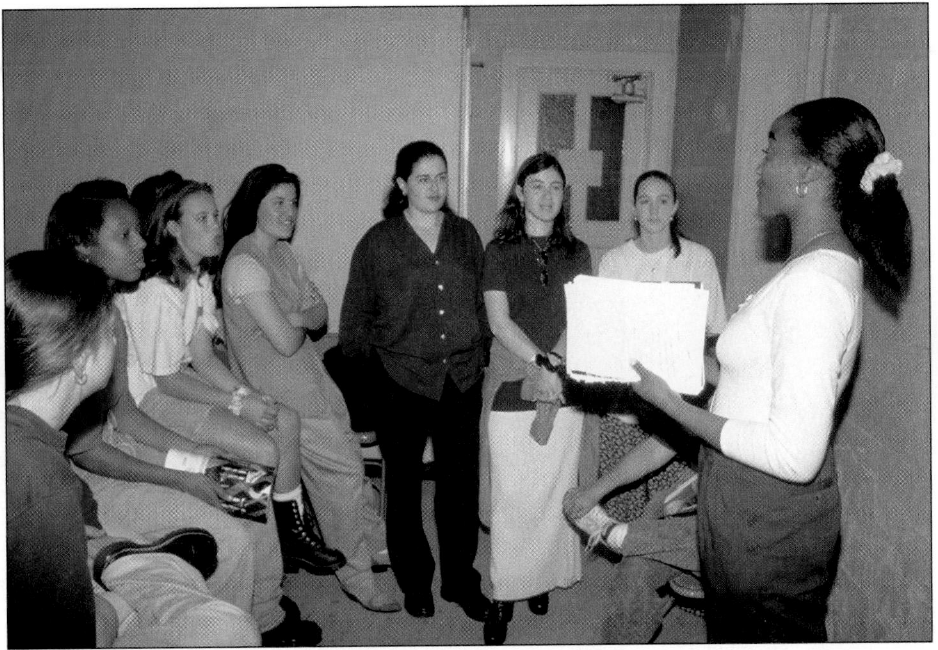

Beginning teachers face many challenges, which can lead to many personal and professional rewards.

Let's see how you did. If you either agreed or strongly agreed with each of the statements, your beliefs are consistent with those generally held by other students in teacher-preparation programs. Let's see what research tells us about these beliefs.

Item 1: When I begin teaching, I will be a better teacher than most of the teachers now in the field. Preservice teachers are optimistic and idealistic, both of which are very positive characteristics. "Prospective teachers report being confident and self-assured in their teaching ability," but unfortunately, "preservice teachers may be unrealistically optimistic about their future teaching performance" (Borko & Putnam, 1996, p. 678). The danger in this perspective occurs when the realities of classrooms shock beginning teachers, who then feel as though "nobody prepared me for this" (Veenman, 1984). Optimism can turn into pessimism or even cynicism; teachers question their career choice; and, as we saw earlier, about one of six beginning teachers quit within the first year.

Increasing Understanding 13.3

What concept is being illustrated by teachers believing they are capable of helping all students to learn and achieve? What do teachers who take responsibility for the success or failure of their instruction do differently than teachers who blame failure on students' lack of intelligence or home environments?

Item 2: As I gain experience in teaching, I expect to become more confident in my ability to help children learn. As with Item 1, most preservice teachers expect to become increasingly confident in their ability to help children learn. Unfortunately, the opposite often occurs. As teachers gain experience, they tend to become more controlling and less democratic in their work with students, becoming less confident that teachers in general can overcome the limitations of home environments and family background (Woolfolk & Hoy, 1990).

As we saw in both Chapters 7 and 11, confidence in their ability to influence learning is essential for teachers, because those that believe they make a difference actually teach differently, taking responsibility for the success or failure of their own instruction (Lee, 2000); they don't blame lack of intelligence, poor home environments, uncooperative administrators, or some other external cause. We are emphasizing this point here in the hope that you won't fall into the same trap that snares many beginning teachers.

Item 3: The most effective teachers are those able to most clearly explain the content they teach to their students. People in general, and preservice teachers in particular, believe that teaching is essentially a process of "telling" or explaining content to students (Holt-

Current views of learning replace telling as an instructional strategy with interactive dialogue between teachers and students.

Reynolds, 1992). This is likely the result of their own personal histories; in most of their school experiences, their teachers lectured.

Teaching is much more complex than simply telling, however, which Suzanne discovered in her first teaching experience. She was lucky; she quickly recognized the problems with talking too much, but many interns and beginning teachers cling to the belief that explaining is the essence of teaching.

Research corroborates Suzanne's experience and the emphasis Dr. Martinez put on questioning. This research consistently indicates that explaining, by itself, is often ineffective for helping students understand topics in depth (Bransford, 1993; Greeno, Collins, & Resnick, 1996). The video episode you saw in Chapter 11 further illustrates this fact. (If you didn't see the video episode, click onto **www.prenhall.com/kauchak,** go to the *Classroom Windows* Module for Chapter 11, and read the written transcript of the lesson.)

For instance, in that lesson we saw that Suzie (one of the students) was provided with at least three clear and accurate solutions to the problem of making the beam balance: Molly's in the group, Marvin's at the board, and the teacher's. In spite of these explanations, she retained the belief that the beam would balance if the number of tiles on each side of the fulcrum was the same. Explaining did little to change Suzie's understanding. She began to understand only when she was directly involved in an interactive question-and-answer session in an interview after the lesson.

The belief that teaching is "telling" is one of the most difficult to dispel, however, and you may not be convinced in spite of what we're saying here and what you saw in the video episode. Please keep this point in mind when you actually begin teaching.

Item 4: I will learn about most of the important aspects of teaching when I get into a classroom. This is another commonly held belief of preservice teachers. Researchers have found that "Beyond a desire for concrete teaching ideas . . . many preservice teachers believe their teacher education classes are little more than hoops they must jump through before getting into their own classrooms, where they will learn the real 'nuts and bolts' about teaching the only way they can learn them, through experience" (Grant, Richard, & Parkay, 1996). This belief in the central importance of experience in learning to teach is also shared by others both inside and outside the profession (Gross, 1999; Neisler, 2000).

Increasing Understanding 13.4

Offer two reasons why students who go through traditional teacher-preparation programs are more successful and more satisfied in their work than those who experience less formal preservice education.

Like most misconceptions, this has more than a grain of truth to it. Experience *is* crucial to learning, as constructivist psychologists continually remind us. While experience in classrooms is essential in learning to teach, it isn't sufficient by itself. In many cases, experience results in repeating the same procedures and techniques year after year, even when they're ineffective (Putnam, Heaton, Prawat, & Remillard, 1992). Needed are research findings describing ways that teachers can help students learn, as well as supportive learning environments where teachers can try these ideas. Research also consistently indicates that students who go through traditional teacher-preparation programs (such as the one you're in) that combine these kinds of experiences are more successful and more satisfied in their work than those who experience less formal preservice education (Darling-Hammond, 2000a). This is one of the reasons you're studying this book.

Item 5: If I thoroughly understand the content I'm teaching, I'll be able to figure out a way of getting it across to students. One of the most pervasive myths in teaching is that knowledge of subject matter is all that is necessary to teach it effectively. Knowledge of content is essential, of course, but learning to teach effectively requires a great deal of additional knowledge—knowledge you will acquire in your teacher-preparation program. Let's look at the different kinds of knowledge you'll learn as you become a professional.

KNOWLEDGE AND LEARNING TO TEACH

■ ■ ■

My kids were off the wall. They wouldn't pay attention, some were disruptive, and those that weren't had their heads down on the desk. I tried enforcing the rules and communicating that I meant business, but it wasn't working.

Linda [a veteran and colleague] saved me. I'm not sure I would have made it through this year if it hadn't been for her. She changed my thinking completely. I was so scared to get the kids involved in lessons, because I was afraid I wouldn't be able to control them, but she said it's just the opposite—kids want to be involved and they want to answer questions, and, if the lesson is any good, they're actually less likely to misbehave. When they act like they don't want to answer questions, it's because they're afraid they won't be able to. "Everyone wants to feel smart," she would say with a laugh. "Plus," she continued, "the more active they are in trying to learn the topic, the more likely they are to truly understand it."

Now, I mostly think about what examples I can use to best illustrate the topics I'm teaching and what I can do to get the kids involved. Wow, what a difference. (Paula, a first-year eighth-grade science teacher.)

■ ■ ■

Let's look again at Paula's comments. She said, "She [Linda] changed my *thinking* completely," and "Now, what I mostly *think* about. . . ." Paula's growth as a teacher is reflected in the differences in the way she *thinks*.

During approximately the last quarter of the 20th century, researchers began to examine differences in the *thinking* of **experts,** *people who are highly knowledgeable and skilled in a field,* compared to **novices,** *people who are inexperienced,* in the same fields. Although the fields varied widely, including areas as diverse as chess, physics, anesthesiology, and teaching, a clear pattern was found. In all cases, the thinking of experts was guided by a great deal of well-organized knowledge, whereas the knowledge of novices either didn't exist or wasn't well-organized (Borko & Putnam, 1996; Bruning, Shraw, & Ronning, 1999). "The accumulation of richly structured and accessible bodies of knowledge allows individuals to engage in expert thinking and action. In studies of teaching, this understanding of expertise has led researchers to devote increased attention to teachers' knowledge and how it is organized" (Borko & Putnam, 1996, p. 674). In essence what teachers know and how their knowledge is organized powerfully affects how teachers view and understand their classrooms and what they do to promote learning.

Research indicates that expert teachers possess at least four different kinds of knowledge (Peterson, 1988; Shulman, 1987):

- Knowledge of content.
- Pedagogical content knowledge.
- General pedagogical knowledge.
- Knowledge of learners and learning.

Let's look at these different kinds of knowledge and see how they can affect your growth as a teacher.

Knowledge of Content

We can't teach what we don't understand. This simple statement is self-evident, and it is well-documented by research examining the relationships between what teachers know and how they teach (Shulman, 1986; Wilson, Shulman, & Richert, 1987). To effectively teach about the American Revolutionary War, for example, a social studies teacher must know not only basic facts about the war but also how it relates to other aspects of history, such as the French and Indian War, our relationship with England prior to the Revolution, and the characteristics of the colonies. The same is true for any topic in any content area.

Pedagogical Content Knowledge

Pedagogical content knowledge is *an understanding of "ways of representing . . . the subject that make it comprehensible to others," and "an understanding of what makes the learning of specific topics easy or difficult . . ."* (Shulman, 1986, p. 9). Pedagogical content knowledge depends on an understanding of a particular topic, such as understanding the factors leading to the American Revolution, but it goes beyond this understanding in that it also includes knowing how to illustrate and explain these factors so they make sense to students.

Teachers who possess pedagogical content knowledge also recognize when topics are hard to understand and illustrate these difficult-to-teach ideas with concrete experiences that make them meaningful. The following are some examples:

- In Chapter 1, David Jackson taught the principle of *inertia* for his eighth-grade science students by using seatbelts in cars, the spin cycle of a clothes washer, and a dog shaking itself off when it came out of a pond.
- In Chapter 10, Suzanne Brush helped her second graders understand graphing by using bar graphs to represent their favorite flavor of jelly bean.
- In Chapter 11, Leslie Nelson used written paragraphs displayed on an overhead to illustrate pronoun cases for her students.

We see the influence of pedagogical content knowledge on Paula's thinking when she commented, "Now, I mostly think about what examples I can use to best illustrate the topics I'm teaching . . . ," and we also see why a thorough understanding of content is important, but not sufficient in itself, in helping learners understand the topics they're studying. Majoring in math doesn't ensure that a teacher will be able to create examples that

Pedagogical content knowledge allows teachers to illustrate difficult-to-learn concepts with concrete examples.

Increasing Understanding 13.5

Describe the pedagogical content knowledge that Suzanne demonstrated in her lesson on longitude and latitude. Be specific in your response.

will help students understand why multiplying two numbers results in a smaller number ($\frac{1}{4} \times \frac{1}{3} = \frac{1}{12}$, for instance), nor does majoring in history ensure that a teacher will think of using a student "crusade" to have extracurricular activities governed by a student council as a metaphor for the real crusades. The ability to do so requires both a clear understanding of content together with pedagogical content knowledge. If either is lacking, teachers often will paraphrase information in learners' textbooks or students will memorize steps that don't make sense to them (such as procedures for graphing equations).

Developing pedagogical content knowledge is one of the most challenging aspects of learning to teach. But throughout your teacher-preparation program, if you are constantly looking for ways of illustrating topics you might teach, then gradually your thinking will develop, and you'll acquire the pedagogical content knowledge that can help you become an expert teacher.

General Pedagogical Knowledge

Knowledge of content and pedagogical content knowledge are "domain specific"; that is, they focus on knowledge of a particular topic or content area, such as multiplying fractions, density, the Crusades, or our judicial system. In comparison, **general pedagogical knowledge** *involves a general understanding of instruction and management that transcends individual topics or subject matter areas* (Borko & Putnam, 1996). Let's look at these two components.

Instructional Strategies Instruction is at the heart of teaching. Expert teachers understand different ways of involving students in learning activities, techniques for checking their understanding, and strategies for keeping lessons running smoothly (Leinhardt & Greeno, 1986). Questioning is perhaps the most important example that exists. Regardless of the content or topic, expert teachers ask questions that get students to think, engage all students as equally as possible (McDougall & Granby, 1996), give them time to think about their responses (Rowe, 1986), and provide prompts and cues when they're unable to answer

stuff. Now, what's this? They expect me to be able to do all this when I first go into a classroom. I have to know what I'm teaching and then all this about learner development, "variety of instructional strategies," motivation, assessment, and I might get tested on all this stuff. Where'd they get this idea that learning to teach was so easy? (Diedra, a preservice education major told she will be accountable for meeting INTASC standards.)

■ ■ ■

Diedra's reaction is understandable. In the past, learning to teach was easier and the demands on beginning teachers were not as great. This has changed (Berliner, 2000). A rapidly expanding body of literature consistently demonstrates that teaching now requires professionals who are highly knowledgeable and skilled.

The profession is responding. Created in 1987, the Interstate New Teacher Assessment and Support Consortium (INTASC) was designed to help states develop better teachers through coordinated efforts of support and assessment. INTASC has raised the bar by setting rigorous standards for new teachers in important areas such as planning, instruction, and motivation. These standards describe what you should know and be able to do when you first walk into a classroom.

At this point, general standards organized around 10 principles have been prepared, and subject area standards and a Test for Teaching Knowledge (TTK) are being developed. These principles are outlined in Table 13.1. To learn more about INTASC, go to the *Web Links* Module of the Companion Website at **http://www.prenhall.com/kauchak.**

The principles are expanded by describing the knowledge, dispositions, and performances teachers are expected to demonstrate. For instance, with respect to the first principle, teachers should understand how students' misconceptions in an area—such as believing that the earth is closer to the sun in the summer (in the northern hemisphere)—can influence their learning (knowledge); teachers should be committed to continuous learning (disposition); and they should use a variety of ways of illustrating ideas to make them understandable to students (performance), such as using demonstrations, pictures, technology, and classroom discussion to illustrate the seasons. Similar knowledge, dispositions, and performances are described for each principle.

The INTASC standards are demanding, but this is as it should be. As we've said throughout this book, if you expect to be treated as a professional, you should have the knowledge and skills that allow you to make the decisions expected of a professional. Being able to meet the INTASC standards is a good beginning.

Advanced Professionalism: National Board Certification

Earlier we saw that licensure is the process that states use to ensure that teachers meet professional standards. In comparison, **certification** is *special recognition by a professional organization indicating that an individual has met certain requirements specified by the organization.*

One important form of certification has been created by the National Board for Professional Teaching Standards (NBPTS). Created in 1987 as an outgrowth of the *Carnegie Forum Report, A Nation Prepared: Teachers for the 21st Century,* the board is composed mostly of K–12 teachers, but it also includes union and business leaders and university faculty. NBPTS seeks to strengthen teaching as a profession and raise the quality of education by recognizing the contibutions of exemplary teachers, compensate them financially, give them increased responsibility, and increase their role in decision making. To learn more about NBPTS, go to the *Web Links* Module of the Companion Website at **http://www.prenhall.com/kauchak.**

Table 13.1 **The INTASC Principles**

Principle	Description
1. Knowledge of subject	The teacher understands the central concepts, tools of inquiry, and structures of the discipline(s) he or she teaches and can create learning experiences that make these aspects of subject matter meaningful for students.
2. Learning and human development	The teacher understands how children learn and develop and can provide learning opportunities that support their intellectual, social and personal development.
3. Adapting instruction	The teacher understands how students differ in their approaches to learning and creates instructional opportunities that are adapted to diverse learners
4. Strategies	The teacher understands and uses a variety of instructional strategies to encourage students' development of critical thinking, problem solving, and performance skills.
5. Motivation and management	The teacher uses an understanding of individual and group motivation and behavior to create a learning environment that encourages positive social interaction, active engagement in learning, and self-motivation.
6. Communication skills	The teacher uses knowledge of effective verbal, nonverbal, and media communication techniques to foster active inquiry, collaboration, and supportive interaction in the classroom.
7. Planning	The teacher plans instruction based upon knowledge of subject matter, students, the community, and curriculum goals.
8. Assessment	The teacher understands and uses formal and informal assessment strategies to evaluate and ensure the continuous intellectual, social, and physical development of the learner.
9. Commitment	The teacher is a reflective practitioner who continually evaluates the effects of his/her choices and actions on others (students, parents, and other professionals in the learning community) and who actively seeks out opportunities to grow professionally.
10. Partnership	The teacher fosters relationships with school colleagues, parents, and agencies in the larger community to support students' learning and well-being.

Source: From Interstate New Teacher Assessment and Support Consortium. (1993). *Model standards for beginning teacher licensing and development: A resource for state dialogues.* Washington, D.C.: Council of Chief State School Officers. Reprinted by permission.

The standards, which grew out of the report *What Teachers Should Know and Be Able to Do*, are directed by five core propositions. The propositions and descriptions are outlined in Table 13.2.

National Board certification has five important characteristics:

- It is designed for experienced teachers. Applicants must have graduated from an accredited college or university and must have taught for at least 3 years.
- Applying for National Board certification is strictly voluntary and independent of any state's licensure. It is intended to indicate a high level of achievement and professionalism.
- Acquiring National Board certification requires that teachers pass a set of exams in their area of specialty, such as math, science, early childhood, or physical education and health.
- Additional evidence, such as videotapes of teaching and a personal portfolio, are used in the assessment process.

Table 13.2 Propositions of the National Board for Professional Teaching Standards

Proposition	Description
1. Teachers are committed to students and their learning.	■ Accomplished teachers believe that all students can learn, and they treat students equitably. ■ Accomplished teachers understand how students develop, and they use accepted learning theory as the basis for their teaching. ■ Accomplished teachers are aware of the influence of context and culture on behavior, and they foster students' self-esteem, motivation, and character.
2. Teachers know the subjects they teach and how to teach those subjects to students.	■ Accomplished teachers have a rich understanding of the subject(s) they teach, and they appreciate how knowledge in their subject is linked to other disciplines and applied to real-world settings. ■ Accomplished teachers know how to make subject matter understandable to students, and they are able to modify their instruction when difficulties arise. ■ Accomplished teachers demonstrate critical and analytic capacities in their teaching, and they develop those capacities in their students.
3. Teachers are responsible for managing and monitoring student learning.	■ Accomplished teachers capture and sustain the interest of their students and use their time effectively. ■ Accomplished teachers are able to use a variety of effective instructional techniques, and they use the techniques appropriately. ■ Accomplished teachers can use multiple methods to assess the progress of students, and they effectively communicate this progress to parents.
4. Teachers think systematically about their practice and learn from experience.	■ Accomplished teachers are models for intellectual curiosity, and they display virtues—honesty, fairness, and respect for diversity—that they seek to inspire in their students. ■ Accomplished teachers use their understanding of students, learning, and instruction to make principled judgments about sound practice, and they are lifelong learners. ■ Accomplished teachers critically examine their practice, and they seek continual professional growth.
5. Teachers are members of learning communities.	■ Accomplished teachers contribute to the effectiveness of the school, and they work collaboratively with their colleagues. ■ Accomplished teachers evaluate school progress, and they utilize community resources. ■ Accomplished teachers work collaboratively with parents, and they involve parents in school activities.

Source: Reprinted with permission from the National Board for Professional Teaching Standards. *What Teachers Should Know and Be Able to Do*, 1994.

- The primary control of the NBPTS is in the hands of practicing teachers, which increases the professionalism of teaching.

Considering that the NBPTS is for veterans, why are we providing this information in this book—one studied by preservice teachers early in their programs? There are four reasons. First, one of the themes of this book has been professionalism, and the NBPTS is a national effort to professionalize teaching. Second, National Board certification can provide a long-term career goal combined with financial incentives for you as a new teacher. Nearly 200 school districts in 39 states have spent millions of dollars to reward teachers who successfully complete the process, and by late 2000, nearly 5,000 teachers had done so, with nearly 10,000 others awaiting word on whether or not they had passed (Blair, 2000b).

National Board certification requires teachers to demonstrate their expertise through exams and classroom performance.

Increasing Understanding 13.9

Identify an example of pedagogical content knowledge, general pedagogical knowledge, and knowledge of learners and learning in the descriptions of the propositions. Be sure to take information directly from the descriptions in your response.

Third, the descriptions in Table 13.2 emphasize the pedagogical content knowledge, general pedagogical knowledge, and knowledge of learners and learning that we discussed earlier in the chapter. The NBPTS recognizes that increasing professionalism requires teachers to be both highly knowledgeable and skilled in their areas of specialization.

Finally, evidence indicates that National Board certification makes a difference. A study comparing teachers who had successfully completed the process to those who had attempted but failed to achieve National Board certification found that the nationally certified teachers scored higher on nearly all measures of teaching expertise. The study involved at least 75 hours of observation of each teacher, together with interviews and samples of student work (Blair, 2000b). National Board certification is a long-term goal that is well worth pursuing and one we're encouraging you to keep in mind as you begin your career.

Increasing Understanding 13.10

Identify at least three similarities between the INTASC principles and the NBPTS propositions. Take information directly from each in identifying these similarities.

Getting Started in the Profession

You now understand the characteristics of people like you—other preservice and beginning teachers, the different kinds of knowledge you need to think and act like a professional, and what it takes to be licensed in any state in the nation. You've also seen what professional organizations expect of you as a beginning teacher and as an expert.

So, when and how do you get started? The answer to when is *now,* and we'll try to answer the question of how in this section as we consider:

- Developing a professional portfolio.
- Becoming marketable.
- Searching for and securing a job.

Portfolios provide a concrete way for beginning teachers to display their developing knowledge and skills.

Beginning Your Professional Portfolio

■ ■ ■

The interview was going okay, but I was uneasy. The principal I was interviewing with was cordial, but she certainly wasn't enthusiastic. "I've had it," I thought to myself. She even quit asking me questions after about 20 minutes. I really wanted the job too.

As I was about to leave, I happened to mention, "Would you like to see my portfolio?" She looked at it for a couple minutes, and then she started asking some probing questions. When she stuck my CD-ROM in her computer and saw me teaching, she really lit up. I got the job! (Greg, a recent graduate and new teacher.)

■ ■ ■

As you begin this section, you might wonder, Why are they talking about a portfolio now when I'm taking my first (or one of my first) courses in education? The answer is simple. The sooner you start on your professional portfolio, the better. A **professional portfolio** is *a collection of work produced by a prospective teacher*. Just as artists use portfolios of produced work to illustrate their talents and accomplishments, teachers use portfolios to document their knowledge and skills. The reason you should start now in thinking about your portfolio is that you may want to include products that you complete early in your program. For instance, suppose you write a particularly good paper for a beginning composition class. You may want to include the paper and the instructor's comments in your portfolio as evidence of your developing ability to communicate in writing. Although this experience will have occurred long before you actively seek a job, it can be a valuable entry nevertheless. The sooner you start thinking about what to include in your portfolio, the less likely you are to omit valuable or important entries.

Portfolios also provide tangible benchmarks that you can use for reflection, and reflection, or thinking about your actions and beliefs, can accelerate your growth as a professional. For instance, suppose you have yourself videotaped teaching a lesson for one of your teaching methods courses. The videotape is a concrete indicator of your skills at that point and provides a tangible basis for your reflection. Later, you may complete another videotaped lesson during an internship experience or student teaching. A comparison of your performance in the two lessons provides a measure of your progress.

Preparing a portfolio typically involves five steps (Martin, 1999):

1. Specify a goal. For example, you're probably taking this course because you've either decided that you want to teach, or you're at least considering teaching. Finding a satisfying job would be a likely goal.
2. Determine how both past and future experiences relate to the goal. For example, you might choose to tutor a student with a reading problem to get professional experience that will make you more marketable.
3. Strategically collect items that provide evidence of your developing knowledge and skill. A video clip of you working with the student would be an excellent entry, for instance.
4. Decide which items in your collection best illustrate your knowledge and skills. For example, since a prospective employer is unlikely to view a bulky collection or series of videotapes, a videotaped lesson is likely to be a better entry than is a clip from a tutoring session.
5. Determine how to best present the items to the person or people connected to your goal, such as the personnel director of a school district in which you want to teach.

As we said earlier, the sooner you start making these decisions, the more complete and effective your portfolio will be.

As you begin, we offer three suggestions:

- Initially, err on the side of including too much in the portfolio. If you think you might use it, include it now. You can always remove an item, but including an item you've discarded is difficult if not impossible.
- Always date the entry. If you want to organize your portfolio chronologically, the dated items will make organizing the information simpler.
- Make all entries and supporting information with clear communication in mind. You're trying to convince a potential employer that you're knowledgeable and skilled, and you want to make his or her decision as easy as possible. A well-organized portfolio creates a positive impression; the opposite occurs with a disorganized one.

Electronic portfolios. As we move farther into the information age, the development of electronic portfolios is becoming more commonplace. They include everything a paper-based product includes, but they do it more efficiently. For example, one CD-ROM disk can hold the equivalent of 300,000 text pages (Lankes, 1995). Typed documents can be scanned into word processing files and stored on floppy disks or CD-ROMs, and video can be digitized and also stored on CD-ROMs. This saves both time and energy. People who want to view a video episode in a paper-based portfolio must find a VCR, review the tape, and put it back into the correct portfolio container. In contrast, video footage in an electronic portfolio can be augmented with text and graphics and accessed with the click of a mouse. This is what got Greg his job. The principal was impressed with both his teaching and the fact that the information in his portfolio was so easy to access.

Electronic portfolios require sophisticated computer equipment, software, and skilled users. In spite of these obstacles, however, it is likely that the expansion of technology will eventually make paper-based portfolios obsolete, so the sooner you develop your technology skills in these areas, the more effective your portfolio will be.

Figure 13.1 **A Sample Résumé**

Your name
Your address
Your phone number
Your e-mail address

Education (Most recent first)

Year:	Degree (For example, B.S. in Education)
	College or University
	Major
	Minor(s)
Year:	Previous college or university coursework
Year:	High School

Teaching Experience (Most recent first)

Dates:	Substitute teaching
	Name of school
Dates:	Internship
	Name of school
Dates:	Field experience
	Name of school

Work Experience: (Most recent first)

Dates:	Employer, job title
	Responsibilities

Extracurricular Activities and Interests

Organizations to which you belong (Highlight leadership positions)
Volunteer work (dates)
Hobbies

Honors and Awards

Scholarships, grants, honor societies

References

You might write "available on request" or you may include names and addresses. (If names and addresses are included, be sure that you have first obtained permission to use the person as a reference.)

Organizing your portfolio. You will want to organize your portfolio to make it accessible to an evaluator. As an organizational guide, put yourself in evaluators' shoes. Remember, they don't know much about you, and you want to make it as easy for them to learn about you as possible. Let communication and ease of access be your guide for organizing the information in your portfolio.

Regardless of whether your portfolio is paper-based or electronic, you will want to start with a title page followed by a table of contents. Then you'll want to include the most impressive entries followed by those that are less significant. Work samples and evidence of performance, such as video clips, are always treated more significantly than testimonial letters, which are often essentially disregarded.

Preparing a résumé. The first item you will want to include in your portfolio is a **résumé,** which is *a document that provides an overview of your background and experience.*

Table 13.3 **Making Yourself Marketable**

Suggestion	Example
Develop a minor area of study	If you're a Spanish major, consider a minor in French. If you're a chemistry major, consider a minor in biology.
Join professional organizations	Most universities have student chapters of the National Education Association as well as student chapters of several other professional organizations. (A directory of professional organizations is on the Website for this book.)
Tutor a child	Parents often seek tutoring help for their children, and it's a way of earning some extra money.
Seek leadership positions	People assessing résumés look for leadership roles, because they suggest effective human-relations skills and the desire to be a lifelong learner.
Do volunteer work	Volunteer work can be enriching, and it indicates a desire to contribute to society.
Become an aide	Schools often hire part-time aides, which can provide valuable experience and a way to earn money.

Increasing Understanding 13.11

Explain how a portfolio and a résumé are different. Be specific in your explanation. What is the purpose of each?

The organization and contents of a résumé can vary, but clarity and simplicity should again be guiding principles. People reading your résumé want to be able to easily access personal information, such as your address and phone number, and they also want to be able to simply summarize your education, work experience, interests, and references. Some people suggest including a description of the type of position you seek and your educational philosophy, whereas others feel that this information detracts from the simplicity and clarity of the résumé. The office of career planning and placement at your college or university will be able to help you in preparing a résumé; a sample résumé is shown in Figure 13.1

Making Yourself Marketable Along with beginning your portfolio, now is also the time to start making yourself marketable. Your portfolio and résumé can be a guide. It makes sense that the more teaching-related experience you can acquire, the more impressive both your portfolio and résumé will be. You can make yourself marketable in several ways. Some examples are included in Table 13.3.

The suggestions in Table 13.3 can become potential portfolio entries, and descriptions of each can be included in your résumé. If you begin now, by the time you complete your teacher-preparation program, you can build both an impressive portfolio and résumé.

Finding a Job

■ ■ ■

I really wish someone had reminded me of these things sooner. When I started, like a lot of others, I didn't take it all too seriously. I'd blow class off now and then, and I didn't always get there on time. I actually did study, but I guess not as hard as I should have.

When I asked Dr. Laslow for a letter of recommendation, he refused. Actually, he said he didn't know me well enough to write a good one. I couldn't believe it. He was nice about it, but he wouldn't write one, advising me to find someone who knew me better and was more familiar with my work. And, a couple others were sort of lukewarm. Now, it's too late. My record is a little spotty and I feel bad about it now, but I can't go back. I used to wonder why Brad and Kelly always seemed to get all the breaks. Now I get it. They just worked at it harder and were more organized. I don't know what I was thinking back then. (Jeremy, a recent graduate without a job.)

■ ■ ■

As with preparing your portfolio and résumé, the time to think about getting a job and developing your professional reputation is *now*. Even though you may be 2 or more years away from graduation, you should keep this long-range goal in mind.

If you are conscientious and professional in your approach to your classwork, and if you systematically develop your portfolio and résumé, finding a job will take care of itself. You will be prepared, and you will have established a professional reputation as a student. Let's look at this issue a bit further.

Developing a Professional Reputation Do you know people who seem to get a lot of breaks? Do you get your share? Do your instructors know you and value the work you do for them? There is usually a reason that certain students are known and valued by their instructors and seem to "get all the breaks." The reason is that they take their schoolwork seriously, they're conscientious, and they're reliable. In other words, as students, they behave professionally. Just as teachers out in the field demonstrate professional behaviors, students do as well. Professors like and value conscientious students, and students like Jeremy bother them—because they just don't seem serious about becoming a first-class teacher. The effort and enthusiasm just aren't there. It's easy to understand why Brad and Kelly got breaks while Jeremy didn't. They probably deserved them.

Your professional relationships with your professors are important. Instructors quickly see through artificial attempts to demonstrate conscientious behavior, to "suck up" or to "beat the system." Students can beat the system if they want to, but professors know it, and ultimately the student is the one who loses. Instructors also understand the difference between students who sincerely ask for explanations of scoring criteria and those who wheedle for points. You obviously have the right to speak your mind, and professors want you to do so—as long as it's done in a spirit of learning.

So what can you do to develop your professional behavior? The following are some suggestions:

- Attend all classes, and be on time. If you must miss, see your professor in advance or explain afterwards.
- Work hard, study diligently, and try to learn as much as possible in your classes.
- Extend your classroom behavior to your life. If the opportunity to learn something exists, take it. For example, travel, especially to other countries, provides opportunities to learn about other cultures and the ways they approach education. Trips like this also make valuable entries on your résumé.
- Turn in required assignments on time and follow the established guidelines or criteria. Even if you disagree with the worth of the assignment, complete it and try to learn from it.
- Take tests when they're scheduled. They can then be scored and returned in a timely way, and you'll receive valuable feedback. Students who continually ask to take tests at special times are perceived as not being committed to their schoolwork.
- Participate in class. Offer comments and ask questions. This is a win–win situation. Your reputation as a student will be enhanced, and you will both enjoy your classes more and learn more from them.

If you sincerely and conscientiously attempt to learn and grow—as with finding a job in general—your professional reputation will take care of itself. Set as your goal being the best student you can be, and your professional development will be improved as well.

Table 13.4 **Projected Changes in Public School Student Enrollment by Grade Level and Geographic Area (1998–2008)**

	Grades K–8	Grades 9–12
Northeast	−3.8%	+11.9%
Midwest	−4.1%	+1.5%
South	+3.2%	+16.3%
West	+10.8%	+28.6%

Source: From *Projection of Education Statistics to 2008* (p. 17), National Center for Education Statistics, 1998, Washington, DC: Author.

Where the Jobs Are Since your ultimate goal is to locate a teaching position that will allow you to utilize your skills and develop as a professional, you need to consider factors such as supply and demand. Job opportunities are greater in some areas than others, and you will want to consider these factors as you begin your professional program.

Geography is one example. As you can see from Table 13.4, student growth patterns vary by geographic area and grade level. In general, the greatest student enrollment increases will occur in the western parts of the country and in secondary education, so this is where the greatest demand for teachers will be.

Increasing Understanding 13.12

Explain the job patterns that have just been described. Why, for example, are more jobs available in the inner city than in the suburbs? Why are more jobs available in math than in English?

Within geographic areas, specific locations also influence teacher supply and demand; job opportunities are much greater in rural and inner-city schools than they are in the suburbs, for example. The specific teaching position you seek will also affect your chances for finding a job. Areas such as audiology, speech pathology, bilingual education, English as a second language, foreign languages (especially Spanish), special education, math, physics, and chemistry need teachers more than areas like English or history (Darling-Hammond, Berry, Haselkorn, & Fideler, 1999). In the chapter-opening vignette, Shelley experienced these patterns. She initially looked for jobs at two suburban schools, but there were no openings. However, she had offers in three different inner-city schools.

What implications do these patterns have for you? First, if you haven't already decided on a major, you shouldn't select one based on job availability alone. To be effective, you must want to teach in the area you select. Don't major in chemistry, for example, if you dislike chemistry. However, if you sincerely like chemistry, you now know that there is a high probability of getting a job in this area.

Second, try to become knowledgeable about where teaching jobs exist. The career placement center at your college or university can help you. Then be flexible about where you'll teach. Your first teaching position may not be exactly where you want, but you can use it to gain experience and as a stepping stone to other positions.

Creating a Credentials File Your college or university will have a placement center designed to help graduates find jobs. An essential service of this center, in addition to providing information about job openings, is to serve as a repository for your credentials file. A **credentials file** is *a collection of important documents you'll need to submit when you apply for a teaching position*. It typically includes background information about you, your résumé, the type of position you're seeking, courses taken, performance evaluations by your cooperating teacher and college or university supervisor, and letters of recommendation (usually three or more). When you apply for a job, you notify the placement center, which will then send your credentials file to the prospective employer. If the district feels there is a potential match after reviewing this file, you'll be contacted for an interview.

Interviews provide opportunities for you to explain your qualifications as well as find out about the position you're applying for.

Interviewing Effectively We've emphasized professional behavior throughout this book and particularly in this chapter. One area in which professional behavior is essential is the interview. This is the setting that almost certainly will determine whether or not you get a job. Some guidelines for interviewing effectively are outlined in Table 13.5.

If you're *genuinely* interested in working with young people, and if you've been conscientious in your teacher-preparation program, the interview will largely take care of itself. Nothing communicates more effectively than a sincere desire to do the job for which you're interviewing.

However, additional preparation can increase the positive impression you make. For example, how would you respond to the following questions, all of which are frequently asked in an interview?

- Why do you want to teach?
- Why do you want to work in this school?
- What is your philosophy of education?
- How would you motivate unmotivated learners?
- How would you handle a classroom management issue?
- How would you organize a unit on (a topic in your area)?
- How would you involve parents or caregivers to help your students learn?

The more specific and concrete you can be in responding to each of the questions, the more positive your impression will be. For instance, in response to the question about your teaching philosophy, the following statement is a specific response that communicates that you're clear about what you would try to do: "I believe that all children can learn, regardless of their backgrounds. I would try my best to make that happen by ensuring that all students are involved in the lessons I teach. I would get them involved by designing interactive learning strategies, using groupwork, and by regularly calling on all of them as often as possible." In contrast, a vague response, such as "I am a humanistic and

Table 13.5 **Guidelines for Interviewing Effectively**

Guideline	Rationale
Be on time.	Nothing creates a worse impression than being late for an interview.
Dress appropriately.	Wear an outfit appropriate for an interview, and be well-groomed. Shorts, jeans, and t-shirts are inappropriate, as is an eyebrow ring. You have the right to dress and groom yourself in any way you choose, but if you are serious about getting a job, you won't demonstrate your freedom of expression during a job interview.
Speak clearly, and use standard English and grammar.	Clear language is correlated with effective teaching, and your verbal ability creates an impression of professional ability.
Sit comfortably and calmly.	Fidgeting, or worse—glancing at your watch—suggests that you'd rather be somewhere else.
Communicate empathy for children and a desire to work with them.	Communicating an understanding of learning, learner development, and instruction demonstrates that you have a professional knowledge base.

Increasing Understanding 13.13

What will determine how able you are to provide a clear and concrete response to an interviewer's question? Hint: Think back to the second major topic of the chapter.

learner-centered teacher" is much less impressive. It's general and vague, and leaves the interviewer with the impression that you're saying some words that you learned in a class.

The more you think about questions such as our earlier examples, the better prepared for the interview you'll be, and the more at ease you'll be during the interview.

Assessing the School The interview process is a two-way street. Not only are you being interviewed, but you are also interviewing the school to determine whether it will be a good place to work and grow as a professional. You want a job, but you also want to find out if the school is the kind of place in which you want to work. When you interview, you also have the right to ask questions of the principal or other people interviewing you. This not only helps answer questions you may have about the position but also communicates that you are thoughtful and are considering the position seriously.

Some factors to look for include the following:

- Commitment and leadership of the principal. The school leadership sets the tone for the school. Does the principal demonstrate caring for students and support for teachers? The answers to these questions are highly inferential, but you can look for evidence in the principal's manner and comments.
- School mission. Does the principal communicate a clear mission for the school? If you have a chance to talk to other teachers, ask them if the teachers feel like they're a team, all working for the benefit of students.
- School climate. Does the emotional climate of the school seem positive? How do office personnel treat students? Do members of the support staff, such as custodians and cafeteria workers, feel like they're part of the team? Is there a positive and upbeat orientation in the school?
- The physical plant. Are there student work products like art and woodshop projects in display cases and on the walls? Do signs and notices on hallway walls communicate that this is a healthy place to learn? Are the classrooms, halls, and restrooms generally clean and free of debris and graffiti?
- The behavior of the students. Are the students generally orderly and polite to each other and to the teachers? Do they seem happy to be there?

Minority teachers bring unique perspectives and valuable cultural insights into their classrooms.

- A mentoring program for teachers. Does the school have a beginning support system, such as a mentoring program for first-year teachers? First-year teachers who participate in formal mentoring programs are more likely to succeed and stay in teaching than those who don't (Edwards & Chronister, 2000; Shoho & Martin, 1999).

These questions are difficult to answer in one visit to the school, but they are important. The working conditions in schools vary dramatically, and they can be the difference between a positive and rewarding first year of teaching compared to a year that makes you reconsider your decision to be a teacher. Poor working conditions are one of the most commonly cited reasons that beginning teachers leave the profession (Edwards & Chronister, 2000).

SURVIVING YOUR FIRST YEAR OF TEACHING

Although your first teaching job is probably 2 or more years away, now is the time to start learning to think like a teacher. This doesn't mean that you should stop thinking like a student; rather, it merely suggests that you expand your thinking while you have time for learning and growth.

At least three areas of concern will likely emerge during your first year of teaching, and beginning to think about them now can help you get a running start in your first job. These areas of concern include:

- Time
- Classroom management
- Uncertainty

Let's look at them.

Reflect on This

INTERVIEWING FOR A POSITION

You're interviewing for a position in a large, inner-city middle school. The leadership team of the school is composed of the school principal, a vice principal, and two assistant principals. Both the principal and vice principal are involved in the interview, which is scheduled for 1 hour.

You've been asked a number of probing questions, such as, "What was the biggest problem you faced in your internship?" "How would you motivate a class of unmotivated learners?" and "How would you enforce rules with students who are disruptive in your class?"

As you respond, the vice principal appears to listen attentively, but the principal appears distracted. He nods and responds in general terms to your answers, but doesn't follow up on any of the questions.

After 45 minutes have passed, the interview seems to be winding down, so you attempt to ask some questions about the school. The principal cuts you off, saying she has a meeting she must attend. She cordially thanks you for coming and quickly leaves the office, 10 minutes before the scheduled end of the interview. The vice principal, on the other hand, asks you to come into his office and says he is willing to try and answer any questions you have. You spend another half hour with him, and he takes you on a tour of the school, during which the discussion of the school and students continues. The principal's name doesn't come up in the discussion, but the physical plant is clean and attractive, the students are orderly as they move between classes, and one who accidently bumps you says, "Oh, excuse me."

1. Based on your total experience—the interview with the administrators and the tour—what is your impression of the school?
2. What might explain the principal's behavior? Offer at least two possibilities.
3. Suppose you had another interview for a job in a second inner-city school. In this case, the principal's behavior was warm and inviting in the interview, but the students appeared to be less well-behaved in the hallways. Which job would you take if you were offered both? Provide a basis for your decision. (Assume that other factors, such as pay and the distance from your home, are similar.)
4. What else might you do to help yourself decide which job to take?

To answer these questions online and receive immediate feedback, go to the Reflect on This Module in Chapter 13 of the Companion Website.

Time

One of the first crunches you'll experience as a beginning teacher is lack of time. You'll feel like you don't have a second to yourself. As Antonio said in one of the excerpts earlier in the chapter, "I've never been so tired in my life. You're in front of kids all day, and then you go home and work all night to get ready for the next day." In the chapter-opening case, Shelley said, "I can't believe how much there is to do—IEPs, progress reports, CPR training, responsibility to look for signs of abuse. When do I teach?"

Is there a solution to this dilemma? If so, what is it? While a perfect solution doesn't exist, one key is *organization*. A great deal of research, dating back to the 1970s, indicates that effective teachers are very well-organized (Bennett, 1978; Rutter, Maughan, Mortimore, Ouston, & Smith, 1979). The students in one of our classes described a first-year teacher that they had visited: "His desk is a mess. Books and papers piled everywhere.

Exploring Diversity

Considering Multiple Perspectives

THE COMPETITION FOR MINORITY TEACHERS

In Chapter 2, we saw that nearly one-third of school-age children in the United States are cultural minorities, compared to only 12 percent of the teaching force (Archer, 2000). The proportion of African American teachers has declined, and the proportion of Latino teachers has increased only slightly; at the same time, the percentage of K–12 students who are members of minority groups is in the midst of a steep incline. Projections indicate that somewhere between 2030 and 2040, cultural minorities will make up more than half of the nation's students.

These trends have resulted in significantly greater efforts to recruit minority teachers. These efforts have been made more difficult by the fact that many African Americans are opting for more lucrative careers in other areas because teaching is no longer viewed as one of their only entrées to the middle class. Because recruiting minority teachers is a challenge, scholarships, loan-forgiveness programs, specific recruitment aimed at bright minority high school and college students, and recruitment of career changers have all been tried in various states.

Because programs for career changers are often successful in recruiting minority teachers, alternative licensure has proven to be another promising avenue for bringing minority teachers into the profession.

These trends and efforts raise at least three issues. The first is need. Educators worry about the implications that a rapidly increasing minority-student population—without a similar increase in the minority teaching force—has for schooling, both for minorities and nonminorities. Many educators believe that minority students need role models that come from their same cultural backgrounds, and they further suggest that minority teachers bring unique perspectives to learning experiences (Archer, 2000a). This position is also supported by theories suggesting that models are most effective when observers perceive the models to be similar to themselves (Pintrich & Schunk, 1996).

He can't find anything there." If he can't find anything there, you can bet that he wastes precious time looking for lesson plans and student papers. If you frequently or even occasionally lament that "I must get organized," now is a good time to start changing your habits. Organization is one of the most essential skills that exist in teaching; it can make the difference between a relatively smooth year and one in which you're continually exhausted.

Classroom Management

Classroom management is consistently identified as one of the most important problems teachers face (Rose & Gallup, 1999); it is one of the primary concerns of beginning teachers (Kellough, 1999); and new teachers often feel ill-equipped to deal with management (Kher-Durlabhji, Lacina-Gifford, Jackson, Guillory, & Yandell, 1997).

Classroom management is never easy, but some guidelines can help. As you move through your program, we're encouraging you to keep the following three ideas in mind:

- Plan for effective management.
- Know your students.
- Use effective instructional strategies.

Let's consider these ideas.

Planning for Effective Management We have emphasized teacher thinking in this book, and nowhere is it more important than in the area of classroom management. Think about and plan for simple procedures, including the following: how students will

However, neither research nor theory suggests that nonminority teachers cannot be effective teachers for minority students; knowledgeable, dedicated, and caring teachers can make a difference for all types of students. Further, research provides few answers to the question of what ratio of nonminority to minority teachers is necessary or sufficient, and no evidence suggests that the percentage of minority teachers must be the same as the percentage of minority students in schools.

The tension between recruitment and standards is a second issue. In the face of increased efforts to recruit minority teachers is a simultaneous effort to raise teaching standards. Associated with raised standards is greater use of standardized tests to screen potential educators, a practice that has a history of negatively and disproportionately affecting minorities.

A third issue involves alternative certification. For example, nearly half of the candidates who have gone through California's alternative program are members of minority groups, as are 41 percent of those who went through the Texas program (National Center for Education Information, 2000). While these statistics are good news with respect to recruiting, alternative certification programs, as we saw in our "Teaching in an Era of Reform" section earlier in the chapter, can be problematic. For instance, first-year *Teach for America* graduates drop out of teaching at a rate three times greater than that for beginning-teacher graduates of traditional programs. If these statistics are representative of alternative licensure programs in general, they're unlikely to solve the lack-of-minority-teachers problem. Further, as we saw earlier, the quality of some alternative licensure programs is low.

However, there is some room for optimism in this area. Trends indicate that the enrollment of African American students in colleges of education increased from 6 percent to 9 percent in the 1990s, suggesting that the downward trend in the African American teaching force might be reversing (Archer, 2000a). However, this increase only slows the diversity gap, and it doesn't address a larger issue that exists in K–12 education: the ability of K–12 schools to produce enough minority graduates who can then go on to become teachers. Surveys indicate that African American, Native American, and Hispanic college graduates are more likely to become teachers than are White graduates. Unfortunately, students in these minority groups are less likely to succeed in and ultimately graduate from high school (Archer, 2000a). Leaders suggest that a nation wanting the teaching force to more nearly reflect the composition of society must first focus its educational efforts on today's elementary and secondary students.

The topic is likely to remain an issue for the foreseeable future.

hand in papers and how you will return them; if and when students will be allowed to get out of their seats to sharpen pencils; how students will get into and out of groups if they do groupwork in your class; and how materials will be distributed and re-stored. In essence, anticipate potential problems and plan accordingly. Making decisions about these issues in advance will simplify the decisions you must make later in cases that can't be anticipated. A number of valuable books are available to help both elementary teachers (for example, Evertson, Emmer, Clements, & Worsham, 2000) as well as secondary teachers (for example, Emmer, Evertson, Clements, & Worsham, 2000) plan for classroom management.

Increasing Understanding 13.14

Planning for effective management closely relates to what other important idea discussed in the previous section? Explain how the two are related.

As you move through your program, keep the issue of management in mind; ask your professors questions, and talk to teachers when you're out in the field. Be a sponge, and take notes on what you see and what the professors and teachers say. As we discussed in the last section, note taking is part of being organized. Because you won't remember everything you hear, taking notes and storing them in a file will give you a leg up on your planning when you begin your first year.

Get to Know Your Students Getting to know your students is important on several levels. It communicates true caring and establishes a human link between you and your students. Knowing your students' names is essential. It communicates that you care about them as people, and you can't teach effectively without knowing them. Commit yourself to knowing all your students by their first name by the end of the first week of school.

Again, watch your professors and teachers out in the field. See how they use students' names in their instruction. You will notice a striking difference in both the instruction

Many of the problems encountered by beginning teachers can be avoided through thorough professional preparation and careful planning.

and the classroom climate when teachers know students' names and address them by name compared to teachers who don't.

Use Effective Instructional Strategies You might wonder why we're discussing "effective instructional strategies" when the issue is classroom management. The answer is simple. Research consistently demonstrates that it is virtually impossible to maintain classroom order in the absence of effective instruction. In other words, if you're not teaching effectively, the likelihood of having classroom management problems increases dramatically.

The active involvement of students in learning activities is one of the most important aspects of effective instruction. Students who are actively involved in learning are much less likely to misbehave than those who are sitting passively or who don't understand the topic. A guiding principle for your instruction should be, *All students want to learn, and they want to participate*. It may not seem like it at times, but students who act like they don't care or don't want to learn are more nearly demonstrating fear that they *can't* learn.

We saw evidence of this in both Paula and Suzanne's comments in vignettes earlier in the chapter. Paula said, "Now, I mostly think about what examples I can best use to illustrate the topics I'm teaching and what I can do to get the kids involved. Wow, what a difference," and Suzanne commented, "Now I understand the stuff Dr. Martinez stressed so much when he was always after us to use concrete examples and to question, question, question. . . . I thought I could just explain everything to them, but they got confused and drifted off so fast I couldn't believe it. As soon as I started asking questions about the lines on the Styrofoam ball, though, they perked right up."

Look for models of effective instruction in the schools you visit, and seize the opportunity to practice getting students involved in learning activities; particularly practice your questioning. Again, these experiences will give you a leg up when you begin your first job.

Planning for management, knowing your students, and teaching effectively won't solve all of your management problems, but they will make a big difference, so big a difference, in fact, that they can largely determine how successful both your internship and your first year of teaching will be.

MENTORING NEW TEACHERS

This ABC News video segment describes a mentoring program for new teachers at Malden Catholic High School in Massachusets. First-year teacher Joe Laferlito explains how mentoring helped him deal with instructional and management issues. Veteran teacher Rich Mazzei describes his role in the process and the benefits of mentoring to him.

Think About This

1. How is mentoring more like teaching? How is it different from traditional classroom teaching?
2. What qualities would you look for in a mentor?
3. In what areas of teaching would a mentor be most helpful? Least helpful?

To answer these questions online and receive immediate feedback, go to the Video Perspectives Module in Chapter 13 of the Companion Website.

Uncertainty

Uncertainty is, without question, one of the most disconcerting experiences in life. Being in a situation and not being quite sure of what you're doing or how you're supposed to act is very unsettling. You will experience many uncertainties during your first year.

Can you anticipate and prepare for them? To a certain extent, yes. One way is to be as well-informed as possible. Learn as much as you can about as many aspects of teaching as possible. A second way to prepare is to ask questions. In general, teachers are very cooperative, and veteran teachers in your school will be willing to answer your questions and give advice.

At this point you're preparing for one of the most challenging and rewarding professions in the world—teaching—and when you complete your program, you'll begin some of the most important work that exists. We hope that your study of this book has helped launch you on your way.

SUMMARY

Characteristics of Beginning Teachers

The teaching population is aging, and the number of beginning teachers is likely to increase significantly in the next 10 years. The population will become increasingly White, female, and younger than the existing population. A greater number of people are entering teaching after they've earned bachelor's degrees than has occurred in the past.

Beginning teachers drop out during their first year at over twice the attrition rate for teachers in general, and significant numbers also leave after their second and third years.

Preservice and beginning teachers tend to be optimistic about their abilities, but their optimism wanes as they get more experience. They tend to believe that the essence of teaching is "explaining" and that most of what they learn about teaching will occur once they get into classrooms.

Knowledge and Learning to Teach

As the professionalism of teaching increases, more emphasis is placed on what teachers know and how they think. Expert teachers know the content of the subjects they teach; they are able to represent the content in ways that are understandable to learners, which is called pedagogical content knowledge; they have general pedagogical knowledge, such as knowing how to manage classrooms and ask questions effectively; and they know how students learn and develop as well as what motivates learners.

Joining the Profession

The majority of teachers are licensed in traditional programs, which are designed and implemented by each state. Alternative licensure is the process of licensing people to teach who have bachelor's degrees in some academic area by having them complete short, intensive training programs combined with a licensing exam.

In an attempt to professionalize teaching, the National Board for Professional Teaching Standards (NBPTS) has established rigorous standards and assessments for teachers who have completed at least 3 years of successful service. Substantive financial rewards exist in most states for teachers who have successfully completed national certification. The Interstate New Teacher Assessment and Support Consortium (INTASC) is conducting a similar effort for beginning teachers.

The more quickly students in preservice programs begin developing a professional portfolio, gathering experiences that make them marketable, and developing their professional reputation, the better equipped they will be to find a job when they graduate.

Surviving Your First Year of Teaching

Lack of time, classroom management, and the uncertainties of a new job are the three most common problems beginning teachers face. Getting organized, becoming well-informed, and developing their teaching skills are the most effective ways teachers have of preparing for both their internship and their first year of teaching. The time to begin this preparation is now.

IMPORTANT CONCEPTS

certification
credentials file
expert
general pedagogical knowledge
licensure
novice
pedagogical content knowledge
professional portfolio
résumé

DISCUSSION QUESTIONS

1. What can preservice teachers do to decrease the likelihood that they will leave the profession? What can school leaders do?
2. The National Board for Professional Teaching Standards and The Interstate New Teacher Assessment and Support Consortium are attempting to increase the professionalism of teaching. How successful are they likely to be? Explain why you believe as you do.
3. Some critics suggest that teaching isn't a profession because it doesn't have a body of knowledge on which to base its decisions. How do you respond to these critics?
4. It was suggested in the chapter that you attempt to establish a professional reputation by being conscientious in your classes and attempting to get along with your professors. Is this reasonable? Is it important? Explain.
5. Several suggestions for making yourself marketable were offered in the chapter. Is it reasonable to expect that preservice teachers involve themselves in these activities? Explain.
6. What are the advantages and disadvantages of developing a professional portfolio? To constructing one using technology?

GOING INTO SCHOOLS

1. Interview a teacher about developing as a professional. Ask him or her the following questions:
   a. Which do you believe is more important in teaching: understanding content, or understanding how to communicate content to students?
   b. Do you believe that if you understand the content you're teaching well enough that you'll be able to get it across to students? Please explain why you do or do not think so.
   c. Are you more or less confident in your ability to get students to learn than you were as a beginning teacher?
   d. Which do you believe is more effective for getting students to understand the topics you're teaching: explaining the topics clearly, or asking good questions?
   e. What were the most important problems you faced during your first year of teaching?
   f. What suggestions would you offer prospective teachers to help them best prepare for their first year of teaching?
2. Interview a new teacher about his or her job-seeking experiences.
   a. Ask to see the teacher's résumé. How does it compare to the one in Figure 13.1?
   b. Did the teacher use a portfolio? If so, what was included in it? How well did it work? What would he or she have done differently?
   c. How valuable are the guidelines found in Table 13.3 for making yourself marketable?
   d. How well did the teacher's interview(s) go? What questions were asked? What advice would he or she give you regarding the guidelines for interviewing found in Table 13.5?
3. Interview a teacher about NBPTS certification. Explain the process and ask the following questions:
   a. Does the basic idea behind NBPTS certification have value? What are its basic strengths and weaknesses?
   b. Share the propositions behind NBPTS certification found in Table 13.2. Which are more valuable? Should any be added?
   c. Describe the evaluation procedures for selecting teachers. Are these adequate? Should any additional be added?
4. Interview a school administrator. Ask him or her how many teachers in the school are licensed through traditional means and through an alternative licensure process. Ask which process—traditional or alternative—seems to be more effective.
5. Interview a school administrator who is involved in hiring new teachers. Ask the following questions:
   a. What kinds of personal characteristics—such as attitudes and personality traits—do you look for in a new teacher?
   b. What kinds of knowledge—such as content, learning, learner development—do you look for in beginning teachers?
   c. How do you react to dress and manner in an interview? What suggestions do you have in this regard?
   d. How important is a prospective teacher's use of standard English and grammar in an interview?
   e. Do you want to see a prospective teacher's portfolio when you interview him or her? If so, what do you look for?

Atlanta, GA 30334
404-657-9000
www.gapsc.com

Hawaii
State Department of Education
Office of Personnel Services
P.O. Box 2360
Honolulu, HI 96804
800-305-5104

Idaho
Department of Education
Teacher Certification and Professional Standards
P.O. Box 83720
Boise, ID 83720-0027
208-232-6884

Illinois
State Teacher Certification Board
Division of Professional Preparation
100 North First Street
Springfield, IL 62777-0001
217-782-2805
www.isbe.state.il.us/homepage.html

Indiana
Professional Standards Board
251 East Ohio Street, Suite 201
Indianapolis, IN 46204-2133
317-232-9010

Iowa
Board of Educational Examiners
Teacher Licensure
Grimes State Office Building
East 14th and Grand
Des Moines, IA 50319-0146
515-281-3245
www.state.ia.us/educate/depteduc/elseced/praclic/license/index.html

Kansas
State Department of Education
Certification and Teacher Education
120 South East 10th Avenue
Topeka, KS 66612-1182
913-296-2288
www.ksbe.state.ks.us/cert/cert.html

Kentucky
Office of Teacher Education and Certification
1024 Capital Center Drive
Frankfort, KY 40601
502-573-4606

Louisiana
State Department of Education
Bureau of Higher Education, Teacher Certification, and Continuing Education
626 North 4th Street
P.O. Box 94064
Baton Rouge, LA 70804-9064
504-342-3490

Maine
Department of Education
Certification Office
23 State House Station
Augusta, ME 04333-0023
207-287-5944

Maryland
State Department of Education
Division of Certification and Accreditation
200 West Baltimore Street
Baltimore, MD 21201
410-767-0412

Massachusetts
Department of Education
Certification and Professional Development Coordination
350 Main Street
P.O. Box 9140
Malden, MA 02148-5023
781-388-3300
www.info.doe.mass.edu/news.html

Michigan
Department of Education
Office of Professional Preparation and Certification Services
608 West Allegan, 3rd Floor
Lansing, MI 48933
517-335-0406
www.mde.state.mi.us

Minnesota
State Department of Children, Families, and Learning
Personnel Licensing
610 Capitol Square Building
550 Cedar Street
St. Paul, MN 55101-2273
612-296-2046

Mississippi
State Department of Education
Office of Educator Licensure
Central High School Building
359 North West Street
P.O. Box 771
Jackson, MS 39205-0771
601-359-3483
http://mdek12.state.ms.us/OVTE/License/license.htm

Missouri
Department of Elementary and Secondary Education
Teacher Certification Office
205 Jefferson Street
P.O. Box 480
Jefferson City, MO 65102-0480
573-751-0051
http://services.dese.state.mo.us/divurbteached/teachcert

Montana
Office of Public Instruction
Teacher Education and Certification
1227 11th Avenue East, Room 210
Box 202501
Helena, MT 59620-2501
406-444-3150

Nebraska
Department of Education
Teacher Education and Certification
301 Centennial Mall South, Box 94987
Lincoln, NE 68509-4987
402-471-0739
http://nde4.nde.state.ne.us/TCERT/TCERT.html

Nevada
Department of Education
Licensure Division
700 East 5th Street
Carson City, NV 89701
702-687-9141

New Hampshire
State Department of Education
Bureau of Credentialing
101 Pleasant Street
Concord, NH 03301-3860
603-271-2407
www.state.nh.us/doe/education.htm

New Jersey
Department of Education
Office of Professional Development and Licensing
Riverview Executive Plaza, Building 100, Rte. 29
Trenton, NJ 08625-0500
609-292-2045

New Mexico
State Department of Education
Professional Licensure Unit
Education Building
Santa Fe, NM 87501-2786
505-827-6587

New York
State Education Department
Office of Teaching
Cultural Education Center, Room 5A47
Nelson A. Rockefeller Empire State Plaza
Albany, NY 12230
518-474-3901
www.nysed.gov/tcert/homepage.htm

North Carolina
Department for Public Instruction
Licensure Section
301 North Wilmington Street
Raleigh, NC 27601-2825
919-733-4125

North Dakota
Department of Public Instruction
Educational Standards and Practices Board
600 East Boulevard Avenue
Bismarck, ND 58505-0540
701-328-2264

Ohio
Department of Education
Division of Professional Development and Licensure
65 South Front Street, Room 412
Columbus, OH 43215-4183
614-466-3593
www.ode.ohio.gov/www/tc/teacher.html

Oklahoma
State Department of Education
Professional Standards Section
Hodge Education Building
2500 North Lincoln Boulevard, Room 212
Oklahoma City, OK 73105-4599
405-521-3337
www.sde.state.ok.us

Oregon
Teacher Standards and Practices Commission
Public Service Building, Suite 105
255 Capitol Street, N.E.
Salem, OR 97310
503-378-3586

Pennsylvania
State Department of Education
Bureau of Teacher Preparation and Certification
333 Market Street, 3rd Floor
Harrisburg, PA 17126-0333
717-787-3356
www.cas.psu.edu/pde.html

Puerto Rico
Department of Education
Certification Office
P.O. Box 190759
San Juan, PR 00919-0759
787-754-0060

Rhode Island
Department of Education
Office of Teacher Preparation, Certification, and Professional Development
Shepard Building
255 Westminster Street
Providence, RI 02903
401-222-2675

St. Croix District
Department of Education
Educational Personnel Services
2133 Hospital Street
St. Croix, VI 00820
340-773-1095

St. Thomas/St. John District
Department of Education
Personnel Services
44-46 Kongens Gade
St. Thomas, VI 00802
340-774-0100

South Carolina
State Department of Education
Office of Organizational Development
Teacher Certification Section
Rutledge Building, Room 702
Columbia, SC 29201
803-734-8466

South Dakota
Division of Education and Cultural Affairs
Office of Policy and Accountability
Kneip Building, 700 Governors Drive
Pierre, SD 57501-2291
605-773-3553
www.state.sd.us/state/executive/deca/account/certif/htm

Tennessee
State Department of Education
Teacher Licensing and Certification
Andrew Johnson Tower, 5th Floor
710 James Robertson Parkway
Nashville, TN 37243-0377
615-532-4880

Texas
State Board of Educator Certification
1001 Trinity Street
Austin, TX 78701-2603
512-469-3001
www.sbec.state.tx.us/sbec/txcert.htm

United States Department of Defense
Dependent Schools 3
Certification Unit
4040 N. Fairfax Drive
Arlington, VA 22203-1634
703-696-3081, ext. 133
www.tmn.com/dodea

Utah
State Office of Education
Certification and Personnel Development
250 East 500 South
Salt Lake City, UT 84111
801-538-7741
www.usoe.k12.ut.us/cert/regs.html

Vermont
State Department of Education
Licensing and Professional Standards
120 State Street
Montpelier, VT 05620
802-828-2445

Virginia
Department of Education
James Monroe Building
P.O. Box 2120
Richmond, VA 23218-2120
804-371-2522
www.pen.k12.va.us/Anthology/VDOE/Compliance/TeachED

Washington
Superintendent of Public Instruction
Professional Education and Certification Office
Old Capitol Building
600 South Washington Street
P.O. Box 47200
Olympia, WA 98504-7200
360-753-6773
http://inform.ospi.wednet.edu/CERT/welcome.html

West Virginia
Department of Education
Office of Professional Preparation
1900 Kanawha Boulevard East
Building #6, Room B-252
Charleston, WV 25305-0330
304-558-7010

Wisconsin
Department of Public Instruction
Teacher Education and Licensing Teams
125 South Webster Street, P.O. Box 7841
Madison, WI 53707-7841
608-266-1879
www.dp.state.wi.us/tcert

Wyoming
Professional Teaching Standards Board
Hathaway Building, 2nd Floor
2300 Capital Avenue
Cheyenne, WY 82002
307-777-6248
www.k12.wy.us

REFERENCES

Abel, M., & Sewell, J. (1999). Stress and burnout in rural and urban secondary school teachers. *The Journal of Educational Research, 92*, 287–294.

Abington School District v. Schempp, 374 U.S. 203 (1963).

Adler, M. (1982). *The Paideia proposal: An educational manifesto*. New York: Macmillan.

Administration on Children, Youth & Families. (1995). *Project Head Start Statistical Fact Sheet*. Washington, DC: Author.

Alexander, B., Crowley, J., Lundin, D., Murdy, V., Palmer, S., & Rabkin, E. (1997, September). E-Comp: A few words about teaching writing with computers. *T.H.E. Journal, 25*, 66–67.

Alexander, P., & Murphy P. (1998). The research base for APA's learner-centered psychological principles. In N. Lambert, & B. McCombs (Eds.), *How students learn: Reforming schools through learner-centered education* (pp. 25–60). Washington, DC: American Psychological Association.

Allison, C. (1995). *Present and past: Essays for teachers in the history of education*. New York: Peter Lang.

Altermatt, E., Jovanovic, J., & Perry, M. (1998). Bias or responsivity? Sex and achievement-level effects on teachers' classroom questioning practices. *Journal of Educational Psychology, 90*(3), 516–527.

American Association for the Advancement of Science. (1989). *Project 2061: Science for all Americans*. Washington, DC: Author.

American Association of University Women. (1992). *How schools shortchange girls*. Annapolis Junction, MD: Author.

American Association of University Women (1993). *Hostile hallways: The AAUW survey on sexual harassment in America's schools*. New York: Louis Harris and Associates.

American Association of University Women. (1998). *Gender gaps: Where schools still fail our children*. Annapolis Junction, MD: Author.

American Association of University Women. (1999). *Separated by sex: A critical look at single sex education for girls*. Annapolis Junction, MD: Author.

American Council of Trustees and Alumni. (2000). *Losing America's memory: Historical illiteracy in the 21st century*. Washington, DC: Author.

Anderson, J. (1988). *The Education of Blacks in the South*. Chapel Hill, NC: University of North Carolina Press.

Apple, M. (1995). *Education and power* (2nd ed.). New York: Rutledge.

Archer, J. (1998). The link to higher scores. *Education Week, 28*(5), 10–14, 18–21.

Archer, J. (2000a). Competition fierce for minority teachers. *Education Week, 19*(18), 32–33.

Archer, J. (2000b). Teachers warned against teaching contracts. *Education Week, 20*(15), 30.

Archer, J., Bradley, A., & Schnaiberg, L. (1999). Urban districts offering teacher-induction programs, study finds. *Education Week, 18*(43), 15.

Arias, M., & Casanova, U. (Eds.). (1993). Bilingual education: Politics, practice, and research. *Ninety-second yearbook of the National Society for the Study of Education, Part 2*. Chicago: University of Chicago Press.

Arnold, M. (1998). 3 kinds of equity. *American School Board Journal, 85*(5), 34–36.

Associated Press. (2000, December 29). Texas legislative panel calls for charter schools moratorium. *Boston Globe*, p. A13.

Babad, E., Bernieri, F., & Rosenthal, R. (1991). Students as judges of teachers' verbal and nonverbal behavior. *American Educational Research Journal, 28*(1), 211–234.

Bailey, W. (1997). *Educational leadership for the 21st century: Organizing schools*. Lancaster, PA: Technomic.

Baker, D., & Stevenson, D. (1986). Mothers' strategies for children's school achievement: Managing the transition to high school. *Sociology of Education, 59*, 156–166.

Ball, D. (1992, Summer). Magical hopes: Manipulatives and the reform of math education. *American Educator*, 28–33.

Bandura, A. (1989). Social cognitive theory. In R. Vasta (Ed.), *Annals of child development* (Vol. 6, pp. 1–60). Greenwich, CT: JAI Press.

Bangert-Drowns, R. (1993). The word processor as an instructional tool: A meta-analysis of word processing in writing instruction. *Review of Educational Research, 63*(1), 69–93.

Banks, J. (1994). *Multiethnic education* (3rd ed.). Boston: Allyn & Bacon.

Banks, J. (1997). Multicultural education: Characteristics and goals. In J. Banks, & C. Banks (Eds.), *Multicultural education: Issues and perspectives*, (3rd ed., pp. 3–32). Boston: Allyn & Bacon.

Barab, S., & Landa, A. (1997). Designing effective interdisciplinary anchors. *Educational Leadership, 54*, 52–55.

Barone, M. (2000). In plain English: Bilingual education flunks out of schools in California. *U.S. News and World Report, 128*(21), 37.

Barr, R., & Parrett, W. (1995). *Hope at last for at-risk youth*. Boston: Allyn & Bacon.

Barr, R., & Parrett, W. (2001). *Hope fulfilled for at-risk youth*. Boston: Allyn & Bacon.

Barth, P., Haycock, K., Jackson, H., Mora, K., Ruiz, P., Robinson, S., & Wilkins, A. (Eds.). (1999). *Dispelling the myth: High poverty schools exceeding expectations*. Washington, DC: The Education Trust.

Battista, M. (1999). The mathematical miseducation of America's youth: Ignoring research and scientific study in education. *Phi Delta Kappan, 80*(6), 425–433.

Beane, J. (1997). *Curriculum integration: Designing the core of democratic education*. New York: Teachers College Press.

Benard, B. (1993). Fostering resilience in kids. *Educational Leadership, 51*(3), 44–48.

Bender, W., & McLaughlin, P. (1997). Violence in the classroom. *Intervention in School & Clinic, 32*(4), 196–198.

Bennett, C. (1990). *Comprehensive multicultural education* (2nd ed.). Boston: Allyn & Bacon.

Bennett, S. (1978). Recent research on teaching: A dream, a belief, and a model. *British Journal of Educational Psychology, 48*, 27–147.

Berk, L. (1996). *Infants, children, and adolescents* (2nd ed.). Boston: Allyn & Bacon.

Berk, L. (2000). *Child development* (5th ed.). Boston: Allyn & Bacon.

Berliner, D. (1984). *Making our schools more effective: Proceedings of three state conferences*. San Francisco: Far West Laboratory.

Berliner, D. (1992, February). *Educational reform in an era of disinformation*. Paper presented at a meeting of the American Association of Colleges for Teacher Education, San Antonio, TX.

Berliner, D. (1994). Expertise: The wonder of exemplary performances. In J. Mangieri, & C. Collins (Eds.), *Creating powerful thinking in teachers and students* (pp. 11–186). Fort Worth, TX: Harcourt Brace.

Berliner, D. (2000). A personal response to those who bash education. *Journal of Teacher Education, 51*, 358–371.

Bernstein, M. (1998). The tyranny of a national curriculum. *Education Week, 17*(19), 40, 42.

Bertman, S. (2000). *Cultural amnesia: America's future and the crisis of memory*. Westport, CT: Praeger.

Bethel School District No. 403 v. Fraser, 106 S. Ct. 3159 (1986).

Bishop, J. (1995). The power of external standards. *American Educator, 19*, 10–14, 17–18, 42–43.

Bishop, J. (1998). The effect of curriculum-based external exit systems on student achievement. *Journal of Economic Education, 29*, 171–182.

Black, S. (1996, September). The pull of magnets. *American School Board Journal*, 35.

Blair, J. (1999). Kellogg begins program to boost service learning. *Education Week, 18*(37), 3.

Blair, J. (2000a). AFT urges new tests, expanded training for teachers. *Education Week, 19*(32), 11.

Blair, J. (2000b). Certification found valid for teachers. *Education Week, 20*(8), 1, 24–25.

Bliss, T. (1992). Alternate certification in Connecticut: Reshaping the profession. *Peabody Journal of Education, 67*, 35–54.

Bloom, B. (1981). *All our children learning*. New York: McGraw-Hill.

Board of Education of the Westside Community School v. Mergens, 496 U.S. 226 (1990).

Bond, H. (1934). *The education of the Negro in the American social order*. New York: Prentice Hall.

Borko, H., & Putnam, R. (1996). Learning to teach. In D. Berliner, & R. Calfee (Eds.), *Handbook of educational psychology* (pp. 673–708). New York: Simon & Schuster Macmillan.

Boser, U. (2000). Teaching to the test? *Education Week, 19*(39), 1, 10.

Bosworth, K. (1995). Caring for others and being cared for: Students talk about caring in school. *Phi Delta Kappan, 76*, 686–693.

Bowman, D. (2000a). Arizona poised to revisit graduation exam. *Education Week, 20*(13), 16, 18.

Bowman, D. (2000b). Charters, vouchers earning mixed report card. *Education Week, 19*(34), 1, 19–21.

Bowman, D. (2000c). Prospects for charter school initiative look dim. *Education Week, 29*(11), 18.

Bowman, D. (2000d). Troubled St. Paul charter school closes early. *Education Week, 19*(40), 3.

Bowman, D. (2000e). Vast majority of charter school studies show positive findings, report states. *Education Week, 20*(10), 18.

Bowman, D. (2000f). White House proposes goals for improving Hispanic education. *Education Week, 19*(41), 9.

Boyer, E. (1995). *The basic school: A community for learning*. Princeton, NJ: The Carnegie Foundation for the Advancement of Teaching.

Bracey, G. (1998). The eighth Bracey Report on the condition of public education. *Phi Delta Kappan, 80*(2), 112–127.

Bracey, G. (1999a). Research: The growing divide. *Phi Delta Kappan, 81*(1), 90.

Bracey, G. (1999b). Top-heavy. *Phi Delta Kappan, 80*(6), 472–473.

Braddock, J. (1990). Tracking the middle grades: National patterns of grouping for instruction. *Phi Delta Kappan, 71*(6), 445–449.

Bradley, A. (1998). Muddle in the middle. *Education Week, 17*(31), 38–42.

Bradley, A. (1999a). Confronting a tough issue: Teacher tenure. *Education Week, 18*(17), 48–52.

Bradley, A. (1999b). Pool of aspiring teachers is growing older. *Education Week, 19*(7), 3.

Bradley, A. (1999c). Science group finds middle school textbooks inadequate. *Education Week, 19*(6), 5.

Bradley, A. (1999d). Zeroing in on teachers. *Education Week, 18*(17), 46–47, 49–52.

Bradley, A. (2000a). Chicago makes deal with feds to hire foreign teachers. *Education Week, 19*(19), 17.

Bradley, A. (2000b). High-tech fields luring teachers from education. *Education Week, 19*(19), 1, 16, 17.

Bradley, A. (2000c). L.A. proposes linking teacher pay to tests. *Education Week, 19*(28), 3.

Bradley, A. (2000d). Massachusetts to test teachers in school with low math scores. *Education Week, 19*(21), 19.

Bradley, A. (2000e). The gatekeeping challenge. *Education Week, 19*(18), 20–26.

Bradley, A. (2000f). Union heads issue standards warning. *Education Week, 19*(42), 1, 20, 21.

Bradley, D., & Switlick, D. (1997). The past and future of special education. In D. Bradley, M. King-Sears, & D. Tessier-Switlick (Eds.), *Teaching students in inclusive settings* (pp. 1–20). Boston: Allyn & Bacon.

Bradley v. Pittsburgh Board of Education, 913 F.2d 1064 (3d Cir. 1990).

Bradsher, M., & Hagan, L. (1995). The kids network: Student-scientists pool resources. *Educational Leadership, 53* (2), 38–43.

Bransford, J. (1993). Who ya gonna call? Thoughts about teaching problem solving. In P. Hallinger, K. Leithwood, & J. Murphy (Eds.), *Cognitive perspectives on educational leadership* (pp. 2–30). New York: Teachers College Press.

Brenner, M., Mayer, R., Moseley, B., Brar, T., Durán, R., Reed, B., & Webb, D. (1997). Learning by understanding: The role of multiple representations in learning algebra. *American Education Research Journal, 34*(4), 663–689.

Brint, S. (1998). *Schools and societies*. Thousand Oaks, CA: Pine Forge Press.

Brody, N. (1992). *Intelligence* (2nd ed.). San Diego: Academic Press.

Brookhart, S. (1997). A theoretical framework for the role of classroom assessment in motivating student effort and achievement. *Applied Measurement In Education, 10*(2), 161–180.

Brophy, J. (1986). Research linking teacher behavior to student achievement: Potential implications for instruction of Chapter 1 students. In B. Williams, P. Richmond, & B. Mason (Eds.), *Designs for Compensatory Education Conference proceedings and papers* (pp. IV-121–IV-179). Washington, DC: Research and Evaluation Associates.

Brophy, J. (1996). *Teaching problem students*. New York: Guilford Press.

Brophy, J., & Alleman, J. (1991). A caveat: Curriculum integration isn't always a good idea. *Educational Leadership, 49*, 66.

Brophy, J., & McCaslin, M. (1992). Teachers' reports of how they perceive and cope with problem students. *Elementary School Journal, 93*(1), 3–68.

Brophy, J., & Rohrkemper, M. (1987). *Teachers' strategies for coping with hostile-aggressive students*. East Lansing: Michigan State University, Institute for Research on Teaching.

Brouillette, L. (2000, April). *What is behind all that rhetoric?: A case study of the creation of a charter school*. Paper presented at the annual meeting of the American Educational Research Association, New Orleans.

Brown, A., & Campione, J. (1986). Psychological theory and the study of learning disabilities. *American Psychologist, 41*, 1059–1068.

Brown, D. (1991). *The effects of state-mandated testing on elementary classroom instruction*. Unpublished doctoral dissertation, University of Tennessee-Knoxville.

Brown v. Bathhe, 416 F. Supp. 1194 (D. Neb., 1976).

Bruning, R., Schraw, G., & Ronning, R. (1999). *Cognitive psychology and instruction* (3rd ed.). Upper Saddle River, NJ: Prentice Hall.

Brunsma, D., & Rockquemoro, K. (1999). Effects of student uniforms on attendance, behavior problems, substance abuse and academic achievement. *Journal of Educational Research, 92*(1), 53–62.

Bullock, A., & Hawl, P. (2001). *Developing a teaching portfolio: A guide for preservice and practicing teachings*. Upper Saddle River, NJ: Merrill Prentice Hall.

Bullough, R. (1989). *First-year teacher: A case study*. New York: Teachers College Press.

Bullough, R. (1999, April). *In praise of children at-risk: Life on the other side of the teacher's desk*. Paper presented at the annual meeting of the American Educational Research Association, Montreal.

Bullough, R. (2001). *Uncertain lives; Children of promise, teachers of hope*. New York: Teachers College Press.

Bullough, R., & Baughman, K. (1997). *"First-year teacher" eight years later: An inquiry into teacher development*. New York: Teachers College Press.

Bushweller, K. (1998). Probing the roots and prevention of youth violence. *American School Board Journal, 85*(12), December, A8–A12.

Button, H., & Provenzo, E. (1983). *History of education in American culture*. New York: Holt, Rinehart & Winston.

Butts, R. (1978). *Public education in the United States*. New York: Holt, Rinehart & Winston.

Butts, R., & Cremin, L. (1953). *A history of education in American culture*. New York: Holt, Rinehart & Winston.

Cahupe, P., & Howley, C. (1992). *Indian nations at risk.* Charleston, W. Va.: Clearinghouse on Rural Education and Small Schools.

Calsyn, C., Gonzales, P., & Frase, T. (1999). *Highlights from TIMSS*. Washington, DC: National Center for Educational Statistics.

Cameron, C., & Lee, K. (1997). Bridging the gap between home and school with voice-mail technology. *Journal of Educational Research*, 90, 182–190.

Campbell, D., Cignetti, P., Melenyzer, B., Nettles, D., & Wyman, R. (2001). *How to develop a professional portfolio: A manual for teachers* (2nd ed.). Boston: Allyn & Bacon.

Campbell, J., & Beaudry, J. (1998). Gender gap linked to differential socialization for high achieving senior mathematics students. *Journal of Educational Research*, *91*(3), 140–147.

Campbell, P., & Clewell, B. (1999). Science, math, and girls. *Education Week*, *19*(2), 50–53.

Carkci, M. (1998, November 8). A classroom challenge I just had to take. *The Washington Post*, p. C3.

Carter, C. (1997). Integrated middle school. Humanities: A process analysis. *Teacher Education Quarterly*, *24*, 55–73.

Carter, C., & Mason, D. (1997, March). *Cognitive effects of integrated curriculum*. Paper presented at the annual conference of the American Educational Research Association, Chicago.

Ceci, S. (1990). *On Intelligence . . . More or less*. Englewood Cliffs, N.J.: Prentice Hall.

Ceci, S., & Williams, W. (1997). Schooling, intelligence, and income. *American Psychologist*, *53*, 185–204.

Centers for Disease Control and Prevention. (1996). *HIV/AIDS surveillance report*. Atlanta, GA: Author.

Chalk v. U.S. District Court Cent. Dist. of California (1988).

Chance, P. (1997). Speaking of differences. *Phi Delta Kappan*, *78*(7) , 506–507.

Chaskin, R., & Rauner, D. (1995). Youth and caring: An introduction. *Phi Delta Kappan*, *76*, 667–674.

Chekles, K. (1997). The first seven . . . and the eighth. *Educational Leadership*, *55*, 8–13.

Children's Defense Fund. (1995). *"The state of America's children" yearbook 1995*. Washington, DC: Author. [Online] Available: *http://www.Tmn.com/CDF/facts.htmL#USChildren*

Children's Defense Fund. (1998). *"The state of America's children" yearbook 1998*. Washington, DC: Author.

Clandinin, J., & Connelly, M. (1996). Teacher as curriculum maker. In P. Jackson, (Ed.), *Handbook of research on curriculum* (pp. 363–401). New York: Macmillan.

Clinkenbeard, P. (1992, April). *Motivation and gifted adolescents: Learning from observing practice*. Paper presented at the annual meeting of the American Educational Research Association, San Francisco.

Cognition and Technology Group at Vanderbilt. (1992). The Jasper Series as an example of anchored instruction: Theory, program description, and assessment data. *Educational Psychologist*, *27*, 291–315.

Cognition and Technology Group at Vanderbilt. (1997). *The Jasper Project: Lessons in curriculum, instruction, assessment, and professional development*. Mahwah, New Jersey: Erlbaum.

Cohen, D. (1993). Perry preschool graduates show dramatic new social gains at 27. *Education Week*, *12*(28), 1, 16–17.

Cohen, E. (1994). Restructuring the classroom: Conditions for productive small group. *Review of Educational Research*, *64*, 1–35.

Coladarci, T., & Cobb, C. (1995, April). *The effects of school size and extracurricular participation on 12th grade academic achievement and self-esteem*. Paper presented at the annual meeting of the American Educational Research Association, San Francisco.

Coles, A. (1997). Poll finds growing support for school choice. *Education Week*, *17*(1), 14.

Coles, A. (1999a). Falling teenage birthrate fuels drop in overall U.S. rate. *Education Week*, *18*(35), 130.

Coles, A. (1999b). Surveys examine sex education programs. *Education Week*, *19*(6), 13.

Coles, A. (1999c). Teenage drug use continues to slide. *Education Week*, *19*(1), 100.

Coles, A. (2000). Drug use more prevalent among rural teenagers, study warns. *Education Week*, *19*(21), 8.

Comer, J. (1994, April). *A brief history and summary of the school development program*. Paper presented at the annual meeting of the American Educational Research Association, San Francisco.

Comer, J., Haynes, N., Joyner, E., & Ben-Avie, M. (1996). *Rallying the whole village: The Comer process for reforming education*. New York: Teachers College Press.

Commonwealth of Pennsylvania v. Douglass, 588 A. 2d 53 (Pa. Super. Ct. 1991).

Compayre, G. (1888). *History of pedagogy*. (W. Payne, Trans.). Boston: Heath.

Conger, R., Conger, K., Elder, G., Lorenz, F., Simons, R., & Whitbeck, L. (1992). A family process model of economic hardship and adjustment of early adolescent boys. *Child Development*, *63*, 526–541.

Consortium for Longitudinal Studies. (1983). *As the twig is bent: Lasting effects of preschool programs*. Hillsdale, NJ: Erlbaum.

Corey, G., Corey, M., & Callahan, P. (1993). *Issues and ethics in the helping professions*. Pacific Grove, CA: Brooks/Cole.

Coughlin, E. (1996, February 16). Not out of Africa. *Chronicle of Higher Education*, A6–A7.

Cremin, L. (1961). *The transformation of the school*. New York: Alfred Knopf.

Cremin, L. (1970). *American education: The colonial experience, 1607–1783*. New York: Harper & Row.

Croasmun, J., Hampton, D., & Herrmann, S. (1999). *Teacher attrition: Is time running out?* [Online]. Horizon Site. The

University of North Carolina. Available: *http://horizon.unc.edu/projects/issues/papers/Hampton.asp*

Cuban, L. (1984). *How teachers taught: Constancy and change in American classrooms: 1890–1980*. White Plains, NY: Longman.

Cuban, L. (1996). Curriculum stability and change. In P. Jackson (Ed.), *Handbook of research on curriculum* (pp. 216–247). New York: Macmillan.

Cuban, L. (1999). The technology puzzle. *Education Week, 19*(43), 47, 68.

Curry, L. (1990). A critique of research on learning styles. *Educational Leadership, 48*(2), 50–52, 54–56.

Curwin, R., & Mendler, A. (1988). *Discipline with dignity*. Alexandria, VA: Association for Supervision and Curriculum Development.

Curwin, R., & Mendler, A. (1988). Packaged discipline programs: Let the buyer beware. *Educational Leadership, 46*(2), 68–71.

Cushner, K., McClelland, A., & Safford, P. (1992). *Human diversity in education*. New York: McGraw-Hill.

Cypher, T., & Willower, D. (1984). The work behavior of secondary school teachers. *Journal of Research & Development, 18*, 19–20.

Dai, D., Moon, S., & Feldhusen, J. (1998). Achievement motivation and gifted students: A social cognitive perspective. *Educational Psychologist, 33*(2/3), 45–63.

Darling-Hammond, L. (1992). Teaching and knowledge: Policy issues posed by alternative certification for teachers. *Peabody Journal of Education, 67*, 123–154.

Darling-Hammond, L. (1995). *The condition of teaching in America: Resources for restructuring*. New York: National Center for Restructuring Education, Schools and Teaching, Teachers College, Columbus University.

Darling-Hammond, L. (1996). *What matters most: Teaching for America's future*. Washington, DC: National Commission on Teaching and America's Future.

Darling-Hammond, L. (1998). *The right to learn*. San Francisco, CA: Jossey-Bass.

Darling-Hammond, L. (2000a). How teacher education matters. *Journal of Teacher Education, 51*(3), 166–173.

Darling-Hammond, L. (2000b). Teacher quality and student achievement: A review of state policy evidence. *Education Policy Analysis Archives, 8*(1), 1–44.

Darling-Hammond, L., Berry, B., Haselkorn, D., & Fideler, E. (1999). Teacher recruitment, selection, and induction: Policy influences on the supply and quality of teachers. In L. Darling-Hammond, & G. Sykes (Eds.), *Teaching as the learning profession. Handbook of policy and practice*. San Francisco: Jossey-Bass.

Darling-Hammond, L., & Sclan, E. (1996). Who teachers are and why: Dilemmas of building a profession for twenty-first century schools. In J. Sikula (Ed.), *Handbook of research on teacher education* (2nd ed., pp. 67–101). New York: Macmillan.

Datnow, A., Hubbard, L., & Conchas, G. (1999, April). *How context mediates policy: The implementation of single gender public schooling in California*. Paper presented at the annual meeting of the American Educational Research Association, Montreal.

Davenport, E., Davison, M., Kuang, H., Ding, S., Kim, S., & Kwak, N. (1998). High school mathematics course-taking by gender and ethnicity. *American Educational Research Journal, 35*(3), 497–514.

Davis, G., & Rimm, S. (1993). *Education of the gifted and talented* (3rd ed.). Upper Saddle River, NJ: Prentice Hall.

Delgado-Gaiton, C. (1992). School matters in the Mexican American home: Socializing children to education. *American Educational Research Journal, 29*(3), 495–516.

deMarrais, K., & LeCompte, M. (1999). *The way schools work* (3rd ed.). New York: Longman.

DeVries, R., & Zan, B. (1995, April). *The sociomoral atmosphere: The first principle of constructivist education*. Paper presented at the annual meeting of the American Educational Research Association, San Francisco.

Dewey, J. (1902). *The child and the curriculum*. Chicago: University of Chicago Press.

Dewey, J. (1906). *Democracy and education*. New York: Macmillan.

Dewey, J. (1923). *The school and society*. Chicago: University of Chicago Press.

Dewey, J. (1938). *Experience and education*. New York: Macmillan.

Diamond, J. (1999). *Guns, germs and steel: The fates of human societies*. New York: W. W. Norton.

Diaz, R. (1990). Bilingualism and cognitive ability: Theory, research, and controversy. In A. Barona, & E. Garcia (Eds.), *Children at risk: Poverty, minority status, and other issues of educational equity* (pp. 91–102). Washington, DC: National Association of School Psychologists.

Diem, R. (1996). Using social studies as the catalyst for curriculum integration: The experience of a secondary school. *Social Education, 60*, 95–98.

Dillon, D. (1989). Showing them that I want them to learn and that I care about who they are: A microethnography of the social organization of a secondary low-track English reading classroom. *American Educational Research Journal, 26*(2), 227–259.

Dobrzynski, J. (1996, July 21). The new jobs: A growing number are good ones. *New York Times*, Section 3, pp. 1, 10–11.

Dochy, F., & McDowell, L. (1997). Introduction: Assessment as a tool for learning. *Studies in Educational Evaluation, 23*(4), 279–298.

Doe v. Renfrow, 635 F.2d 582 (7th Cir. 1980).

Dowling-Sendor, B. (1999, April). Struggling with set-asides. *American School Board Journal, 186*(4), 20, 22, 63.

Doyle, D. (1997). Education and character. *Phi Delta Kappan, 78*(6), 440–443.

Doyle, D. (1999). De facto national standards. *Education Week, 18*(42), 36, 56.

Doyle, W. (1986). Classroom organization and management. In M. Wittrock (Ed.), *Handbook of research on teaching* (3rd ed., pp. 392–431). New York: Macmillan.

Dulude-Lay, C. (2000). *The confounding effect of the dimensions of classroom life on the narratives of student teachers*. Unpublished document, University of Utah.

Dworkin, R. (1998, October 23). Affirming affirmative action. *New York Review of Books*, 91–102.

Echevarria, J., & Graves, A. (1998). *Sheltered content instruction*. Boston, MA: Allyn & Bacon.

Education vital signs. (1998). *American School Board Journal, 185*(12), A1–A30.

Education vital signs. (1999). *American School Board Journal, 186*(12), A1–A28.

Educational Excellence for All Children Act of 1999. (1999). *Education Week, 18*(39), 28–54.

Educational Testing Service. (1999). *Principles of learning and teaching test bulletin*. Princeton, NJ: Author.

Edwards, V., & Chronister, G. (Eds.). (2000). Who should teach? The states decide. *Education Week, 19*(18), 8–9.

Egan, D. (1997, September 26). Critics claim history textbook is trying to "brainwash" kids. *Salt Lake Tribune*, B1, B3.

Eggen, P. (1998, April). *A comparison of inner-city middle school teachers' classroom practices and their expressed beliefs about learning and effective instruction*. Paper presented at the annual meeting of the American Educational Research Association, San Diego.

Eggen, P., & Kauchak, D. (2001). *Educational psychology: Windows on classrooms* (5th ed.). Upper Saddle River, NJ: Prentice Hall.

Eisenberg, N., Martin, C., & Fabes, R. (1996). Gender development and gender effects. In D. Berliner, & R. Calfee (Eds.), *Handbook of educational psychology*. New York: Macmillan.

Eisner, E. (1985). *The educational imagination: On the design and evaluation of school programs* (2nd ed.). New York: Macmillan.

Elam, S., Rose, L., & Gallup, A. (1995). The 27th annual Phi Delta Kappa/Gallup Poll. *Phi Delta Kappan, 77*(55).

Elliot, M. (1998). School finance and opportunities to learn: Does money well spent enhance students' achievement? *Sociology of Education, 71*(3), 223–245.

Ellis, S., Dowdy, B., Graham, P., & Jones, R. (1992, April). *Parental support of planning skills in the context of homework and family demands*. Paper presented at the annual meeting of the American Educational Research Association, San Francisco.

Emmer, E., Evertson, C., Clements, B., & Worsham, M. (2000). *Classroom management for secondary teachers* (5th ed.). Needham Heights, MA: Allyn & Bacon.

Engle v. Vitale, 370 U.S. 421 (1962).

Epstein, J. (1990). School and family connections: Theory, research, and implications for integrating sociologies of education and family. In D. Unger , & M. Sussman (Eds.), *Families in community settings: Interdisciplinary perspectives* (pp. 99–126). New York: Haworth Press.

Evertson, C. (1982). Differences in instructional activities in higher- and lower-achieving junior high English and math classes. *Elementary School Journal, 82*, 329–350.

Evertson, C., Emmer, E., Clements, B., & Worsham, M. (2000). *Classroom management for elementary teachers* (5th ed.). Needham Heights, MA: Allyn & Bacon.

Fagen v. Summers 498 F.2d 1227 (Wyo. 1972).

Fatemi, E. (1999). Building the digital curriculum. *Education Week, 19*(4), 5–12.

Federal Interagency Forum on Child and Family Statistics. (1997). *America's children: Key national indicators of well-being*. Washington, DC: Author.

Feingold, A. (1995). Gender differences in personality: A meta-analysis. *Psychological Bulletin, 116*, 429–456.

Feldman, S. (2000). True merit pay. *Education Week, 19*(26), 21.

Ferguson, R. (1991). Paying for public education: New evidence on how and why money matters. *Harvard Journal on Legislation, 28*, 465–498.

Fideler, E., & Haselkorn, D. (1999). *Learning the ropes: Urban teacher induction programs and practices in the United States*. Belmont, MA: Recruiting New Teacher, Inc.

Fischer, L., Schimmel, D., & Kelly, C. (1999). *Teachers and the law*. New York: Longman.

Fiske, E., & Ladd, H. (2000). A distant laboratory. *Education Week, 19*(56), 38.

Fleischfresser v. Directors of School District No. 200. 15 F.3d 680 (7th Cir. 1994).

Forcier, R. (1999). *The computer as an educational tool* (2nd ed.). Columbus, OH: Merrill.

Foster, M. (1992). Sociolinguistics and the African-American community: Implications for literacy. *Theory into Practice, 31*(4), 303–311.

Fuchs, D., & Fuchs, L. (1994). Inclusive schools movement and the radicalization of special education reform. *Exceptional Children, 60*, 294–309.

Furlan, C. (1999). States tackle internet-filter rules for schools. *Education Week, 17*(43), 22, 28.

Furlan, C. (2000). Satellite broadcasts seek to enliven study of history. *Education Week, 19*(26), 8.

Furtado, L. (1997, November). *Interdisciplinary curriculum*. Paper presented at the annual meeting of the California Educational Research Association, Santa Barbara, CA.

Gallagher, J. (1998). Accountability for gifted students. *Phi Delta Kappan, 79*(10), 739–742.

Galley, M. (1999). New school curriculum seeks to combat anti-gay bias. *Education Week, 19*(10), 6.

Galley, M. (2000a). Male preschool teachers face skepticism but earn acceptance. *Education Week, 19*(20), 1, 10.

Galley, M. (2000b). Report charts growth in special education. *Education Week, 19*(32), 35.

Garber, H. (1988). *Milwaukee Project: Preventing mental retardation in children at risk*. Washington, DC: American Association on Mental Retardation.

Garcia, E. (1993). Language, culture and education. In *Review of Research in Education* (Vol. 19). Washington, DC: American Educational Research Association.

Gardner, H. (1983). *Frames of mind: The theory of multiple intelligences*. New York: Basic Books.

Gardner, H. (1995). *"Multiple intelligences"* as a catalyst. *English Journal, 84*(8), 16–26.

Gardner, H., & Hatch, T. (1989). Multiple intelligences go to school. *Educational Researcher, 18*(8), 4–10.

Gay, G. (1997). Educational equality for students of color. In J. Banks, & C. Banks (Eds.), *Multicultural education: Issues and perspectives* (3rd ed., pp. 195–228). Boston: Allyn & Bacon.

Gehring, J. (1999a). Displays entangle Ten Commandments, First Amendment. *Education Week, 19*(15), 7.

Gehring, J. (1999b). Groups endorse guidelines on using the Bible in instruction. *Education Week, 19*(12), 7.

Gehring, J. (2000a). Massachusetts teachers blast state tests in new TV ads. *Education Week, 20*(12), 1, 22.

Gehring, J. (2000b). Schools' Bible courses "taught wrong" report says. *Education Week, 19*(19), 10.

Geiger, K. (1993). A safe haven for children. *Education Week, 12*(24), 15.

Gentry, C. (1995). Educational technology: A question of meaning. In G. Anglin (Ed.), *Instructional technology: Past, present, and future* (2nd ed., pp. 1–10). Englewood, CO: Libraries Unlimited.

Gewertz, C. (2000a). Levy to stay in N.Y.C., Ackerman quits D.C. *Education Week, 19*(37), 3.

Gewertz, C. (2000b). More districts add summer coursework. *Educational Leadership, 19*(30), 1, 12.

Gewertz, C. (2000c). Wisconsin study finds benefits in classes of 15 or fewer students. *Education Week, 19*(31), 10.

Gibsen, R. (1998, July 3). Growth, diversity alter face of religion in U.S. *Salt Lake City Tribune, 256*(182), pp. A1, A10.

Gibson, P. (1989). Gay male and lesbian youth suicide. In M. Feinleib (Ed.), *Report of the secretary's task force on youth suicide* (pp. 3–142). Washington, DC: U.S. Department of Health and Human Services.

Gibson, S., & Dembo, M. (1984). Teacher efficacy: A construct validation. *Journal of Educational Psychology, 76*, 569–582.

Gladney, L., & Greene, B. (1997, March). *Descriptions of motivation among African American high school students for their favorite and least favorite classes*. Paper presented at the annual meeting of the American Educational Research Association, Chicago.

Goldhaber, D. (1999). School choice: An examination of the empirical evidence on achievement, parental decision making and equity. *Educational Researcher, 28*(9), 16–25.

Gollnick, D., & Chinn, P. (2002). *Multi-cultural education in a pluralistic society* (6th ed.). New York: Merrill/Macmillan.

Good, T., & Brophy, J. (1986). School effects. In M. Wittrock (Ed.), *Handbook of research on teaching* (3rd ed., pp. 570–604). New York: Macmillan.

Good, T., & Brophy, J. (1997). *Looking in classrooms* (7th ed.). New York: HarperCollins.

Good, T., & Marshall, S. (1984). Do students learn more in heterogeneous or homogeneous groups? In P. Peterson, L. Wilkinson, & M. Hallinan (Eds.), *The social context of instruction: Group organization and group process* (pp. 15–38). San Diego: Academic Press.

Goodenow, C. (1992, April). *School motivation, engagement, and sense of belonging among urban adolescent students*. Paper presented at the annual meeting of the American Educational Research Association, San Francisco.

Goodlad, J. (1984). *A place called school*. New York: McGraw-Hill.

Gordon, J. (1993). *Why did you select teaching as a career? Teachers of color tell their stories* (Tech. Rep. No. 143). Washington, DC. (ERIC Document Reproduction Service No. ED 363 653).

Gordon, T. (1999). Retention is no way to boost reading. *Education Week, 18*(40), 42, 44.

Gorman, J., & Balter, L. (1997). Culturally sensitive parent education: A critical review of quantitative research. *Review of Educational Research, 67*, 339–369.

Gracenin, D. (1993). On their own terms. *The Executive Educator, 15*(10), 31–34.

Grant, L., & Rothenberg, J. (1986). The social enhancement of ability differences: Teacher-student interactions in first- and second-grade reading groups. *Elementary School Journal, 87*, 29–49.

Grant, P., Richard, K., & Parkay, F. (1996, April). *Using video cases to promote reflection among preservice teachers: A qualitative inquiry*. Paper presented at the annual meeting of the American Educational Research Association, New York.

Greene, J. (2000). Why school choice can promote integration. *Education Week, 19*(31), 52, 72.

Greenfield, P. (1994). Independence and interdependence as developmental scripts: Implications for theory, research, and practice. In P. Greenfield, & R. Cocking (Eds.), *Cross-cultural roots of minority child development*. Hillsdale, NJ: Erlbaum.

Greeno, J., Collins, A., & Resnick, L. (1996). Cognition and learning. In D. Berliner, & R. Calfee (Eds.), *Handbook of educational psychology* (pp. 15–46). New York: Macmillan.

Greenwald, R., Hedges, L., & Laine, R. (1996, Fall). The effects of school resources on student achievement. *Review of Educational Research*, 361–396.

Gresham, A., Hess, F., Maranto, R., & Milliman, S. (2000). Desert bloom: Arizona's free market in education. *Phi Delta Kappan, 81*(10), 751–757.

Gross, M. (1999). *The conspiracy of ignorance: The failure of American public schools*. New York: HarperCollins.

Gruhn, W., & Douglass, H. (1971). *The modern junior high school* (3rd ed.). New York: Ronald Press.

Gursky, D. (1999). Wired . . . but not plugged in? *American Teacher, 84*(2), 10, 19.

Gutek, B. (1991). *An historical introduction to American education* (2nd ed.). Prospect Heights, IL: Waveland Press.

Hale, E. (1998, February 14). Cyber gap costs women at work. *Gannett News Service, in Salt Lake City Tribune*, pp. A1, A4.

Hallahan, D., & Kauffman, J. (1997). *Exceptional children* (7th ed.). Needham Heights, MA: Allyn & Bacon.

Hallinan, M. (1984). Summary and implications. In P. Peterson, L. Wilkinson, & M. Hallinan (Eds.), *The social context of instruction: Group organization and group processes* (pp. 229–240). San Diego: Academic Press.

Hamilton, V. (1972). *W.E.B. Dubois: A biography*. New York: Crowell.

Hamm, J., & Coleman, H. (1997, March). *Adolescent strategies for coping with cultural diversity: Variability and youth outcomes*. Paper presented at the annual meeting of the American Educational Research Association, Chicago.

Hampshire, H. (1966). *Philosophy of mind*. New York: Harper & Row.

Hanushek, E. (1996). A more complete picture of school resource policies. *Review of Educational Research*, 66(3), 397–410.

Hardman, M., Drew, C., & Egan, W. (1999). *Human exceptionality* (7th ed.). Needham Heights, MA: Allyn & Bacon.

Harp, L. (1993). Advocates of year-round schooling shift focus to educational advantages. *Education Week, 12*(24), 1, 17.

Harry, B. (1992). An ethnographic study of cross-cultural communication with Puerto Rican American families in the special education system. *American Educational Research Journal, 29*(3), 471–488.

Hartnett, P., & Gelman, R. (1998). Early understandings of numbers: Paths or barriers to the construction of new understandings. *Learning and Instruction*, 8(4), 341–374.

Haschak, J. (1992). It happens in the huddle. In J. Lounsbury (Ed.), *Connecting the curriculum through interdisciplinary instruction*. Columbus, OH: National Middle School Association. (ERIC Document Reproduction Service No. ED 362 262)

Hauser, R. (1999). What if we ended social promotion? *Education Week, 18*(7), 37, 64.

Hawisher, G. (1989). Research and recommendations for computers and compositions. In G. Hawisher, & C. Selfe (Eds.), *Critical perspectives on computers and composition instruction*. New York: Teachers College Press.

Haycock, K. (1998). Good teaching matters . . . a lot. *Thinking K–16, 3*(2). Washington, DC: The Education Trust.

Hayes, J. (1996). A new framework for understanding cognition and affect in writing. In C. Levy, & S. Ransdell, (Eds.), *The science of writing* (pp. 1–28). Mahwah, NJ: Erlbaum.

Haynes, N., & Comer, J. (1995, April). *The school development program (SDP): Lessons from the past*. Paper presented at the annual meeting of the American Educational Research Association, San Francisco.

Hazelwood School District v. Kuhlmeier (1988).

Heath, S. (1982). Questioning at home and at school: A comparative study. In G. Spindler (Ed.), *Doing the ethnography of schooling*. New York: Holt, Rinehart & Winston.

Heath, S. (1983). *Ways with words: Language, life, and work in communities and classrooms*. New York: Cambridge University Press.

Heath, S. (1989). Oral and literate traditions among black Americans living in poverty. *American Psychologist, 44*, 367–373.

Hechinger, F. (1992). *Fateful choices: Healthy youth for the 21st century*. New York: Cornegal's Corporation.

Hendrie, C. (1998a). Judge ends desegregation case in Cleveland. *Education Week, 17*(38), 30.

Hendrie, C. (1998b). New magnet schools policies sidestep an old issue: Race. *Education Week, 17*(39), 10.

Hendrie, C. (1999). Harvard study finds increase in segregation. *Education Week, 18*(41), 6.

Hernstein, R., & Murray, C. (1994). *The bell curve*. New York: Free Press.

Heward, W. (1996). *Exceptional children* (5th ed.). Upper Saddle River, NJ: Merrill/Prentice Hall.

Heward, W. (2000). *Exceptional children* (6th ed.). Upper Saddle River, NJ: Merrill/Prentice Hall.

Hewlett, S. (1991). *When the bough breaks: The cost of neglecting our children*. New York: Basic Books.

Hiebert, E., & Raphael, T. (1996). Psychological perspectives on literacy and extensions to educational practice. In D. Berliner, & R. Calfee (Eds.), *Handbook of educational psychology* (pp. 550–602). New York: Macmillan.

Hill, D. (1999). Everyone gets to play at Indiana middle school. *Education Week, 18*(37), 6–7.

Hill, D. (2000). Test case. *Education Week, 19*(25), 34–38.

Hillocks, G., Jr. (1999). *Ways of thinking, ways of teaching*. New York: Teachers College Press.

Hirsch, E. D. (1987). *Cultural literacy: What every American needs to know*. Boston: Houghton-Mifflin.

Hirsch, E. D. (Ed.). (1994). *What your third grader needs to know: Fundamentals of a good third-grade education (Core knowledge series)*. New York: Delta.

Hirsch, E. D. (Ed.). (1995). *What your 6th grader needs to know: Fundamentals of a good sixth-grade education (Core knowledge series: Resource books for grades one through six)*. New York: Delta.

Hirsch, E. D. (1996). *The schools we need and why we don't have them*. New York: Doubleday.

Hirsch, E. D. (2000). The tests we need and why we don't quite have them. *Education Week, 19*(21), 40–41, 64.

Hoff, D. (1998). On Capital Hill, Congress picks up bilingual education debate. *Education Week, 17*(37), 20.

Hoff, D. (1999). Goals push for 2000 falls short. *Education Week, 19*(15), 1, 10.

Hoff, D. (2000a). Conservative group seeks to end state NAEP program. *Education Week, 19*(29), 29.

Hoff, D. (2000b). Gap widens between black and white students on NAEP. *Education Week, 20*(1), 6–7.

Hoff, D. (2000c). Massachusetts to put math teachers to the test. *Education Week, 19*(38), 16, 18.

Hoff, D. (2000d). NAEP weighed as measure of accountability. *Education Week, 19*(26), 1, 20.

Holland, A., & Andre, T. (1987). Participation in extracurricular activities in secondary schools. *Review of Educational Research, 20*, 437–466.

Holt-Reynolds, D. (1992). Personal history-based beliefs as relevant prior knowledge in coursework: Can we practice what we teach? *American Educational Research Journal, 29*, 325–349.

Hoover-Dempsey, K., Bassler, O., & Burow, R. (1995). Parents' reported involvement in students' homework: Strategies and practices. *Elementary School Journal, 95*(5), 435–449.

Hoover-Dempsey, K., & Sandler, H. (1997). Why do parents become involved in their children's education? *Review of Educational Research, 67*(1), 3–42.

Hudley, C. (1992, April). *The reduction of peer-directed aggression among highly aggressive African American boys*. Paper presented at the annual meeting of the American Educational Research Association, San Francisco.

Hudley, C. (1997). Teacher practices and student motivation in a middle school program for African-American males. *Urban Education, 32*, 304–319.

Hvitfeldt, C. (1986). Traditional culture, perceptual style, and learning: The classroom behavior of Hmong adults. *Adult Education Quarterly, 36*(2), 65–77.

Illig, D. (1996). *Reducing class size: A review of the literature and options for consideration*. Sacramento, CA: California Research Bureau.

Ingersoll, R. (1997). *The status of teaching as a profession: 1990–1991*. Washington DC: U.S. Department of Education.

Ingraham v. Wright, 430 U.S. 651 (1977).

Institute for Social Research. (1998). *Monitoring the future*. Ann Arbor, MI: University of Michigan.

International Society for Technology in Education. (1998). *National educational technology standards for students*. Eugene, OR: ISTE.

Interstate New Teacher Assessment and Support Consortium. (1993). *Model standards for beginning teacher licensing and development: A resource for state dialogues*. Washington, DC: Council of Chief State School Officers.

Jackson, P. (1968). *Life in classrooms*. New York: Holt, Rinehart & Winston.

Jackson, P. (1990). *Life in classrooms* (2nd ed.). New York: Teachers College Press.

Jacobsen, D. (1999). *Philosophy in classroom teaching: Bridging the gap*. Upper Saddle River, NJ: Prentice Hall.

Jacobsen, D., Eggen, P., & Kauchak, D. (1999). *Methods for teaching* (5th ed.). Columbus, OH: Merrill.

Jacobson, L. (1999). A kinder, gentler student body. *Education Week, 18*(42), 1, 22–23.

Jacobson, L. (2000a). Huge middle school has big job in feeling smaller to its students. *Education Week, 19*(35), 1, 16–17.

Jacobson, L. (2000b). Plans for universal preschool gain ground in New York state. *Education Week, 20*(8), 1, 31.

Jacobson, L. (2000c). Study: Program started in infancy has positive effect in adult years. *Education Week, 19*(9), 6.

Jacoby, R., & Glauberman, N. (Eds.). (1995). *The bell curve debate: History, documents, opinions*. New York: Random House.

Jehng, J. (1997). The psycho-social processes and cognitive effects of peer-based collaborative interactions with computers. *Journal of Educational Computing Research, 17*(1), 19–46.

Jencks, C., & Phillips, M. (Eds.). (1998). *The black-white test score gap*. Washington, DC: Brookings Institution Press.

Jennings, J. (2000). Title I—A success. *Education Week, 19*(20), 30.

Jennings, M. (2000). Attendance technology easing recordkeeping burden. *Education Week, 19*(35), 7.

Jenson, W., Sloane, H., & Young, K. (1988). *Applied behavior analysis in education*. Upper Saddle River, NJ: Prentice Hall.

Jerald, C., & Orlofsky, G. (1999). Raising the bar on school technology. *Education Week, 19*(4), 58–62.

Johnson, D., & Johnson, R. (1996). Cooperation and the use of technology. In D. Jonassen (Ed.), *Handbook of research for educational communications and technology* (pp. 1017–1042). New York: Macmillan.

Johnson, V. (1994, Winter). Parent centers send clear message. *Equity and Choice*, 42–44.

Johnston, P. (1998). Report finds no easy solution for disparities in school funding. *Education Week, 17*(41), 16.

Johnston, R. (1994). Policy details who paddles students and with what. *Education Week, 14*(11), 17–18.

Johnston, R. (2000a). As the U.S. Hispanic population soars, raising performance becomes vital. *Education Week, 19*(27), 18–19.

Johnston, R. (2000b). Bumper summer school crop yields mixed test results. *Education Week, 20*(1), 10.

Johnston, R. (2000c). Federal data highlight disparities in discipline. *Education Week, 19*(41), 3.

Johnston, R. (2000d). In a Texas district, test scores for minority students have soared. *Education Week, 19*(30), 14–15.

Johnston, R. (2000e). N.C. district to integrate by income. *Education Week, 19*(33), 1, 19.

Jordan, W., & Brooks, W. (2000, April). *Mending the safety net: A preliminary analysis of the twilight school*. Paper presented at the annual meeting of the American Educational Research Association, New Orleans.

Julyan, C. (1989). National Geographic Kids Network: Real science in the elementary classroom. *Classroom Computer Learning, 10*(2), 30–41.

Kaestle, C. (1983). *Pillars of the republic: Common schools and American society, 1780–1860*. New York: Hill & Wang.

Kagan, D. (1992). Professional growth among preservice and beginning teachers. *Review of Educational Research, 62*, 129–169.

Kahlenberg, R. (1999). Economic school desegregation. *Education Week, 18(29)*, 31, 52.

Kahne, J., & Westheimer, J. (1996). In the service of what? The politics of service learning. *Phi Delta Kappan, 77*(9), 593–599.

Kamerman, S., & Kamerman, A. (1995). *Starting right*. New York: Oxford University Press.

Kann, L., Warren, W., Collins, J., Ross, J., Collins, B., & Kalbe, L. (1993). Results from the national school-based 1991 Youth Risk Behavior Survey and progress toward achieving related health objectives for the nation. *Public Health Reports, 108*, Supplement 1, pp. 47–55.

Karweit, N. (1989). Time and learning: A review. In R. Slavin (Ed.), *School and classroom organization*. Hillsdale, NJ: Erlbaum.

Kauchak, D., & Burbank, M. D. (2000, April). *Case studies of minority teacher development*. Paper presented at the annual meeting of the American Educational Research Association, New Orleans.

Kauchak, D., & Eggen, P. (1998). *Learning and teaching: Research-based methods* (3rd ed.). Needham Heights, MA: Allyn & Bacon.

Kedar-Voivodas, G. (1983). The impact of elementary children's school roles and sex roles on teacher attitudes: An interactional analysis. *Review of Educational Research, 20*, 417.

Keller, B. (1999). Women superintendents: Few and far between. *Education Week, 19*(11), 1, 22–23.

Keller, B., & Coles, A. (1999, September 8). Kansas evolution controversy gives rise to national debate. *Educational Week, 19*(1), 1, 24–25.

Kellogg, R. (1994). *The psychology of writing*. New York: Oxford Press.

Kellogg, R., & Mueller, S. (1993). Performance amplification and process restructuring in computer-based writing. *International Journal of Man-Machine Studies, 39*, 33–49.

Kellough, R. (1999). *Surviving your first year of teaching: Guidelines for success*. Upper Saddle River, NJ: Prentice Hall.

Kerman, S. (1979). Teacher expectations and student achievement. *Phi Delta Kappan, 60*, 70–72.

Kher-Durlabhji, N., Lacina-Gifford, L., Jackson, L., Guillory, R., & Yandell, S. (1997, March). *Preservice teachers' knowledge of effective classroom management strategies*. Paper presented at the annual meeting of the American Educational Research Association, Chicago.

Kim, D., Solomon, D., & Roberts, W. (1995, April). *Classroom practices that enhance students' sense of community*. Paper presented at the annual meeting of the American Educational Research Association, San Francisco.

King-Sears, M. (1997). Disability: Legalities and labels. In D. Bradley, M. King-Sears, & D. Tessier-Switlick (Eds.), *Inclusive settings: From theory to practice* (pp. 21–55). Boston: Allyn & Bacon.

Kirst, M. (1995, December). Recent research on intergovernmental relations in education policy. *Educational Researchers*, 18–22.

Knapp, M., Shields, P., & Turnbull, B. (1995). Academic challenge in high-poverty classrooms. *Phi Delta Kappan, 76*, 770–776.

Kochenberger-Stroeher, S. (1994). Sixteen kindergartners' gender-related views of careers. *Elementary School Journal, 95* (1), 95–103.

Kogan, N. (1994). Cognitive styles. In R. Sternberg (Ed.), *Encyclopedia of human intelligence*. New York: Macmillan.

Kohn, A. (1996). *Beyond discipline: From compliance to community*. Alexandria, VA: Association for Supervision and Curriculum Development.

Kohn, A. (1997). How not to teach values. *Phi Delta Kappan, 78*(6), 429–439.

Kohn, A. (1999). Direct drilling. *Education Week, 18*(30), 43.

Kohn, A. (2000). Burnt at the high stakes. *Journal of Teacher Education, 51*(4), 315–327.

Konstantopoulos, S. (1997, March). *Hispanic-white differences in central tendency and proportions of high- and low-scoring individuals*. Paper presented at the annual meeting of the American Educational Research Association, Chicago.

Kopp, W. (2000). Ten years of Teach for America. *Education Week, 19*(41), 48, 52, 53.

Kounin, J. (1970). *Discipline and group management in classrooms*. New York: Holt, Rinehart & Winston.

Kozol, J. (1991). *Savage inequalities*. New York: Crown.

Kramer, L., & Colvin, C. (1991, April). *Rules, responsibilities, and respect: The school lives of marginal students*. Paper presented at the annual meeting of the American Educational Research Association, Chicago.

Kramer, R. (1991). *Ed school follies: The miseducation of America's teachers*. New York: Free Press.

Kramer-Schlosser, L. (1992). Teacher distance and student disengagement: School lives on the margin. *Journal of Teacher Education, 43*(2), 128–140.

Krashen, S. (1996). *Under attack: The case against bilingual education*. Culver City, CA: Language Education Associates.

Kuh, D., & Vesper, N. (1999, April). *Do computers enhance or detract from student learning?* Paper presented at the annual meeting of the American Educational Research Association, Montreal.

Kunen, J. (1996, April 29). The end of integration, *Time, 147*(118), 39–45.

Labaree, D. (1992). Power, knowledge, and the rationalization of teaching: A genealogy of the movement to professionalize teaching. *Harvard Educational Review, 62*, 123–154.

Labaree, D. (1999). The chronic failure of curriculum reform. *Education Week, 18*(36), 42–44.

Ladson-Billings, J. (1994). *The dreamkeepers*. San Francisco: Jossey-Bass.

Lambert, N., & McCombs, B. (Eds.). (1998). *How students learn: Reforming schools through learner-centered education*. Washington, DC: American Psychological Association.

Landry, D., Kaeser, L., & Richards, C. (1999). Abstinence promotion and the provision of information about contraception in public school district sexuality education policies. *Family Planning Perspectives, 31*, 280–286.

Lankes, A. (1995). Electronic portfolios: A new idea in assessment. *ERIC Digest*. (EDO-IR-95-9).

Larrivee, B., Semmel, M., & Gerber, M. (1997). Case studies of six schools varying in effectiveness for students with learning disabilities. *Elementary School Journal*, 98(1), 27–50.

Lawrence-Lightfoot, S. (1983). Teaching from the perspectives of teachers. In L. Shulman, & G. Sykes (Eds.), *Handbook of teaching and policy* (pp. 239–260). New York: Longman.

Lawton, M. (1997). Feds position national tests on fast track. *Education Week, 16*(41), 1, 34.

Leach, P. (1995). *Children first*. New York: Viking.

Leadership (1994). *American School Board Journal, 81*(12), A18–A22.

Lee, V. (2000). Using hierarchical linear modeling to study social contexts: The case of school effects. *Educational Psychologist, 35*, 125–141.

Lee, V., & Smith, J. (1999). Social support and achievement for young adolescents in Chicago: The role of school academic press. *American Educational Research Journal, 36*(4), 907–946.

Lee v. Weismann, 112 S. Ct. 29649 (1992).

Leinhardt, G., & Greeno, J. (1986). The cognitive skill of teaching. *Journal of Educational Psychology, 78*, 75–95.

Levin, H. (1988, April). *Structuring schools for greater effectiveness with educationally disadvantaged or at-risk students*. Paper presented at the annual meeting of the American Educational Research Association, San Francisco.

Lewis, R., & Doorlag, D. (1999). *Teaching special students in general education classrooms*. Columbus, OH: Merrill.

Lind, M. (1995). *The next American nation*. New York: Free Press.

Linn, R. (2000). Assessments and accountability. *Educational Researcher, 29*, 4–14.

Lipka, J. (with G. Mohatt and the Ciulistet Group). (1998). *Transforming the culture of schools*. New Jersey: Lawrence Erlbaum.

Loehlin, J. (1989). Partitioning environmental and genetic contributions to behavioral development. *American Psychologist, 44*, 1285–1292.

López, G., & Scribner, J. (1999, April). *Discourses of involvement: A critical review of parent involvement research*. Paper presented at the annual meeting of the American Educational Research Association, Montreal.

Lortie, D. (1975). *Schoolteacher: a sociological study*. Chicago: University of Chicago Press.

Louis Harris. (1993). *The Metropolitan Life survey of the American teacher, 1993*. New York: Louis Harris and Associates.

Louis Harris and Associates. (1996). *The Metropolitan Life survey of the American teacher, 1996: Students voice their opinions on: Violence, social tension, and equality among teens, Part I*. New York: Met Life.

Lumsdaine, A. A. (1964). Educational technology: Issues and problems. In P. C. Lange (Ed.), *Programmed instruction: The sixty-sixth yearbook of the National Society for the Study of Education*. Chicago: University of Chicago Press.

Ma, L. (1999). *Knowing and teaching elementary mathematics: Teachers' understanding of fundamental mathematics in China and the United States*. Hillsdale, NJ: Earlbaum.

Mael, F. (1998). Single-sex and coeducational schooling: Relationships to socioemotional and academic development. *Review of Educational Research*, 68(2), 101–129.

Mailloux v. Kiley, 323 F. Supp. 1387 (D. Mass. 1971), 448 F.2d 1242 (lst Cir. 1971).

Manning, M., & Baruth, L. (1995). *Students at risk*. Boston: Allyn & Bacon.

Manno, B. (1995, March). The new school wars: Battles over outcome-based education. *Phi Delta Kappan, 76*(4), 522–529.

Manzo, K. (2000a). Algebra textbooks come up short in Project 2061 review. *Education Week, 19*(34), 5.

Manzo, K. (2000b). Book binds. *Education Week, 19*(17), 29–33.

Marks, J. (1995). *Human biodiversity: Genes, race, and history*. New York: Aldine de Gruyter

Marshall, H. (1992). Seeing, redefining, and supporting student learning. In H. Marshall (Ed.), *Redefining student learning: Roots of educational change* (pp. 1–32). Norwood, NJ: Ablex.

Martin, D. (1999). *The portfolio planner: Making professional portfolios work for you*. Upper Saddle River, NJ: Prentice Hall.

Marzano, R., Kendall, J., & Gaddy, B. (1999). Deciding on "essential knowledge," *Education Week, 18*(32), 49, 68.

Maslow, A. (1968). *Toward a psychology of being* (2nd ed.). New York: Van Nostrand.

Maslow, A. (1970). *Motivation and personality* (2nd ed.). New York: Harper & Row.

Mayer, R. (1998). Cognitive theory for education: What teachers need to know. In N. Lambert, & B. McCombs (Eds.), *How students learn: Reforming schools through learner-centered education* (pp. 353–377). Washington, DC: American Psychological Association.

Mayer, R. (1999). *The promise of educational psychology: Learning in the content areas*. Upper Saddle River, NJ: Prentice Hall.

McAdams, R. (1994, July). Mark, yen, buck, pound: Money talks. *American School Board Journal*, 35–36.

McCarthy, J. (1991, April). *Classroom environments which facilitate innovative strategies for teaching and learning*. Paper presented at the annual meeting of the American Educational Research Association, Chicago.

McCaslin, M., & Good, T. (1992). Compliant cognition: The misalliance of management and instructional goals in current school reform. *Educational Researcher, 21*(3), 4–17.

McCaslin, M., & Good, T. (1996). The informal curriculum. In D. Berliner, & R. Calfee (Eds.), *Handbook of educational psychology* (pp. 622–670). New York: Macmillan.

McCombs, B. (1998). Integrating metacognition, affect, and motivation in improving teacher education. In N. Lambert, & B. McCombs (Eds.), *How students learn: Reforming schools through learner-centered education* (pp. 379–408). Washington, DC: American Psychological Association.

McCutcheon, G. (1982). How do elementary school teachers plan? The nature of planning and influences on it. In W. Doyle, & T. Good (Eds.), *Focus on teaching* (pp. 260–279). Chicago: University of Chicago Press.

McDermott, J. (1994). Buddhism. *Encarta* [CD-ROM]. Bellevue, WA: Microsoft.

McDougall, D., & Granby, C. (1996). How expectations of questioning method affects undergraduates' preparation for class. *Journal of Experimental Education, 65*, 43–54.

McIntosh, J. (1996). *U.S.A. suicide: 1994 official final data*. Washington, DC: American Association of Suicidology.

McIntyre, D., Byrd, D., & Foxx, S. (1996). Field and laboratory experiences. In T. Sikula, & E. Guyton, (Eds.), *Handbook of research on teacher education* (2nd ed., pp. 171–192). New York: Macmillan.

McLoyd, V. (1998). Socioeconomic disadvantages and child development. *American Psychologist, 53*, 185–204.

McNeal, R. (1997). High school extracurricular activities: Closed structures and stratified patterns of participation. *Journal of Educational Research, 91*(5), 183–190.

Means, B., & Knapp, M. (1991). Introduction: Rethinking teaching for disadvantaged students. In B. Means, C. Chelemer, & M. Knapp (Eds.), *Teaching advanced skills to at-risk students* (pp. 1–27). San Francisco: Jossey-Bass.

Mehrabian, A., & Ferris, S. (1967). Inference of attitude from nonverbal behavior in two channels. *Journal of Consulting Psychology, 31*, 248–252.

Melnick, S., & Pullin, D. (2000). Can you take dictation? Prescribing teacher quality through testing. *Journal of Teacher Education, 51*(4), 262–275.

Mercer, J. (1973). *Labeling the mentally retarded*. Berkeley: University of California Press.

Metropolitan Life Insurance Company. (1995). *The American teacher 1984–1995: Old problems, new challenges*. New York: Author.

Metropolitan Life Survey of the American Teacher: 1984–1995. (1995). New York: Louis Harris & Associates.

Metz, M. (1978). *Classrooms and corridors: The crisis of authority in desegregated secondary schools*. Los Angeles: University of California Press.

Mickelson, R., & Heath, D. (1999, April). *The effects of segregation and tracking on African American high school seniors' academic achievement, occupational aspirations, and interracial social networks in Charlotte, North Carolina*. Paper presented at the annual meeting of the American Educational Research Association, Montreal.

Miller, D., Barbetta, P., & Heron, T. (1994). START tutoring: Designing, training, implementing, adapting, and evaluating tutoring programs for school and home settings. In R. Gardner, D. Sianato, J. Cooper, W. Heward, T. Heron, J. Eshleman, & T. Grossi (Eds.), *Behavior analysis in education: Focus on measurably superior instruction* (pp. 265–282). Pacific Grove, CA: Brooks/Cole.

Miller, S., Leinhardt, G., & Zigmond, N. (1988). Influencing engagement through accommodation: An ethnographic study of at-risk students. *American Educational Research Journal, 25*, 465–487.

Mishel, L., & Frankel, D. (1991). *The state of working America: 1990–1991 edition*. Armonk, NY: M.E. Sharpe.

Missouri Department of Elementary and Secondary Education.(1995). *The show-me standards*. Columbus, MO: Author.

Molnar, A., Percy, S., Smith, P., & Zahorik, J. (1998). *1997–98 results of the Student Achievement Guarantee in Education (SAGE) program*. Milwaukee, WI: University of Wisconsin-Milwaukee.

More families in poverty. (1993). *Executive Educator, 15*, 9–10.

Morine-Dershimer, G. (1985). *Talking, listening, and learning in elementary classrooms*. New York: Longman.

Morine-Dershimer, G., & Reeve, P. (1994). Prospective teachers' images of management. *Action in Teacher Education, 16*(1), 29–40.

Morris v. Douglas County School District (1965).

Morrison, G. (1993). *Contemporary curriculum K–8*. Boston: Allyn & Bacon.

Morrison, G., Lowther, D., & DeMuelle, L. (1999). *Integrating computer technology into the classroom*. Columbus, OH: Merrill.

Morrison v. State Board of Education, 461 F.2d 375 (Cal. 1969).

Morton, E. (1988). *To touch the wind: An introduction to native American philosophy and beliefs*. Dubuque, IA: Kendall/Hunt.

Mozert v. Hawkins County Public Schools, 827 F.2d 1058 (6th Cir., 1987), cert. denied, 108 S. Ct. 1029 (1988).

Murnane, R., & Tyler, J. (2000). The increasing role of the GED in American education. *Education Week, 19(34)*, 48, 64.

Murray, F. (1986, May). *Necessity: The developmental component in reasoning*. Paper presented at the sixteenth annual meeting, Jean Piaget Society, Philadelphia.

Murray, K. (1994). Copyright and the educator. *Phi Delta Kappan, 75*(7), 552–555.

National Association for Year-Round Education. (1998). *Status of year-round schooling*. [Online]. Available: *http://www.NAYRE.org*

National Association of State Boards of Education (1995). *State education governance at a glance*. Alexandria, VA: Author.

National Board for Professional Teaching Standards. (1994). *Toward high and rigorous standards for the teaching profession*. Detroit: Author.

National Center for Education Information. (2000). *Alternative routes to teaching accelerate in just the last two years*. Washington, DC: Author.

National Center for Education Statistics. (1995). *Digest of educational statistics, 1995*. Washington DC: U.S. Department of Education, Office of Educational Research and Improvement.

National Center for Education Statistics. (1996). *Digest of educational statistics*. Washington, DC: Department of Education.

National Center for Education Statistics. (1997a). *America's teachers; Profile of a profession, 1993–1994*. Washington, DC: U.S. Department of Education.

National Center for Education Statistics. (1997b). *Violence and discipline problems in U.S. public schools, 1996–1997*. Washington, DC: Author.

National Center for Education Statistics. (1998a). *Digest of education statistics*. Washington, DC: U.S. Department of Education.

National Center for Education Statistics. (1998b). *Digest of education statistics, 1998*. [Online]. Available: *http://nces.ed.gov/pubsearch/pubsinfo.asp?pubid=1999036*

National Center for Education Statistics. (1998c). *Projection of education statistics to 2008*. Washington, DC: Author.

National Center for Education Statistics. (1999). *Digest of education statistics*. Washington, DC: U.S. Department of Education.

National Commission on Children. (1991). *Speaking of kids*. Washington, DC: Author.

National Commission on Excellence in Education. (1983). *A nation at risk: The imperative for educational reform*. Washington, DC: Government Printing Office.

National Commission on Teaching and America's Future (NCTAF). (1996). *What matters most: Teaching and America's future*. Washington, DC: Author.

National Council for the Social Studies. (1994). *Expectations of excellence: Curriculum standards for the social studies*. Washington, DC: Author.

National Council of Teachers of Mathematics. (1989). *Curriculum and evaluation standards for school mathematics*. Reston, VA: Author.

National Council of Teachers of Mathematics. (2000). *Principles and standards for school mathematics*. Reston, VA: Author.

National Education Association. (1993). *Status of the American public school teacher*. Washington DC: Author.

National Education Association (1995). *Focus on Hispanics*. Washington, DC: Author.

National Education Association (1996). *Rankings of the states, 1995*. Washington, DC: Author.

National Education Association. (1997a). *1997 resolutions*. [Online]. Available: *http://www.nea.org/resolutions/97/97e-2.html*

National Education Association. (1997b). *Estimates of school statistics*. [Online]. Available: *http://www.nea.org/s*

National Education Association. (1997c). *Rankings of the states, 1997*. Washington, DC: Author.

National Education Association. (1997d). *Status of the American public school teacher (1995–1996)*. Washington, DC: Author.

National Education Association Research. (1998). *Status of public education in rural areas and small towns: A comparative analysis*. [Online]. Available: *http://www.nea.org/publiced/rural.html*

National Education Commission on Time and Learning. (1994). *Prisoners of time: A report of the National Education Commission on time and learning*. Washington, DC: U.S. Government Printing Office.

National Joint Committee on Learning Disabilities. (1994). Learning disabilities: Issues on definition. A position paper of the National Joint Committee in Learning Disabilities. In *Collective perspectives on issues affecting learning disability: Position papers and statements*. Austin, TX: PRO-ED.

National Parent Teacher Association. (1998). *National standards for Parent/Family Involvement Programs*. Chicago: Author.

National Parent Teacher Association. (2000). *Standards for Parent/Family Involvement Programs*. [Online]. Available: *http://www.pta.org/programs/INVSTAND*

National Research Council. (1996). *National science education standards*. Washington, DC: National Academy Press.

National Telecommunications and Information Administration. (1999). *Falling through the net: Defining the digital divide*. [Online]. Available: *http://www.ntia.doc.gov/ntiahome/fttn99/contents.html*

Neale, D., Pace, A., & Case, A. (1983, April). *The influence of training, experience, and organizational environment on teachers' use of the systematic planning model*. Paper presented at the annual meeting of the American Educational Research Association, New Orleans.

Neisler, O. (2000). How does teacher education need to change to meet the needs of America's schools at the start of the 21st century? *Journal of Teacher Education, 51*, 248–255.

Nelson, C. (1999, April). *Litigation and the politics of equity: Testing the school finance process over time and across states*. Paper presented at the annual meeting of the American Educational Research Association, Montreal.

New Jersey v. T.L.O., 105 S. Ct. 733 (1985).

Newby, T., Stepich, D., Lehman, J., & Russell, J. (2000). *Instructional technology and teaching and learning* (2nd ed.). Columbus, OH: Merrill.

Newman, J. (1998). *America's teachers*. New York: Longman.

Nieto, S. (1992). *Affirming diversity*. New York: Longman.

Nieto, S. (1996). *Affirming diversity* (2nd ed.). New York: Longman.

Noblit, G., Rogers, D., & McCadden, B. (1995). In the meantime: The possibilities of caring. *Phi Delta Kappan*, 76, 680–685.

Noddings, N. (1992). *The challenge to care in schools: An alternate approach*. New York: Teachers College Press.

Noddings, N. (1995). Teaching the themes of care. *Phi Delta Kappan, 76*, 675–679.

Nord, W., & Haynes, C. (1998). *Taking religion seriously across the curriculum*. Alexandria, VA: Association for Supervision and Curriculum Development.

Nyberg, K., McMillin, J., O'Neill-Rood, N., & Florence, J. (1997). Ethnic differences in academic retracking: A four-year longitudinal study. *Journal of Educational Research, 91*(1), 33–41.

Nystrand, M., & Gamoran, A. (1989, March). *Instructional discourse and student engagement*. Paper presented at the annual meeting of the American Educational Research Association, San Francisco.

Oakes, J. (1985). *Keeping track: How schools structure inequality*. New Haven, CN: Yale University Press.

Oakes, J. (1992). Can tracking research inform practice? *Educational Researcher, 21*(4), 12–21.

Oakes, J. (1995). Matchmaking: The dynamics of high school teaching decisions. *American Educational Research Journal, 32*(1), 3–33.

Oakes, J., & Lipton, M. (1999). *Teaching to change the world*. Boston: McGraw-Hill.

O'Brien, V., Kopola, M., & Martinez-Pons, M. (1999). Mathematics self-efficacy, ethnic identity, gender, and career interests related to mathematics and science. *Journal of Educational Research, 92*(4), 231–235.

Odden, A., & Clune, W. (1998). School finance systems: Aging structures in need of renovation. *Educational Evaluation and Policy Analyses, 20*(3), 158–177.

Odden, A., Monk, D., Nakib, Y., & Picus, L. (1995, November). The story of the education dollar: No academy awards and no fiscal smoking guns, *Phi Delta Kappan, 77*(2), 161–168.

Office of Bilingual Education and Minority Affairs. (1999). *Facts about limited English proficiency students*. Washington, DC: U.S. Department of Education. [Online]. Available: *http://www.ed.gov/offices/OBEMLA/rileyfact.html*

Ogbu, J. (1987). Variability in minority school performance: A problem in search of an explanation. *Anthropology and Education Quarterly*, 18, 312–334.

Ogbu, J., & Simons, H. (1998). Voluntary and involuntary minorities: A cultural-ecological theory of school performance with some implications for education. *Anthropology & Education Quarterly, 29*(2), 155–188.

Olson, L. (1999a). A closer look: What makes a good report card? *Education Week, 18*(17), 29.

Olson, L. (1999b). Report cards for schools. *Education Week, 18*(17), 28–36.

Olson, L. (1999c). Shining a spotlight on results. *Education Week, 18*(17), 8–10.

Olson, L. (2000a). Finding and keeping competent teachers. *Education Week, 19*(18), 12–18.

Olson, L. (2000b). Taking a different road to teaching. *Education Week, 19*(18), 35.

Olson, L. (2000c). Worries of a standards "backlash" grow. *Education Week, 19*(30), 1, 12–13.

Oregon Department of Education. (1996). *Grade level common curriculum goals, grades 6–8 content and performance standards*. Salem, OR: Author.

Ormrod, J. (2000). *Educational psychology* (3rd ed.). Columbus, OH: Merrill.

Ornstein, A. (1993, August). Leaders and losers. *Executive Educator*, 28–30.

Osborne, J. (1996). Beyond constructivism. *Science Education, 80*, 53–81.

Owston, R., & Wideman, H. (1997). Word processors and children's writing in a high-computer-access setting. *Journal of Research on Computing in Education, 30*(2), 202–217.

Ozmon, H., & Craver, S. (1995). *Philosophical foundations of education*. Upper Saddle River, NJ: Prentice Hall.

Palmer, P. (1998). *The courage to teach. Exploring the inner landscape of a teacher's life*. San Francisco: Jossey-Bass.

Paris, S. (1998). Why learner-centered assessment is better than high-stakes testing. In N. Lambert, & B. McCombs (Eds.), *How students learn: Reforming schools through learner-centered education* (pp. 189–209). Washington, DC: American Psychological Association.

Park, C. (1997, March). *A comparative study of learning style preferences: Asian-American and Anglo students in secondary schools*. Paper presented at the annual meeting of the American Educational Research Association, Chicago.

Pea, R., Tinker, R., Linn, M., Means, B., Bransford, J., Roschelle, J., Hsi, S., Brophy, S., & Songer, N. (1999). Toward a learning technologies knowledge network. *Educational Technology Research & Development, 47*(2), 19–38.

Peng, S., & Lee, R. (1992, April). *Home variables, parent-child activities, and academic achievement: A study of 1988 eighth graders*. Paper presented at the annual meeting of the American Educational Research Association, San Francisco.

People for the American Way. (1991). *Attacks on the freedom to learn 1990–1991 report*. Washington, DC: Author.

Peregoy, S., & Boyle, O. (1997). *Reading, writing, and learning in ESL* (2nd ed.). New York: Longman.

Perkins, D. (1995). *Outsmarting IQ*. New York: Free Press.

Perry, R. (1985). Instructor expressiveness: Implications for improving teaching. In J. Donald, & A. Sullivan (Eds.), *Using research to improve teaching* (pp. 35–49). San Francisco: Jossey-Bass.

Perry, R., Magnusson, J., Parsonson, K., & Dickens, W. (1986). Perceived control in the college classroom: Limitations in instructor expressiveness due to noncontingent feedback and lecture content. *Journal of Educational Psychology, 78*, 96–107.

Peterson, P. (1988). Teachers' and students' cognitional knowledge for classroom teaching and learning. *Educational Research, 17*, 5–14.

Phillips, K. (1990). *The politics of rich and poor*. New York: Random House.

Piaget, J. (1952). *Origins of intelligence in children*. New York: International Universities Press.

Piaget, J. (1970). *The science of education and the psychology of the child*. New York: Orion Press.

Pickering v. Board of Education, 225 N.E.2d 1 (Ill. 1967); 391 U.S. 563 (1968).

Pintrich, P., & Schunk, D. (1996). *Motivation in education: Theory, research, and applications*. Upper Saddle River, NJ: Prentice Hall.

Pogrow, S. (1990). Challenging at-risk students: Findings from the HOTS Program. *Phi Delta Kappan, 71*(5), 389–397.

Pogrow, S. (1996). Reforming the wannabe reformers: Why education reforms almost always end up making things worse. *Phi Delta Kappan, 77*, 656–663.

Poole, M., Okeafor, K., & Sloan, E. (1989, April). *Teachers' interactions, personal efficacy, and change implementation*. Paper presented at the annual meeting of the American Educational Research Association, San Francisco.

Portner, J. (1993). Prevention efforts in junior high found not to curb drug use in high school. *Education Week, 12*(40), 9.

Portner, J. (1999a). Florida's four-pronged attack on teen smoking pays off. *Education Week, 18*(41), 70.

Portner, J. (1999b). Schools ratchet up the rules on student clothing, threats. *Education Week 18*(35), 6–70.

Portner, J. (2000a). Complex set of ills spur rising teen suicide rate. *Education Week, 19*(31), 1, 22–31.

Portner, J. (2000b). Fearful teachers buy insurance against liability. *Education Week, 19*(20), 1, 18.

Portner, J. (2000c). Maryland study finds benefits in "integrated instruction" method. *Education Week, 19*(37), 10.

Posner, G. (1992). *Analyzing the curriculum*. New York: McGraw-Hill.

Powell, R., McLaughlin, H., Savage, T., & Zehm, S. (2001). *Classroom management*. Columbus, OH: Merrill.

Pratton, J., & Hales, L. (1986). The effects of active participation on student learning. *Journal of Educational Research, 79*, 210–215.

Prawat, R. (1998). Current self-regulation views of learning and motivation viewed through a Deweyan lens: The problems with dualism. *American Educational Research Journal, 35*, 199–224.

Probst, R., Anderson, R., Brinnin, J., Leggett, J., & Irvin, J. (1997). *Elements of literature: Second course*. Austin, TX: Holt, Rinehart and Winston.

Proefriedt, W. (1999). Sorry, John. I'm not who you thought I was. *Education Week, 19*(15), 28, 30.

Provenzo, E., & Gotthoffer, D. (2000). *Quick guide to the Internet for education*. Boston: Allyn & Bacon.

Public Agenda. (1994). *First things first: What Americans expect from the public schools*. New York: Author.

Pulliam, J., & Van Patten, J. (1995). *History of education in America* (6th ed.). Englewood Cliffs, NJ: Merrill.

Pulliam, J., & Van Patten, J. (1999). *History of education in America* (7th ed.). Englewood Cliffs, NJ: Merrill.

Purkey, S., & Smith, M. (1983). Effective schools: A review. *Elementary School Journal, 83*, 427–452.

Putnam, R., Heaton, R., Prawat, R., & Remillard, J. (1992). Teaching mathematics for understanding: Discussing case studies of four fifth-grade teachers. *Elementary School Journal, 93*, 213–228.

Quality counts (1999). *Education Week, 18*(17), 121.

Radd, T. (1998). Developing an inviting classroom climate through a comprehensive behavior-management plan. *Journal of Invitational Theory and Practice, 5*, 19–30.

Rafferty, Y. (1995, Spring). The legal rights and educational problems of homeless children and youth. *Educational Evaluation and Policy Analysis*, 39–61.

Ravitch, D. (1983). *The troubled crusade: American education, 1945–1980*. New York: Basic Books.

Ravitch, D. (1990, October 24). Multiculturalism, yes, particularism, no. *Chronicle of Higher Education*, A44.

Ravitch, D. (2000). *Left back: A century of failed school reforms*. New York: Simon and Schuster.

Ray v. School District of DeSoto County, 666 F. Supp. 1524 (M.D., Fla. 1987).

Reckase, M. (1997, March). *Constructs assessed by portfolios: How do they differ from those assessed by other educational tests?* Paper presented at the annual meeting of the National Educational Research Association, Chicago.

Regents of the University of California v. Bakke, 438 U.S. 265 (1978).

Reich, R. (1995, February). Class anxieties. *Harper's*, 4–5.

Reinhard, B. (1997). Ohio Supreme Court will allow Cleveland voucher program to begin its second year. *Education Week, 16*(41), 9.

Reinhard, B. (1998). Milwaukee choice program returns to Wisconsin Supreme Court. *Education Week, 17*(26), 2.

Reynolds, M. (Ed.). (1989). *Knowledge base for the beginning teacher*. New York: Pergamon Press.

Rich, D. (1987). *Teachers and parents: An adult-to-adult approach*. Washington, DC: National Education Association.

Richard, A. (2000a). L.A. Board taps Romer for top job. *Education Week, 19*(40), 1, 12–13.

Richard, A. (2000b). Studies cite lack of diversity in top position. *Education Week*, 19(25), 3.

Richardson, A. (1999). Pay soars for school chiefs in big districts. *Education Week, 19*(10), 1, 13.

Richardson, J. (1995). Critics target state teacher tenure laws. *Education Week, 15*(4), 315–327.

Riordan, C. (1996). *Equality and achievement: An introduction to the sociology of education*. New York: Longman.

Riordan, C. (1999). The silent gender gap. *Education Week, 19*(12), 46, 49.

Robelen, E. (2000). L.A. set to retain 4th and 8th graders based on state exam. *Education Week, 19*(37), 24.

Robinson, G. (1990). Synthesis of research on the effects of class size. *Educational Leadership, 47*, 80–88, 90.

Roblyer, M., & Edwards, J. (2000). *Integrating educational technology into teaching* (2nd ed.). Upper Saddle River, NJ: Prentice Hall.

Rogers, C. (1967). Learning to be free. In C. Rogers, & B. Stevens (Eds.), *The problem of being human*. Lafayette, CA: Real People Press.

Rogers, D. (1991, April). *Conceptions of caring in a fourth-grade classroom*. Paper presented at the annual meeting of the American Educational Research Association, Chicago.

Rose, L., & Gallup, A. (1998). The 30th annual Phi Delta Kappan/Gallup Poll of the public's attitudes toward the public schools. *Kappan, 80*(1), 41–56.

Rose, L., & Gallup, A. (1999). The 31st annual Phi Delta Kappan/Gallup Poll of the public's attitudes toward the public schools. *Phi Delta Kappan, 81*, 41–56.

Rose, L., & Gallup, A. (2000). The 32nd annual Phi Delta Kappan/Gallup Poll of the public's attitudes toward the public schools. *Phi Delta Kappa, 82*, 41–56.

Rosenshine, B. (1997, March). *The case for explicit, teacher-led, cognitive strategy instruction*. Paper presented at the Annual Meeting of the American Educational Research Association, Chicago.

Ross, S., Smith, L., Loks, L., & McNelie, M. (1994). Math and reading instruction in tracked first-grade classes. *Elementary School Journal*, 95(2), 105–118.

Roth, K. (1994). Second thoughts about interdisciplinary studies. *American Educator, 18*, 44–48.

Rothman, R. (1990). New study confirms income, education linked to parent involvement in schools. *Education Week*, 9(31), 10.

Rothman, R. (1991). Schools stress speeding up, not slowing down. *Education Week*, 9(1), 11, 15.

Rothstein, R. (1998). What does education cost? *American School Board Journal*, 85(9), 30–33.

Rottier, K. (1995, October). If kids ruled the world: Icons. *Educational Leadership*, 53(2), 51–53.

Rouse, C. (1997). *Private school vouchers and student achievement: An evaluation of the Milwaukee parental choice program*. Princeton, NJ: Princeton University.

Rowan, B. (1994). Comparing teachers' work with work in other occupations: Notes on the professional status of teaching. *Educational Researcher, 23*(6), 4–17, 21.

Rowe, M. (1986). Wait-time: Slowing down may be a way of speeding up. *Journal of Teacher Education, 37*(1), 43–50.

Rutherford, F., & Algren, A. (1990). *Science for all Americans*. New York: Oxford University Press.

Rutter, M., Maughan, B., Mortimore, P., Ouston, J., & Smith, A. (1979). *Fifteen thousand hours*. Cambridge, MA: Harvard University Press.

Ryan, K. (1992). *The roller coaster year*. New York: HarperCollins.

Ryan, K., & Bohlin, K. (2000). Teacher education's empty suit: Why is targeted preparation on character development and the teaching of core ethical values missing? *Education Week, 19*(26), 41–42.

Ryan, R., & Deci, E. (1998, April). *Intrinsic and extrinsic motivations: Classic definitions and new directions*. Paper presented at the annual meeting of the American Educational Research Association, San Diego.

Sabo, D., Miller, K., Farrell, M., Barnes, G., & Melnick, M. (1998). The women's sports foundation report: Sport and teen pregnancy. *Volleyball, 26*(3), 20–23.

Sack, J. (1999a). All classes of spec. ed. teachers in demand throughout nation. *Education Week, 18*(28), 1, 12, 14, 15.

Sack, J. (1999b). Riley says it's time to rethink high schools. *Education Week, 19*(3), 20.

Sack, J. (2000a). IDEA opens doors, fans controversies. *Education Week, 20*(13), 1, 22–27.

Sack, J. (2000b). Riley endorses "dual immersion" programs. *Education Week, 19*(28), 34.

Sadker, M., Sadker, D., & Klein, S. (1991). The issue of gender in elementary and secondary education. In G. Grant (Ed.), *Review of research in education* (Vol. 17, pp. 269–334). Washington, DC: American Educational Research Association.

Sadker, M., Sadker, D., & Long, L. (1997). Gender and educational equality. In J. Banks, & C. Banks (Eds.), *Multicultural education: Issues and perspectives* (3rd ed., pp. 131–149). Boston: Allyn & Bacon.

Sanders, M., & Jordan, W. (1997, March). *Breaking barriers to student success*. Paper presented at the annual meeting of the American Educational Research Association, Chicago.

Sandham, J. (2000). Home sweet school. *Education Week, 19*(20), 24–29.

Sarason, S. (1993). *You are thinking of teaching? Opportunities, problems, realities*. San Francisco: Jossey-Bass.

Sarason, S. (1997). *How schools might be governed and why*. New York: Teachers College Press.

Sato, N., & McLaughlin, M. (1992). Context matters: Teaching in Japan and in the United States. *Phi Delta Kappan, 73*, 359–366.

Sauter, R. (1995). Standing up to violence. *Phi Delta Kappan, 76*, K1–K12.

Scarcella, R. (1990). *Teaching language-minority students in the multicultural classroom*. Upper Saddle River, NJ: Prentice Hall.

Schiff, M., Duyme, M., Dumaret, A., & Tomkiewicz, S. (1982). How much could we boost scholastic achievement and IQ scores? A direct answer from a French adoption agency. *Cognition, 12*, 165–192.

Schlessinger, A. (1992). *The disuniting of America*. New York: Norton.

Schmidt, P. (1994). Magnets' efficiency as desegregation tool questioned. *Education Week, 13*(19), 1, 16.

Schnaiberg, L. (1998). Uncertainty follows vote on Proposition 227. *Education Week, 17*(39), 1, 21.

Schnaiberg, L. (1999a). Arizona looks to its neighbor in crafting plan to take to voters. *Education Week, 18*(38), 9.

Schnaiberg, L. (1999b). Calif's year on the bilingual battleground. *Education Week, 18*(38), 1, 9, 10.

Schnaiberg, L. (2000). Charter schools: Choice, diversity may be at odds. *Education Week, 19*(35), 1, 18–20.

Schoen, H., Fey, J., Hirsch, C., & Coxford, A. (1999). Issues and options in the math wars. *Phi Delta Kappan, 80*(6), 444–453.

School Board of Nassau County v. Arline (1987).

Schorr, J. (1993, December). Class action: What Clinton's National Service Program could learn from "Teach for America." *Phi Delta Kappan, 74*, 315–318.

Schramm, S. (1997, March). *Related webs of meaning between the disciplines: Perceptions of secondary students who experienced an integrated curriculum*. Paper presented at the annual meeting of the American Educational Research Association, Chicago.

Schunk, D. (1987). Peer models and children's behavioral change. *Review of Educational Research, 57*, 149–174.

Schunk, D. (2000). *Learning theories* (3rd ed.). Columbus, OH: Merrill.

Sears, J. (1991). Helping students understand and accept sexual diversity. *Educational Leadership, 49*(1), 54–56.

Sears, J. (1993). Responding to the sexual diversity of faculty and students: Sexual praxis and the critically reflective administrator. In C. Capper (Ed.), *Educational administration in a pluralistic society*. Albany, NY: SUNY Press.

Sebring, P., & Bryk, A. (2000). School leadership and the bottom line in Chicago. *Phi Delta Kappan, 81*(6), 440–443.

Seels, B. B., & Richey, R. C. (1994). *Instructional technology: The definition and domains of the field*. Washington, DC: Association for Educational Communications and Technology.

Senftleber, R., & Eggen, P. (1999, April). *A comparison of achievement and attitudes in a three-year integrated versus traditional middle-school science program*. Paper presented at the annual meeting of the American Educational Research Association, Montreal.

Sergiovanni, T. (1991). *The principalship: A reflective practice perspective* (2nd ed.). Boston: Allyn & Bacon.

Sergiovanni, T., Burlingame, M., Coombs, F., & Thurstone, P. (1999). *Educational governance and administration* (4th ed.). Boston: Allyn & Bacon.

Sewall, G. (2000). History 2000: Why the older textbooks may be better than the new. *Education Week, 19*(38), 36, 52.

Sexuality Information and Education Council of the United States and Advocates for Youth. (1999). *SIECUS/Advocates for Youth survey of American's views on sexuality education.* Washington, DC: Author.

Shakeshaft, C., Mandel, L., Johnson, Y., Sawyer, J., Hergenrother, M., & Barber, E. (1997). Boys call me cow. *Educational Leadership, 55*(2), 22–25.

Shepard, L., & Smith, M. (1990). Synthesis of research on grade retention. *Educational Leadership, 47*(8), 84–88.

Shields, P., & Shaver, D. (1990, April). The *mismatch between the school and home cultures of academically at-risk students.* Paper presented at the annual meeting of the American Educational Research Association, Boston.

Shoho, A., & Martin, N. (1999, April). *A comparison of alienation among alternatively and traditionally certified teachers.* Paper presented at the annual meeting of the American Educational Research Association, Montreal.

Shuell, T. (1996). Teaching and learning in a classroom context. In D. Berliner, & R. Calfee (Eds.), *Handbook of educational psychology* (pp. 726–764). New York: Simon & Schuster Macmillan.

Shulman, D. (1992). Alternative to certification: Are we on the right track? *Policy Briefs, 17,* 6–7.

Shulman, L. (1986). Those who understand: Knowledge growth in teaching. *Educational Researcher, 15*(2), 4–14.

Shulman, L. (1987). Knowledge and teaching: Foundations of the new reform. *Harvard Educational Review, 57,* 1–22.

Shumow, L., & Harris, W. (1994, April). *Teachers' thinking about home-school relations in low-income urban communities.* Paper presented at the annual meeting of the American Educational Research Association, San Diego.

Shumow, L., & Harris, W. (1998, April). *Teachers' thinking about home-school relations in low-income urban communities.* Paper presented at the annual meeting of the American Educational Research Association, San Diego.

Skiba, R., & Peterson, R. (1999). The dark side of zero tolerance. *Phi Delta Kappan,* 80(5), 372–376, 381–382.

Slavin, R., & Karweit, N. (1982). *School organizational vs. developmental effects on attendance among young adolescents.* Paper presented at the annual meeting of the American Psychological Association, Washington, DC.

Slavin, R., Karweit, N., & Madden, N. (Eds.). (1989). *Effective programs for students at risk.* Needham Heights, MA: Allyn & Bacon.

Slavin, R., Karweit, N., & Madden, N. (Eds.). (1997). *Effective programs for students at risk* (2nd ed.). Boston, MA: Allyn & Bacon.

Slavin, R., Madden, N., Dolan, L., Wasik, B., Ross, S., Smith, L., & Dianda, M. (1996). Success for all: A summary of research. *Journal of Education for Students Placed At Risk, 1*(1), 41–76.

Smith v. Board of School Commissioners of Mobile County (1985).

Smyth, J. (1997). Teaching and social policy: Images of teaching for democratic change. In B. Biddle, T. Good, & I. Goodson (Eds.), (pp. 1081–1143). *International handbook of teachers and teaching* (Vol. 2). Boston: Kluwer.

Snyder, T. (1999). *Digest of education statistics, 1998.* Washington, DC: National Center for Educational Statistics.

Snyderman, M., & Rothman, S. (1987). Survey of expert opinion on intelligence and aptitude testing. *American Psychologist, 42,* 137–144.

Sokol-Katz, J., & Braddock, J. (2000, April). *Interscholastic sport participation and school engagement: Do they deter dropouts?* Paper presented at the annual meeting of the American Educational Research Association, New Orleans.

Sommers, C. (2000). *The war against boys: How misguided feminism is harming our young men.* New York: Simon & Schuster.

Sorensen, S., Brewer, D., Carroll, S., & Bryton, E. (1993). *Increasing Hispanic participation in higher education: A desirable investment.* Santa Monica, CA: Rand.

Soulé, H. (2000). Dumping old computers. *Education Week, 29*(36), 37, 40.

Spiro, R., Feltovich, P., Jacobson, M., & Coulson, R. (1992). Knowledge representation, content specification, and the development of skill in situation-specific knowledge assembly: Some constructivist issues as they relate to cognitive flexibility theory and hypertext. In T. Duffy, & D. Jonassen (Eds.), *Constructivism and the technology of instruction: A conversation* (pp. 121–127). Hillsdale, NJ: Erlbaum.

Sprigle, J., & Schoefer, L. (1985). Longitudinal evaluation of the effects of two compensatory preschool programs on fourth-through sixth-grade students. *Developmental Psychology, 21,* 702–708.

Spring, J. (1997). *The American school, 1642–1996.* New York: McGraw-Hill.

Stainback, S., & Stainback, W. (Eds.). (1992). *Curriculum considerations in inclusive classrooms.* Baltimore: Broakes.

Stein, M., & Carnine, D. (1999). Designing and delivering effective mathematics instruction. In R. Stevens (Ed.), *Teaching in American schools* (pp. 245–270). Columbus, OH: Merrill.

Stepp, L. (1996, January 4). Cliques or gangs? *Washington Post,* p. C5.

Sternberg, R. (1986). *Intelligence applied: Understanding and increasing your intellectual skills.* San Diego, CA: Harcourt Brace Jovanovich.

Stevens-Smith, R., & Remley, S. (1994). Drugs, AIDS, and teens: Intervention and the school counselor. *The School Counselor, 41,* 180–183.

Stigler, J., Gonzales, P., Kawanaka, T., Knoll, T., & Serrano, A. (1999). *The TIMSS videotape classroom study: Methods and finding from an exploratory research project on eighth-grade mathematics instruction in Germany, Japan, and the United States* (NCES 990074). Washington, DC: U.S. Department of Education, National Center for Educational Statistics.

Stipek, D. (1996). Motivation and instruction. In D. Berliner, & R. Calfee (Eds.), *Handbook of Educational Psychology* (pp. 85–113). New York: Macmillan.

Stipek, D. (1998). *Motivation to learn* (3rd ed.). Needham Heights, MA: Allyn & Bacon.

Stoddart, T. (1999, April). *Language acquisition through science inquiry*. Symposium presented at the annual meeting of the American Educational Research Association, Montreal.

Stoddart, T., Connell, M., Stofflett, R., & Peck, D. (1993). Reconstructing elementary teacher candidates' understanding of mathematics and science content. *Teaching and Teacher Education*, *9*, 229–241.

Stodolsky, S. (1988). *The subject matters: Classroom activity in math and social studies*. Chicago: University of Chicago Press.

Stone v. Graham 449 U.S. 39 (1981).

Strapp, L. (1996). Teen parenting: One school system's efforts to help mothers and their babies. *Equity and Excellence in Education*, *29*(1), 86–90.

Streitmatt, J. (1997). An exploratory study of risk-taking and attitudes in a girls-only middle school math class. *Elementary School Journal*, *98*(1), 15–26.

Strudler, N., McKinney, M., Jones, P., & Quinn, L. (1999). First year teachers use of technology: Preparation, expectations and realities. *Journal of Technology and Teacher Education*, *7*(2), 112–129.

Subotnik, R. (1997). Teaching gifted students in a multicultural society. In J. Banks, & C. Banks (Eds.), *Multicultural education: Issues and perspectives* (3rd ed., pp. 361–382). Boston: Allyn & Bacon.

Swain, J., McEwin, C., & Irvin, J. (1998). Responsive middle level sports programs. *Middle School Journal*, *30*(2), 72–74.

Takaki, R. (1993). *A different mirror: A history of multicultural education*. Boston: Allyn & Bacon.

Taxman v. Board of Education of Township of Piscataway, 91 F.3d 1547 (3d Cir. 1996).

Taylor, B., & Levine, D. (1991, January). Effective school projects and school-based management. *Phi Delta Kappan*, *72*(5), 394–397.

Tharp, R. (1989). Psychocultural variables and constants: Effects on teaching and learning in schools. *American Psychologist*, *44*(2), 349–359.

Tinker v. Des Moines Community School District, 393 U.S. 503 (1969).

Tobin, K. (1987). Role of wait-time in higher cognitive level learning. *Review of Educational Research*, *57*(1), 69–95.

Toch, T. (1991). *In the name of excellence*. New York: Oxford University Press.

Toch, T. (1998, April 27). Education bazaar. *U.S. News and World Report*, *124*(16), 35–46.

Tollefson, N. (2000). Classroom applications of cognitive theories of motivation. *Educational Psychology Review*, *12*, 63–84.

Tomlinson, C., Callahan, C., & Moon, T. (1998, April). *Teachers learning to create environments responsive to academically diverse classroom populations*. Paper presented at the annual meeting of the American Educational Research Association, San Diego.

Toppin, R., & Levine, L. (1992, April). *"Stranger in their presence": Being and becoming a teacher of color*. Paper presented at the annual meeting of the American Educational Research Association, San Francisco.

Torrance, E. (1983). Status of creative women past, present, future. *Creative Child and Adult Quarterly*, *8*, 135–144.

Triandis, H. (1995). *Individualism and collectivism*. Boulder, CO: Westview Press.

Trotter, A. (1999a). Preparing teachers for the digital age. *Education Week*, *19*(4), 37–43.

Trotter, A. (1999b). Technology and its continual rise and fall. *Education Week*, *18*(36), 30–31.

Trotter, A. (2000). Home computer used primarily for learning, families say in survey. *Education Week*, *19*(30), 6.

Trotter, A. (2001a). Army's new cyber-school opens doors for online learners. *Education Week*, *26*(16), 6.

Trotter, A. (2001b). New law directs schools to install filtering devices. *Education Week*, *20*(16), 32.

Tschannen-Moran, M., Woolfolk-Hoy, A., & Hoy, W. (1998). Teacher efficacy: Its meaning and measure. *Review of Educational Research*, *68*(2), 202–248.

Tucker, M., & Codding, J. (1998). *Standards for our schools: How to set them, measure them and reach them*. San Francisco: Jossey-Bass.

Tuckman, B. (1998). Using tests as an incentive to motivate procrastinators to study. *Journal of Experimental Education*, *66*(2), 141–147.

Turnbull, A., Turnbull, H. R., Shank, M., & Leal, D. (1999). *Exceptional lives* (2nd ed.). Upper Saddle River, NJ: Prentice Hall.

Tyack, P., & Cuban, L. (1995). *Tinkering toward Utopia*. Cambridge, MA: Harvard University Press.

Tyson, H. (1999). A load off the teacher's back. *Phi Delta Kappan*, *80*(5), K1–K8.

U.S. Advisory Commission on Intergovernmental Relations. (1994). *Significant features of fiscal federalism*. Washington, DC: Author.

U.S. Bureau of Census. (1990). *Statistical abstract of the United States* (110th ed.). Washington, DC: U.S. Government Printing Office.

U.S. Bureau of Census. (1996a). *Statistical Abstract of the United States* (116th ed.). Washington, DC: U.S. Government Printing Office.

U.S. Bureau of Census. (1996b). *Statistics*. Washington, DC: Author.

U.S. Bureau of Census. (1997). *Poverty rate: Below the poverty line by race and ethnicity*. Washington, DC: Author.

U.S. Bureau of Census. (1998a). Money, income in the United States: 1998. *Current population survey*. [Online]. Available: *http://www.census.gov/hhes/income95/inmed2.html*

U.S. Bureau of Census. (1998b). *Statistics*. Washington, DC: Author.

U.S. Bureau of Indian Affairs. (1974). Government schools for Indians (1881). In S. Cohen (Ed.), *Education in the United States: A documentary history* (1734–1756) (Vol. 3). New York: Random House.

U.S. Department of Education. (1993). *Schools and staffing survey, 1990–1991*. Washington DC: National Center for Education Statistics.

U.S. Department of Education. (1994). *The national educational goals*. Washington, DC: Author.

U.S. Department of Education. (1995). *Digest of education statistics*. Washington, DC: U.S. Government Printing Office.

U.S. Department of Education. (1996a). *Digest of education statistics*. Washington, DC: U.S. Government Printing Office.

U.S. Department of Education. (1996b). *The condition of education, 1996*. Washington, DC: U.S. Government Printing Office.

U.S. Department of Education. (1996c). *Youth indicators*. Washington, DC: National Center for Education Statistics.

U.S. Department of Education. (1997). *Nineteenth annual report to Congress on the implementation of the Individuals With Disabilities Act*. Washington, DC: U.S. Government Printing Office.

U.S. Department of Education. (1998a). *Advanced telecommunications in U.S.: Public school survey*. Washington, DC: National Center for Education Statistics.

U.S. Department of Education. (1998b). *Early warning, timely response: A guide to safe schools*. Washington DC: Author.

U.S. Department of Education. (1998c). *Indicators of school crime and safety*. Washington, DC: National Center for Education Statistics.

U.S. Department of Education. (1998d). *National assessment of educational progress in reading*. Washington, DC: Author.

U.S. Department of Education. (1998e). *The baccalaureate and beyond*. Washington, DC: National Center for Education Statistics.

U.S. Department of Education. (1999a). *Digest of education statistics, 1998*. Washington, DC: U.S. Government Printing Office.

U.S. Department of Education. (1999b). *Statistics in brief: Revenues and expenditures for public elementary and secondary education: School year 1996–1997*. Washington, DC: National Center for Education Statistics.

U.S. Department of Education. (1999c). *Study of education resources and federal funding: Preliminary report*. Washington, DC: Author.

U.S. Department of Education guidelines on religion in the schools. (1995). *Education Week, 15*(48), 30.

U.S. Department of Health and Human Services. (1996). Teen births decline. *Public Health Reports, 31*(1), 95.

U.S. Department of Health and Human Services, National Center on Child Abuse and Neglect. (1996). *Child maltreatment 1994: Reports from the states to the National Center on Child Abuse and Neglect*. Washington DC: U.S. Government Printing Office.

U.S. Department of Health and Human Services. (1997). *Head Start program performance measures: Second progress report*. Washington, DC: Author.

U.S. Government Printing Office. (1975). *Historical statistics of the United States: Colonial times to 1970* (Vol. I). Washington, DC: Author.

Vallance, E. (1995). The public curriculum of orderly images. *Educational Researcher, 24*, 4–13.

Vars, G. (1996). The effects of interdisciplinary curriculum and instruction. In P. Hlebowitsh, & R. Wraga (Eds.), *Annual review of research for school leaders* (pp. 147–164). Reston, VA: National Association of Secondary School Principals.

Veenman, S. (1984). Perceived problems of beginning teachers. *Review of Educational Research, 54*, 143–178.

Venezky, R. (1992). Textbooks in school and society. In P. Jackson (Ed.), *Handbook of research on curriculum* (pp. 436–464). New York: Macmillan.

Verstegen, D. (1994, November). The new wave of school finance litigation. *Phi Delta Kappan*, 243–250.

Viadero, D. (1996). Middle school gains over 25 years chronicled. *Education Week, 15*(33), 7.

Viadero, D. (1999a). Education Department is set to release its list of recommended math programs. *Education Week, 19*(6), 1, 14.

Viadero, D. (1999b). Study highlights benefits, shortcomings of magnet programs. *Education Week, 18*(39), 9.

Viadero, D. (1999c). Tennessee class-size study finds long-term benefits. *Education Week, 18*(34), 5.

Viadero, D. (2000a). High-stakes tests lead debate at researchers' gathering. *Education Week, 19*(34), 6.

Viadero, D. (2000b). Lags in minority achievement defy traditional explanations. *Education Week, 19*(28), 1, 18–19, 21.

Viadero, D., & Johnston, R. (2000). Lifting minority achievement: Complex answers. *Education Week, 19*(30), 1, 14–16.

Villegas, A. (1991). *Culturally responsive pedagogy for the 1990s and beyond*. Princeton, NJ: Educational Testing Service.

Virginia Board of Education. (1995). *United States history and social science standards of learning*. Richmond, VA: Author.

Vissing, Y., Schroepfer, D., & Bloise, F. (1994). Homeless students, heroic students. *Phi Delta Kappan, 75*, 535–539.

Waggoner, D. (1995, November). Are current home speakers of non-English languages learning English? *Numbers and Needs*, 5.

Walberg, H. (1991). Improving school science in advanced and developing countries. *Review of Educational Research, 61*, 25–70.

Walberg, H., & Niemiec, R. (1994, May). Is Chicago school reform working? *Phi Delta Kappan, 13*, 713–715.

Walsh, M. (1998a). Appeals court allows student-led graduation prayers. *Education Week, 17*(38), 7.

Walsh, M. (1998b). Green light for school vouchers? *Education Week, 18*(12), 1–19.

Walsh, M. (1998c). Judge defines church-state rules for Alabama. *Education Week, 17*(10), 1, 16.

Walsh, M. (1998d). Religious freedom amendment fails in house vote. *Education Week, 17*(39), 22.

Walsh, M. (1998e). Religious schools welcome back on-site Title I services. *Education Week, 17*(41), 8.

Walsh. M. (1999a). Appeals court tosses out ruling in Alabama religious-expression case. *Education Week, 18*(43), 1, 10.

Walsh, M. (1999b). Tax credits pass muster in Arizona. *Education Week, 18*(21), 1, 20.

Walsh, M. (2000a). Church-state rulings cut both ways. *Education Week, 19*(42), 1, 40–41.

Walsh, M. (2000b). Grades are for students' eyes only, federal appeals court rules. *Education Week, 20*(1), 26.

Walsh, M. (2000c). Voucher initiatives defeated in Calif., Mich. *Education Week, 29*(11), 14, 18.

Wang, M., Haertel, G., & Walberg, H. (1993). Toward a knowledge base for school learning. *Review of Educational Research, 63*(3), 249–294.

Wang, M., Haertel, G., & Walberg, H. (1995, April). *Educational resilience: An emerging construct*. Paper presented at the annual meeting of the American Educational Research Association, San Francisco.

Washington, B. (1932). *Selected speeches of Booker T. Washington*. New York: Doubleday.

Wasserstein, P. (1995). What middle schoolers say about their schoolwork. *Educational Leadership, 53*(1), 41–43.

Watson, B., & Konicek, R. (1990). Teaching for conceptual change: Confronting children's experience. *Phi Delta Kappan, 71*, 680–685.

Waxman, H., & Huang, S. (1996). Motivation and learning environment differences in inner-city middle school students. *Journal of Educational Research, 90*(2), 93–102.

Waxman, H., Huang, S., Anderson, L., & Weinstein, T. (1997). Classroom process differences in inner-city elementary schools. *Journal of Educational Research, 91*(1), 49–59.

Weaver, L., & Padron, Y. (1997, March). *Mainstream classroom teachers' observations of ESL teachers' instruction*. Paper presented at the annual meeting of the American Educational Research Association, Chicago.

Wechsler, D. (1991). The *Wechsler Intelligence Scale for Children-Third Edition-WISC-III*. San Antonio, TX: Psychological Corporation.

Weinstein, C., & Mignano, A. (1993). *Elementary classroom management*. New York: McGraw-Hill.

Weinstein, R. (1998). Promoting positive expectations in schooling. In N. Lambert, & B. McCombs (Eds.), *How students learn: Reforming schools through learner-centered education* (pp. 81–111). Washington, DC: American Psychological Association.

Wenglinksy, H. (1997). *When money matters*. Princeton, NJ: Educational Testing Service.

Wenglinsky, Y. (1998). Finance equalization and within-school equity: The relationship between education spending and the social distribution of achievement. *Educational Evaluation and Policy Analyses, 20*(4), 269–283.

West, E. (1972). *The black American and education*. Columbus, OH: Merrill.

Westheimer, J., & Kahne, J. (2000). Service learning required. *Education Week 19*(20), 52, 32.

Whimbey, A. (1980). Students can learn to be better problem solvers. *Educational Leadership, 37*, 560–565.

White, K. (1997a). Arkansas backs off extracurricular GPA requirement. *Education Week, 17*(5), 9.

White, K. (1997b). Few U.S. schools use technology well, 2 studies report. *Education Week, 17*(7), 6.

White, K. (1999a). Girls' sports: "The best of times, the worst of times." *Education Week, 19*(7), 16–17.

White, K. (1999b). L.A. to ease requirements for promotion. *Education Week, 19*(16), 1, 17.

White, K., & Johnston, R. (1999). Summer school: Amid successes, concerns persist. *Education Week, 19*(3), 1, 8–9.

Wiggins, G. (1996/97). Practicing what we preach in designing authentic assessment. *Educational Leadership, 54*(4), 18–25.

Wildavsky, B. (1999, September 27). Achievement testing gets its day in court. *U.S. News and World Report, 22–23*.

Williams, S., Bareiss, R., & Reiser, B. (1996, April). *Ask Jasper: A multimedia publishing and performance support environment for design*. Paper presented at the annual meeting of the American Educational Research Association, New York.

Willingham, W., & Cole, N. (1997). *Gender and fair assessment*. Mahweh, NJ: Lawrence Erlbaum.

Wilson, S., Shulman, L., & Richert, A. (1987). 150 different ways of knowing: Representations of knowledge in teaching. In J. Calderhead (Ed.), *Exploring teacher thinking* (pp. 104–124). London: Cassel.

Winitzky, N. (1994). Multicultural and mainstreamed classrooms. In R. Arends (Ed.), *Learning to teach* (3rd ed., pp. 132–170). New York: McGraw-Hill.

Winograd, K. (1998). Rethinking theory after practice: Education professor as elementary teacher. *Journal of Teacher Education, 49*(4), 296–303.

Wong-Fillmore, L. (1992). When learning a second language means losing the first. *Education, 6*(2), 4–11.

Wong-Fillmore, L., & Meyer, L. (1996). The curriculum and linguistic minorities. In P. Jackson (Ed.), *Handbook of research on curriculum* (pp. 626–658). New York: Macmillan.

Wood, T., Cobb, P., & Yackel, E. (1992). Change in learning mathematics: Change in teaching mathematics. In H. Marshall (Ed.), *Redefining student learning: Roots of educational change* (pp. 177–205). Norwood, NJ: Ablex.

Woolfolk, A., & Hoy, W. (1990). Socialization of student teachers. *American Educational Research Journal, 27*, 279–300.

Worthen, B. (1993). Critical issues that will determine the future of alternative assessment. *Phi Delta Kappan, 74*, 444–454.

Wynne, E. (1997, March). *Moral education and character education: A comparison/contrast.* Paper presented at the annual meeting of the American Educational Research Association, Chicago.

Yee, A. (1995). Evolution of the nature–nurture controversy: Response to J. Philipps Rushton. *Educational Psychology Review, 7*(4), 381–394.

Young, B., & Smith, T. (1999). *The condition of education, 1996: Issues in focus: The social context of education.* Washington, DC: U.S. Department of Education. [Online]. Available: *http://NCES.ed.gov/pubs/ce/c9700.html*

Young, M., & Scribner, J. (1997, March). *The synergy of parental involvement and student engagement at the secondary level: Relationships of consequence in Mexican-American communities*. Paper presented at the annual meeting of the American Educational Research Association, Chicago.

Zahorik, J. (1991). Teaching style and textbooks. *Teaching and Teacher Education, 7*, 185–196.

Zehr, M. (1999a). Moving teachers along a competency continuum. *Education Week, 19*(4), 41.

Zehr, M. (1999b). Texas exit exam under challenge in federal court. *Education Week, 19*(15), 1, 14–15.

Zehr, M. (2000a). Arizona curtails bilingual education. *Education Week, 20*(11), 1, 21.

Zehr, M. (2000b). Campaigns to curtail bilingual ed. advance in Colorado, Arizona. *Education Week, 19*(39), 19.

Zehr, M. (2000c). National standards on technology education released. *Education Week, 19*(31), 18.

Zehr, M. (2000d). N.C. same-sex classes dropped. *Education Week, 19*(32), 40.

Zehr, M. (2000e). Un día nuevo for schools. *Education Week, 20*(12), 38–45.

Zeldin, A., & Pajares, F. (2000). Against the odds: Self-efficacy beliefs of women in mathematical, scientific, and technological careers. *American Educational Research Journal, 37*(1), 215–246.

Zirkel, P. (1999). Urinalysis? *Phi Delta Kappan, 80*(5), 409–410.

Zollars, N. (2000). Schools need rules when it comes to students with disabilities. *Education Week, 19*(25), 1, 46, 48.

Zumwalt, K. (1990). *Alternate routes to teaching: Three alternative approaches*. New York: Teachers College, Columbia University.

GLOSSARY

Ability grouping. The process of placing students of similar abilities together as part of an effort to match instruction to the needs of different groups.

Academic freedom. Teachers' rights to choose both content and teaching methods based on their professional judgment.

Academies. Secondary schools that developed during the 1700s and focused on the practical needs of a growing nation; math, navigation, astronomy, bookkeeping, logic, and rhetoric were all taught. These schools ultimately evolved into college-prep institutions.

Acceleration. A form of individualization within gifted and talented programs that keeps the curriculum the same but allows students to move through it more quickly.

Accountability. Requiring students to demonstrate that they have met specified standards or that they demonstrate understanding of the topics they study as measured by standardized tests; teachers are also held responsible for students' performance.

Adaptive fit. A concept in special education in which the degree to which a student is able to cope with the requirements of a school setting and the extent to which the school is able to accommodate the student's special needs are assessed.

Administrators. Individuals who are responsible for the day-to-day operation of a school.

Advanced placement classes. Courses students take in high school that allow them to earn college credit, thereby making college less time-consuming and expensive.

Alternating-day block schedule. An alternate form of secondary scheduling in which classes are approximately 90 to 100 minutes long, students take eight classes a semester, and classes meet every other day.

Alternative assessments. Assessments that directly measure student performance through "real life" tasks.

Assessment. The process of gathering information and making conclusions about student learning. Means of assessment may include traditional tests, written papers, and projects.

Assimilation. An approach to multicultural education that attempted to bring different minorities into the mainstream of American life by both teaching the three Rs and inculcating White middle-class values and morals.

Assistive technology. Technology that includes adaptive tools that help students with disabilities learn and perform better in daily life as well as in accomplishing school tasks.

At-risk students. Students in danger of failing to complete their education with the skills necessary to survive in modern society.

Autonomy. Being in control of one's own existence, identified as a basic need in people by researchers who study human motivation.

Axiology. A branch of philosophy that considers values and ethics.

Behavior disorder. A condition in which students display serious and persistent age-inappropriate behaviors that result in social conflict, personal unhappiness, and school failure.

Behaviorism. A view of learning that focuses on specific and observable behaviors and the factors that influence those behaviors.

Between-class ability grouping. A type of ability grouping that divides all students in a given grade into high, medium, and low groups with instruction adapted to the needs of each group.

Block grants. A form of federal assistance that provides states and districts with funds with few federal restrictions.

Block schedules. An alternate form of secondary scheduling that increases the length of classes, often doubling typical periods. The basic purpose of block scheduling is to minimize disruptions caused by bells and transitions and to provide teachers with extended periods of time for teaching along with greater flexibility.

Brown v. Board of Education of Topeka. An important Supreme Court decision that ruled that separate educational facilities are inherently unequal and that racially segregated schools generated "a feeling of inferiority."

Buckley Amendment. A constitutional amendment that made school records more open and accessible to parents.

Bulletin boards. Serve as electronic message centers for a given topic; people can read the comments of others and leave their own messages.

Caring. An important dimension of teaching that refers to teachers' abilities to empathize with and invest in the protection and development of young people.

Categorical grants. A form of federal assistance that targets money for specific groups and designated purposes.

Censorship. The process of prohibiting the use of certain books in libraries or in literature classes in schools.

Certification. Special recognition by a professional organization indicating that an individual has met certain requirements specified by the organization.

Character education. An educational position suggesting that values, such as honesty and citizenship, should be emphasized, taught, and rewarded.

Charter schools. Alternative public schools that are independently operated but publicly funded and operated under a charter or special contract.

Chat rooms. Expanded, collective versions of e-mail.

Classroom management. Teachers' abilities to create and maintain orderly classrooms.

Common school movement. A historical attempt in the 1800s to make education available to all children in the United States. Began with the goal of universal elementary education.

Compensatory education programs. Government attempts to create equal educational opportunities for disadvantaged youth (such as Head Start and Title I).

Comprehensive high school. An approach to secondary education in which all students are housed under the same school roof but different tracks are provided for different students. The hope was that the diverse student body would be integrated by sports and other extracurricular activities.

Computer literacy. An initial goal of educational technology that focused on helping students understand how to operate computers.

Cooperative learning. A teaching strategy that involves students working together in groups small enough so that everyone can participate in a clearly assigned task.

Copyright laws. Federal laws designed to protect the intellectual property of authors, including printed matter, videos, and computer software.

Credentials file. A collection of important documents that teachers need to submit when they apply for teaching positions.

Culturally responsive teaching. Acknowledges cultural diversity in classrooms and accommodates this diversity in instruction.

Culture. Refers to the attitudes, values, customs, and behavior patterns that characterize a social group.

Curriculum. The content, skills, values, and attitudes students learn in school.

Databases. Computer programs that allow users to store, organize, and manipulate information, including both text and numerical data.

Development. The physical changes in children as well as changes in the way they think and relate to their peers that result from maturation and experience.

Developmental programs. Educational programs designed to accommodate children's developmental differences by allowing them to acquire skills and abilities at their own pace through direct experiences.

Disability. A functional limitation or an inability to do something specific, such as hear or walk.

Discovery learning. A teaching strategy in which teachers identify a content goal, arrange information so that patterns can be found, and guide students to the goal.

Distance education. A catch-all term for a number of organized instructional programs in which teachers and learners are physically separated.

Early childhood education. A range of educational programs for young children including infant intervention and enrichment programs, nursery schools, public and private prekindergartens and kindergartens, and federally funded Project Head Start.

Effective school. A school in which learning for all students is maximized.

Electronic mail (e-mail). A technology system that allows a message to be sent via telecommunication from one person to one or more other people.

English as a Second Language (ESL). A general instructional approach involving programs where students are provided with supplementary English instruction or modified instruction in content areas (also called "sheltered English programs").

English Classical School. A free secondary school, established in Boston in 1821, designed to meet the needs of boys not planning to attend college.

English High School. Evolved from English Classical School in 1824 with a practical curriculum including English, math, history, science, geography, bookkeeping, and surveying.

Enrichment. An approach to dealing with students who are gifted and talented that provides richer and varied content through strategies that supplement usual grade-level work.

Epistemology. A branch of philosophy that deals with the question of *how* we come to know what we know.

Equitable distribution. The practice of calling on all students—both volunteers and non-volunteers—as equally as possible.

Essentialism. An educational philosophy suggesting that a critical core of information exists that all people should possess, so education should emphasize basic skills and academic subjects.

Establishment clause of the First Amendment. Prohibits the establishment of a national religion in the United States.

Ethics. A description of moral standards for good behavior, such as being honest or treating peers with courtesy and respect. Ethics provides a set of principles that can be used to decide whether or not acts are right or wrong.

Ethnicity. Refers to a person's ancestry or the way individuals identify themselves with the nation from which they or their ancestors came. Members of an ethnic group have a common history, language (although sometimes not spoken), customs, and traditions.

Exceptionality. A special education classification in which differences are such that special help and resources are needed to help students reach their full potential.

Existentialism. A traditional philosophy suggesting that humanity isn't part of an orderly universe, so individuals create their own existence in their own unique way.

Experts. People who are highly experienced, knowledgeable, and skilled in a field.

Explicit curriculum. The part of the curriculum that includes what teachers are expected to teach, what learners are expected to learn, and what schools are held accountable for.

Extracurriculum. The part of the curriculum that includes learning experiences (such as sports and clubs) that extend beyond the core of students' formal studies.

Faculty psychology. A view of learning suggesting that mental discipline and exercising powers of the mind are important.

Fair-use guidelines. Specify legal limitations in the educational use of copyrighted print, video, and software materials.

Feedback. Information about current performance that can be used to increase future learning.

Field dependence/independence. A learning-style difference that targets an individual's ability to identify relevant information in a complex and potentially confusing background. Field-dependent people see patterns as wholes; field-independent people are able to analyze complex patterns into their constituent parts.

Four-by-four block schedule. An alternate form of secondary scheduling in which students take four classes a day that are approximately 90 to 100 minutes long. Courses that took a year in the traditional system are completed in one semester in the four-by-four plan.

Free exercise clause of the First Amendment. Prohibits the government from interfering with individuals' rights to hold and freely practice religion.

Gender-role identity differences. Expectations and beliefs about appropriate roles and behaviors of the two sexes.

General pedagogical knowledge. An understanding of general factors that increase learning, such as classroom management and questioning.

Gifted and talented. Students who are gifted and talented are those at the upper end of the ability continuum who need supplemental help to realize their full potential.

Goals. The content teachers want students to understand or the skills teachers want students to acquire in the lessons that are taught.

Grade retention. The process of making students repeat a grade if they don't meet certain criteria.

Handicap. A limitation that an individual experiences in a particular environment, such as a person in a wheelchair attempting to enter a building.

Head Start. A federal compensatory preschool education program designed to help 3- and 4-year-old disadvantaged students enter school ready to learn.

High-collective-efficacy schools. Schools in which most of the teachers are high in personal teaching efficacy.

High-impact teachers. Effective teachers for students placed at risk who create caring, personal learning environments and assume responsibility for their students' progress.

High-stakes tests. Tests used to determine whether or not students will be promoted from one grade to another, graduate from high school, or have access to specific fields of study.

Hypermedia. A system of information representation in which data—text, graphics, audio, or video—are stored in interlinked nodes.

Icons. Technology pictures that act as symbols for some action or item.

Idealism. A traditional philosophy asserting that the physical world is constantly changing, so ideas are the only reliable form of reality.

Immersion programs. A bilingual education approach in which students learn English by being "immersed" in classrooms where English is the only language spoken.

Implicit curriculum. Sometimes called the "hidden curriculum," this is a part of the curriculum that represents its unstated and sometimes unintended aspects.

Impulsive students. A learning-style difference in which students perform better on activities requiring factual information. Impulsive students work quickly but make errors.

***In loco parentis*.** Legal principle that requires teachers to use the same judgment and care as parents in protecting the children under their supervision.

Inclusion. A comprehensive approach to educating students with exceptionalities that advocates a total, systematic, and coordinated web of services.

Instruction. The processes used to help students learn the curriculum.

Instructional alignment. A description of the congruence between goals, learning activities, practice in the form of assignments and homework, and assessment.

Integrated curriculum. An approach to curriculum development that emphasizes combining concepts and skills across disciplines.

Intelligence. Often thought of in three dimensions: the capacity to acquire knowledge; the ability to think and reason in the abstract; and the ability to solve problems.

Internet. A spider web of interconnections between millions of computers that allows tens of millions of people to communicate and share information worldwide.

Intrinsic rewards. Rewards that are personally satisfying for emotional or intellectual reasons.

Junior high schools. A separate kind of school created to provide a unique academic curriculum for early adolescent youth. Initially created in 1909, these are being replaced increasingly by middle schools.

Latchkey children. Children who go home to empty houses after school and who are left alone until parents arrive home from work.

Latin Grammar School. Established in Boston in 1635, this was the first secondary school in the Colonies. Initially a colonial college preparatory school, it was designed to help students prepare for the ministry, with law added later as a second college option.

Learner-centered instruction. An approach to instruction in which teachers guide learners toward an understanding of the topics they study rather than merely explaining content to them.

Learning (behaviorist view). A change in observable behavior that occurs as a result of experience.

Learning (cognitive view). A change in a person's mental representations of the world that may or may not result in an immediate change in behavior.

Learning disabilities. An exceptionality in which a student has difficulty in acquiring and using listening, speaking, reading, writing, reasoning, and/or mathematical abilities.

Learning style. A preferred way of learning or processing information.

Least-restrictive environment (LRE). A requirement of the Education for All Handicapped Children Act that places students in as normal an educational setting as possible while still meeting their special academic, social, and physical needs.

Licensure. The process by which a state evaluates the credentials of prospective teachers to ensure that they meet the professional standards set by the state education agency.

Limited English proficiency (LEP). A classification for nonnative English speakers for whom speaking English is not a comfortable and automatic process.

Local school boards. Groups of lay citizens responsible for setting policies that determine how districts operate.

Logic. A branch of philosophy that examines the processes of deriving valid conclusions from basic principles.

Low-impact teachers. Teachers who are ineffective for students placed at risk because they are more authoritarian, distance themselves from students, and place primary responsibility for learning on students.

Magnet schools. Attempt to integrate White and minority students by attracting them to schools with quality instruction or innovative programs.

Mainstreaming. A practice in special education of moving students with exceptionalities from segregated settings into regular classrooms.

Maintenance language programs. An approach in bilingual education in which a learner's first language is maintained by continuing with reading and writing activities in the first language while English is introduced.

Mental retardation. A categorization within special education that has two important criteria: limitations in intellectual functioning, as indicated by difficulties in learning, and problems with adaptive skills, such as communication, self-care, and social ability.

Metaphysics (ontology). A branch of philosophy that examines *what* we know.

Middle class. A socioeconomic status (SES) that includes managers, administrators, and white-collar workers who perform nonmanual work.

Middle schools. A recent hybrid of junior high schools that typically includes grades 6–8, and attempts to meet the developmental needs of adolescents and provide a curriculum that helps them make the transition from elementary to high school.

Modeling. The tendency of people to imitate behaviors that they observe in others (suggesting that teachers should behave in ways they would like their students to imitate).

Moral education. An educational position emphasizing the development of students' moral reasoning without establishing a preset list of values that learners should acquire.

Multicultural education. A catch-all term for a variety of strategies that schools use to accommodate cultural differences and provide educational opportunities for all students.

Multiple intelligences (MI). A theory of intelligence posited by Howard Gardner that suggests that overall intelligence is composed of eight relatively independent dimensions.

Nature view of intelligence. Asserts that intelligence or ability is determined solely by genetics.

Negligence. Occurs when teachers fail to exercise sufficient care in protecting students from injury.

Normal schools. Two- or four-year institutions developed in the early 1800s to prepare prospective teachers. These schools were replaced by the present system of higher education in which teacher education is part of a larger college or university.

Normative philosophy. A description of the way education, architecture, medicine, or any other profession ought to practice.

Notoriety. The extent to which a teacher's behavior becomes known and controversial.

Novices. People who are unskilled, inexperienced, and lack knowledge in a field.

Nurture view of intelligence. Emphasizes the influence of the environment on intelligence.

Obedience model of management. An approach to classroom management that teaches students to follow rules and obey authority using rewards and punishment.

Old Deluder Satan Act. A landmark piece of legislation, the Massachusetts Act of 1647 was designed to create scripture-literate citizens in order to thwart Satan's trickery.

Ontology (metaphysics). A branch of philosophy that examines *what* we know.

Outcomes-based education (OBE). An approach to curriculum design that attempts to describe curriculum in terms of objectives and results.

Overlapping. Refers to expert teachers' ability to attend to more than one activity at a time.

Pedagogical content knowledge. An understanding of ways of representing a topic to make it comprehensible to others and an understanding of what makes the learning of specific topics easy or difficult.

Perennialism. An educational philosophy suggesting that nature is constant, so education should focus on the classic intellectual pursuits of history.

Performance assessment. A type of alternative assessment that asks learners to demonstrate their competence in a life-like situation.

Personal teaching efficacy. A teacher's belief that he or she can promote learning in all students regardless of their backgrounds.

Philosophy. An academic area described as a search for wisdom.

Philosophy of education. A type of philosophy that guides professional practice and provides a framework for thinking about educational issues.

Physical conditions of teaching. The school facility and the equipment and materials it contains.

Portfolio assessment. A type of alternative assessment in which teachers evaluate collections of student work using preset criteria.

Portfolios. Collections of students' or teachers' work.

Postmodernism. An educational philosophy suggesting that many of the institutions in our society, including schools, are used by those in power to control and marginalize those who lack power.

Poverty. A level of yearly income that the federal government defines as less than $16,000 for a family of four.

Pragmatism. A traditional philosophy that rejects the idea of absolute, unchanging truth, instead asserting that truth is what works.

Principal. The individual given the ultimate responsibility for the school's operation.

Professional ethics. Moral principles adopted by a group to provide guidelines for right conduct.

Professional portfolio. A collection of work produced by a prospective teacher.

Progressive education. A philosophy of education developed during the early 1900s that featured a child-centered curriculum that encouraged individual problem solving.

Progressivism. An educational philosophy emphasizing curriculum that focuses on real-world problem solving and individual development.

Psychological conditions of teaching. The emotional makeup of students and colleagues together with the behaviors they display.

Questioning frequency. The number of questions teachers ask during the course of a lesson.

Realism. A traditional philosophy asserting that the features of the universe exist whether or not a human being is there to perceive them.

Reduction in force. Also called "riffing," this involves the elimination of teaching positions because of declining student populations or funds.

Reflective practitioner. Involves constantly evaluating the effectiveness of one's practice. Self-reflection as a teacher is the first step to understanding one's practice, enabling the teacher to see how modifications may be made for improvement.

Reflective students. A learning-style difference in which students analyze and deliberate before answering. Reflective students think more and consider alternatives before they answer.

Reforms. Suggested changes in teaching and teacher preparation intended to increase the amount that students learn.

Resilient students. Students placed at risk who have been able to rise above these conditions to succeed in school and in other aspects of life.

Responsibility model of management. An approach to classroom management that attempts to create orderly classrooms by explaining reasons for rules and applying logical consequences for behavior.

Résumé. A document that provides an overview of a teacher's background and experience.

Separate but equal. The segregation policy of separate but equal resulted in separate schools with different curricula, different teaching methods, different teachers, and different resources.

Service learning. An aspect of curriculum that involves students in social-service projects.

Sexual harassment. Unwanted and unwelcome sexual behavior that interferes with a student's life.

Simulations. Types of software that model a real or imaginary system in order to help learners understand the system.

Single-gender classes and schools. Segregate students by gender for part or all of the day.

Site-based decision making. A reform movement that places more responsibility for governance at the school level.

Social institution. An organization with established structures and rules designed to promote certain goals.

Socioeconomic status (SES). A system for categorizing students that combines parents' incomes, occupations, and levels of education.

Software. Programs written in a computer language that tell the computer what to do and are used to deliver instruction.

Special education. Refers to instruction designed to meet the unique needs of students with exceptionalities.

Spreadsheets. Programs that organize and manipulate numerical data.

Standards. Statements specifying what students will know and what skills they will have upon completing an area of study, such as an Algebra I course.

Standards-based education. The process of focusing curriculum and instruction on predetermined standards.

State tax-credit plan. Parents are given tax credits for money they spend on private-school tuition. This is a variation of the voucher plan, in which parents are given vouchers to pursue alternatives to public schools.

State board of education. The legal governing body that exercises general control and supervision of the schools in a state.

State office of education. The administrative branch that is responsible for implementing policy on a day-to-day basis.

Superintendent. A school district's head administrative officer who (along with his or her staff) is responsible for implementing the school board's policy in the district's schools.

Teacher-centered instruction. An approach to instruction in which teachers carefully specify objectives, present the content to be learned, and actively direct learning activities.

Teacher effectiveness research. A body of knowledge describing differences in the actions of teachers whose students achieve higher than expected for their grade and ability levels compared to teachers whose students achieve lower than expected for their grade and ability levels.

Technician. A person who uses specific skills to complete well-defined tasks, such as an electrician wiring an outlet.

Technology. A combination of the processes and tools involved in addressing educational needs and problems, with an emphasis on applying the most current tools.

Tenure. Legal safeguard that provides job security by preventing teacher dismissal without cause.

Theory. A set of related principles that are based on observation and are used to explain additional observations.

Title I. A federal compensatory education program targeting low-income students in elementary and secondary schools.

Title IX. Legislation created to eliminate gender bias in schools and states.

Tracking. A comprehensive form of ability grouping at the secondary level that places students in different classes or curricula on the basis of ability.

Transition programs. An approach to bilingual education in which students learn to read in their first language and are given supplementary instruction in "English as a Second Language." Once English is mastered, students are placed in regular classrooms and the first language is discontinued.

Tutorials. Technology applications designed to deliver an entire integrated instructional sequence similar to a teacher's instruction on the topic.

Underclass. A term used to describe people with low incomes who have difficulty coping with economic problems.

Uniform Resource Locator (URL). A series of letters and/or symbols that act as an address for a site on the Internet.

Upper class. A socioeconomic status (SES) category that includes the smallest segment of the population (approximately 15 percent or less) and is composed of highly educated (usually a college degree), highly paid (yearly income above $100,000) professionals.

Voucher. A check or piece of paper that parents can use to purchase educational services. Designed to provide parents with alternatives to regular public education.

Wait-time. A period of silence after a question is asked that allows students a few seconds to think about their answers.

War on Poverty. The federal government's increased involvement in social programs designed to eradicate poverty during the 1960s.

Website. Location on the World Wide Web identified with a Uniform Resource Locator (URL) and designed around a function or theme.

Within-class grouping. Involves ability grouping within one classroom at the elementary level, particularly in reading and math.

Withitness. Refers to expert teachers' ability to be aware of the multiple activities students are simultaneously doing in a classroom and being able to communicate that awareness to them.

Year-round schooling. An alternate form of annual scheduling in which students spend 3 months in school and 1 month off rather than the traditional 9–3 pattern.

Zero-tolerance programs. An approach to school discipline that punishes offenses, such as school disruptions, drugs, and weapons, with automatic suspensions.

NAME INDEX

SUBJECT INDEX